MEASURES OF JOB SATISFACTION, ORGANISATIONAL COMMITMENT, MENTAL HEALTH AND JOB-RELATED WELL-BEING

MEASURES OF JOB SATISFACTION, ORGANISATIONAL COMMITMENT, MENTAL HEALTH AND JOB-RELATED WELL-BEING

A Benchmarking Manual

Second Edition

Chris Stride, Toby D. Wall and Nick Catley

John Wiley & Sons, Ltd

Other Wiley Editorial Offices

John Wiley & Sons Inc., 111 River Street, Hoboken, NJ 07030, USA

Jossey-Bass, 989 Market Street, San Francisco, CA 94103-1741, USA

Wiley-VCH Verlag GmbH, Boschstr. 12, D-69469 Weinheim, Germany

John Wiley & Sons Australia Ltd, 42 McDougall Street, Milton, Queensland 4064, Australia

John Wiley & Sons (Asia) Pte Ltd, 2 Clementi Loop #02-01, Jin Xing Distripark, Singapore 129809

John Wiley & Sons Canada Ltd, 6045 Freemont Blvd, Mississauga, ONT, L5R 4J3, Canada

Wiley also publishes its books in a variety of electronic formats. Some content that appears in print may not
be available in electronic books.

Anniversary Logo Design: Richard J. Pacifico

Library of Congress Cataloging-in-Publication Data

British Library Cataloguing in Publication Data

A catalogue record for this book is available from the British Library

ISBN 978-0-470-05981-4 (pbk)

Typeset in 10/12pt Palatino by SNP Best-set Typesetter Ltd., Hong Kong
Printed and bound in Great Britain by TJ International, Padstow, Cornwall.
This book is printed on acid-free paper responsibly manufactured from sustainable forestry in which at least
two trees are planted for each one used for paper production.

CONTENTS

ABOUT THE AUTHORS

Chris Stride obtained his first degree in Mathematics and Statistics and his Ph.D in Statistics at the University of Warwick, England. He is the statistician at the Institute of Work Psychology, University of Sheffield.

Toby D. Wall obtained his first degree and his Ph.D in Psychology from the University of Nottingham, England. He is Professor of Psychology at the University of Sheffield, where he was the former director of the Institute of Work Psychology and ESRC Centre for Organisation and Innovation.

Nick Catley obtained both his first degree and his M.Sc in Economics at the University of Warwick, England. He is an auditor at the National Audit Office, London.

ACKNOWLEDGEMENTS

This manual builds on an earlier version, which involved other authors, namely Chris Clegg, Sean Mullarkey and Peter Warr, whose contributions live on through these pages. The development of a manual such as this also involves collating information from many different sources, and hence the co-operation of numerous people. We are very grateful, therefore, to the many colleagues who have made available their time and research data. Without their collaboration, the project would not have been possible.

Among current and former colleagues and students from the Institute of Work Psychology and associated departments, we wish particularly to thank: Yesim Aras, Christian Aspinall, Sam Axelby, Carolyn Axtell, Kamal Birdi, Linda Booth, Carol Borrill, Anna Brockhurst, Melanie Brutsche, Angie Carter, Catherine Cassell, Carla Cavanagh, Kate Charles, Nik Chmiel, Julie Culham, Toni Dietmann, Steven Fleck, Lavinia Foye, Manny Gill, Melanie Gray, Emma Guy, Linda Hall, Mandy Harte, Craig Hartley, Fiona Hayes, Clare Haynes, Kate Hollis, David Holman, Fleur Hubert, Amy Hukin, Paul Jackson, Vivian Karavia, Kate Lambert, Rebecca Lawthom, Des Leach, Chrysanthi Lekka, Emer Lynam, Sam Mitchell, Polly Morgan, Sara Nadin, Nadia Nagamootoo, Sharon Parker, Malcolm Patterson, Kathryn Pepper, Margaret Sanders, Helen Smith, Christine Sprigg, Peter Totterdell, Chris Turgoose, Mel Walls, Simon Walne, Jane Ward, Susannah Wells, Michael West, Alison Whybrow, Stephen Wood and Stephen Wright.

Equally we are indebted to researchers elsewhere who have provided data for this manual, including: John Cordery, University of Western Australia; Susan Grey-Taylor, University of Hertfordshire; Ronny Lardner, the Keil Centre, Edinburgh; David Morrison, University of Western Australia; Lawrence Smith, University of Leeds; and John Wilson, University of Nottingham.

CHAPTER 1

INTRODUCTION

The aim of this manual is to provide benchmarking information for four widely-used measures of employee affective reactions at work. Although psychologists and others have been very industrious in developing such measures and establishing their reliability and validity, they have fallen short in supporting those instruments with adequate comparative data.

The paucity of benchmarking information is not difficult to explain. The development of a measure is a relatively self-contained task that can be accomplished by an individual or small group of people within a short period of time. Indeed, it is often undertaken as part of a larger substantive study. To obtain comparable information from a wide range of different settings, however, is a much more demanding (and intrinsically less interesting) task, which typically requires the collection of responses from large numbers of users over longer periods of time. Such data do not accumulate naturally as a function of the subsequent use of measures, be this for practical or research purposes, because authors rarely include sufficient detail in their publications.

Nonetheless, gathering information on identical instruments across samples can be almost as important as developing a measure in the first place. This is because scores on scales of employee emotional reaction have no natural or absolute meaning. A mean score of 4.15 for Job-related Anxiety–Contentment for one group of employees, for example, is of limited value by itself; but when set against a score of, say, 3.41 for another group engaged on similar work, it becomes much more interpretable. Such comparisons can be used by the practitioner or researcher for diagnostic or benchmarking purposes. Many organisations now routinely carry out employee opinion surveys incorporating such measures to inform their development plans, but in the absence of systematic comparative data they do not gain the degree of benefit from those exercises that they otherwise might.

The importance of such comparative data is firmly established in measurement theory, and is well-catered for in many areas of research and practice. Intelligence test scores, for instance, are firmly anchored in normative data, as are those for leading personality scales. Equivalent progress is needed for measures of job satisfaction, organisational commitment, mental health and well-being, if the full potential of the scales that have been constructed is to be realised. This manual represents one small step towards meeting that need.

MEASURES COVERED

The four measures, including their subscales and/or alternative versions, are:

1. **Job Satisfaction:** A 15-item scale (Warr, Cook & Wall, 1979) yielding both an overall scale score and two subscale scores, thus providing three measures:
   Overall Job Satisfaction (15 items)
   Intrinsic Job Satisfaction (7 items)
   Extrinsic Job Satisfaction (8 items)
2. **Organisational Commitment:** A 9-item overall scale (Cook & Wall, 1980), which has also been used in a shorter 6-item form. The original 9-item scale had three 3-item subscales, namely Organisational Identification, Organisational Loyalty and Organisational Involvement. Of these, however, only Organisational Identification has shown the level of internal consistency reliability expected for all samples, and hence we omitted benchmarking data for the other subscales. Thus we present information for three measures:
   Organisational Commitment (9 items)
   Organisational Commitment (6 items)
   Organisational Identification (3 items)
3. **Mental Health:** The General Health Questionnaire (GHQ-12; Goldberg, 1972), a 12-item scale designed to detect minor psychiatric disorder (sometimes referred to as strain), which has been scored in two main ways:
   GHQ-12 original 'case' scoring method
   GHQ-12 Likert scoring method
4. **Job-related Well-being:** Two scales (Warr, 1996), each of which has three main variants depending upon the number of items and the response scale used:
   Job-related Anxiety–Contentment (6 items, 5-point response scale)
   Job-related Anxiety (3 items, 5-point response scale)
   Job-related Depression–Enthusiasm (6 items, 5-point response scale)
   Job-related Depression (3 items, 5-point response scale)
   Job-related Anxiety (3 items, 6-point response scale)
   Job-related Depression (3 items, 6-point response scale)

CHOICE OF MEASURES

The identification of instruments to include in the manual was determined largely by their frequency of use. This is partly because the extent of use of instruments is indicative of their theoretical and practical value. More pragmatically, however, it is also because benchmarking data become available only after instruments have been used with a large number and variety of respondents for whom there is also information about characteristics such as their age, gender and job.

To the data sets used for the original manual, we have been able to find a further 54 meeting our criteria (see below), which had data for at least one, but more usually two or more of the measures covered here. As befits this far larger and wide-ranging sample, this second edition includes a further measure (of Organisational Commitment), and for each measure features additional tables giving descriptive data broken down by the Office for National Statistics' systems for classifying organisations and individuals' occupations (see below and overleaf respectively).

INTENDED USES

The manual is intended for use by occupational and organisational psychologists, management consultants and in-house practitioners who are involved in auditing, monitoring or evaluating organisations through the use of attitude surveys. Individuals in managerial or trade union positions involved in organisational audits of employee attitudes will also benefit. The provision of benchmarking data should lead to better diagnosis of organisational problems and, by implication, better solutions.

THE COMBINED DATA SET AND
ORGANISATIONAL CLASSIFICATION

The 82 data sets from which the benchmarking data were obtained are described in Table 1.1 (see pp. 6–11). Collectively, those data sets include in excess of 57300 respondents from more than 170 different organisations.

To specify an organisation's industrial sector we used the 2003 UK Standard Industrial Classification of Economic Activities (SIC 2003; Office for National Statistics, 2003). This distinguishes 17 Major Industrial Sectors, ordered from A to Q; of these, 13 appear in our sample, namely:

C   Mining and quarrying
D   Manufacturing
E   Electricity, gas and water supply
F   Construction
G   Wholesale and retail trade; repair of motor vehicles, motorcycles and personal and household goods
H   Hotels and restaurants

I   Transport, storage and communication
J   Financial intermediation
K   Real estate, renting and business activities
L   Public administration and defence; compulsory social security
M   Education
N   Health and social work
O   Other community, social and personal service activities

OCCUPATIONAL AND OTHER CLASSIFICATIONS OF INDIVIDUALS

Job satisfaction, organisational commitment, mental health and job-related well-being are all known to vary according to individuals' occupations, gender and age. These factors were used to classify the data for benchmarking purposes.

To specify an individual's occupation we used the UK Standard Occupational Classification (SOC; Office for National Statistics, 2000). This distinguishes nine Major Occupational Groups, namely:

1. Managers and Senior Officials
2. Professional Occupations
3. Associate Professional and Technical Occupations
4. Administrative and Secretarial Occupations
5. Skilled Trades Occupations
6. Personal Service Occupations
7. Sales and Customer Service Occupations
8. Process, Plant and Machine Operatives
9. Elementary Occupations

Note that the wording describing all but categories 2 and 3 differs slightly from that used in the previous version of UKSOC (Government Statistical Service,1990), which was used in the first edition of this manual.

A second method was designed to focus on individuals from industrial sectors prominently represented in the overall data set examined here, specifically workers from manufacturing organisations (N = 15661) and those working within the NHS (N = 24930). The occupational groups within these sectors identified as having sufficient numbers to be suitable for benchmarking purposes are as follows:

Manufacturing Organisations (using the UKSOC described above)

1. Managers and Senior Officials
2. Professional Occupations

3. Associate Professional and Technical Occupations
4. Administrative and Secretarial Occupations
5. Skilled Trades Occupations
6. Process, Plant and Machine Operatives
7. Elementary Occupations

NHS Trusts

1. Managers
2. Doctors
3. Nurses
4. Professions Allied to Medicine (e.g. physiotherapists, radiographers)
5. Professional and Technical Staff (e.g. phlebotomists, scientists)
6. Administrative Staff (e.g. secretaries, clerks)
7. Ancillary Staff (e.g. porters, domestics)

For each of the occupational groups, the data are further broken down first according to respondents' gender, and second by their age (groupings are 16–29 years, 30–39 years, 40–49 years and 50–65 years).

NATURE OF THE STATISTICS PRESENTED

For each instrument, we present information by sample (i.e. study data set), industrial classification and occupational group (as described above).

For each sample, we first provide descriptive statistics in terms of the average scale score (mean value) and standard deviation (sd, an index of variation around the mean). We also report the internal reliability of the scale (Cronbach's (1951) alpha coefficient of internal consistency), which indicates the degree to which responses to items in the scale are homogenous or consistent with one another (i.e. positively interrelated). An alpha coefficient of 0.70 is usually regarded as adequate for research and practical purposes, though higher values (0.80 or more) are desirable. That minimum threshold is met, and typically well exceeded, by each of the instruments in almost all of the samples described here.

Descriptive statistics (means and standard deviations) are also presented for each industrial sector, and then for each occupational group, further broken down by age and gender.

In providing data of this kind, we have been careful not to claim that they are 'norms'. The use of the term 'norm' would imply that the descriptive statistics were demonstrably representative, or characteristic, of a known population. As is evident from the summary of the data sets in Table 1.1 (pp. 6–11), this is not necessarily the case.

Table 1.1   Data sets used to derive benchmarking data

Sample	Study organisation(s)	Respondent characteristics	Sector(s)	N
1	Manufacture of electronic machinery	Assemblers/Line Workers, Supervisors, Managers	D	163
2	Manufacture of clothing	Sewing Machinists, Supervisors, Secretaries and Administrative Staff, Managers	D	915
3	Manufacture of electronic process control systems	Assemblers/Line Workers, Stores, Despatch and Production Control Clerks, Supervisors, Secretaries and Administrative Staff, Managers	D	164
4	Collection, purification and distribution of water	General Managers	E	101
5	Chemical process control plant	Plant Operatives, Engineers, Ancillary Staff, Supervisors, Managers	D	351
6	NHS hospitals (23 Trusts)	Managers, Doctors, Nurses, Professions Allied to Medicine (e.g. physiotherapists), Professional and Technical Staff (e.g. scientists), Administrative Staff, Ancillary Staff (e.g. porters)	N	20957
7	City Council	Clerical Officers and Assistants, Information Officers, Managers	L	838
8	Manufacture of glassware and ceramics	Furnace Operatives, Kiln Setters, Glaziers	D	916
9	Manufacture of wire and wire products	Assemblers/Line Workers, Supervisors, Managers	D	756
10	Manufacture of heavy plant machinery	Assemblers/Line Workers, Supervisors, Managers	D	783
11	Chemical process control plant	Plant Operatives, Engineers, Ancillary Staff, Supervisors, Managers	D	339
12	Mail sorting office	Postal Workers, Mail Sorters	I	407

Table 1.1   Continued

Sample	Study organisation(s)	Respondent characteristics	Sector(s)	N
13	Manufacturing (68 companies)	Plant and Machine Operatives, Engineers, Supervisors, Ancillary Staff	D	6699
14	Local Authority	Managers, Clerical Officers, Welfare Community Workers, Teachers, Archivists, other occupations	L	4955
15	Meat processing and production	Slaughterhouse Workers	D	581
16	Manufacture of steel	Furnace Operatives, Metal Rollers, Stores and Despatch Clerks, Sales Staff, Supervisors, Managers.	D	462
17	Manufacture of steel	Process Operatives, Supervisors, Managers	D	378
18	Film processing and photographic activities	Process Operatives, Ancillary Staff, Supervisors, Managers	K	51
19	Manufacture of car interiors	Assemblers/Line Workers, Supervisors, Managers	D	42
20	Manufacture of tungsten and carbide products	Smith and Forge Workers, Process Operatives, Supervisors, Managers	D	56
21	Manufacture of mining and pneumatic drills	Smith and Forge Workers, Process Operatives, Supervisors, Managers	D	73
22	Manufacturing of wire and wire products	Process Operatives, Supervisors, Managers	D	396
23	Patent office	Clerks, Managers, Professional Staff	L	171
24	Civil Service administrative office	Administrative Officers and Assistants	L	73
25	Wholesale of building and construction products	Managers	G	67
26	Banking and financial services	Bank Managers, Computer Programmers	J	74
27	Manufacture of metal products	Smith and Forge Workers, Supervisors, Managers	D	145
28	Manufacture of metal products	Machine Operatives, Supervisors, Managers	D	84

Table 1.1 Continued

Sample	Study organisation(s)	Respondent characteristics	Sector(s)	N
29	Professional association	Psychologists	M	870
30	Financial service call centre	Call Centre Agents	J	831
31	Call centre of private healthcare organisation	Call Centre Agents	N	464
32	Private healthcare organisation administrative centre	Brokers, Telephone Salespersons	N	121
33	Call centre of private healthcare organisation	Call Centre Agents, General Office Assistants, Customer Care Managers	N	254
34	Bus company	Bus and Coach Drivers	I	213
35	Police Force	Constables, Sergeants, Inspectors	L	357
36	Mixed Industries (3 companies): Airline; Civil Service department; Local Authority	Many types of occupation	I, L	1351
37	Railway track and infrastructure maintenance	Rail Construction and Maintenance Operatives, Metal Workers, Welders, Forge Workers, Office Assistants, Construction Managers	F	618
38	Manufacture of heavy plant vehicles	Assemblers, Goods Handling, Machine Operatives, Metal Workers, Welding, Office Assistants, Managers	D	424
39	University	University Lecturers	M	32
40	Mixed industries (predominantly publishing)	Authors, Writers, Journalists, Graphic Designers	D	65
41	Civil Service social work activities	Cleaners, Administrative Officers and Assistants, Housing Officers, Probation Officers, Senior Officers	N	313

Table 1.1 Continued

Sample	Study organisation(s)	Respondent characteristics	Sector(s)	N
42	NHS Hospital Trust	Managers, Doctors, Nurses, Professions Allied to Medicine, Professional and Technical Staff, Administrative Staff, Ancillary Staff	N	2988
43	Civil Service policy unit	Administrative Officers, Legal Professionals, PR Officers, Senior Officials	L	325
44	Manufacture of chemical products	Machine Operatives, Chemical Process Operatives, Office Clerks, Financial Clerks, Technicians, Engineers, Chemists, Production Managers	D	217
45	Postal and courier services	Postal Workers and Mail Sorters, Transport Clerks, Financial Clerks, Buyers, Technicians, Transport and Distribution Managers	I	232
46	Processing of tea and coffee	Cleaners, Process Operatives, Administrative Officers, Technicians, Managers	D	387
47	Manufacture of machinery	Engineering Technicians, Office Clerks	D	441
48	Police Force	Constables, Sergeants, Administrative Officers	L	154
49	Railway track and infrastructure maintenance	Rail Construction and Maintenance Operatives, Welders, Electricians, Surveyors	F	160
50	Mixed industries (3 companies): Manufacture of confectionary; Manufacture of aircraft; Electricity distribution	Food and Drink Process Operatives, Sales Representatives, Works Managers, Office Managers	D, E	118
51	Public transport provider	Call Centre Agents	I	50
52	Manufacture of food and drink	Process Operatives, Maintenance Fitters	D	106

Table 1.1   Continued

Sample	Study organisation(s)	Respondent characteristics	Sector(s)	N
53	Retail of fashion accessories	Sales Assistants, Retail and Wholesale Managers	G	172
54	Manufacture of medical and surgical equipment	Process Operatives, Stores, Administrative Officers, Technicians, Managers	D	193
55	Higher education	Teachers, Vocational Trainers, Office Assistants, Office Managers	M	95
56	Banking and financial services	Counter Clerks, Financial Clerks, IT Technicians, Chartered Secretaries, Financial Managers	J	125
57	Secondary education	Teachers	M	92
58	Manufacture of petroleum products	Riggers, Machine Operatives, Process Operatives	D	53
59	Manufacture of aircraft parts	Metal Workers, Production and Maintenance Fitters, Business Professionals	D	88
60	Business logistics and consultancy	Clerks	K	25
61	Manufacture of tobacco products	Sales Representatives, Marketing and Sales Managers	D	45
62	NHS Hospital Trust	Managers, Doctors, Nurses, Professional and Technical Staff, Administrative Staff, Ancillary Staff	N	643
63	Local Authority	Senior Officials	L	46
64	Local Authority	Clerical Officers and Assistants, Senior Officials	L	189
65	Film processing and photographic activities	Packers, Inspectors and Testers, Chemical Process Operatives	K	236
66	Mixed industries (2 companies): Manufacture of steel; Film processing	Goods Handling, Inspectors and Testers, Metal-making Process Operatives, Chemical Process Operatives, Technicians, Works Managers	D, K	194
67	2 Financial service call centres	Call Centre Agents, Call Centre Managers	J	162
68	Public utility	Plumbers, Heating and Ventilation Engineers	E	97

Table 1.1   Continued

Sample	Study organisation(s)	Respondent characteristics	Sector(s)	N
69	Banking and financial services	Counter Clerks	J	47
70	20 Call centres (serving companies from mixed industries)	Call Centre Agents, Office Assistants, Managers	E, G, H, I, J, K, L, N	1140
71	Wholesale of metal and metal ores	Goods Handling and Stores, HGV Drivers, Secretaries, IT Technicians, Accountants, Sales and Marketing Managers, Works and Process Managers	G	489
72	NHS Ambulance Trust	Communication Operatives	N	53
73	Religious organisation (Christian)	Clergy	O	77
74	Extraction of oil and gas	Managers	C	72
75	Mixed industries (5 companies): Business and management consultancy (4); Architectural/ engineering activities	Secretaries, Management Consultants, Psychologists, Chartered Secretaries, Personnel and Training Managers, Financial Managers	K	128
76	NHS Hospital Trust	Managers, Doctors, Nurses, Professional and Technical Staff, Administrative Staff, Ancillary Staff	N	289
77	Retail chemist	Dispensers, Pharmacists	G	20
78	Estate agency	Estate Agents	K	32
79	Railway track and infrastructure maintenance	Rail Construction and Maintenance Operatives	F	109
80	Mixed industries (2 companies): Post and telecommunications; Financial intermediation	Postal Workers and Mail Sorters, Financial Managers, Chartered Secretaries	I, J	115
81	Manufacture of pottery	Office Clerks and Assistants, Production, Works and Maintenance Managers	D	130
82	Social work	Housing and Welfare Officers	N	109

Nonetheless, the data may be considered 'normative' in the more general sense in that there is little reason to believe that they are strongly biased. It might be suggested that, because the responses inevitably come from organisations which have agreed to take part in surveys, either for their own or for research purposes, then it is possible that average scores will differ from those organisations which might refuse such involvement. By the same token, however, future work using the present instruments will necessarily involve such 'volunteer' organisations. Thus the data in this manual, though not demonstrably true norms, are likely to provide useful comparisons for future work.

CHAPTER 2

JOB SATISFACTION

ORIGIN AND APPLICATIONS

This job satisfaction measure was developed by Warr, Cook and Wall (1979) as a robust instrument that is easily completed by employees at all levels and is psychometrically sound. It can be scored to provide a single index of Overall Job Satisfaction, or separate indices of Intrinsic and Extrinsic Job Satisfaction.

Intrinsic Job Satisfaction covers people's affective reactions to job features that are integral to the work itself (e.g. variety, opportunity to use one's skills, autonomy); whereas Extrinsic Job Satisfaction covers features external to the work itself (e.g. pay, the way the firm is managed). In the original development of the measure on two samples of shop-floor employees, these two subscales, gh psychometrically distinguishable, were found to intercorrelate highly ($r = 0.72$), and similar levels of association have been shown subsequently.

The scale has been used with a wide range of employees including those working in: primary healthcare (Sutherland & Cooper, 1992); shop-floor manufacturing jobs (Clegg, Wall & Kemp, 1987; Cooper & Bramwell, 1992; Epitropaki & Martin, 2005; Patterson, Warr & West, 2004; Wall & Clegg, 1981; Wall et al. 1990); education (Cooper & Kelly, 1993; Travers & Cooper, 1993); the service sector (Cordery et al. 1993; Martin et al. 2005); construction work (Sutherland & Davidson, 1993); and off-shore oil installations (Sutherland & Flin, 1989).

Studies have found the scale to be sensitive to: job control and occupational achievement (Petrides & Furnham, 2006); role ambiguity and role conflict (O'Driscoll & Beehr, 1994); leader–member exchange (Epitropaki & Martin, 2005); lean manufacturing practices (Mullarkey, Jackson & Parker, 1995); work pacing (Corbett et al. 1989); work design (Kemp et al. 1983; Noblet et al. 2006; Wall & Clegg, 1981; Wall et al., 1990); technological differences (Wall 1987); and technological uncertainty (Mullarkey et al. 1997).

PERMISSIONS, AVAILABILITY AND QUALIFICATIONS

There are no specific restrictions on the use of this measure. It is freely available for use by psychologists or other practitioners involved in organisational survey research.

SCALE ITEMS AND RESPONSE OPTIONS

The Job Satisfaction Scale consists of 15 items, and respondents are asked to indicate on a seven-point response scale the extent to which they are satisfied or dissatisfied with each. The Intrinsic Job Satisfaction subscale comprises seven items (items 2, 4, 6, 8, 10, 12, 14); and the Extrinsic Job Satisfaction subscale is made up of eight items (items 1, 3, 5, 7, 9, 11, 13 and 15). There are no reverse scored items. The measure is as follows:

Please indicate how satisfied or dissatisfied you feel with each of these features of your present job by placing a tick in the appropriate box.

How satisfied or dissatisfied are you with:	1 I'm extremely dissatisfied	2 I'm very dissatisfied	3 I'm moderately dissatisfied	4 I'm not sure	5 I'm moderately satisfied	6 I'm very satisfied	7 I'm extremely satisfied
1. The physical working conditions?	[ ]	[ ]	[ ]	[ ]	[ ]	[ ]	[ ]
2. The freedom to choose your own method of working?	[ ]	[ ]	[ ]	[ ]	[ ]	[ ]	[ ]
3. Your fellow workers?	[ ]	[ ]	[ ]	[ ]	[ ]	[ ]	[ ]
4. The recognition you get for good work?	[ ]	[ ]	[ ]	[ ]	[ ]	[ ]	[ ]
5. Your immediate boss?	[ ]	[ ]	[ ]	[ ]	[ ]	[ ]	[ ]
6. The amount of responsibility you are given?	[ ]	[ ]	[ ]	[ ]	[ ]	[ ]	[ ]
7. Your rate of pay?	[ ]	[ ]	[ ]	[ ]	[ ]	[ ]	[ ]
8. Your opportunity to use your abilities?	[ ]	[ ]	[ ]	[ ]	[ ]	[ ]	[ ]
9. Industrial relations between management and workers in your firm?	[ ]	[ ]	[ ]	[ ]	[ ]	[ ]	[ ]

(continued)

Please indicate how satisfied or dissatisfied you feel with each of these features of your present job by placing a tick in the appropriate box.

	1 I'm extremely dissatisfied	2 I'm very dissatisfied	3 I'm moderately dissatisfied	4 I'm not sure	5 I'm moderately satisfied	6 I'm very satisfied	7 I'm extremely satisfied
10. Your chance of promotion?	[ ]	[ ]	[ ]	[ ]	[ ]	[ ]	[ ]
11. The way the organisation is managed?	[ ]	[ ]	[ ]	[ ]	[ ]	[ ]	[ ]
12. The attention paid to suggestions you make?	[ ]	[ ]	[ ]	[ ]	[ ]	[ ]	[ ]
13. Your hours of work?	[ ]	[ ]	[ ]	[ ]	[ ]	[ ]	[ ]
14. The amount of variety in your job?	[ ]	[ ]	[ ]	[ ]	[ ]	[ ]	[ ]
15. Your job security?	[ ]	[ ]	[ ]	[ ]	[ ]	[ ]	[ ]

SCORING

Originally, scoring was by summation across items. Thus the range of possible scores for Overall Job Satisfaction was 15–105 (all 15 items), for Intrinsic Job Satisfaction 7–49 (all seven even-numbered items), and for Extrinsic Job Satisfaction 8–56 (all eight odd-numbered items). The limitations of this method are that the omission of a response to even a single item invalidates a respondent's score, and that there is no direct comparability between scale scores for Intrinsic and Extrinsic Satisfaction.

For the above reasons, scoring practice in the studies included here has been to calculate the mean item score, and to require responses to a minimum of 12 items for Overall Job Satisfaction, five items for Intrinsic Job Satisfaction and six items for Extrinsic Job Satisfaction. In practice very few missing responses arise on this scale, and comparisons between the two methods (requiring responses to all items versus allowing missing responses on up to three items) show no meaningful differences in terms of means and standard deviations.

INTERNAL RELIABILITY AND DESCRIPTIVE STATISTICS

The following tables present the internal reliabilities and benchmarking data for the scales. The first six tables cover Overall Job Satisfaction, and show, respectively:

Table 2.1 – descriptive statistics and internal reliabilities (Cronbach's (1951) alpha coefficient of internal consistency) by sample

Table 2.2 – descriptive statistics for the SIC Major Industrial Sectors

Table 2.3 – descriptive statistics for the SOC Major Occupational Groups by gender

Table 2.4 – descriptive statistics for the SOC Major Occupational Groups by age

Table 2.5 – descriptive statistics for the selected occupational groups by gender

Table 2.6 – descriptive statistics for the selected occupational groups by age.

Tables 2.7–2.12 and Tables 2.13–2.18 present the corresponding information for Intrinsic Job Satisfaction and Extrinsic Job Satisfaction respectively.

INTERNAL RELIABILITY AND DESCRIPTIVE STATISTICS
(Tables 2.1–2.6)

Table 2.1   Overall Job Satisfaction: Descriptive statistics and internal reliability (alpha) by sample[†]

Sample and organisation	n	mean	s.d.	n[‡]	alpha
1 Manufacturing – electronic machinery	162	4.65	0.82	154	0.87
2 Manufacturing – clothing	906	3.87	0.91	836	0.88
3 Manufacturing – electronics	160	4.93	0.73	147	0.88
4 Water authority	101	4.90	0.64	101	0.85
6 NHS hospitals	20694	4.51	0.86	19101	0.87
7 City Council	835	4.47	0.95	809	0.89
9 Manufacturing – wire	745	4.24	0.94	693	0.89
11 Manufacturing – chemicals	338	4.30	0.94	322	0.90
12 Mail sorting office	404	3.76	1.03	390	0.91
13 Manufacturing – various	6579	4.51	1.08	6317	0.92
14 Local Authority	4442	4.35	0.95	4117	0.88
15 Manufacturing – food/drink	574	3.98	0.98	342	0.89
18 Film processing	51	4.23	0.80	49	0.89
19 Manufacturing – vehicle parts	42	4.16	0.95	40	0.93
20 Manufacturing – metal	56	4.47	0.97	56	0.92
21 Manufacturing – metal products	73	3.93	0.89	65	0.87
22 Manufacturing – wire	386	4.30	1.01	368	0.92
23 Patent office	169	4.53	0.80	164	0.88
25 Wholesale – building products	66	4.34	0.77	63	0.83
27 Manufacturing – metal products	144	4.38	0.92	140	0.91
28 Manufacturing – metal products	83	4.09	0.90	81	0.87
29 Professional association	853	4.55	0.99	785	0.89
30 Financial service call centre	830	4.43	0.86	807	0.88
31 Private healthcare call centre	454	4.54	0.90	426	0.90
32 Private healthcare administration	121	4.93	0.94	121	0.92
35 Police Force	353	4.55	0.79	342	0.88
36 Mixed industries	1030	4.53	0.95	970	0.91
37 Railway maintenance	613	4.54	1.02	568	0.93
38 Manufacturing – heavy plant	422	4.16	0.98	409	0.90
39 University	32	4.86	1.01	32	0.92
41 Civil Service – social work	313	4.33	1.02	290	0.90
42 NHS Hospital Trust	2936	4.68	0.90	2750	0.89
45 Postal services	232	5.04	1.05	219	0.90
46 Manufacturing – food/drink	374	4.61	0.80	350	0.89
48 Police Force	153	3.95	0.85	146	0.87
53 Retail – fashion accessories	171	4.32	1.08	170	0.92
54 Manufacturing – medical equipment	187	4.11	0.89	176	0.89
55 Higher education	94	4.08	1.14	88	0.93
60 Logistics and consultancy	25	3.49	0.98	23	0.86
61 Manufacturing – tobacco products	45	4.61	0.76	44	0.87
63 Local Authority	45	4.52	0.90	36	0.87
65 Film processing	225	4.50	0.86	202	0.90
68 Public utility	96	4.16	0.90	93	0.90

Table 2.1 Continued

Sample and organisation	n	mean	s.d.	n[‡]	alpha
69 Banking	47	5.03	0.79	47	0.89
70 Mixed industries call centres	1133	4.22	1.02	1078	0.91
71 Wholesale – metal	488	4.63	1.01	467	0.93
72 NHS Ambulance Trust	53	4.59	0.88	49	0.91
75 NHS Hospital Trust	287	4.59	0.96	275	0.91
80 Mixed industries	112	4.53	1.06	101	0.93
82 Social work	108	4.74	1.01	104	0.93

[†] Details of the samples/organisations are shown in Table 1.1, pp. 6–11.
[‡] Sample sizes for alpha coefficients are smaller than for the sample as a whole because of listwise deletion for missing values.

Table 2.2 Overall Job Satisfaction: Descriptive statistics for UK SIC major industrial sectors and overall

Standard Industrial Classification of company	n	mean	s.d.
D Manufacturing	11276	4.38	1.04
E Electricity, gas and water supply	350	4.43	0.94
F Construction	613	4.54	1.02
G Wholesale and retail trade[†]	801	4.49	1.02
H Hotels and restaurants	96	4.19	1.02
I Transport, storage and communication	1401	4.20	1.12
J Financial intermediation	1215	4.47	0.90
K Real estate, renting and business activities	318	4.39	0.90
L Public administration and defence; compulsory social security	6784	4.40	0.94
M Education	979	4.51	1.01
N Health and social work	25009	4.53	0.87
Total	48842	4.47	0.94

[†] Includes repair of motor vehicles, motorcycles and household and personal goods.

Table 2.3 Overall Job Satisfaction: Descriptive statistics for SOC major occupational groups by gender and overall

Major occupational group	Female			Male			All		
	n	*mean*	*s.d.*	*n*	*mean*	*s.d.*	*n*	*mean*	*s.d.*
Managers and senior officials	2006	4.68	0.93	3314	4.78	0.93	5320	4.74	0.93
Professional occupations	3010	4.52	0.88	2649	4.48	0.88	5659	4.50	0.88
Associate professional and technical	13241	4.55	0.84	3084	4.39	0.91	16325	4.52	0.86
Administrative and secretarial	5051	4.59	0.89	1472	4.45	0.96	6523	4.55	0.91
Skilled trades	277	4.07	1.02	1155	4.18	0.99	1432	4.16	0.99
Personal service	94	4.64	0.84	84	4.45	1.27	178	4.55	1.07
Sales and customer service	1766	4.38	0.95	865	4.30	1.00	2631	4.35	0.96
Process, plant and machine operatives	1786	4.25	0.94	4081	4.13	1.06	5867	4.17	1.03
Elementary occupations	1441	4.56	0.99	1876	4.10	1.11	3317	4.30	1.09

Table 2.4 Overall Job Satisfaction: Descriptive statistics for SOC major occupational groups by age

Major occupational group	16–29			30–39			40–49			50–65		
	n	mean	s.d.	n	mean	s.d.	n	mean	s.d.	n	mean	s.d.
Managers and senior officials	702	4.65	0.93	1673	4.66	0.92	1803	4.75	0.93	1110	4.93	0.94
Professional occupations	859	4.39	0.78	1580	4.49	0.83	1867	4.50	0.89	1316	4.58	0.97
Associate professional and technical	3359	4.48	0.84	5409	4.46	0.85	4514	4.52	0.86	2875	4.67	0.86
Administrative and secretarial	1572	4.48	0.92	1674	4.55	0.91	1775	4.54	0.91	1466	4.66	0.90
Skilled trades	330	4.03	1.02	390	4.10	0.94	398	4.15	1.03	300	4.42	0.97
Personal service	74	4.66	1.04	52	4.25	1.07	37	4.66	1.03	13	–	–
Sales and customer service	1309	4.28	0.96	764	4.43	0.96	387	4.40	0.96	158	4.52	0.96
Process, plant and machine operatives	1774	4.03	0.97	1690	4.10	1.04	1391	4.24	1.05	1064	4.49	1.03
Elementary occupations	626	4.17	1.05	853	4.23	1.09	866	4.29	1.06	972	4.49	1.08

– Too few respondents (<20) to warrant descriptive statistics.

Table 2.5 Overall Job Satisfaction: Descriptive statistics for selected occupational groups by gender and overall

Selected occupational group	Female			Male			All		
	n	mean	s.d.	n	mean	s.d.	n	mean	s.d.
NHS Trusts									
Managers	1032	4.84	0.85	790	4.76	0.89	1822	4.80	0.87
Doctors	933	4.54	0.76	1682	4.56	0.83	2615	4.55	0.80
Nurses	8224	4.52	0.84	842	4.30	0.92	9066	4.50	0.85
Professions allied to medicine	2864	4.70	0.77	435	4.56	0.83	3299	4.68	0.78
Professional and technical staff	1024	4.36	0.85	641	4.29	0.91	1665	4.33	0.88
Administrative staff	3415	4.55	0.86	401	4.37	0.96	3816	4.53	0.87
Ancillary staff	968	4.58	0.96	683	3.97	1.09	1651	4.32	1.06
Manufacturing organisations									
Managers and senior officials	326	4.94	0.88	1569	4.91	0.91	1895	4.91	0.91
Professional occupations	24	4.70	0.64	226	4.44	0.88	250	4.46	0.86
Associate professional and technical	49	4.61	0.94	158	4.46	0.92	207	4.50	0.92
Administrative and secretarial	616	4.76	0.95	395	4.43	0.96	1011	4.63	0.97
Skilled trades	169	3.89	1.01	759	4.15	0.95	928	4.10	0.96
Process, plant and machine operatives	1637	4.22	0.95	3743	4.11	1.06	5380	4.15	1.03
Elementary occupations	211	4.71	0.99	641	4.51	1.08	852	4.56	1.06

Table 2.6 Overall Job Satisfaction: Descriptive statistics for selected occupational groups by age

Selected occupational group	16–29			30–39			40–49			50–65		
	n	mean	s.d.	n	mean	s.d.	n	mean	s.d.	n	mean	s.d.
NHS Trusts												
Managers	190	4.69	0.81	614	4.72	0.87	636	4.84	0.85	377	4.94	0.92
Doctors	592	4.36	0.72	815	4.53	0.77	695	4.62	0.83	493	4.72	0.88
Nurses	1668	4.37	0.82	3134	4.44	0.85	2480	4.53	0.85	1667	4.68	0.86
Professions allied to medicine	887	4.70	0.79	996	4.61	0.78	857	4.67	0.79	535	4.82	0.73
Professional and technical staff	379	4.30	0.83	534	4.27	0.86	481	4.34	0.89	263	4.48	0.93
Administrative staff	697	4.45	0.86	879	4.50	0.86	1122	4.53	0.86	1058	4.62	0.88
Ancillary staff	193	4.11	1.03	364	4.23	1.03	440	4.30	1.05	627	4.46	1.07
Manufacturing organisations												
Managers and senior officials	276	4.82	0.90	585	4.77	0.92	661	4.96	0.90	454	5.11	0.87
Professional occupations	77	4.52	0.75	87	4.44	0.87	54	4.40	0.93	37	4.54	0.98
Associate professional and technical	68	4.53	1.04	50	4.43	0.92	51	4.45	0.82	33	4.68	0.90
Administrative and secretarial	404	4.44	0.97	262	4.73	0.94	221	4.68	0.97	168	4.80	0.96
Skilled trades	221	3.87	1.00	245	4.01	0.94	243	4.11	0.99	207	4.48	0.86
Process, plant and machine operatives	1710	4.02	0.97	1529	4.09	1.05	1261	4.22	1.05	949	4.47	1.04
Elementary occupations	265	4.47	0.99	218	4.55	1.08	203	4.50	1.04	193	4.86	1.08

INTERNAL RELIABILITY AND DESCRIPTIVE STATISTICS
(Tables 2.7–2.12)

Table 2.7 Intrinsic Job Satisfaction: Descriptive statistics and internal reliability (alpha) by sample[†]

Sample and organisation	n	mean	s.d.	$n^{‡}$	alpha
1 Manufacturing – electronic machinery	163	4.35	1.01	159	0.85
2 Manufacturing – clothing	910	3.82	1.03	868	0.84
3 Manufacturing – electronics	163	4.85	0.88	154	0.85
4 Water authority	101	5.14	0.73	101	0.83
5 Manufacturing – chemicals	350	4.51	1.00	340	0.85
6 NHS hospitals	20746	4.59	1.03	19531	0.85
7 City Council	835	4.46	1.14	814	0.87
8 Manufacturing – glassware	882	4.31	1.04	843	0.87
9 Manufacturing – wire	747	4.40	1.06	714	0.83
10 Manufacturing – heavy plant	780	4.39	1.01	768	0.86
11 Manufacturing – chemicals	338	4.43	1.06	328	0.87
12 Mail sorting office	404	3.73	1.20	399	0.88
13 Manufacturing – various	6583	4.45	1.22	6445	0.88
14 Local Authority	4446	4.40	1.12	4278	0.85
15 Manufacturing – food/drink	574	3.95	1.21	349	0.86
16 Manufacturing – steel	461	4.70	0.95	452	0.85
17 Manufacturing – steel	186	4.31	0.80	182	0.78
18 Film processing	51	4.18	0.90	51	0.82
19 Manufacturing – vehicle parts	42	4.03	1.10	41	0.90
20 Manufacturing – metal	56	4.42	1.11	56	0.89
21 Manufacturing – metal products	72	4.20	1.03	67	0.81
22 Manufacturing – wire	387	4.35	1.06	377	0.86
23 Patent office	169	4.54	0.91	169	0.84
24 Civil Service – administration	73	4.45	1.04	71	0.86
25 Wholesale – building products	66	4.57	0.81	65	0.75
27 Manufacturing – metal products	144	4.28	1.11	142	0.88
28 Manufacturing – metal products	83	4.30	0.97	81	0.80
29 Professional association	862	4.64	1.17	814	0.87
30 Financial service call centre	831	4.07	1.11	816	0.88
31 Private healthcare call centre	454	4.23	1.10	438	0.87
32 Private healthcare administration	121	4.81	1.11	121	0.89
35 Police Force	353	4.65	0.89	345	0.83
36 Mixed industries	1030	4.42	1.07	997	0.86
37 Railway maintenance	614	4.54	1.14	591	0.90
38 Manufacturing – heavy plant	422	4.07	1.13	415	0.87
39 University	32	4.93	1.21	32	0.91
40 Mixed industries	64	5.07	1.08	62	0.88
41 Civil Service – social work	313	4.39	1.15	297	0.86
42 NHS Hospital Trust	2942	4.68	1.04	2796	0.86
44 Manufacturing – chemicals	212	4.68	1.01	212	0.89
45 Postal services	232	5.04	1.22	223	0.87
46 Manufacturing – food/drink	385	4.42	0.88	366	0.83
47 Manufacturing – machinery	436	3.95	1.32	426	0.88
48 Police Force	153	3.88	1.01	147	0.85

Table 2.7 Continued

Sample and organisation	n	mean	s.d.	n[‡]	alpha
53 Retail – fashion accessories	172	4.27	1.14	170	0.86
54 Manufacturing – medical equipment	187	4.05	0.99	181	0.81
55 Higher education	94	4.28	1.33	91	0.92
59 Manufacturing – aircraft parts	86	5.10	0.93	85	0.86
60 Logistics and consultancy	25	3.46	1.23	23	0.85
61 Manufacturing – tobacco products	45	4.60	0.92	44	0.84
62 NHS Hospital Trust	586	4.71	1.05	543	0.88
63 Local Authority	46	4.74	1.01	40	0.83
64 Local Authority	187	4.53	1.06	185	0.87
65 Film processing	225	4.49	0.94	216	0.85
68 Public utility	96	4.08	0.96	94	0.83
69 Banking	47	4.92	0.97	47	0.88
70 Mixed industries call centres	1132	3.87	1.24	1101	0.89
71 Wholesale – metal	488	4.53	1.11	477	0.89
72 NHS Ambulance Trust	53	4.47	1.01	49	0.87
76 NHS Hospital Trust	287	4.55	1.09	280	0.88
80 Mixed industries	113	4.50	1.16	104	0.90
82 Social work	108	4.80	1.09	106	0.89

[†]Details of the samples/organisations are shown in Table 1.1, pp. 6–11.
[‡]Sample sizes for alpha coefficients are smaller than for the sample as a whole because of list-wise deletion for missing values.

Table 2.8 Intrinsic Job Satisfaction: Descriptive statistics for UK SIC major industrial sectors and overall

Standard industrial classification of company	n	mean	s.d.
D Manufacturing	14758	4.36	1.15
E Electricity, gas and water supply	350	4.33	1.18
F Construction	614	4.54	1.14
G Wholesale and retail trade[†]	802	4.40	1.13
H Hotels and restaurants	96	3.89	1.21
I Transport, storage and communication	1401	4.07	1.30
J Financial intermediation	1215	4.13	1.15
K Real estate, renting and business activities	318	4.36	1.00
L Public admin and defence; compulsory social security	7050	4.42	1.10
M Education	988	4.62	1.19
N Health and social work	25653	4.60	1.04
Total	53245	4.48	1.10

[†]Includes repair of motor vehicles, motorcycles and household and personal goods.

Table 2.9 Intrinsic Job Satisfaction: Descriptive statistics for SOC major occupational groups by gender and overall

Major occupational group	Female			Male			All		
	n	mean	s.d.	n	mean	s.d.	n	mean	s.d.
Managers and senior officials	2057	4.77	1.09	3475	4.90	1.07	5532	4.85	1.08
Professional occupations	3037	4.62	1.02	2967	4.62	1.02	6004	4.62	1.02
Associate professional and technical	13623	4.61	1.00	3524	4.38	1.12	17147	4.56	1.03
Administrative and secretarial	5385	4.57	1.06	1866	4.41	1.11	7251	4.53	1.08
Skilled trades	301	4.07	1.17	1298	4.26	1.11	1599	4.22	1.12
Personal service	94	4.64	0.88	84	4.39	1.41	178	4.52	1.17
Sales and customer service	1764	4.05	1.15	867	4.00	1.22	2631	4.03	1.18
Process, plant and machine operatives	2025	4.16	1.03	5701	4.15	1.14	7726	4.15	1.12
Elementary occupations	1462	4.53	1.12	1939	4.09	1.24	3401	4.28	1.21

Table 2.10 Intrinsic Job Satisfaction: Descriptive statistics for SOC major occupational groups by age

Major occupational group	16–29			30–39			40–49			50–65		
	n	mean	s.d.	n	mean	s.d.	n	mean	s.d.	n	mean	s.d.
Managers and senior officials	731	4.67	1.09	1735	4.74	1.07	1877	4.89	1.08	1162	5.06	1.06
Professional occupations	948	4.49	0.92	1656	4.59	0.97	1962	4.63	1.03	1412	4.71	1.12
Associate professional and technical	3504	4.50	1.01	5672	4.49	1.03	4736	4.58	1.03	3065	4.73	1.01
Administrative and secretarial	1755	4.38	1.09	1861	4.50	1.09	1997	4.55	1.08	1600	4.71	1.02
Skilled trades	357	4.01	1.19	436	4.16	1.08	454	4.25	1.15	341	4.52	1.03
Personal service	74	4.60	1.07	52	4.18	1.23	37	4.74	1.16	13	–	–
Sales and customer service	1309	3.94	1.18	763	4.13	1.16	388	4.09	1.16	158	4.26	1.19
Process, plant and machine operatives	2158	3.96	1.06	2277	4.06	1.11	1914	4.27	1.13	1415	4.50	1.10
Elementary occupations	648	4.06	1.19	879	4.18	1.21	881	4.29	1.20	992	4.55	1.19

– Too few respondents (<20) to warrant descriptive statistics.

Table 2.11 Intrinsic Job Satisfaction: Descriptive statistics for selected occupational groups by gender and overall

Selected occupational group	Female			Male			All		
	n	mean	s.d.	n	mean	s.d.	n	mean	s.d.
NHS Trusts									
Managers	1057	5.02	1.01	813	4.93	1.03	1870	4.98	1.02
Doctors	938	4.67	0.90	1689	4.73	0.96	2627	4.71	0.94
Nurses	8414	4.58	0.99	901	4.37	1.09	9315	4.56	1.00
Professions allied to medicine	2966	4.80	0.93	453	4.64	1.01	3419	4.78	0.94
Professional and technical staff	1025	4.35	1.04	641	4.31	1.12	1666	4.34	1.07
Administrative staff	3539	4.58	1.04	421	4.40	1.15	3960	4.56	1.05
Ancillary staff	986	4.55	1.10	692	4.01	1.26	1678	4.33	1.20
Manufacturing organisations									
Managers and senior officials	347	4.92	1.00	1684	5.03	1.05	2031	5.01	1.04
Professional occupations	42	4.58	0.88	536	4.57	0.94	578	4.57	0.93
Associate professional and technical	137	4.62	1.13	521	4.04	1.27	658	4.16	1.26
Administrative and secretarial	760	4.63	1.09	608	4.41	1.09	1368	4.53	1.10
Skilled trades	192	3.95	1.16	897	4.26	1.08	1089	4.21	1.10
Process, plant and machine operatives	1876	4.13	1.03	5362	4.14	1.15	7238	4.14	1.12
Elementary occupations	214	4.62	1.08	694	4.44	1.18	908	4.48	1.16

Table 2.12 Intrinsic Job Satisfaction: Descriptive statistics for selected occupational groups by age

Selected occupational group	16–29			30–39			40–49			50–65		
	n	mean	s.d.	n	mean	s.d.	n	mean	s.d.	n	mean	s.d.
NHS Trusts												
Managers	199	4.76	0.97	635	4.89	1.03	648	5.04	0.99	383	5.14	1.04
Doctors	590	4.48	0.87	819	4.69	0.90	698	4.81	0.95	500	4.89	1.03
Nurses	1714	4.40	0.98	3223	4.50	1.00	2552	4.62	0.99	1709	4.75	0.98
Professions allied to medicine	911	4.76	0.95	1043	4.69	0.95	884	4.78	0.96	556	4.94	0.86
Professional and technical staff	379	4.24	1.02	534	4.26	1.05	482	4.37	1.08	263	4.55	1.13
Administrative staff	725	4.40	1.06	905	4.49	1.06	1172	4.57	1.05	1099	4.71	1.03
Ancillary staff	196	4.02	1.15	372	4.19	1.16	446	4.29	1.22	637	4.53	1.18
Manufacturing organisations												
Managers and senior officials	296	4.85	1.04	621	4.81	1.07	713	5.10	1.02	487	5.24	0.98
Professional occupations	168	4.54	0.82	159	4.50	0.99	144	4.59	0.95	123	4.73	0.99
Associate professional and technical	143	4.31	1.23	177	3.93	1.27	173	4.12	1.24	159	4.35	1.30
Administrative and secretarial	504	4.29	1.13	343	4.61	1.08	333	4.64	1.08	231	4.73	1.02
Skilled trades	246	3.87	1.18	288	4.13	1.09	298	4.26	1.11	248	4.61	0.93
Process, plant and machine operatives	2094	3.95	1.06	2115	4.05	1.12	1784	4.26	1.14	1300	4.49	1.11
Elementary occupations	284	4.35	1.12	236	4.44	1.19	212	4.47	1.12	202	4.87	1.10

INTERNAL RELIABILITY AND DESCRIPTIVE STATISTICS
(Tables 2.13–2.18)

Table 2.13 Extrinsic Job Satisfaction: Descriptive statistics and internal reliability (alpha) by sample[†]

	Sample and organisation	n	mean	s.d.	n[‡]	alpha
1	Manufacturing – electronic machinery	163	4.92	0.78	156	0.71
2	Manufacturing – clothing	910	3.92	0.92	863	0.77
3	Manufacturing – electronics	160	5.00	0.70	153	0.74
4	Water authority	101	4.69	0.63	101	0.64
6	NHS hospitals	20740	4.45	0.83	19863	0.71
7	City Council	836	4.49	0.89	821	0.73
9	Manufacturing – wire	748	4.11	0.96	718	0.78
11	Manufacturing – chemicals	338	4.19	0.94	330	0.77
12	Mail sorting office	404	3.78	0.99	395	0.80
13	Manufacturing – various	6590	4.56	1.07	6413	0.83
14	Local Authority	4450	4.31	0.92	4224	0.73
15	Manufacturing – food/drink	578	4.01	0.95	559	0.69
18	Film processing	51	4.27	0.78	49	0.78
19	Manufacturing – vehicle parts	42	4.27	0.91	41	0.84
20	Manufacturing – metal	56	4.51	0.94	56	0.83
21	Manufacturing – metal products	73	3.68	0.96	71	0.81
22	Manufacturing – wire	386	4.27	1.07	377	0.84
23	Patent office	169	4.52	0.81	164	0.74
25	Wholesale – building products	66	4.14	0.87	63	0.70
27	Manufacturing – metal products	144	4.46	0.85	141	0.80
28	Manufacturing – metal products	83	3.90	0.97	82	0.81
29	Professional association	853	4.48	0.95	815	0.75
30	Financial service call centre	830	4.74	0.79	819	0.71
31	Private healthcare call centre	454	4.80	0.83	438	0.78
32	Private healthcare administration	121	5.04	0.85	121	0.79
35	Police Force	353	4.45	0.81	348	0.74
36	Mixed industries	1033	4.63	0.94	994	0.80
37	Railway maintenance	613	4.54	0.99	586	0.83
38	Manufacturing – heavy plant	422	4.24	0.98	414	0.80
39	University	32	4.79	0.93	32	0.79
41	Civil Service – social work	313	4.27	1.01	302	0.78
42	NHS Hospital Trust	2941	4.67	0.87	2848	0.76
45	Postal services	232	5.05	1.01	228	0.77
46	Manufacturing – food/drink	374	4.77	0.83	366	0.80
48	Police Force	153	4.00	0.85	152	0.71
51	Public transport call centre	49	4.05	1.10	48	0.83
53	Retail – fashion accessories	171	4.38	1.10	171	0.83
54	Manufacturing – medical equipment	187	4.16	0.90	181	0.78
55	Higher education	94	3.92	1.07	90	0.81
60	Logistics and consultancy	25	3.52	0.93	24	0.70
61	Manufacturing – tobacco products	45	4.61	0.75	44	0.72

Table 2.13   Continued

Sample and organisation	n	mean	s.d.	n[‡]	alpha
63 Local Authority	45	4.32	0.93	41	0.70
65 Film processing	226	4.49	0.89	209	0.80
68 Public utility	96	4.23	0.96	94	0.84
69 Banking	47	5.12	0.71	47	0.70
70 Mixed industries call centres	1135	4.52	0.93	1103	0.77
71 Wholesale – metal	488	4.72	1.00	477	0.86
72 NHS Ambulance Trust	53	4.68	0.89	53	0.80
76 NHS Hospital Trust	288	4.62	0.93	281	0.78
80 Mixed industries	115	4.52	1.09	104	0.86
82 Social work	108	4.70	1.00	106	0.84

[†]Details of the samples/organisations are shown in Table 1.1, pp. 6–11.
[‡]Sample sizes for alpha coefficients are smaller than for the sample as a whole because of list-wise deletion for missing values.

Table 2.14   Extrinsic Job Satisfaction: Descriptive statistics for UK SIC major industrial sectors and overall

Standard Industrial Classification of company	n	mean	s.d.
D Manufacturing	11299	4.41	1.05
E Electricity, gas and water supply	350	4.51	0.86
F Construction	613	4.54	0.99
G Wholesale and retail trade[†]	801	4.57	1.02
H Hotels and restaurants	97	4.44	0.93
I Transport, storage and communication	1454	4.31	1.08
J Financial intermediation	1216	4.77	0.82
K Real estate, renting and business activities	319	4.40	0.92
L Public admin and defence; compulsory social security	6795	4.38	0.91
M Education	979	4.43	0.98
N Health and social work	25061	4.48	0.85
Total	48984	4.46	0.92

[†]Includes repair of motor vehicles, motorcycles and household and personal goods.

Table 2.15 Extrinsic Job Satisfaction: Descriptive statistics for SOC major occupational groups by gender and overall

Major occupational group	Female			Male			All		
	n	mean	s.d.	n	mean	s.d.	n	mean	s.d.
Managers and senior officials	2008	4.60	0.89	3315	4.69	0.90	5323	4.65	0.90
Professional occupations	3017	4.43	0.87	2659	4.37	0.86	5676	4.40	0.87
Associate professional and technical	13261	4.50	0.82	3085	4.35	0.87	16346	4.47	0.83
Administrative and secretarial	5063	4.61	0.86	1472	4.50	0.93	6535	4.58	0.88
Skilled trades	280	4.13	0.99	1155	4.17	1.01	1435	4.16	1.00
Personal service	94	4.65	0.92	84	4.50	1.23	178	4.58	1.08
Sales and customer service	1797	4.65	0.90	887	4.56	0.92	2684	4.62	0.91
Process, plant and machine operatives	1797	4.34	0.98	4085	4.18	1.08	5882	4.23	1.05
Elementary occupations	1451	4.58	0.98	1880	4.12	1.10	3331	4.32	1.07

Table 2.16 Extrinsic Job Satisfaction: Descriptive statistics for SOC major occupational groups by age

Major occupational group	16–29			30–39			40–49			50–65		
	n	mean	s.d.	n	mean	s.d.	n	mean	s.d.	n	mean	s.d.
Managers and senior officials	703	4.65	0.89	1674	4.59	0.88	1805	4.63	0.90	1109	4.82	0.92
Professional occupations	859	4.31	0.81	1585	4.40	0.83	1873	4.38	0.87	1322	4.47	0.94
Associate professional and technical	3359	4.46	0.81	5412	4.42	0.82	4517	4.46	0.83	2888	4.61	0.85
Administrative and secretarial	1573	4.58	0.88	1674	4.59	0.86	1777	4.54	0.89	1475	4.63	0.88
Skilled trades	331	4.11	1.00	391	4.12	0.97	398	4.12	1.03	301	4.36	1.01
Personal service	74	4.71	1.13	52	4.32	1.01	37	4.59	0.98	13	–	–
Sales and customer service	1347	4.57	0.91	776	4.68	0.90	389	4.67	0.90	159	4.73	0.87
Process, plant and machine operatives	1777	4.15	0.99	1696	4.18	1.08	1395	4.26	1.07	1067	4.52	1.06
Elementary occupations	627	4.27	1.03	855	4.28	1.08	872	4.30	1.05	977	4.43	1.09

–Too few respondents (<20) to warrant descriptive statistics.

Table 2.17 Extrinsic Job Satisfaction: Descriptive statistics for selected occupational groups by gender and overall

Selected occupational group	Female			Male			All		
	n	mean	s.d.	n	mean	s.d.	n	mean	s.d.
NHS Trusts									
Managers	1034	4.67	0.83	790	4.62	0.86	1824	4.65	0.84
Doctors	934	4.44	0.77	1691	4.41	0.83	2625	4.42	0.81
Nurses	8243	4.47	0.83	842	4.25	0.88	9085	4.45	0.83
Professions allied to medicine	2864	4.63	0.75	436	4.48	0.79	3300	4.61	0.75
Professional and technical staff	1025	4.36	0.81	641	4.27	0.85	1666	4.33	0.82
Administrative staff	3423	4.53	0.82	401	4.35	0.91	3824	4.51	0.83
Ancillary staff	977	4.59	0.94	685	3.93	1.06	1662	4.32	1.05
Manufacturing organisations									
Managers and senior officials	326	4.95	0.86	1570	4.82	0.90	1896	4.84	0.90
Professional occupations	24	4.61	0.75	226	4.44	0.89	250	4.46	0.87
Associate professional and technical	49	4.62	0.98	158	4.49	0.94	207	4.52	0.95
Administrative and secretarial	619	4.89	0.92	395	4.52	0.93	1014	4.74	0.94
Skilled trades	170	3.95	1.01	759	4.13	0.97	929	4.09	0.98
Process, plant and machine operatives	1648	4.32	0.99	3747	4.17	1.08	5395	4.21	1.06
Elementary occupations	211	4.77	1.02	641	4.56	1.08	852	4.61	1.07

Table 2.18 Extrinsic Job Satisfaction: Descriptive statistics for selected occupational groups by age

Selected occupational group	16–29			30–39			40–49			50–65		
	n	mean	s.d.	n	mean	s.d.	n	mean	s.d.	n	mean	s.d.
NHS Trusts												
Managers	191	4.62	0.80	615	4.57	0.83	637	4.66	0.82	376	4.78	0.90
Doctors	592	4.26	0.75	819	4.40	0.78	698	4.46	0.82	496	4.59	0.86
Nurses	1668	4.34	0.78	3136	4.40	0.82	2482	4.46	0.84	1680	4.63	0.86
Professions allied to medicine	887	4.65	0.76	997	4.54	0.75	857	4.59	0.76	535	4.72	0.74
Professional and technical staff	379	4.36	0.80	534	4.28	0.82	482	4.31	0.83	263	4.43	0.86
Administrative staff	698	4.48	0.82	879	4.51	0.80	1123	4.49	0.82	1064	4.56	0.86
Ancillary staff	194	4.18	1.00	365	4.27	1.03	445	4.30	1.03	631	4.40	1.06
Manufacturing organisations												
Managers and senior officials	276	4.80	0.89	585	4.73	0.90	662	4.85	0.89	454	5.01	0.88
Professional occupations	77	4.53	0.83	87	4.49	0.81	54	4.31	0.99	37	4.46	0.93
Associate professional and technical	68	4.56	1.06	50	4.45	0.96	51	4.49	0.81	33	4.69	0.96
Administrative and secretarial	404	4.61	0.94	262	4.82	0.92	222	4.75	0.96	170	4.85	0.95
Skilled trades	222	3.97	0.98	245	4.01	0.99	243	4.07	1.00	207	4.40	0.92
Process, plant and machine operatives	1713	4.14	1.00	1535	4.17	1.09	1265	4.24	1.08	952	4.50	1.07
Elementary occupations	265	4.56	1.00	218	4.64	1.07	203	4.53	1.03	193	4.83	1.16

ORGANISATIONAL COMMITMENT

ORIGIN AND APPLICATIONS

This measure of organisational commitment was developed by Cook and Wall (1980) as a robust instrument easily completed by employees at all levels and which is psychometrically sound. It can be scored to provide a single index of Overall Organisational Commitment, the original version containing nine items and a shorter six-item version having emerged. The original scale was designed to yield separate indices of Organisational Identification, Organisational Loyalty, and Organisational Involvement, but only the first of these has proven consistently reliable across samples.

The overall concept of organisational commitment refers to people's affective reactions to their employing organisation as a whole. This is made up of the three components originally specified by Buchanan (1974): (1) Organisational Identification represents pride in the organisation and internalisation of its goals and values; (2) Organisational Loyalty reflects affection for and attachment to the organisation, a sense of belongingness manifested as a wish to stay; and (3) Organisational Involvement refers to engagement with the work itself because of its contribution to the organisation as a whole. The instrument corresponds closely to two other measures of organisational commitment developed in the USA, which cover the same three components, namely Porter et al.'s (1974) Organisational Commitment Questionnaire, and Meyer and Allen's (1984) Affective Commitment Scale.

The present instrument has been used with a wide range of employees including: public sector employees (Gould-Williams, 2003, 2004); shop-floor manufacturing workers (Fenton-O'Creevy et al. 1997; Matthews & Shepherd, 2002; Parker, 2003); call centre and service sector employees (Biggs & Swailes, 2006); and employees of NHS Trusts (Borrill et al., 1998; Hicks-Clarke & Iles, 2000). The above studies have found the scale to be sensitive to a wide range of factors including: human resource management practices; flexible working hours; organisational justice; interpersonal trust; employment status (agency versus permanent employees); and reported organisational performance. Additional correlates include:

reported job performance (De Cuyper & De Witte, 2006); and autonomy and proactivity at work (Parker, Williams & Turner, 2006).

PERMISSIONS, AVAILABILITY AND QUALIFICATIONS

There are no specific restrictions on the use of this measure. It is freely available for use by psychologists or other practitioners involved in organisational survey research.

SCALE ITEMS AND RESPONSE OPTIONS

The Organisational Commitment Scale consists of nine items, and respondents are asked to indicate on a five-point response scale the extent to which they agree or disagree with each statement. The items and response scale are as follows:

Please indicate on this scale how much you agree or disagree with each statement by placing a tick in the appropriate box.

	1	2	3	4	5
	Strongly disagree	Disagree	Neither agree nor disagree	Agree	Strongly agree
1. I am quite proud to be able to tell people who it is I work for.	[ ]	[ ]	[ ]	[ ]	[ ]
2. I sometimes feel like leaving this employment for good.	[ ]	[ ]	[ ]	[ ]	[ ]
3. I'm not willing to put myself out just to help the organisation.	[ ]	[ ]	[ ]	[ ]	[ ]
4. Even if the firm were not doing too well financially, I would be reluctant to change to another employer.	[ ]	[ ]	[ ]	[ ]	[ ]
5. I feel myself to be part of the organisation.	[ ]	[ ]	[ ]	[ ]	[ ]
6. In my work I like to feel I am making some effort, not just for myself but for the organisation as well.	[ ]	[ ]	[ ]	[ ]	[ ]
7. The offer of a bit more money with another employer would not seriously make me think of changing my job.	[ ]	[ ]	[ ]	[ ]	[ ]
8. I would not recommend a close friend to join our staff.	[ ]	[ ]	[ ]	[ ]	[ ]
9. To know that my own work had made a contribution to the good of the organisation would please me.	[ ]	[ ]	[ ]	[ ]	[ ]

The Overall Organisational Commitment measure can be constructed using all nine items, or as a six-item subscale using items 1, 2, 3, 4, 5 and 7. The three subscales measuring the separate components of commitment each have three items, which for Organisational Identification comprise items 1, 5 and 8; for Organisational Loyalty are items 2, 4, 7; and for Organisational Involvement are items 3, 6 and 9. However, the latter two subscales have been excluded from this manual due to the substantial number of studies for which they displayed weak internal consistency reliability.

Note that items 2, 3 and 8 are negatively phrased and consequently are reverse-scored.

SCORING

Originally, scoring was by summation across items. Thus the range of possible scores for Overall Organisational Commitment was either 9–45 (for the 9-item version) or 6–30 (for the 6-item version), and for the 3-item Organisational Identification subscale was from 3 to 15. The limitation of this method is that the omission of a response to even a single item invalidates a respondent's score.

For the above reason the scoring practice in this manual has been to calculate the mean item score, and to require responses to a minimum of seven items for the 9-item measure of Overall Organisational Commitment, four items for the 6-item measure of Overall Organisational Commitment and two items for the 3-item Organisational Identification subscale. In practice, very few missing responses arise, and comparisons between the two methods (requiring responses to all items versus allowing missing responses on up to two items) show no meaningful differences in terms of means and standard deviations.

INTERNAL RELIABILITY AND DESCRIPTIVE STATISTICS

The following tables present the internal reliabilities and benchmarking data for the scales. The first six Tables cover Overall Organisational Commitment (9-item version), and show, respectively:

Table 3.1 – descriptive statistics and internal reliabilities (Cronbach's (1951) alpha coefficient of internal consistency) by sample
Table 3.2 – descriptive statistics for the SIC major industrial sectors
Table 3.3 – descriptive statistics for the SOC major occupational groups by gender

Table 3.4 – descriptive statistics for the SOC major occupational groups by age

Table 3.5 – descriptive statistics for the selected occupational groups by gender;

Table 3.6 – descriptive statistics for the selected occupational groups by age

Tables 3.7–3.12 and 3.13–3.18 present the corresponding information for Overall Organisational Commitment (6-item version) and Organisational Identification respectively.

OVERALL ORGANISATIONAL COMMITMENT (9-ITEM SCALE)

INTERNAL RELIABILITY AND DESCRIPTIVE STATISTICS
(Tables 3.1–3.6)

Table 3.1 Organisational Commitment (9-item scale): Descriptive statistics and internal reliability (alpha) by sample[†]

Sample and Organisation	n	mean	s.d.	n[‡]	alpha
2 Manufacturing – clothing	914	3.07	0.68	892	0.81
13 Manufacturing – various	6600	3.59	0.69	6444	0.77
16 Manufacturing – steel	459	3.50	0.71	455	0.86
19 Manufacturing – vehicle parts	42	3.50	0.55	41	0.79
20 Manufacturing – metal	56	3.53	0.65	55	0.85
27 Manufacturing – metal products	142	3.66	0.60	140	0.78
36 Mixed industries	325	3.56	0.76	259	0.87
48 Police Force	154	3.09	0.68	153	0.81
53 Retail – fashion accessories	172	3.28	0.76	170	0.85
55 Higher education	94	3.37	0.67	91	0.81
56 Banking	125	4.01	0.68	122	0.86
78 Estate agency	32	3.78	0.58	29	0.80
79 Railway maintenance	109	3.43	0.81	103	0.83
80 Mixed industries	114	3.47	0.58	107	0.74

[†]Details of the samples/organisations are shown in Table 1.1, pp. 6–11.
[‡]Sample sizes for alpha coefficients are smaller than for the sample as a whole because of list-wise deletion for missing values.

Table 3.2 Organisational Commitment (9-item scale): Descriptive statistics for UK SIC major industrial sectors and overall

Standard Industrial Classification of company	n	mean	s.d.
D Manufacturing	8213	3.53	0.71
F Construction	109	3.43	0.81
G Wholesale and retail trade[†]	172	3.28	0.76
I Transport, storage and communication	382	3.51	0.75
J Financial intermediation	182	3.91	0.64
K Real estate, renting and business activities	32	3.78	0.58
L Public admin and defence; compulsory social security	154	3.09	0.68
M Education	94	3.37	0.67
Total	9338	3.52	0.71

[†]Includes repair of motor vehicles, motorcycles and household and personal goods.

Table 3.3 Organisational Commitment (9-item scale): Descriptive statistics for SOC major occupational groups by gender and overall

Major occupational group	Female			Male			All		
	n	mean	s.d.	n	mean	s.d.	n	mean	s.d.
Managers and senior officials	339	3.75	0.62	1419	3.88	0.62	1758	3.86	0.62
Professional occupations	62	3.40	0.65	281	3.29	0.54	343	3.31	0.56
Associate professional and technical	146	3.29	0.69	272	3.35	0.66	418	3.33	0.67
Administrative and secretarial	593	3.65	0.67	414	3.59	0.73	1007	3.62	0.69
Skilled trades	171	3.20	0.68	341	3.32	0.58	512	3.28	0.62
Personal service	78	3.77	0.69	42	3.82	0.88	120	3.79	0.76
Sales and customer service	185	3.31	0.71	156	3.31	0.66	341	3.31	0.68
Process, plant and machine operatives	1031	3.25	0.67	2430	3.46	0.76	3461	3.40	0.74
Elementary occupations	189	3.51	0.56	503	3.54	0.68	692	3.53	0.65

Table 3.4 Organisational Commitment (9-item scale): Descriptive statistics for SOC major occupational groups by age

Major occupational group	16–29			30–39			40–49			50–65		
	n	mean	s.d.	n	mean	s.d.	n	mean	s.d.	n	mean	s.d.
Managers and senior officials	271	3.73	0.64	540	3.74	0.60	610	3.95	0.60	416	3.96	0.60
Professional occupations	81	3.22	0.48	87	3.30	0.49	107	3.39	0.57	88	3.35	0.65
Associate professional and technical	107	3.32	0.56	118	3.22	0.69	126	3.34	0.73	66	3.48	0.62
Administrative and secretarial	385	3.44	0.71	275	3.67	0.65	227	3.73	0.64	167	3.78	0.71
Skilled trades	153	2.98	0.67	106	3.24	0.57	121	3.43	0.54	137	3.51	0.50
Personal service	72	3.70	0.80	35	3.81	0.66	6	–	–	5	–	–
Sales and customer service	210	3.22	0.69	73	3.35	0.70	34	3.58	0.56	20	3.62	0.45
Process, plant and machine operatives	1204	3.22	0.72	951	3.36	0.76	820	3.51	0.71	691	3.68	0.68
Elementary occupations	221	3.43	0.62	162	3.57	0.66	171	3.52	0.66	170	3.62	0.63

– Too few respondents (<20) to warrant descriptive statistics.

Table 3.5 Organisational Commitment (9-item scale): Descriptive statistics for selected occupational groups by gender and overall

Selected occupational group	Female			Male			All		
	n	mean	s.d.	n	mean	s.d.	n	mean	s.d.
Manufacturing organisations									
Managers and senior officials	292	3.76	0.61	1319	3.88	0.62	1611	3.86	0.62
Professional occupations	18	–	–	252	3.32	0.52	270	3.31	0.53
Associate professional and technical	41	3.22	0.52	119	3.40	0.46	160	3.35	0.48
Administrative and secretarial	560	3.65	0.68	390	3.57	0.72	950	3.61	0.70
Skilled trades	171	3.20	0.68	341	3.32	0.58	512	3.28	0.62
Process, plant and machine operatives	1031	3.25	0.67	2321	3.46	0.76	3352	3.40	0.74
Elementary occupations	198	3.50	0.55	506	3.56	0.65	704	3.54	0.62

– Too few respondents (<20) to warrant descriptive statistics.

Table 3.6 Organisational Commitment (9-item scale): Descriptive statistics for selected occupational groups by age

Selected occupational group	16–29			30–39			40–49			50–65		
	n	mean	s.d.	n	mean	s.d.	n	mean	s.d.	n	mean	s.d.
Manufacturing organisations												
Managers and senior officials	246	3.72	0.65	493	3.75	0.60	564	3.95	0.61	395	3.96	0.60
Professional occupations	76	3.21	0.45	74	3.31	0.44	82	3.36	0.56	58	3.45	0.62
Associate professional and technical	60	3.18	0.40	38	3.35	0.46	36	3.43	0.50	30	3.61	0.55
Administrative and secretarial	377	3.43	0.71	252	3.66	0.65	213	3.72	0.65	159	3.79	0.71
Skilled trades	153	2.98	0.67	106	3.24	0.57	121	3.43	0.54	137	3.51	0.50
Process, plant and machine operatives	1188	3.22	0.72	924	3.36	0.76	782	3.51	0.70	664	3.69	0.67
Elementary occupations	232	3.42	0.61	171	3.58	0.62	168	3.55	0.61	165	3.64	0.62

ORGANISATIONAL COMMITMENT
(6-ITEM SCALE)

INTERNAL RELIABILITY AND DESCRIPTIVE STATISTICS
(Tables 3.7–3.12)

Table 3.7   Organisational Commitment (6-item scale): Descriptive statistics and internal reliability (alpha) by sample[†]

Sample and organisation		n	mean	s.d.	n[‡]	alpha
2	Manufacturing – clothing	914	2.93	0.73	896	0.72
6	NHS hospitals	20708	3.15	0.72	20294	0.78
8	Manufacturing – glassware	887	3.17	0.71	855	0.75
9	Manufacturing – wire	748	3.29	0.72	737	0.75
10	Manufacturing – heavy plant	774	3.69	0.65	764	0.72
12	Mail sorting office	402	3.19	0.75	221	0.66
13	Manufacturing – various	6613	3.45	0.77	6484	0.69
14	Local Authority	3368	3.32	0.67	3246	0.72
16	Manufacturing – steel	460	3.38	0.76	457	0.80
17	Manufacturing – steel	375	3.46	0.67	374	0.78
18	Film processing	51	3.42	0.72	51	0.77
19	Manufacturing – vehicle parts	42	3.36	0.61	41	0.71
20	Manufacturing – metal	56	3.40	0.70	55	0.78
22	Manufacturing – wire	390	3.39	0.73	388	0.74
25	Wholesale – building products	67	3.33	0.66	66	0.78
27	Manufacturing – metal products	142	3.51	0.67	140	0.70
36	Mixed industries	326	3.45	0.84	261	0.84
46	Manufacturing – food/drink	374	3.35	0.59	369	0.67
48	Police Force	154	2.89	0.79	153	0.78
50	Mixed industries	115	3.51	0.70	113	0.72
53	Retail – fashion accessories	172	3.14	0.81	170	0.79
55	Higher education	94	3.20	0.74	92	0.75
56	Banking	125	3.83	0.77	122	0.81
60	Logistics and consultancy	24	2.78	0.74	24	0.70
65	Film processing	233	3.45	0.66	228	0.78
72	NHS Ambulance Trust	53	3.49	0.64	49	0.71
74	Extraction of oil and gas	72	3.38	0.75	72	0.83
78	Estate agency	32	3.67	0.64	31	0.75
79	Railway maintenance	109	3.36	0.85	104	0.77
80	Mixed industries	114	3.41	0.62	107	0.63
82	Social work	108	3.40	0.83	107	0.81

[†] Details of the samples/organisations are shown in Table 1.1, pp. 6–11.
[‡] Sample sizes for alpha coefficients are smaller than for the sample as a whole because of list-wise deletion for missing values.

Table 3.8   Organisational Commitment (6-item scale): Descriptive statistics for UK SIC major industrial sectors and overall

Standard Industrial Classification of company		n	mean	s.d.
C	Mining and quarrying	72	3.38	0.75
D	Manufacturing	11874	3.39	0.76
E	Electricity, gas and water supply	16	–	–
F	Construction	109	3.36	0.85
G	Wholesale and retail trade[†]	239	3.20	0.77
I	Transport, storage and communication	785	3.30	0.79
J	Financial intermediation	182	3.76	0.71
K	Real estate, renting and business activities	340	3.42	0.70
L	Public admin and defence; compulsory social security	3522	3.30	0.68
M	Education	94	3.20	0.74
N	Health and social work	20869	3.15	0.72
Total		38102	3.25	0.74

[†]Includes repair of motor vehicles, motorcycles and household and personal goods.
– Too few respondents (<20) to warrant descriptive statistics.

Table 3.9 Organisational Commitment (6-item scale): Descriptive statistics for SOC major occupational groups by gender and overall

Major occupational group	Female			Male			All		
	n	mean	s.d.	n	mean	s.d.	n	mean	s.d.
Managers and senior officials	1708	3.45	0.71	2786	3.60	0.76	4494	3.55	0.75
Professional occupations	1600	3.10	0.66	2157	3.18	0.76	3757	3.15	0.72
Associate professional and technical	11550	3.12	0.68	2272	3.14	0.78	13822	3.12	0.70
Administrative and secretarial	3704	3.30	0.72	878	3.28	0.80	4582	3.30	0.74
Skilled trades	276	3.16	0.70	633	3.19	0.70	909	3.18	0.70
Personal service	84	3.64	0.74	82	3.67	0.79	166	3.65	0.77
Sales and customer service	187	3.18	0.78	162	3.19	0.70	349	3.19	0.74
Process, plant and machine operatives	1643	3.18	0.70	4665	3.37	0.78	6308	3.32	0.76
Elementary occupations	1169	3.30	0.69	1532	3.16	0.78	2701	3.22	0.75

Table 3.10 Organisational Commitment (6-item scale): Descriptive statistics for SOC major occupational groups by age

Major occupational group	16–29			30–39			40–49			50–65		
	n	*mean*	*s.d.*	*n*	*mean*	*s.d.*	*n*	*mean*	*s.d.*	*n*	*mean*	*s.d.*
Managers and senior officials	612	3.35	0.74	1444	3.45	0.71	1540	3.61	0.74	969	3.73	0.75
Professional occupations	700	2.85	0.67	1126	3.09	0.69	1156	3.25	0.69	767	3.35	0.75
Associate professional and technical	2862	3.02	0.67	4490	3.04	0.70	3795	3.18	0.71	2507	3.31	0.68
Administrative and secretarial	1089	3.16	0.73	1099	3.28	0.73	1272	3.33	0.73	1113	3.42	0.74
Skilled trades	232	2.94	0.71	203	3.11	0.67	241	3.34	0.68	231	3.34	0.64
Personal service	74	3.60	0.86	49	3.55	0.72	30	3.86	0.58	11	–	–
Sales and customer service	214	3.08	0.76	74	3.23	0.74	36	3.45	0.63	21	3.53	0.47
Process, plant and machine operatives	1809	3.14	0.76	1864	3.29	0.77	1537	3.43	0.74	1196	3.56	0.72
Elementary occupations	535	3.09	0.72	692	3.17	0.74	718	3.24	0.74	760	3.35	0.74

– Too few respondents (<20) to warrant descriptive statistics.

Table 3.11 Organisational Commitment (6-item scale): Descriptive statistics for selected occupational groups by gender and overall

Selected occupational group	Female			Male			All		
	n	mean	s.d.	n	mean	s.d.	n	mean	s.d.
NHS Trusts									
Managers	891	3.46	0.71	734	3.49	0.80	1625	3.47	0.75
Doctors	829	2.95	0.71	1521	3.15	0.80	2350	3.08	0.77
Nurses	7219	3.09	0.69	690	2.94	0.80	7909	3.07	0.70
Professions allied to medicine	2491	3.14	0.64	377	3.15	0.76	2868	3.14	0.66
Professional and technical staff	875	3.10	0.68	566	3.15	0.76	1441	3.12	0.71
Administrative staff	2885	3.25	0.71	348	3.12	0.80	3233	3.24	0.72
Ancillary staff	749	3.31	0.71	586	3.01	0.82	1335	3.18	0.77
Manufacturing organisations									
Managers and senior officials	329	3.59	0.72	1518	3.73	0.71	1847	3.71	0.72
Professional occupations	25	3.12	0.67	424	3.27	0.64	449	3.27	0.65
Associate professional and technical	61	3.10	0.55	232	3.39	0.59	293	3.33	0.59
Administrative and secretarial	648	3.52	0.75	434	3.38	0.82	1082	3.47	0.78
Skilled trades	173	3.09	0.73	455	3.12	0.66	628	3.11	0.68
Process, plant and machine operatives	1494	3.15	0.70	4458	3.37	0.78	5952	3.31	0.76
Elementary occupations	203	3.32	0.65	613	3.35	0.73	816	3.34	0.71

Table 3.12 Organisational Commitment (6-item scale): Descriptive statistics for selected occupational groups by age

Selected occupational group	16–29			30–39			40–49			50–65		
	n	mean	s.d.	n	mean	s.d.	n	mean	s.d.	n	mean	s.d.
NHS Trusts												
Managers	180	3.18	0.73	549	3.41	0.71	550	3.52	0.74	343	3.65	0.80
Doctors	512	2.73	0.67	746	3.03	0.73	630	3.24	0.77	442	3.34	0.80
Nurses	1524	2.95	0.66	2743	2.99	0.70	2096	3.14	0.71	1431	3.26	0.68
Professions allied to medicine	747	3.08	0.63	866	3.07	0.64	757	3.15	0.67	471	3.36	0.65
Professional and technical staff	340	3.00	0.68	456	3.10	0.68	413	3.17	0.73	225	3.23	0.77
Administrative staff	598	3.08	0.69	734	3.18	0.70	952	3.26	0.72	897	3.36	0.72
Ancillary staff	173	3.01	0.73	301	3.10	0.74	361	3.17	0.79	480	3.31	0.76
Manufacturing organisations												
Managers and senior officials	280	3.47	0.76	550	3.58	0.69	648	3.80	0.70	455	3.89	0.66
Professional occupations	110	3.13	0.57	121	3.21	0.57	128	3.31	0.65	110	3.41	0.72
Associate professional and technical	74	3.09	0.57	71	3.27	0.58	85	3.47	0.59	61	3.54	0.57
Administrative and secretarial	431	3.26	0.78	274	3.51	0.75	246	3.59	0.71	180	3.70	0.80
Skilled trades	169	2.83	0.70	130	3.06	0.64	146	3.23	0.67	184	3.33	0.59
Process, plant and machine operatives	1766	3.13	0.76	1749	3.28	0.77	1438	3.42	0.74	1112	3.57	0.72
Elementary occupations	262	3.21	0.68	204	3.37	0.71	191	3.38	0.70	186	3.45	0.72

INTERNAL RELIABILITY AND DESCRIPTIVE STATISTICS
(Tables 3.13–3.18)

Table 3.13 Organisational Identification: Descriptive statistics and internal reliability (alpha) by sample[†]

Sample and organisation		n	mean	s.d.	n[‡]	alpha
2	Manufacturing – clothing	914	3.03	0.88	907	0.71
13	Manufacturing – various	6623	3.62	0.85	6565	0.60
16	Manufacturing – steel	460	3.51	0.87	458	0.79
19	Manufacturing – vehicle parts	42	3.48	0.77	42	0.78
20	Manufacturing – metal	56	3.48	0.79	56	0.74
27	Manufacturing – metal products	144	3.78	0.73	140	0.66
30	Financial service call centre	830	3.58	0.74	627	0.67
36	Mixed industries	1035	3.54	0.85	1017	0.77
48	Police Force	154	2.84	0.92	154	0.75
53	Retail – fashion accessories	172	3.36	0.86	172	0.67
54	Manufacturing – medical equipment	192	3.24	0.77	189	0.64
55	Higher education	94	3.39	0.95	94	0.85
56	Banking	125	4.11	0.80	124	0.80
69	Banking	47	3.53	0.69	46	0.66
78	Estate agency	32	3.95	0.75	29	0.61
79	Railway maintenance	109	3.46	0.94	107	0.65
80	Mixed industries	114	3.55	0.80	111	0.63

[†]Details of the samples/organisations are shown in Table 1.1, pp. 6–11.
[‡]Sample sizes for alpha coefficients are smaller than for the sample as a whole because of listwise deletion for missing values.

Table 3.14 Organisational Identification: Descriptive statistics for UK SIC major industrial sectors and overall

Standard Industrial Classification of company		n	mean	s.d.
D	Manufacturing	8431	3.54	0.87
F	Construction	109	3.46	0.94
G	Wholesale and retail trade[†]	172	3.36	0.86
I	Transport, storage and communication	383	3.58	0.90
J	Financial intermediation	1059	3.66	0.76
K	Real estate, renting and business activities	32	3.95	0.75
L	Public admin and defence; compulsory social security	863	3.37	0.88
M	Education	94	3.39	0.95
Total		11143	3.54	0.87

[†]Includes repair of motor vehicles, motorcycles and household and personal goods.

Table 3.15 Organisational Identification: Descriptive statistics for SOC major occupational groups by gender and overall

Major occupational group	Female			Male			All		
	n	mean	s.d.	n	mean	s.d.	n	mean	s.d.
Managers and senior officials	346	3.86	0.74	1432	3.95	0.75	1778	3.94	0.75
Professional occupations	62	3.38	0.94	290	3.28	0.71	352	3.30	0.75
Associate professional and technical	155	3.26	0.94	283	3.33	0.85	438	3.31	0.88
Administrative and secretarial	1005	3.63	0.80	718	3.56	0.86	1723	3.60	0.83
Skilled trades	171	3.14	0.90	346	3.36	0.74	517	3.29	0.80
Personal service	78	3.89	0.84	42	3.94	0.89	120	3.91	0.85
Sales and customer service	729	3.56	0.76	437	3.47	0.79	1166	3.53	0.77
Process, plant and machine operatives	1154	3.23	0.85	2460	3.45	0.94	3614	3.38	0.92
Elementary occupations	192	3.59	0.67	522	3.55	0.86	714	3.56	0.81

Table 3.16 Organisational Identification: Descriptive statistics for SOC major occupational groups by age

Major occupational group	16–29			30–39			40–49			50–65		
	n	mean	s.d.	n	mean	s.d.	n	mean	s.d.	n	mean	s.d.
Managers and senior officials	272	3.83	0.79	545	3.84	0.76	620	4.03	0.73	419	4.00	0.69
Professional occupations	83	3.28	0.64	88	3.36	0.64	107	3.36	0.76	94	3.24	0.89
Associate professional and technical	112	3.41	0.73	126	3.20	0.96	130	3.23	0.96	69	3.43	0.74
Administrative and secretarial	550	3.52	0.84	502	3.61	0.80	434	3.62	0.81	268	3.69	0.88
Skilled trades	153	2.90	0.88	110	3.28	0.72	122	3.43	0.70	137	3.58	0.66
Personal service	72	3.82	0.88	35	3.90	0.82	6	–	–	5	–	–
Sales and customer service	668	3.44	0.76	309	3.62	0.76	143	3.65	0.77	41	3.85	0.55
Process, plant and machine operatives	1255	3.21	0.90	1000	3.37	0.94	850	3.45	0.90	708	3.66	0.87
Elementary occupations	230	3.47	0.82	169	3.64	0.79	175	3.53	0.81	171	3.62	0.82

– Too few respondents (<20) to warrant descriptive statistics.

Table 3.17 Organisational Identification: Descriptive statistics for selected occupational groups by gender and overall

Selected occupational group	Female			Male			All		
	n	mean	s.d.	n	mean	s.d.	n	mean	s.d.
Manufacturing organisations									
Managers and senior officials	297	3.87	0.72	1331	3.94	0.76	1628	3.93	0.75
Professional occupations	18	–	–	255	3.31	0.67	273	3.29	0.69
Associate professional and technical	43	3.28	0.70	120	3.49	0.60	163	3.44	0.64
Administrative and secretarial	571	3.69	0.81	390	3.59	0.89	961	3.65	0.84
Skilled trades	171	3.14	0.90	346	3.36	0.74	517	3.29	0.80
Process, plant and machine operatives	1154	3.23	0.85	2351	3.45	0.94	3505	3.38	0.92
Elementary occupations	201	3.58	0.65	524	3.59	0.81	725	3.59	0.77

–Too few respondents (<20) to warrant descriptive statistics.

Table 3.18 Organisational Identification: Descriptive statistics for selected occupational groups by age

Selected occupational group	16–29			30–39			40–49			50–65		
	n	mean	s.d.	n	mean	s.d.	n	mean	s.d.	n	mean	s.d.
Manufacturing organisations												
Managers and senior officials	246	3.82	0.80	498	3.83	0.77	572	4.02	0.74	398	4.00	0.69
Professional occupations	77	3.28	0.60	75	3.36	0.58	82	3.32	0.74	59	3.30	0.82
Associate professional and technical	61	3.28	0.62	39	3.50	0.70	37	3.46	0.60	30	3.64	0.56
Administrative and secretarial	381	3.51	0.86	255	3.69	0.79	216	3.70	0.84	160	3.80	0.86
Skilled trades	153	2.90	0.88	110	3.28	0.72	122	3.43	0.70	137	3.58	0.66
Process, plant and machine operatives	1239	3.21	0.90	973	3.37	0.94	812	3.46	0.90	681	3.67	0.86
Elementary occupations	240	3.48	0.79	178	3.65	0.74	172	3.59	0.73	166	3.67	0.80

MENTAL HEALTH

ORIGIN AND APPLICATIONS

The General Health Questionnaire (Goldberg, 1972) was developed as a self-administered screening test for detecting minor psychiatric disorder in the general population. It covers feelings of strain, depression, inability to cope, anxiety-based insomnia, lack of confidence and other psychological problems; and focuses on state, rather than trait, disorder. It is a measure of general or 'context free', rather than 'job-specific', well-being (see Warr, 1987; Warr, 1996).

There are four main versions of the General Health Questionnaire (GHQ). The original full GHQ has 60 items. From this were developed, in parallel, two shortened versions: the GHQ-30, comprising the 30 most discriminating items from the original 60 (i.e. those most strongly associated with psychiatric assessment); and the GHQ-12, made up of the best 12 of those 30 items. There is also a 28-item version (Goldberg & Hillier, 1979), which differentiates among four dimensions of mental health, namely somatic symptoms, anxiety and insomnia, social dysfunction and severe depression. This includes items from the above versions, but also some new ones.

The GHQ-12 is the version most widely used in occupational settings. This is for two main reasons: first, being a brief instrument, it can be accommodated easily along with other outcome measures of interest (e.g. job satisfaction, organisational commitment) in both questionnaire and interview-based surveys; and second, it has been shown to be essentially as valid as the longer versions. Validity studies of the GHQ-12 include those by Williams, Goldberg and Mari (1987), Goldberg and Williams (1988), Goldberg et al. (1997) and Hardy et al. (1999).

There are many instances of the use of the GHQ-12 in occupational research for the measurement of minor psychiatric disorder, or 'strain'. Studies have found it to be sensitive to: absence (Hardy, Woods & Wall, 2003); employment status (Banks et al. 1980; Pernice & Long, 1996; Viinamaki et al. 1993; Warr, 1987); work conditions and technology (Noblet et al., 2006; Prosser et al. 1996; Wall et al., 1987); work design and re-design (Bond & Bunce, 2003;

Dollard & Winefield, 1995; Evans et al., 2006; Wall & Clegg, 1980); organisational factors (Wall & Clegg, 1981); and occupational level (Borrill et al., 1998; Wall et al., 1997).

PERMISSIONS, AVAILABILITY AND QUALIFICATIONS

The GHQ is intended for use by medical doctors, clinical psychologists and similarly qualified practitioners, or by researchers and practitioners under their supervision. The copyright for this scale is held by Professor D Goldberg, although all reproduction, publication, and distribution rights are owned by the National Foundation for Educational Research (NFER), whose permission must be obtained before reproducing or using the scale for research or other purposes. Anyone wishing to use the instrument in an occupational setting should contact NFER for advice on registering to use the GHQ (see address below).

SCALE ITEMS AND RESPONSE OPTIONS

The GHQ-12 is made up of six negatively worded and six positively worded items, with individualised response scales. Respondents are asked to indicate the extent to which they have recently experienced change in the particular symptom or feeling in question. For copyright reasons only six items and their associated response scales can be reproduced. These are given below.

Have you recently:

Been able to concentrate on whatever you're doing?	better than usual	same as usual	less than usual	much less than usual
	[ ]	[ ]	[ ]	[ ]
Lost much sleep over worry?	not at all	no more than usual	rather more than usual	much more than usual
	[ ]	[ ]	[ ]	[ ]
Felt that you are playing a useful part in things?	more so than usual	same as usual	less than usual	much less than usual
	[ ]	[ ]	[ ]	[ ]
Felt that you couldn't overcome your difficulties?	not at all	no more than usual	rather more than usual	much more than usual
	[ ]	[ ]	[ ]	[ ]
Been able to face up to your problems?	more so than usual	same as usual	less than usual	much less than usual
	[ ]	[ ]	[ ]	[ ]
Been losing confidence in yourself?	not at all	no more than usual	rather more than usual	much more than usual
	[ ]	[ ]	[ ]	[ ]

SCORING METHODS

There are two main ways of scoring the GHQ-12; one is the original 'case classification' or 'GHQ method' and the other the 'Likert method'.

GHQ Method. The GHQ method involves scoring each item for the presence or absence of the symptom described. A response indicating deterioration is scored 1; and a response showing no change or improvement is scored 0. Thus, for the first item, 'Been able to concentrate on whatever you're doing', a response of 'better than usual' or 'same as usual' scores 0; whereas 'less than usual' or 'much less than usual' is scored 1. The scale score is simply the sum of item scores, indicating the number of symptoms reported as having deteriorated over the last month (maximum 12). The scale score is then used to distinguish between probable 'case' and 'non-case', that is whether or not the individual would be classified as suffering from minor psychiatric disorder on the basis of psychiatric assessment. The threshold for case classification has varied across studies, in some being defined as a sum score equal to or greater than 3, and in others as a score equal to or greater than 4.

Likert Method. With the Likert scoring method, item responses are assigned scores of 0, 1, 2 or 3 as appropriate, with 0 representing improvement or absence of the symptom; 1 no change; and so on. Thus, for the fourth item above, 'Felt that you couldn't overcome your difficulties', a response of 'not at all' scores 0, 'no more than usual' 1, 'rather more than usual' 2, and 'much more than usual' 3. The scale score is the mean item score; and responses to all 12 items are required.

The Likert method uses more of the information in the response scales and its distribution often makes it a more appropriate measure to use in studies employing parametric statistics. While there is thus some advantage in adopting this method, evidence suggests that, with regard to internal relia-bility, and for the purposes of identifying cases, there is little difference between the two methods (see Goldberg & Williams, 1988; Goldberg et al., 1997).

INTERNAL RELIABILITY AND DESCRIPTIVE STATISTICS

The following tables present the benchmarking data for each of the two scoring methods for the GHQ-12.

The first eight tables present the information for the GHQ scoring method:

Table 4.1 – descriptive statistics and 'case' rate by sample
Table 4.2 – descriptive statistics and 'case' rate for the major industrial
  sectors

Table 4.3 – descriptive statistics and 'case' rate by SOC major occupational groups

Table 4.4 – descriptive statistics and 'case' rate for SOC major occupational groups by gender

Table 4.5 – descriptive statistics and 'case' rate for SOC major occupational groups by age

Table 4.6 – descriptive statistics and 'case' rate for selected occupational groups

Table 4.7 – descriptive statistics and 'case' rate for selected occupational group by gender

Table 4.8 – descriptive statistics and 'case' rate for selected occupational groups by age.

Note that Table 4.1 does not include information about internal reliability, since this is inappropriate given the dichotomous scoring of the response in question.

Tables 4.9–4.14 provide the corresponding values for the Likert scoring method (including internal reliabilities in Table 4.9).

GHQ SCORING METHOD: DESCRIPTIVE STATISTICS
(Tables 4.1–4.8)

Table 4.1   GHQ-12 – GHQ scoring method: Descriptive statistics and 'case' rates by sample[†]

Sample and organisation		n	mean[‡]	s.d.[‡]	% >= 3	% >= 4
1	Manufacturing – electronic mcchinery	155	2.01	2.93	29.0	22.6
2	Manufacturing – clothing	860	2.72	3.17	39.5	30.9
3	Manufacturing – electronics	155	1.56	2.61	21.3	17.4
4	Water authority	100	2.74	2.89	39.0	32.0
5	Manufacturing – chemicals	341	1.80	2.69	26.7	20.2
6	NHS hospitals	20549	2.32	3.09	33.6	26.6
7	City Council	830	2.93	3.59	38.2	33.3
8	Manufacturing – glassware	854	1.88	2.74	26.7	21.1
9	Manufacturing – wire	728	1.46	2.45	19.8	14.6
10	Manufacturing – heavy plant	768	1.18	2.40	15.4	11.5
11	Manufacturing – chemicals	332	1.63	2.56	24.1	18.1
12	Mail sorting office	392	2.33	3.20	32.1	25.3
13	Manufacturing – various	6403	1.77	2.65	26.3	20.0
14	Local Authority	4351	3.62	3.76	49.6	41.6
16	Manufacturing – steel	458	1.16	2.28	15.9	11.8
17	Manufacturing – steel	373	1.13	2.30	15.0	12.1
18	Film processing	51	1.20	2.05	19.6	13.7
19	Manufacturing – vehicle parts	41	1.07	2.28	12.2	7.3
20	Manufacturing – metal	56	1.04	2.07	16.1	8.9
22	Manufacturing – wire	380	1.48	2.29	20.8	16.3
24	Civil Service – administration	6	–	–	–	–
25	Wholesale – building products	66	2.58	3.50	33.3	28.8
26	Banking	73	2.03	2.77	30.1	26.0
27	Manufacturing – metal products	144	1.31	2.12	18.8	13.9
29	Professional association	842	3.13	3.56	42.6	34.6
30	Financial service call centre	626	2.16	2.97	31.0	25.2
34	Bus company	206	1.29	2.35	18.0	12.1
36	Mixed industries	1028	2.16	3.19	29.6	23.8
40	Mixed industries	61	1.93	3.00	29.5	21.3
41	Civil Service – social work	307	3.90	3.78	52.1	44.6
42	NHS Hospital Trust	2869	2.04	3.00	29.0	23.3
44	Manufacturing – chemicals	212	1.64	2.77	23.1	17.5
46	Manufacturing – food/drink	246	0.83	1.79	8.9	6.9
48	Police Force	152	3.91	3.59	53.9	47.4
52	Manufacturing – food/drink	106	1.49	2.75	21.7	18.9
54	Manufacturing – medical equipment	179	2.28	2.73	32.4	25.1
57	Secondary education	86	1.97	2.65	30.2	22.1
58	Manufacturing – petroleum	52	1.69	1.94	26.9	15.4
60	Logistics and consultancy	25	3.28	3.67	48.0	32.0
61	Manufacturing – tobacco products	45	1.91	2.70	24.4	17.8
62	NHS Hospital Trust	616	2.02	3.10	28.6	23.2
63	Local Authority	43	2.95	2.84	46.5	41.9

Table 4.1 Continued

Sample and organisation	n	mean[†]	s.d.[‡]	% >= 3	% >= 4
64 Local authority	184	1.91	3.09	24.5	22.3
69 Banking	46	1.98	3.18	23.9	21.7
70 Mixed industries call centres	1095	2.87	3.44	39.3	32.1
72 NHS Ambulance Trust	52	2.02	3.13	28.8	21.2
73 Religious organisation	74	1.97	2.63	29.7	17.6
76 NHS Hospital Trust	279	2.15	3.13	28.3	23.3
78 Estate agency	30	1.57	2.57	23.3	16.7
81 Manufacturing – pottery	105	2.25	2.73	32.4	23.8
82 Social work	107	3.28	3.63	43.0	37.4

[†]Details of the samples/organisations are shown in Table 1.1, pp. 6–11.
[‡]Note that means and s.d.s are reported for reasons of consistency with tables elsewhere, but, because of the nature and distribution of values using this scoring method, they should be treated with caution and only as indicative.
–Too few respondents (<20) to warrant descriptive statistics.

Table 4.2 GHQ-12 – GHQ scoring method: Descriptive statistics and 'case' rates for UK SIC major industrial sectors and overall

Standard Industrial Classification of company	n	mean[†]	s.d.[‡]	% >= 3	% >= 4
D Manufacturing	13054	1.72	2.64	24.8	19.0
E Electricity, gas and water supply	248	2.74	3.17	39.5	33.1
G Wholesale and retail trade[†]	136	2.86	3.68	37.5	30.9
H Hotels and restaurants	93	2.26	2.78	31.2	25.8
I Transport, storage and communication	1295	2.34	3.25	31.7	24.9
J Financial intermediation	1015	2.31	3.04	32.9	26.6
K Real estate, renting and business activities	122	1.83	2.76	27.9	19.7
L Public admin and defence; compulsory social security	6353	3.32	3.69	45.2	38.2
M Education	928	3.03	3.50	41.5	33.4
N Health and social work	24821	2.30	3.10	33.2	26.3
O Other social and personal service activities	74	1.97	2.63	29.7	17.6
Total	48139	2.30	3.12	32.6	26.0

[†]Includes repair of motor vehicles, motorcycles and household and personal goods.
[‡]Note that means and s.d.s are reported for reasons of consistency with tables elsewhere, but, because of the nature and distribution of values using this scoring method, they should be treated with caution and only as indicative.

Table 4.3 GHQ-12 – GHQ scoring method: Descriptive statistics and 'case' rates for SOC major occupational groups

Major occupational group	n	mean[‡]	s.d.[‡]	% >= 3	%> = 4
Managers and senior officials	5018	2.66	3.24	38.3	31.0
Professional occupations	5999	2.78	3.39	39.1	31.3
Associate professional and technical	16280	2.42	3.17	34.6	27.7
Administrative and secretarial	6685	2.09	3.03	29.5	23.5
Skilled trades	1039	2.22	3.09	31.5	24.8
Personal service	174	2.17	3.09	32.8	23.6
Sales and customer service	1729	2.53	3.25	34.9	28.2
Process, plant and machine operatives	6582	1.60	2.57	22.7	17.4
Elementary occupations	3054	1.85	2.85	26.7	20.9

[‡] Note that means and s.d.s are reported for reasons of consistency with tables elsewhere, but, because of the nature and distribution of values using this scoring method, they should be treated with caution and only as indicative.

Table 4.4 GHQ-12 – GHQ scoring method: Descriptive statistics and 'case' rates for SOC major occupational groups by gender

Major occupational group	Female					Male				
	n	mean†	s.d.‡	% >= 3	% >= 4	n	mean†	s.d.‡	% >= 3	% >= 4
Managers and senior officials	1956	3.09	3.50	43.3	37.1	3062	2.38	3.04	35.1	27.2
Professional occupations	2993	3.22	3.58	45.0	37.0	3006	2.36	3.13	33.3	25.5
Associate professional and technical	13355	2.41	3.16	34.6	27.6	2925	2.49	3.20	34.8	28.4
Administrative and secretarial	5119	2.05	3.02	29.0	22.8	1566	2.20	3.06	31.3	25.9
Skilled trades	260	3.01	3.63	40.8	33.5	779	1.96	2.84	28.4	22.0
Personal service	92	1.66	2.81	21.7	18.5	82	2.74	3.30	45.1	29.3
Sales and customer service	1197	2.63	3.33	36.0	28.8	532	2.30	3.06	32.3	26.7
Process, plant and machine operatives	1599	2.02	2.84	29.0	22.4	4983	1.47	2.46	20.8	15.8
Elementary occupations	1397	1.65	2.75	23.7	19.0	1657	2.01	2.93	29.1	22.5

‡Note that means and s.d.s are reported for reasons of consistency with tables elsewhere, but, because of the nature and distribution of values using this scoring method, they should be treated with caution and only as indicative.

Table 4.5 GHQ-12 – GHQ scoring method: Descriptive statistics and 'case' rates for SOC major occupational groups by age

Major occupational group	16–29					30–39				
	n	mean[‡]	s.d.[‡]	% >= 3	% >= 4	n	mean[‡]	s.d.[‡]	% >= 3	% >= 4
Managers and senior officials	637	2.52	2.98	37.4	30.8	1548	2.87	3.42	40.1	33.0
Professional occupations	953	2.52	3.09	36.1	27.9	1670	2.71	3.27	39.2	30.6
Associate professional and technical	3332	2.47	2.98	37.1	28.8	5333	2.57	3.24	36.6	29.8
Administrative and secretarial	1618	2.29	3.01	33.9	26.6	1676	2.15	3.08	29.9	23.6
Skilled trades	242	2.64	3.33	39.7	31.4	249	2.53	3.25	33.3	28.1
Personal service	73	1.49	2.35	24.7	16.4	53	3.13	4.00	35.8	32.1
Sales and customer service	788	2.56	3.13	37.3	28.6	529	2.39	3.19	30.8	25.7
Process, plant and machine operatives	1828	1.77	2.59	26.3	19.7	1957	1.70	2.71	23.8	18.9
Elementary occupations	567	2.20	2.96	31.7	25.9	774	1.90	2.86	27.4	20.9

Major occupational group	40–49					50–65				
	n	mean[‡]	s.d.[‡]	% >= 3	% >= 4	n	mean[‡]	s.d.[‡]	% >= 3	% >= 4
Managers and senior officials	1750	2.73	3.26	40.1	32.2	1065	2.20	3.07	31.5	25.1
Professional occupations	1951	3.06	3.55	43.0	34.3	1401	2.67	3.48	35.7	29.9
Associate professional and technical	4514	2.45	3.26	33.9	27.4	2940	2.09	3.10	29.5	23.4
Administrative and secretarial	1843	2.19	3.15	31.4	25.2	1514	1.72	2.82	23.0	18.5
Skilled trades	302	2.10	3.10	28.1	22.2	244	1.67	2.61	25.4	18.9
Personal service	34	2.35	2.73	44.1	26.5	16	–	–	–	–
Sales and customer service	291	2.71	3.51	36.4	31.6	120	2.39	3.52	31.7	26.7
Process, plant and machine operatives	1647	1.55	2.52	21.8	16.5	1261	1.23	2.33	16.5	12.7
Elementary occupations	800	2.04	3.03	29.1	23.6	913	1.43	2.57	20.9	15.6

[‡]Note that means and s.d.s are reported for reasons of consistency with tables elsewhere, but, because of the nature and distribution of values using this scoring method, they should be treated with caution and only as indicative.
–Too few respondents (<20) to warrant descriptive statistics.

Table 4.6   GHQ-12 – GHQ scoring method: Descriptive statistics and 'case' rates for selected occupational groups

Selected occupational group	n	mean[‡]	s.d.[‡]	% >= 3	% >= 4
NHS Trusts					
Managers	1853	2.79	3.28	40.4	33.0
Doctors	2609	2.37	3.08	34.3	26.0
Nurses	9202	2.41	3.16	34.6	27.8
Professions allied to medicine	3400	2.29	3.05	33.4	26.0
Professional and technical staff	1651	2.11	2.97	30.2	23.8
Administrative staff	3927	1.99	2.92	28.8	22.8
Ancillary staff	1648	1.70	2.78	24.8	19.4
Manufacturing organisations					
Managers and senior officials	2004	2.02	2.77	30.5	23.0
Professional occupations	611	1.64	2.57	23.2	18.2
Associate professional and technical	410	1.74	2.67	25.4	18.8
Administrative and secretarial	1251	1.81	2.73	26.2	19.4
Skilled trades	754	1.84	2.76	26.7	20.3
Process, plant and machine operatives	6333	1.61	2.58	22.9	17.6
Elementary occupations	875	1.71	2.62	25.0	19.5

[‡]Note that means and s.d.s are reported for reasons of consistency with tables elsewhere, but, because of the nature and distribution of values using this scoring method, they should be treated with caution and only as indicative.

Table 4.7 GHQ-12 – GHQ method: Descriptive statistics and 'case' rates for selected occupational groups by gender

Selected occupational group	Female					Male				
	n	mean‡	s.d.‡	% >= 3	% >= 4	n	mean‡	s.d.‡	% >= 3	% >= 4
NHS Trusts										
Managers	1044	2.99	3.40	42.9	36.1	809	2.55	3.11	37.1	29.0
Doctors	928	2.66	3.27	38.5	31.0	1681	2.20	2.97	31.9	23.3
Nurses	8314	2.39	3.15	34.4	27.6	888	2.62	3.27	36.1	29.6
Professions allied to medicine	2948	2.28	3.05	33.4	25.6	452	2.33	3.07	33.4	28.3
Professional and technical staff	1017	2.03	2.92	29.0	23.0	634	2.24	3.04	32.2	25.1
Administrative staff	3509	1.95	2.90	28.0	21.9	418	2.40	3.08	35.4	29.7
Ancillary staff	972	1.49	2.63	21.7	17.4	676	2.00	2.96	29.3	22.2
Manufacturing organisations										
Managers and senior officials	349	2.07	3.02	28.1	23.5	1655	2.01	2.72	31.0	22.9
Professional occupations	44	2.02	3.02	27.3	22.7	567	1.60	2.54	22.9	17.8
Associate professional and technical	106	2.20	2.92	34.0	26.4	304	1.58	2.56	22.4	16.1
Administrative and secretarial	755	1.82	2.86	26.1	18.7	496	1.80	2.51	26.4	20.6
Skilled trades	157	2.90	3.53	41.4	33.1	597	1.56	2.44	22.8	16.9
Process, plant and machine operatives	1592	2.01	2.84	29.0	22.4	4741	1.48	2.47	20.9	16.0
Elementary occupations	210	1.78	2.85	24.3	20.0	665	1.68	2.54	25.3	19.4

‡Note that means and s.d.s are reported for reasons of consistency with tables elsewhere, but, because of the nature and distribution of values using this scoring method, they should be treated with caution and only as indicative.

Table 4.8 GHQ-12 – GHQ scoring method: Descriptive statistics and 'case' rates for selected occupational groups by age

Selected occupational group	16–29					30–39				
	n	mean‡	s.d.‡	% >= 3	% >= 4	n	mean‡	s.d.‡	% >= 3	% >= 4
NHS Trusts										
Managers	198	2.89	3.10	40.4	36.4	627	3.02	3.45	41.8	35.4
Doctors	586	2.59	3.16	36.3	28.3	815	2.37	3.04	35.2	26.1
Nurses	1699	2.55	3.01	38.2	30.3	3191	2.59	3.23	37.2	30.4
Professions allied to medicine	913	2.41	2.91	36.6	28.1	1034	2.32	3.15	33.0	25.8
Professional and technical staff	376	2.22	2.87	33.5	25.3	527	2.08	2.89	30.7	23.9
Administrative staff	721	2.30	2.98	35.2	27.3	898	2.12	3.04	29.6	23.9
Ancillary staff	192	2.34	3.13	35.4	27.1	363	1.74	2.75	25.1	19.6
Manufacturing organisations										
Managers and senior officials	303	1.97	2.75	30.0	22.4	603	2.15	2.87	32.3	24.5
Professional occupations	174	1.60	2.30	23.6	17.2	172	1.58	2.54	22.1	18.0
Associate professional and technical	108	1.90	2.71	28.7	19.4	97	1.54	2.45	20.6	15.5
Administrative and secretarial	524	2.10	2.82	30.7	23.7	302	1.52	2.37	23.5	14.9
Skilled trades	178	2.48	3.17	38.8	29.8	173	1.91	2.77	25.4	21.4
Process, plant and machine operatives	1794	1.77	2.58	26.4	19.8	1880	1.71	2.72	24.1	19.1
Elementary occupations	277	1.73	2.43	26.0	20.6	225	1.90	2.85	26.2	21.3

Table 4.8 Continued

Selected occupational group	40–49					50–65				
	n	mean[‡]	s.d.[‡]	% >= 3	% >= 4	n	mean[‡]	s.d.[‡]	% >= 3	% >= 4
NHS Trusts										
Managers	642	2.75	3.18	41.7	32.2	382	2.44	3.25	35.3	28.5
Doctors	693	2.46	3.14	36.4	27.7	496	1.96	2.94	27.6	21.2
Nurses	2522	2.39	3.25	33.3	26.5	1679	2.00	3.03	28.3	22.4
Professions allied to medicine	880	2.27	3.09	32.7	25.5	550	2.09	3.08	30.0	23.8
Professional and technical staff	479	2.26	3.17	30.1	25.1	261	1.77	2.86	25.3	19.5
Administrative staff	1154	2.08	3.01	30.8	24.4	1096	1.66	2.71	22.5	17.9
Ancillary staff	445	1.95	2.99	27.6	23.6	624	1.33	2.48	19.9	14.3
Manufacturing organisations										
Managers and senior officials	708	2.08	2.75	32.1	24.2	474	1.68	2.66	24.1	18.1
Professional occupations	150	1.67	2.85	22.7	17.3	130	1.63	2.63	23.1	18.5
Associate professional and technical	102	1.84	2.69	27.5	22.5	98	1.60	2.76	24.5	17.3
Administrative and secretarial	278	1.89	2.87	27.3	21.6	192	1.33	2.55	17.2	13.0
Skilled trades	207	1.71	2.85	22.2	16.9	197	1.37	2.18	21.3	14.7
Process, plant and machine operatives	1581	1.56	2.54	21.8	16.6	1187	1.24	2.34	16.5	13.0
Elementary occupations	204	1.82	2.81	26.0	20.1	194	1.26	2.28	19.6	14.4

[‡]Note that means and s.d.s are reported for reasons of consistency with tables elsewhere, but, because of the nature and distribution of values using this scoring method, they should be treated with caution and only as indicative.

GENERAL HEALTH QUESTIONNAIRE (GHQ-12): LIKERT SCORING METHOD

INTERNAL RELIABILITY AND DESCRIPTIVE STATISTICS
(Tables 4.9–4.14)

Table 4.9   GHQ-12 – Likert scoring method: Descriptive statistics and internal reliability (alpha) by sample[†]

Sample and organisation	n	mean	s.d.	alpha[‡]
1 Manufacturing – electronic machinery	155	0.92	0.47	0.89
2 Manufacturing – clothing	860	1.10	0.49	0.88
3 Manufacturing – electronics	155	0.84	0.44	0.87
4 Water authority	100	0.99	0.43	0.88
5 Manufacturing – chemicals	341	0.90	0.41	0.88
6 NHS hospitals	20549	1.01	0.46	0.89
7 City Council	830	1.10	0.54	0.92
8 Manufacturing – glassware	854	0.94	0.44	0.88
9 Manufacturing – wire	728	0.89	0.39	0.86
10 Manufacturing – heavy plant	768	0.82	0.40	0.89
11 Manufacturing – chemicals	332	0.94	0.38	0.87
12 Mail sorting office	392	1.00	0.49	0.90
13 Manufacturing – various	6403	0.89	0.43	0.87
14 Local Authority	4351	1.20	0.56	0.92
16 Manufacturing – steel	458	0.83	0.37	0.87
17 Manufacturing – steel	373	0.84	0.36	0.87
18 Film processing	51	0.86	0.36	0.86
19 Manufacturing – vehicle parts	41	0.78	0.36	0.87
20 Manufacturing – metal	56	0.82	0.32	0.82
22 Manufacturing – wire	380	0.87	0.38	0.86
24 Civil Service – administration	6	–	–	–
25 Wholesale – building products	66	1.01	0.51	0.92
26 Banking	73	0.92	0.41	0.87
27 Manufacturing – metal products	144	0.88	0.35	0.83
29 Professional association	842	1.14	0.51	0.91
30 Financial service call centre	626	0.96	0.46	0.89
34 Bus company	206	0.85	0.40	0.88
36 Mixed industries	1028	0.98	0.49	0.91
40 Mixed industries	61	0.88	0.46	0.90
41 Civil Service – social work	307	1.22	0.57	0.92
42 NHS Hospital Trust	2869	0.97	0.45	0.90
44 Manufacturing – chemicals	212	0.90	0.41	0.89
46 Manufacturing – food/drink	246	0.79	0.31	0.83
48 Police Force	152	1.23	0.50	0.90
52 Manufacturing – food/drink	106	0.78	0.53	0.92
54 Manufacturing – medical equipment	179	0.97	0.43	0.85
57 Secondary education	86	0.99	0.41	0.88
58 Manufacturing – petroleum	52	0.91	0.34	0.81
60 Logistics and consultancy	25	1.07	0.53	0.87
61 Manufacturing – tobacco products	45	0.91	0.38	0.84
62 NHS Hospital Trust	616	0.97	0.47	0.91
63 Local Authority	43	1.07	0.38	0.79
64 Local Authority	184	0.96	0.46	0.91

Table 4.9   Continued

Sample and organisation	n	mean	s.d.	alpha[‡]
69 Banking	46	0.94	0.44	0.90
70 Mixed industries call centres	1095	1.10	0.51	0.91
72 NHS Ambulance Trust	52	1.02	0.49	0.91
73 Religious organisation	74	0.94	0.38	0.85
76 NHS Hospital Trust	279	1.01	0.47	0.90
78 Estate agency	30	0.89	0.42	0.84
81 Manufacturing – pottery	105	1.03	0.38	0.84
82 Social work	107	1.12	0.59	0.92

[†] Details of the samples/organisations are shown in Table 1.1, pp. 6–11.
[‡] Sample sizes for alpha coefficients are identical to those for the respective sample since a complete set of responses is required to calculate the scale score.
– Too few respondents (<20) to warrant descriptive statistics.

Table 4.10   GHQ-12 – Likert scoring method: Descriptive statistics for UK SIC major industrial sectors and overall

Standard Industrial Classification of company	n	mean	s.d.
D Manufacturing	13054	0.90	0.43
E Electricity, gas and water supply	248	1.05	0.49
G Wholesale and retail trade[†]	136	1.08	0.54
H Hotels and restaurants	93	1.01	0.39
I Transport, storage and communication	1295	1.00	0.50
J Financial intermediation	1015	0.98	0.47
K Real estate, renting and business activities	122	0.92	0.42
L Public admin and defence; compulsory social security	6353	1.16	0.55
M Education	928	1.13	0.50
N Health and social work	24821	1.01	0.46
O Other community, social and personal service activities	74	0.94	0.38
Total	48139	1.00	0.48

[†] Includes repair of motor vehicles, motorcycles and household and personal goods.

Table 4.11 GHQ-12 – Likert scoring method: Descriptive statistics for SOC major occupational groups by gender and overall

Major occupational group	Female			Male			All		
	n	mean	s.d.	n	mean	s.d.	n	mean	s.d.
Managers and senior officials	1956	1.10	0.53	3062	0.98	0.46	5018	1.03	0.49
Professional occupations	2993	1.15	0.52	3006	1.01	0.46	5999	1.08	0.50
Associate professional and technical	13355	1.03	0.47	2925	1.03	0.47	16280	1.03	0.47
Administrative and secretarial	5119	0.97	0.47	1566	0.97	0.47	6685	0.97	0.47
Skilled trades	260	1.15	0.56	779	0.96	0.44	1039	1.00	0.48
Personal service	92	0.87	0.48	82	1.03	0.57	174	0.94	0.53
Sales and customer service	1197	1.05	0.50	532	0.99	0.48	1729	1.03	0.49
Process, plant and machine operatives	1599	0.97	0.46	4983	0.86	0.41	6582	0.89	0.43
Elementary occupations	1397	0.90	0.44	1657	0.94	0.46	3054	0.92	0.45

Table 4.12 GHQ-12 – Likert scoring method: Descriptive statistics for SOC major occupational groups by age

Major occupational group	16–29			30–39			40–49			50–65		
	n	mean	s.d.	n	mean	s.d.	n	mean	s.d.	n	mean	s.d.
Managers and senior officials	637	0.97	0.45	1548	1.06	0.52	1750	1.05	0.49	1065	0.96	0.47
Professional occupations	953	1.03	0.47	1670	1.06	0.48	1951	1.14	0.51	1401	1.07	0.51
Associate professional and technical	3332	1.02	0.45	5333	1.05	0.48	4514	1.04	0.48	2940	0.98	0.47
Administrative and secretarial	1618	0.98	0.48	1676	0.98	0.48	1843	1.00	0.48	1514	0.93	0.43
Skilled trades	242	1.06	0.53	249	1.05	0.48	302	1.00	0.49	244	0.92	0.41
Personal service	73	0.79	0.42	53	1.13	0.64	34	1.03	0.48	13	–	–
Sales and customer service	788	1.02	0.49	529	1.02	0.48	291	1.09	0.51	120	1.04	0.54
Process, plant and machine operatives	1828	0.90	0.43	1957	0.89	0.44	1647	0.89	0.41	1261	0.83	0.40
Elementary occupations	567	0.96	0.48	774	0.93	0.45	800	0.96	0.47	913	0.86	0.42

– Too few respondents (<20) to warrant descriptive statistics.

Table 4.13 GHQ-12 – Likert scoring method: Descriptive statistics for selected occupational groups by gender and overall

Selected occupational group	Female			Male			All		
	n	mean	s.d.	n	mean	s.d.	n	mean	s.d.
NHS Trusts									
Managers	1044	1.07	0.50	809	1.02	0.47	1853	1.05	0.49
Doctors	928	1.08	0.47	1681	1.00	0.43	2609	1.03	0.44
Nurses	8314	1.02	0.47	888	1.05	0.49	9202	1.03	0.47
Professions allied to medicine	2948	1.00	0.44	452	1.00	0.45	3400	1.00	0.44
Professional and technical staff	1017	0.97	0.45	634	1.00	0.45	1651	0.98	0.45
Administrative staff	3509	0.95	0.45	418	0.98	0.47	3927	0.96	0.45
Ancillary staff	972	0.87	0.44	676	0.95	0.47	1648	0.90	0.45
Manufacturing organisations									
Managers and senior officials	349	0.93	0.48	1655	0.91	0.42	2004	0.91	0.43
Professional occupations	44	0.95	0.44	567	0.88	0.40	611	0.89	0.40
Associate professional and technical	106	0.96	0.44	304	0.88	0.40	410	0.90	0.41
Administrative and secretarial	755	0.92	0.46	496	0.91	0.40	1251	0.91	0.44
Skilled trades	157	1.14	0.54	597	0.91	0.38	754	0.96	0.43
Process, plant and machine operatives	1592	0.97	0.46	4741	0.86	0.41	6333	0.89	0.43
Elementary occupations	210	0.91	0.44	665	0.88	0.41	875	0.89	0.41

Table 4.14 GHQ-12 – Likert scoring method: Descriptive statistics for selected occupational groups by age

Selected occupational group	16–29			30–39			40–49			50–65		
	n	mean	s.d.	n	mean	s.d.	n	mean	s.d.	n	mean	s.d.
NHS Trusts												
Managers	198	1.02	0.45	627	1.09	0.51	642	1.05	0.46	382	1.00	0.50
Doctors	586	1.05	0.47	815	1.03	0.44	693	1.05	0.43	496	0.98	0.43
Nurses	1699	1.04	0.46	3191	1.05	0.47	2522	1.03	0.48	1679	0.97	0.46
Professions allied to medicine	913	0.99	0.42	1034	1.01	0.46	880	1.01	0.44	550	0.99	0.44
Professional and technical staff	376	0.98	0.44	527	0.98	0.43	479	1.01	0.48	261	0.95	0.43
Administrative staff	721	0.98	0.47	898	0.98	0.47	1154	0.97	0.47	1096	0.92	0.42
Ancillary staff	192	0.98	0.52	363	0.92	0.44	445	0.95	0.48	624	0.85	0.41
Manufacturing organisations												
Managers and senior officials	303	0.89	0.44	603	0.94	0.44	708	0.93	0.42	474	0.87	0.42
Professional occupations	174	0.86	0.36	172	0.87	0.40	150	0.91	0.43	130	0.92	0.41
Associate professional and technical	108	0.91	0.44	97	0.88	0.39	102	0.94	0.38	98	0.87	0.42
Administrative and secretarial	524	0.94	0.46	302	0.86	0.40	278	0.95	0.45	192	0.87	0.40
Skilled trades	178	1.05	0.49	173	0.97	0.42	207	0.93	0.46	197	0.89	0.34
Process, plant and machine operatives	1794	0.90	0.43	1880	0.89	0.45	1581	0.89	0.42	1187	0.83	0.40
Elementary occupations	277	0.89	0.40	225	0.91	0.46	204	0.93	0.43	194	0.83	0.35

JOB-RELATED WELL-BEING

This chapter provides reliabilities and descriptive statistics for three pairs of short scales of job-related well-being, namely:

1. Job-related Anxiety–Contentment (6 items, 5-point response scale); and Job-related Depression–Enthusiasm (6 items, 5-point response scale).
2. Job-related Anxiety (3 items, 5-point response scale); and Job-related Depression (3 items, 5-point response scale).
3. Job-related Anxiety (3 items, 6-point response scale); and Job-related Depression (3 items, 6-point response scale).

All three pairs of scales derive directly from Warr's (1987, 1990a) original measures of Job-related Anxiety–Contentment and Job-related Depression–Enthusiasm (6 items, 6-point response scale). As indicated by the way they have been labelled, the scales differ from the originals only in respect of the number of items and response formats used. Thus a description of the origin and applications of Warr's measures is provided as the background to all three pairs of measures of interest here. Benchmarking information for the original measures is not presented, as insufficient information for this purpose is available.

ORIGIN AND APPLICATIONS

Two key considerations underlay the development of Warr's original scales. The first was that the scales should map directly on to axes of psychological well-being as identified within a broader theoretical framework. In line with others' conceptual analyses (e.g. Thayer, 1989; Watson, Clark & Tellegen, 1988), Warr (1990a) identified two axes of psychological well-being in a notional space associated with orthogonal dimensions of pleasure and arousal. These are represented in Figure 5.1 on the next page.

The second consideration relates to the focus of the measures. A distinction was drawn between 'job-specific' and 'context-free' well-being. The scales of current interest were designed to measure the former, that is people's

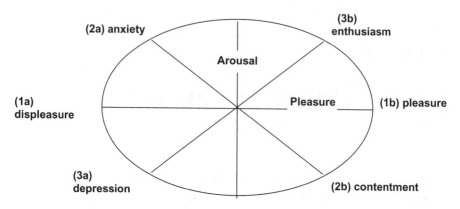

Figure 5.1   Axes of psychological well-being (from Warr, 1990a)

job-related well-being, rather than their well-being more generally (as represented, for example, by the GHQ-12; see Chapter 4).

Warr noted that, with respect to job-related well-being, the pleasure–displeasure axis (1a–1b) was well represented by existing job satisfaction scales (e.g. Chapter 2). He also described an instrument to measure the vertical axis of arousal (Warr, 1990a, p. 210). The measures of present interest, however, are those corresponding to the two diagonal axes of Anxiety–Contentment (2a–2b) and Depression–Enthusiasm (3a–3b) respectively.

The general instructions and items for each of the scales are listed below. Three of the six adjectives in each scale are positive and three negative. In the original application, answers were given on a response scale with six options running from 'never' to 'all the time' (as shown below for the third pair of scales described). Responses were scored so that higher values represent greater contentment (i.e. lower anxiety) or greater enthusiasm (i.e. lower depression).

Both scales have been shown to be sensitive to job level and self-employment status. People in higher level jobs report significantly more positive scores on the Job-related Depression–Enthusiasm scale (i.e. more enthusiasm, less depression) compared with those in lower level jobs, but also significantly lower scores on Job-related Anxiety–Contentment (i.e. less contentment, more anxiety). This pattern of well-being is also found among self-employed individuals (Birdi, Warr & Oswald, 1995; Warr, 1990b; Warr, 1994). Job-related Depression–Enthusiasm has been shown to predict absence at work better than does Job-related Anxiety–Contentment (Hardy, Woods & Wall, 2003). Both measures of job-related well-being have been shown to be sensitive to job demands (Sevastos, Smith & Cordery, 1992; Sprigg & Jackson, 2006; Totterdell, Wood & Wall, 2006; Warr, 1990b), leader behaviour (van Dierendonck et al. 2004), and to machine pacing (Mullarkey et al., 1997). Other published studies that have used the measures include those by Cooksey and Soutar (2006), Epitropaki and Martin (2005), Daniels et al. (1997), Daniels and Guppy (1997), Holman, Chiswick and Totterdell (2002), Parker (2003), Rogelberg et al. (2006) and Schalk, Keunen and Meijer (1995).

CORE ITEMS

The three pairs of measures of present interest all use the same general instructions and set of items, which are as follows:

Thinking of the past few weeks, how much of the time has your job made you feel each of the following?

1. Tense	4. Optimistic	7. Worried	10. Contented
2. Miserable	5. Calm	8. Enthusiastic	11. Gloomy
3. Depressed	6. Relaxed	9. Uneasy	12. Cheerful

The Anxiety–Contentment scale consists of items 1, 5, 6, 7, 9 and 10; and the Depression–Enthusiasm scale of items 2, 3, 4, 8, 11 and 12.

Sevastos, Smith and Cordery (1992) evaluated the original measures, and found support for the factor structure and reliabilities originally reported. However, they proposed minor changes to the items, noting that small psychometric gains were achieved, in their sample, by replacing items 9 (uneasy), 10 (contented) and 12 (cheerful) with 'anxious', 'comfortable' and 'motivated' respectively. Most of the data reported in this chapter are based on the original items, though a minority of users have incorporated the suggested modifications. The two sets of items are here treated as equivalent, as the evidence suggests that they are equivalent with respect to internal reliability and descriptive statistics.

PERMISSIONS, AVAILABILITY AND QUALIFICATIONS

There are no specific restrictions on the use of this measure. It is freely available for use by psychologists or other practitioners involved in organisational survey research.

SCALE ITEMS, RESPONSE OPTIONS AND SCORING

Few researchers have used the scales in exactly their original form, and this has resulted in the existence of the three variants we report on here. These are differentiated by choice of items, response scale and scoring direction.

Job-related Anxiety–Contentment and Job-related Depression–Enthusiasm (6 items, 5-point response scale)

This version of the two scales is the most similar to the original, differing only in that it uses a 5- rather than 6-point response scale. Thus Job-related Anxiety–Contentment comprises the same six adjectives as given above (1, 5, 6, 7, 9, 10), as does the Job-related Depression–Enthusiasm scale (2, 3, 4, 8, 11, 12). The response scale is as follows:

1	2	3	4	5
Never	Occasionally	Some of the time	Most of the time	All of the time

Negative items (1, 2, 3, 7, 9, 11) are reverse scored, and responses are averaged across the items (a minimum of four per scale is required) to provide a scale score. Thus higher scores represent greater contentment (less anxiety) and greater enthusiasm (less depression).

Job-related Anxiety and Job-related Depression (3 items, 5-point response scale)

The second version uses only the six negative core items, three for each scale. Thus for Job-related Anxiety the items are 1, 7 and 9; and for Job-related Depression they are 2, 3 and 11. The above 5-point response format is used, but items are not reverse-scored. Thus higher scores represent greater Job-related Anxiety or Depression. Responses are averaged across items, with a minimum of two per scale being required.

Job-related Anxiety and Job-related Depression (3 items, 6-point response scale)

The third and final version of the original scales is identical to that described immediately above, except that it uses the original 6-point response format (see below). Thus, the items for Job-related Anxiety are 1, 7 and 9; and for Job-related Depression they are 2, 3 and 11. Items are not reverse scored, scale scores are calculated as the average of item scores (a minimum of two per scale), and thus higher scores represent greater Job-related Anxiety or Job-related Depression. The response scale is as follows:

1	2	3	4	5	6
Never	Occasionally	Some of the time	Much of the time	Most of the time	All of the time

INTERNAL RELIABILITY AND DESCRIPTIVE STATISTICS

The following tables present the internal reliabilities and descriptive statistics for each form of the scales.

The first six tables cover Job-related Anxiety–Contentment (6 item, 5-point response scale), presenting:

Table 5.1 – descriptive statistics and internal reliabilities (Cronbach's (1951) alpha coefficient of internal consistency) by sample
Table 5.2 – descriptive statistics for the SIC major industrial sectors
Table 5.3 – descriptive statistics for the SOC major occupational groups by gender and overall
Table 5.4 – descriptive statistics for the SOC major occupational groups by age
Table 5.5 – descriptive statistics for the selected occupational groups by gender and overall
Table 5.6 – descriptive statistics for the selected occupational groups by age.

The corresponding information for Job-related Depression–Enthusiasm (6 item, 5-point response scale) is presented in Tables 5.7–5.12; that for Job-related Anxiety (3 items, 5-point response scale) in Tables 5.13–5.18; and that for Job-related Depression (3 items, 5-point response scale) in Tables 5.19–5.24.

For the last two versions of these scales (Job-related Anxiety – 3 items with 6-point response scale; Job-Related Depression – 3 items with 6-point response scale), more limited information is provided, since this data comes exclusively from the three of our samples of NHS Trust employees where this 6-point response scale was used. Given the small number of samples involved we have not tabulated the internal reliabilities by sample (they ranged from 0.85 to 0.89 for Job-related Anxiety and from 0.86 to 0.87 for

Job-related Depression). Thus, for Job-related Anxiety, Table 5.25 presents descriptive statistics for selected NHS occupational group by gender and overall; and Table 5.26 shows descriptive statistics for selected NHS occupational group by age. Tables 5.27 and 5.28 provide the corresponding information for Job-related Depression.

INTERNAL RELIABILITY AND DESCRIPTIVE STATISTICS
(Tables 5.1–5.6)

Table 5.1 Job-related Anxiety–Contentment (6 items, 5-point response scale): Descriptive statistics and internal reliability (alpha) by sample[†]

Sample and organisation	n	mean	s.d.	n[‡]	alpha
1 Manufacturing – electronic machinery	163	3.53	0.66	162	0.75
2 Manufacturing – clothing	912	2.80	0.74	899	0.79
3 Manufacturing – electronics	162	3.33	0.65	159	0.71
5 Manufacturing – chemicals	348	3.38	0.65	345	0.77
9 Manufacturing – wire	742	3.17	0.69	728	0.77
10 Manufacturing – heavy plant	777	3.49	0.71	772	0.81
11 Manufacturing – chemicals	336	3.26	0.68	332	0.81
16 Manufacturing – steel	461	3.24	0.64	457	0.77
19 Manufacturing – vehicle parts	42	3.34	0.64	42	0.81
20 Manufacturing – metal	56	3.33	0.73	56	0.79
22 Manufacturing – wire	388	3.17	0.70	384	0.74
23 Patent office	162	3.80	0.61	157	0.76
25 Wholesale – building products	66	3.20	0.78	66	0.88
27 Manufacturing – metal products	143	3.38	0.70	53	0.81
28 Manufacturing – metal products	84	2.88	0.72	83	0.77
29 Professional association	856	2.98	0.74	833	0.89
30 Financial service call centre	829	3.34	0.73	809	0.82
31 Private healthcare call centre	461	3.27	0.71	450	0.81
32 Private healthcare administration	120	3.15	0.72	120	0.83
33 Private healthcare call centre	249	3.37	0.72	247	0.83
36 Mixed industries	1033	3.28	0.79	995	0.87
37 Railway maintenance	610	3.19	0.83	597	0.88
38 Manufacturing – heavy plant	420	3.16	0.74	410	0.78
40 Mixed industries	64	3.23	0.78	63	0.89
43 Civil Service – policy unit	316	3.14	0.70	310	0.81
44 Manufacturing – chemicals	214	3.31	0.66	214	0.82
46 Manufacturing – food/drink	369	3.29	0.66	364	0.76
49 Railway maintenance	156	3.23	0.80	153	0.82
51 Public transport call centre	49	3.04	0.75	47	0.82
52 Manufacturing – food/drink	106	3.68	0.82	105	0.84
53 Retail – fashion accessories	172	3.50	0.70	171	0.78
55 Higher education	94	2.83	0.83	93	0.91
56 Banking	125	3.26	0.72	119	0.84
57 Secondary education	92	3.17	0.66	92	0.78
59 Manufacturing – aircraft parts	85	3.32	0.76	85	0.83
60 Logistics and consultancy	24	2.92	0.85	23	0.81
61 Manufacturing – tobacco products	45	3.29	0.64	44	0.81
66 Mixed industries	75	3.26	0.69	74	0.77
67 Financial services call centres	161	3.14	0.78	159	0.84
69 Banking	46	3.40	0.65	46	0.82
70 Mixed industries call centres	1135	3.09	0.77	1112	0.83
71 Wholesale – metal	473	3.26	0.71	464	0.81
72 NHS Ambulance Trust	52	3.37	0.86	52	0.90

Table 5.1   Continued

Sample and organisation	n	mean	s.d.	n[‡]	alpha
73 Religious organisation	76	3.38	0.63	76	0.84
75 Mixed industries	124	3.40	0.63	124	0.80
77 Retail chemist	20	3.21	0.91	19	0.88
78 Estate agency	32	3.38	0.70	31	0.82
81 Manufacturing – pottery	111	3.09	0.70	108	0.81
82 Social work	107	3.09	0.81	105	0.87

[†]Details of the samples/organisations are shown in Table 1.1, pp. 6–11.
[‡]Sample sizes for alpha coefficients are smaller than for the sample as a whole because of list-wise deletion for missing values.

Table 5.2   Job-related Anxiety–Contentment (6 items, 5-point response scale): Descriptive statistics for UK SIC major industrial sectors and overall

Standard Industrial Classification of company	n	mean	s.d.
D Manufacturing	6066	3.22	0.73
E Electricity, gas and water supply	154	3.09	0.74
F Construction	766	3.20	0.82
G Wholesale and retail trade[†]	806	3.28	0.73
H Hotels and restaurants	98	3.17	0.69
I Transport, storage and communication	761	3.17	0.82
J Financial intermediation	1443	3.28	0.73
K Real estate, renting and business activities	233	3.29	0.69
L Public admin and defence; compulsory social security	1266	3.27	0.77
M Education	1042	2.98	0.74
N Health and social work	1032	3.26	0.75
O Other social and personal service activities	76	3.38	0.63
Total	13743	3.22	0.75

[†]Includes repair of motor vehicles, motorcycles and household and personal goods.

Table 5.3 Job-related Anxiety–Contentment (6 items, 5-point response scale): Descriptive statistics for SOC major occupational groups by gender and overall

Major occupational group	Female			Male			All		
	n	mean	s.d.	n	mean	s.d.	n	mean	s.d.
Managers and senior officials	217	3.16	0.70	811	3.19	0.72	1028	3.18	0.72
Professional occupations	807	2.98	0.71	809	3.22	0.73	1616	3.10	0.73
Associate professional and technical	267	3.19	0.75	374	3.27	0.71	641	3.24	0.73
Administrative and secretarial	1008	3.26	0.76	742	3.26	0.72	1750	3.26	0.75
Skilled trades	190	2.89	0.80	736	3.23	0.73	926	3.16	0.76
Personal service	78	3.58	0.69	42	3.44	0.71	120	3.53	0.70
Sales and customer service	1975	3.20	0.75	957	3.30	0.78	2932	3.23	0.76
Process, plant and machine operatives	964	3.02	0.76	2927	3.32	0.74	3891	3.25	0.75
Elementary occupations	20	3.39	0.63	297	3.19	0.73	317	3.21	0.73

Table 5.4 Job-related Anxiety–Contentment (6 items, 5-point response scale): Descriptive statistics for SOC major occupational groups by age

Major occupational group	16–29			30–39			40–49			50–65		
	n	mean	s.d.	n	mean	s.d.	n	mean	s.d.	n	mean	s.d.
Managers and senior officials	192	3.20	0.71	324	3.13	0.68	303	3.19	0.74	198	3.28	0.74
Professional occupations	186	3.16	0.68	354	3.02	0.72	502	3.12	0.70	573	3.11	0.78
Associate professional and technical	159	3.15	0.76	191	3.25	0.69	159	3.23	0.75	112	3.36	0.73
Administrative and secretarial	561	3.26	0.76	490	3.26	0.72	412	3.27	0.76	248	3.29	0.74
Skilled trades	215	2.97	0.75	263	3.08	0.73	250	3.26	0.77	181	3.34	0.71
Personal service	72	3.48	0.71	35	3.63	0.70	6	–	–	5	–	–
Sales and customer service	1499	3.25	0.75	850	3.24	0.76	397	3.17	0.79	165	3.28	0.80
Process, plant and machine operatives	1026	3.09	0.76	1131	3.27	0.74	998	3.28	0.75	628	3.45	0.70
Elementary occupations	75	3.05	0.68	93	3.11	0.71	74	3.28	0.76	69	3.42	0.75

– Too few respondents (<20) to warrant descriptive statistics.

Table 5.5 Job-related Anxiety–Contentment (6 items, 5-point response scale): Descriptive statistics for selected occupational groups by gender and overall

Selected occupational group	Female			Male			All		
	n	mean	s.d.	n	mean	s.d.	n	mean	s.d.
Manufacturing organisations									
Managers and senior officials	82	3.13	0.64	361	3.15	0.67	443	3.15	0.66
Professional occupations	31	3.15	0.75	325	3.24	0.64	356	3.23	0.65
Associate professional and technical	78	3.11	0.78	187	3.30	0.68	265	3.25	0.72
Administrative and secretarial	196	3.26	0.76	152	3.17	0.64	348	3.22	0.71
Skilled trades	187	2.88	0.79	602	3.23	0.72	789	3.15	0.75
Process, plant and machine operatives	960	3.02	0.76	2531	3.33	0.72	3491	3.25	0.75
Elementary occupations	16	–	–	146	3.23	0.68	162	3.24	0.67

– Too few respondents (<20) to warrant descriptive statistics.

Table 5.6 Job-related Anxiety–Contentment (6 items, 5-point response scale): Descriptive statistics for selected occupational groups by age

Selected occupational group	16–29			30–39			40–49			50–65		
	n	mean	s.d.	n	mean	s.d.	n	mean	s.d.	n	mean	s.d.
Manufacturing organisations												
Managers and senior officials	73	3.16	0.62	129	3.09	0.64	150	3.14	0.69	95	3.28	0.68
Professional occupations	115	3.23	0.65	89	3.19	0.63	89	3.23	0.62	71	3.31	0.70
Associate professional and technical	59	3.26	0.72	58	3.18	0.74	69	3.22	0.67	72	3.32	0.77
Administrative and secretarial	170	3.18	0.73	62	3.16	0.73	71	3.26	0.70	44	3.48	0.58
Skilled trades	194	2.97	0.76	214	3.09	0.73	213	3.23	0.77	152	3.30	0.69
Process, plant and machine operatives	967	3.08	0.76	1010	3.28	0.73	886	3.29	0.73	534	3.46	0.70
Elementary occupations	43	3.21	0.65	46	3.03	0.73	35	3.29	0.69	33	3.45	0.69

JOB-RELATED DEPRESSION–ENTHUSIASM
(6 ITEMS, 5-POINT RESPONSE SCALE)

INTERNAL RELIABILITY AND DESCRIPTIVE STATISTICS
(Tables 5.7–5.12)

Table 5.7 Job-related Depression–Enthusiasm (6 items, 5-point response scale): Descriptive statistics and internal reliability (alpha) by sample[†]

Sample and organisation	n	mean	s.d.	n[‡]	alpha
2 Manufacturing – clothing	912	2.96	0.72	893	0.78
9 Manufacturing – wire	741	3.30	0.79	726	0.82
10 Manufacturing – heavy plant	778	3.54	0.69	770	0.80
11 Manufacturing – chemicals	336	3.43	0.77	334	0.85
16 Manufacturing – steel	461	3.53	0.73	453	0.83
19 Manufacturing – vehicle parts	42	3.37	0.76	42	0.84
20 Manufacturing – metal	56	3.50	0.73	56	0.81
22 Manufacturing – wire	387	3.29	0.81	378	0.83
25 Wholesale – building products	66	3.49	0.63	66	0.81
27 Manufacturing – metal products	142	3.49	0.76	53	0.82
28 Manufacturing – metal products	84	3.10	0.70	84	0.78
29 Professional association	857	3.61	0.71	846	0.87
30 Financial service call centre	830	3.40	0.77	797	0.85
31 Private healthcare call centre	462	3.38	0.79	445	0.85
32 Private healthcare administration	120	3.60	0.79	119	0.89
33 Private healthcare call centre	250	3.43	0.79	247	0.87
36 Mixed industries	1034	3.55	0.84	1009	0.89
37 Railway maintenance	609	3.51	0.80	593	0.86
38 Manufacturing – heavy plant	420	3.22	0.81	412	0.82
40 Mixed industries	64	3.89	0.73	64	0.90
43 Civil Service – policy unit	316	3.48	0.75	301	0.85
44 Manufacturing – chemicals	214	3.51	0.72	213	0.86
46 Manufacturing – food/drink	367	3.43	0.62	358	0.71
49 Railway maintenance	156	3.24	0.86	151	0.84
51 Public transport call centre	50	3.14	0.76	48	0.86
52 Manufacturing – food/drink	106	3.43	0.79	106	0.80
53 Retail – fashion accessories	172	3.58	0.80	172	0.82
55 Higher education	94	3.48	0.77	92	0.88
56 Banking	125	3.85	0.77	120	0.89
57 Secondary education	92	3.79	0.63	90	0.81
59 Manufacturing – aircraft parts	85	3.88	0.70	85	0.83
60 Logistics and consultancy	24	2.94	0.72	23	0.72
61 Manufacturing – tobacco products	45	3.79	0.65	45	0.84
66 Mixed industries	75	3.47	0.83	74	0.89
67 Financial service call centres	161	3.22	0.84	158	0.87
69 Banking	46	3.63	0.63	46	0.82
70 Mixed industries call centres	1136	3.18	0.80	1113	0.85
71 Wholesale – metal	473	3.53	0.75	458	0.83
72 NHS Ambulance Trust	52	3.44	0.85	51	0.85
73 Religious organisation	75	3.74	0.67	74	0.88
75 Mixed industries	124	3.86	0.67	117	0.87
77 Retail chemist	20	3.34	0.90	19	0.83
78 Estate agency	32	4.01	0.49	31	0.61
81 Manufacturing – pottery	110	3.28	0.76	106	0.84
82 Social work	107	3.52	0.84	107	0.90

[†] Details of the samples/organisations are shown in Table 1.1, pp. 6–11.
[‡] Sample sizes for alpha coefficients are smaller than for the sample as a whole because of list-wise deletion for missing values.

Table 5.8 Job-related Depression–Enthusiasm (6 items, 5-point response scale): Descriptive statistics for UK SIC major industrial sectors and overall

Standard Industrial Classification of company	n	mean	s.d.
D Manufacturing	5388	3.34	0.77
E Electricity, gas and water supply	154	3.15	0.79
F Construction	765	3.46	0.82
G Wholesale and retail trade[†]	807	3.49	0.76
H Hotels and restaurants	98	3.23	0.73
I Transport, storage and communication	762	3.30	0.89
J Financial intermediation	1444	3.42	0.78
K Real estate, renting and business activities	233	3.66	0.77
L Public admin and defence; compulsory social security	1105	3.47	0.81
M Education	1043	3.62	0.71
N Health and social work	1034	3.44	0.80
O Other social and personal service activities	75	3.74	0.67
Total	12908	3.41	0.79

[†]Includes repair of motor vehicles, motorcycles and household and personal goods.

Table 5.9 Job-related Depression–Enthusiasm (6 items, 5-point response scale): Descriptive statistics for SOC major occupational groups by gender and overall

Major occupational group	Female			Male			All		
	n	mean	s.d.	n	mean	s.d.	n	mean	s.d.
Managers and senior officials	213	3.61	0.73	781	3.74	0.70	994	3.72	0.71
Professional occupations	789	3.59	0.70	661	3.60	0.70	1450	3.59	0.70
Associate professional and technical	265	3.62	0.76	301	3.61	0.70	566	3.61	0.73
Administrative and secretarial	949	3.48	0.81	675	3.47	0.77	1624	3.48	0.79
Skilled trades	190	3.14	0.78	710	3.36	0.78	900	3.31	0.78
Personal service	78	3.93	0.72	42	4.04	0.82	120	3.97	0.75
Sales and customer service	1976	3.32	0.78	960	3.30	0.84	2936	3.31	0.80
Process, plant and machine operatives	828	3.11	0.74	2696	3.34	0.79	3524	3.29	0.78
Elementary occupations	20	3.63	0.73	285	3.26	0.75	305	3.28	0.75

Table 5.10 Job-related Depression–Enthusiasm (6 items, 5-point response scale): Descriptive statistics for SOC major occupational groups by age

Major occupational group	16–29			30–39			40–49			50–65		
	n	mean	s.d.	n	mean	s.d.	n	mean	s.d.	n	mean	s.d.
Managers and senior officials	175	3.60	0.72	309	3.67	0.67	301	3.77	0.71	198	3.83	0.71
Professional occupations	143	3.56	0.62	323	3.57	0.67	451	3.60	0.69	535	3.61	0.74
Associate professional and technical	131	3.54	0.73	176	3.58	0.74	145	3.62	0.70	96	3.82	0.74
Administrative and secretarial	504	3.35	0.83	462	3.53	0.79	390	3.54	0.76	232	3.56	0.73
Skilled trades	209	3.04	0.83	259	3.31	0.76	239	3.36	0.73	176	3.61	0.70
Personal service	72	3.91	0.77	35	4.00	0.78	6	–	–	5	–	–
Sales and customer service	1502	3.27	0.81	850	3.36	0.80	398	3.32	0.77	165	3.49	0.77
Process, plant and machine operatives	943	3.17	0.80	1022	3.28	0.78	890	3.34	0.78	571	3.49	0.70
Elementary occupations	72	3.22	0.73	86	3.17	0.76	74	3.45	0.77	67	3.35	0.70

–Too few respondents (<20) to warrant descriptive statistics.

Table 5.11 Job-related Depression–Enthusiasm (6 items, 5-point response scale): Descriptive statistics for selected occupational groups by gender and overall

Selected occupational group	Female			Male			All		
	n	mean	s.d.	n	mean	s.d.	n	mean	s.d.
Manufacturing organisations									
Managers and senior officials	79	3.57	0.68	343	3.68	0.70	422	3.66	0.70
Professional occupations	22	3.44	0.70	243	3.51	0.65	265	3.51	0.66
Associate professional and technical	76	3.62	0.80	114	3.62	0.66	190	3.62	0.72
Administrative and secretarial	172	3.42	0.79	123	3.27	0.68	295	3.35	0.75
Skilled trades	187	3.12	0.78	576	3.32	0.78	763	3.27	0.78
Process, plant and machine operatives	824	3.11	0.74	2301	3.35	0.77	3125	3.29	0.77
Elementary occupations	16	–	–	134	3.32	0.75	150	3.34	0.75

– Too few respondents (<20) to warrant descriptive statistics.

Table 5.12 Job-related Depression–Enthusiasm (6 items, 5-point response scale): Descriptive statistics for selected occupational groups by age

Selected occupational group	16–29			30–39			40–49			50–65		
	n	mean	s.d.	n	mean	s.d.	n	mean	s.d.	n	mean	s.d.
Manufacturing organisations												
Managers and senior officials	65	3.52	0.70	118	3.59	0.64	148	3.73	0.74	95	3.78	0.69
Professional occupations	71	3.45	0.58	67	3.58	0.63	80	3.52	0.67	57	3.50	0.73
Associate professional and technical	31	3.49	0.69	43	3.54	0.71	55	3.64	0.65	56	3.80	0.80
Administrative and secretarial	151	3.30	0.79	53	3.37	0.74	59	3.46	0.69	33	3.42	0.70
Skilled trades	188	2.98	0.82	210	3.25	0.75	202	3.34	0.75	147	3.58	0.70
Process, plant and machine operatives	884	3.15	0.80	902	3.29	0.76	778	3.36	0.76	477	3.51	0.69
Elementary occupations	40	3.40	0.81	39	3.01	0.75	35	3.56	0.74	31	3.48	0.61

INTERNAL RELIABILITY AND DESCRIPTIVE STATISTICS
(Tables 5.13–5.18)

Table 5.13 Job-related Anxiety (3 items, 5-point response scale): Descriptive statistics and internal reliability (alpha) by sample[†]

Sample and organisation	n	mean	s.d.	n[‡]	alpha
1 Manufacturing – electronic machinery	163	2.12	0.70	162	0.70
2 Manufacturing – clothing	912	2.91	0.86	906	0.74
3 Manufacturing – electronics	162	2.43	0.74	160	0.69
5 Manufacturing – chemicals	348	2.27	0.71	345	0.78
8 Manufacturing – glassware	877	2.43	1.02	866	0.88
9 Manufacturing – wire	744	2.44	0.80	732	0.76
10 Manufacturing – heavy plant	777	2.12	0.81	773	0.79
11 Manufacturing – chemicals	336	2.43	0.75	334	0.78
12 Mail sorting office	402	2.21	0.94	401	0.83
16 Manufacturing – steel	461	2.38	0.73	458	0.77
17 Manufacturing – steel	374	1.96	0.83	370	0.85
18 Film processing	51	1.99	0.61	50	0.70
19 Manufacturing – vehicle parts	42	2.16	0.71	42	0.80
20 Manufacturing – metal	56	2.32	0.77	56	0.73
21 Manufacturing – metal products	73	2.27	0.69	72	0.75
22 Manufacturing – wire	388	2.40	0.78	386	0.67
23 Patent Office	162	1.68	0.68	161	0.82
25 Wholesale – building products	66	2.49	0.87	66	0.86
27 Manufacturing – metal products	143	2.26	0.84	139	0.80
28 Manufacturing – metal products	84	2.85	0.84	84	0.75
29 Professional association	860	2.65	0.77	845	0.89
30 Financial service call centre	830	2.26	0.78	822	0.79
31 Private healthcare call centre	461	2.30	0.78	453	0.78
32 Private healthcare administration	120	2.58	0.82	120	0.81
33 Private healthcare call centre	250	2.22	0.83	248	0.82
35 Police Force	353	1.90	0.82	352	0.84
36 Mixed industries	1034	2.43	0.85	1013	0.84
37 Railway maintenance	612	2.40	0.89	602	0.85
38 Manufacturing – heavy plant	420	2.30	0.87	415	0.78
40 Mixed industries	64	2.38	0.84	64	0.88
43 Civil Service – policy unit	316	2.45	0.80	311	0.82
44 Manufacturing – chemicals	214	2.35	0.69	214	0.78
46 Manufacturing – food/drink	381	2.26	0.77	378	0.75
49 Railway maintenance	157	2.24	0.87	154	0.79
51 Public transport call centre	50	2.67	0.83	47	0.74
52 Manufacturing – food/drink	106	1.73	0.79	106	0.81
53 Retail – fashion accessories	172	2.09	0.78	171	0.74
54 Manufacturing – medical equipment	186	2.28	0.88	183	0.79
55 Higher education	94	2.80	0.84	93	0.87
56 Banking	125	2.52	0.82	121	0.81
57 Secondary education	92	2.63	0.82	92	0.87
59 Manufacturing – aircraft parts	85	2.23	0.88	85	0.85
60 Logistics and consultancy	24	2.64	1.04	24	0.83

Table 5.13   Continued

Sample and organisation	n	mean	s.d.	n‡	alpha
61 Manufacturing – tobacco products	45	2.37	0.65	44	0.79
66 Mixed industries	190	2.29	0.78	190	0.75
67 Financial service call centres	161	2.42	0.87	160	0.82
69 Banking	46	2.20	0.83	46	0.85
70 Mixed industries call centres	1135	2.32	0.85	1123	0.81
71 Wholesale – metal	473	2.29	0.75	467	0.78
72 NHS Ambulance Trust	53	2.26	0.89	53	0.85
73 Religious organisation	76	2.25	0.59	76	0.69
75 Mixed industries	124	2.30	0.63	124	0.70
77 Retail chemist	20	2.33	1.06	19	0.93
78 Estate agency	32	2.41	0.72	31	0.56
81 Manufacturing – pottery	111	2.36	0.79	110	0.81
82 Social work	108	2.56	0.82	105	0.80

†Details of the samples/organisations are shown in Table 1.1, pp. 6–11.
‡Sample sizes for alpha coefficients are smaller than for the sample as a whole because of list-wise deletion for missing values.

Table 5.14   Job-related Anxiety (3 items, 5-point response scale): Descriptive statistics for UK SIC major industrial sectors and overall

Standard Industrial Classification of company	n	mean	s.d.
D Manufacturing	7659	2.37	0.86
E Electricity, gas and water supply	153	2.31	0.83
F Construction	769	2.37	0.89
G Wholesale and retail trade†	807	2.28	0.79
H Hotels and restaurants	98	2.19	0.82
I Transport, storage and communication	1163	2.35	0.91
J Financial intermediation	1444	2.29	0.80
K Real estate, renting and business activities	330	2.32	0.75
L Public admin and defence; compulsory social security	1621	2.25	0.86
M Education	1046	2.66	0.78
N Health and social work	1035	2.34	0.82
O Other social and personal service activities	76	2.25	0.59
Total	16201	2.36	0.85

†Includes repair of motor vehicles, motorcycles and household and personal goods.

Table 5.15 Job-related Anxiety (3 items, 5-point response scale): Descriptive statistics for SOC major occupational groups by gender and overall

Major occupational group	Female			Male			All		
	n	mean	s.d.	n	mean	s.d.	n	mean	s.d.
Managers and senior officials	233	2.53	0.75	917	2.46	0.77	1150	2.47	0.77
Professional occupations	820	2.66	0.76	1001	2.38	0.82	1821	2.50	0.81
Associate professional and technical	345	2.39	0.84	689	2.16	0.82	1034	2.24	0.83
Administrative and secretarial	1070	2.36	0.83	760	2.36	0.80	1830	2.36	0.82
Skilled trades	191	2.79	0.92	833	2.35	0.84	1024	2.44	0.87
Personal service	78	2.28	0.75	42	2.41	0.79	120	2.33	0.77
Sales and customer service	1974	2.34	0.81	959	2.25	0.86	2933	2.31	0.83
Process, plant and machine operatives	1292	2.58	0.92	3706	2.24	0.86	4998	2.33	0.89
Elementary occupations	90	2.23	0.90	609	2.24	0.88	699	2.24	0.88

Table 5.16 Job-related Anxiety (3 items, 5-point response scale): Descriptive statistics for SOC major occupational groups by age

Major occupational group	16–29			30–39			40–49			50–65		
	n	mean	s.d.	n	mean	s.d.	n	mean	s.d.	n	mean	s.d.
Managers and senior officials	202	2.44	0.77	363	2.50	0.73	353	2.49	0.77	220	2.37	0.79
Professional occupations	230	2.43	0.82	408	2.53	0.82	561	2.48	0.77	619	2.54	0.83
Associate professional and technical	249	2.32	0.88	380	2.18	0.81	255	2.21	0.84	126	2.29	0.79
Administrative and secretarial	594	2.29	0.83	507	2.35	0.79	432	2.40	0.83	257	2.41	0.80
Skilled trades	226	2.61	0.90	286	2.46	0.87	284	2.35	0.89	210	2.39	0.79
Personal service	72	2.34	0.79	35	2.28	0.76	6	–	–	5	–	–
Sales and customer service	1501	2.29	0.83	849	2.33	0.81	397	2.36	0.87	165	2.28	0.81
Process, plant and machine operatives	1267	2.46	0.92	1510	2.25	0.87	1263	2.32	0.88	831	2.25	0.84
Elementary occupations	185	2.39	0.95	231	2.31	0.85	148	2.17	0.85	127	2.01	0.85

–Too few respondents (<20) to warrant descriptive statistics.

Table 5.17 Job-related Anxiety (3 items, 5-point response scale): Descriptive statistics for selected occupational groups by gender and overall

Selected occupational group	Female			Male			All		
	n	mean	s.d.	n	mean	s.d.	n	mean	s.d.
Manufacturing organisations									
Managers and senior officials	96	2.58	0.75	447	2.48	0.75	543	2.50	0.75
Professional occupations	38	2.50	0.84	451	2.34	0.77	489	2.35	0.78
Associate professional and technical	92	2.50	0.86	220	2.30	0.72	312	2.36	0.77
Administrative and secretarial	255	2.38	0.77	171	2.46	0.80	426	2.41	0.78
Skilled trades	188	2.80	0.92	698	2.34	0.84	886	2.44	0.88
Process, plant and machine operatives	1282	2.58	0.92	3226	2.25	0.86	4508	2.34	0.89
Elementary occupations	20	2.33	0.79	205	2.33	0.77	225	2.33	0.77

Table 5.18 Job-related Anxiety (3 items, 5-point response scale): Descriptive statistics for selected occupational groups by age

Selected occupational group	16–29			30–39			40–49			50–65		
	n	mean	s.d.	n	mean	s.d.	n	mean	s.d.	n	mean	s.d.
Manufacturing organisations												
Managers and senior officials	82	2.50	0.77	159	2.53	0.72	187	2.54	0.76	116	2.34	0.76
Professional occupations	144	2.30	0.78	124	2.38	0.81	121	2.34	0.71	107	2.38	0.81
Associate professional and technical	67	2.47	0.85	71	2.35	0.72	84	2.30	0.73	81	2.34	0.82
Administrative and secretarial	204	2.33	0.77	78	2.47	0.82	90	2.56	0.78	52	2.33	0.78
Skilled trades	205	2.61	0.91	237	2.41	0.88	246	2.37	0.89	181	2.44	0.79
Process, plant and machine operatives	1202	2.48	0.92	1343	2.26	0.87	1128	2.31	0.87	723	2.25	0.86
Elementary occupations	60	2.43	0.89	69	2.46	0.79	46	2.28	0.75	43	2.12	0.64

JOB-RELATED DEPRESSION (3 ITEMS, 5-POINT RESPONSE SCALE)

INTERNAL RELIABILITY AND DESCRIPTIVE STATISTICS
(Tables 5.19–5.24)

Table 5.19 Job-related Depression (3 items, 5-point response scale): Descriptive statistics and internal reliability (alpha) by sample[†]

Sample and organisation	n	mean	s.d.	n[‡]	alpha
2 Manufacturing – clothing	913	2.68	0.96	902	0.83
8 Manufacturing – glassware	875	2.29	1.06	861	0.90
9 Manufacturing – wire	744	2.22	0.95	734	0.85
10 Manufacturing – heavy plant	779	1.88	0.80	775	0.83
11 Manufacturing – chemicals	337	2.07	0.84	335	0.84
12 Mail sorting office	402	2.32	1.07	400	0.92
16 Manufacturing – steel	461	2.01	0.80	460	0.81
17 Manufacturing – steel	374	1.93	0.88	371	0.89
18 Film processing	51	1.83	0.73	51	0.80
19 Manufacturing – vehicle parts	42	2.02	0.90	42	0.89
20 Manufacturing – metal	56	1.99	0.82	56	0.86
21 Manufacturing – metal products	73	1.95	0.81	73	0.83
22 Manufacturing – wire	388	2.25	0.95	387	0.84
25 Wholesale – building products	66	2.01	0.78	66	0.84
27 Manufacturing – metal products	142	2.08	0.94	142	0.85
28 Manufacturing – metal products	84	2.49	0.90	84	0.88
29 Professional association	858	1.77	0.82	848	0.89
30 Financial service call centre	829	2.03	0.89	824	0.86
31 Private healthcare call centre	462	2.04	0.93	449	0.87
32 Private healthcare administration	120	2.11	0.97	119	0.90
33 Private healthcare call centre	250	2.01	0.92	249	0.89
36 Mixed industries	1034	1.97	0.93	1019	0.90
37 Railway maintenance	610	1.98	0.92	601	0.89
38 Manufacturing – heavy plant	420	2.21	1.00	416	0.87
40 Mixed industries	64	1.63	0.80	64	0.92
43 Civil service – policy unit	316	1.97	0.86	308	0.87
44 Manufacturing – chemicals	214	1.96	0.81	213	0.84
46 Manufacturing – food/drink	382	2.06	0.84	373	0.83
49 Railway maintenance	156	2.12	1.03	155	0.86
51 Public transport call centre	50	2.49	0.89	49	0.82
52 Manufacturing – food/drink	106	1.75	0.92	106	0.89
53 Retail – fashion accessories	172	2.00	0.94	172	0.82
54 Manufacturing – medical equipment	185	2.25	1.02	182	0.86
55 Higher education	93	2.07	0.85	93	0.87
56 Banking	124	1.90	0.92	121	0.86
57 Secondary education	92	1.68	0.70	90	0.85
59 Manufacturing – aircraft parts	85	1.59	0.85	85	0.88
60 Logistics and consultancy	24	2.60	1.12	24	0.88
61 Manufacturing – tobacco products	45	1.72	0.76	45	0.87
65 Film processing	226	1.97	0.88	224	0.83
66 Mixed industries	189	1.94	0.84	188	0.85
67 Financial services call centres	161	2.21	0.97	159	0.86

Table 5.19   Continued

Sample and organisation	n	mean	s.d.	n[‡]	alpha
69 Banking	46	1.69	0.75	46	0.87
70 Mixed industries call centres	1136	2.20	0.95	1129	0.87
71 Wholesale – metal	475	1.97	0.84	466	0.85
72 NHS Ambulance Trust	53	1.89	0.93	53	0.90
73 Religious organisation	75	1.74	0.73	74	0.86
75 Mixed industries	124	1.67	0.76	120	0.85
77 Retail chemist	20	1.90	1.16	20	0.97
78 Estate agency	32	1.67	0.70	32	0.86
81 Manufacturing – pottery	110	1.93	0.89	109	0.89
82 Social work	107	2.06	1.00	107	0.92

[†]Details of the samples/organisations are shown in Table 1.1, pp. 6–11.
[‡]Sample sizes for alpha coefficients are smaller than for the sample as a whole because of list-wise deletion for missing values.

Table 5.20   Job-related Depression (3 items 5-point response scale): Descriptive statistics for UK SIC major industrial sectors and overall

Standard Industrial Classification of company	n	mean	s.d.
D Manufacturing	6986	2.16	0.95
E Electricity, gas and water supply	154	2.21	0.96
F Construction	766	2.01	0.95
G Wholesale and retail trade[†]	809	2.00	0.89
H Hotels and restaurants	98	2.18	0.93
I Transport, storage and communication	1163	2.23	1.01
J Financial intermediation	1442	2.04	0.90
K Real estate, renting and business activities	555	1.92	0.88
L Public admin and defence; compulsory social security	1106	1.99	0.92
M Education	1043	1.79	0.82
N Health and social work	1035	2.03	0.93
O Other community, social and personal service activities	75	1.74	0.73
Total	15232	2.08	0.94

[†]Includes repair of motor vehicles, motorcycles and household and personal goods.

Table 5.21 Job-related Depression (3 items 5-point response scale): Descriptive statistics for SOC major occupational groups by gender and overall

Major occupational group	Female			Male			All		
	n	mean	s.d.	n	mean	s.d.	n	mean	s.d.
Managers and senior officials	228	1.99	0.84	881	1.83	0.76	1109	1.87	0.78
Professional occupations	798	1.81	0.82	855	1.92	0.84	1653	1.87	0.83
Associate professional and technical	279	1.99	0.91	334	1.88	0.79	613	1.93	0.84
Administrative and secretarial	1010	1.97	0.93	694	1.99	0.87	1704	1.98	0.91
Skilled trades	192	2.49	1.00	807	2.14	0.94	999	2.21	0.97
Personal service	78	1.76	0.80	42	1.74	0.94	120	1.76	0.85
Sales and customer service	1973	2.11	0.92	961	2.15	0.97	2934	2.12	0.94
Process, plant and machine operatives	1297	2.38	1.00	3528	2.11	0.96	4825	2.18	0.98
Elementary occupations	106	2.29	1.09	601	2.27	1.00	707	2.27	1.01

Table 5.22 Job-related Depression (3 items 5-point response scale): Descriptive statistics for SOC major occupational groups by age

Major occupational group	16–29			30–39			40–49			50–65		
	n	mean	s.d.	n	mean	s.d.	n	mean	s.d.	n	mean	s.d.
Managers and senior officials	185	1.96	0.80	345	1.89	0.74	347	1.88	0.77	220	1.70	0.78
Professional occupations	187	1.97	0.79	377	1.86	0.84	509	1.84	0.81	580	1.86	0.85
Associate professional and technical	139	2.10	0.85	189	1.97	0.84	160	1.83	0.81	105	1.70	0.80
Administrative and secretarial	538	2.08	0.98	478	1.93	0.89	409	1.95	0.87	242	1.88	0.84
Skilled trades	221	2.59	1.05	282	2.19	0.94	273	2.10	0.90	205	1.94	0.83
Personal service	72	1.80	0.90	35	1.74	0.80	6	–	–	5	–	–
Sales and customer service	1501	2.20	0.96	850	2.06	0.90	398	2.05	0.91	164	1.93	0.87
Process, plant and machine operatives	1207	2.36	1.00	1459	2.14	0.96	1205	2.12	0.96	823	1.99	0.91
Elementary occupations	189	2.55	1.02	231	2.34	1.02	151	2.08	0.98	126	1.99	0.96

–Too few respondents (<20) to warrant descriptive statistics.

Table 5.23 Job-related Depression (3 items 5-point response scale): Descriptive statistics for selected occupational groups by gender and overall

Selected occupational group	Female			Male			All		
	n	mean	s.d.	n	mean	s.d.	n	mean	s.d.
Manufacturing organisations									
Managers and senior officials	93	2.00	0.77	429	1.91	0.74	522	1.93	0.74
Professional occupations	29	1.99	0.72	371	1.98	0.81	400	1.98	0.80
Associate professional and technical	90	2.02	0.98	147	1.81	0.71	237	1.89	0.83
Administrative and secretarial	231	2.01	0.93	142	2.18	0.87	373	2.07	0.91
Skilled trades	189	2.51	1.00	672	2.17	0.95	861	2.25	0.97
Process, plant and machine operatives	1146	2.43	1.00	2999	2.11	0.96	4145	2.20	0.98
Elementary occupations	20	2.03	0.98	192	2.22	0.96	212	2.20	0.96

Table 5.24 Job-related Depression (3 items 5-point response scale): Descriptive statistics for selected occupational groups by age

Selected occupational group	16–29			30–39			40–49			50–65		
	n	mean	s.d.	n	mean	s.d.	n	mean	s.d.	n	mean	s.d.
Manufacturing organisations												
Managers and senior officials	74	1.97	0.73	148	1.97	0.68	185	1.97	0.78	116	1.73	0.74
Professional occupations	101	2.04	0.75	102	2.00	0.83	112	1.91	0.77	94	1.95	0.84
Associate professional and technical	39	2.12	0.86	56	1.99	0.80	70	1.80	0.77	65	1.71	0.84
Administrative and secretarial	185	2.07	0.93	69	2.10	0.97	78	2.07	0.92	41	2.01	0.83
Skilled trades	200	2.64	1.04	233	2.23	0.96	235	2.12	0.90	176	1.99	0.84
Process, plant and machine operatives	1118	2.39	1.01	1236	2.15	0.95	1023	2.13	0.95	665	2.01	0.93
Elementary occupations	57	2.42	0.98	62	2.38	1.03	46	1.97	1.00	40	1.95	0.83

JOB-RELATED ANXIETY (3 ITEMS, 6-POINT RESPONSE SCALE)

DESCRIPTIVE STATISTICS
(Tables 5.25 and 5.26)

Table 5.25 Job-related Anxiety (3 items, 6-point response scale): Descriptive statistics for selected occupational groups by gender and overall

Selected occupational group	Female			Male			All		
	n	mean	s.d.	n	mean	s.d.	n	mean	s.d.
NHS Trusts									
Managers	886	2.35	0.93	694	2.29	0.93	1580	2.33	0.93
Doctors	727	2.30	0.84	1350	2.17	0.81	2077	2.21	0.82
Nurses	6955	2.13	0.90	712	2.33	0.98	7667	2.15	0.91
Professions Allied to Medicine	2509	2.11	0.86	361	2.22	0.94	2870	2.12	0.87
Professional and Technical Staff	823	1.95	0.90	516	1.99	0.87	1339	1.97	0.88
Administrative Staff	2949	1.92	0.91	355	2.02	0.97	3304	1.93	0.92
Ancillary Staff	711	1.73	0.89	516	1.94	1.02	1227	1.82	0.95

Table 5.26 Job-related Anxiety (3 items, 6-point response scale): Descriptive statistics for selected occupational groups by age

Selected occupational group	16–29			30–39			40–49			50–65		
	n	mean	s.d.	n	mean	s.d.	n	mean	s.d.	n	mean	s.d.
NHS Trusts												
Managers	164	2.31	0.97	530	2.42	1.01	550	2.34	0.84	333	2.16	0.91
Doctors	443	2.36	0.88	645	2.19	0.81	560	2.23	0.78	416	2.07	0.80
Nurses	1362	2.18	0.89	2666	2.19	0.92	2103	2.17	0.93	1441	2.02	0.88
Professions allied to medicine	740	2.15	0.87	878	2.15	0.90	748	2.11	0.85	481	2.05	0.84
Professional and technical staff	302	1.94	0.87	421	1.99	0.91	391	1.95	0.83	220	1.98	0.95
Administrative staff	594	2.06	1.00	753	2.00	0.99	990	1.90	0.90	923	1.84	0.82
Ancillary staff	134	1.91	1.00	267	1.83	0.90	331	1.84	1.03	480	1.77	0.92

JOB-RELATED DEPRESSION (3 ITEMS, 6-POINT RESPONSE SCALE)

DESCRIPTIVE STATISTICS
(Tables 5.27 and 5.28)

Table 5.27 Job-related Depression (3 items, 6-point response scale): Descriptive statistics for selected occupational groups by gender and overall

Selected occupational group	Female			Male			All		
	n	mean	s.d.	n	mean	s.d.	n	mean	s.d.
NHS Trusts									
Managers	886	1.85	0.95	693	1.85	0.92	1579	1.85	0.94
Doctors	727	1.86	0.90	1349	1.75	0.81	2076	1.79	0.84
Nurses	6950	1.80	0.91	711	1.98	1.00	7661	1.82	0.92
Professions allied to medicine	2510	1.71	0.85	361	1.79	0.91	2871	1.72	0.86
Professional and technical staff	823	1.75	0.93	516	1.77	0.91	1339	1.76	0.92
Administrative staff	2947	1.71	0.93	355	1.92	1.08	3302	1.74	0.95
Ancillary staff	714	1.66	0.94	517	1.88	1.03	1231	1.75	0.98

Table **5.28** Job-related Depression (3 items, 6-point response scale): Descriptive statistics for selected occupational groups by age

Selected occupational group	16–29			30–39			40–49			50–65		
	n	mean	s.d.	n	mean	s.d.	n	mean	s.d.	n	mean	s.d.
NHS Trusts												
Managers	164	1.98	1.03	529	1.95	1.04	550	1.82	0.85	333	1.68	0.82
Doctors	444	2.01	0.93	644	1.74	0.82	559	1.75	0.81	416	1.68	0.80
Nurses	1362	1.91	0.94	2664	1.86	0.95	2101	1.81	0.92	1439	1.67	0.83
Professions allied to medicine	741	1.76	0.89	878	1.78	0.92	749	1.68	0.81	480	1.63	0.76
Professional and technical staff	302	1.84	0.97	421	1.75	0.94	391	1.73	0.88	220	1.68	0.89
Administrative staff	594	1.99	1.11	752	1.79	1.00	988	1.69	0.91	924	1.60	0.80
Ancillary staff	134	2.02	1.11	267	1.79	0.95	332	1.75	1.02	483	1.66	0.93

REFERENCES

Banks MH, Clegg CW, Jackson PR et al. (1980). The use of the General Health Questionnaire as an indicator of mental health in occupational settings. *Journal of Occupational Psychology*, **53**, 187–194.

Biggs D & Swailes S (2006). Relations, commitment and satisfaction in agency workers and permanent workers. *Employee Relations*, **28**, 130–143.

Birdi K, Warr PB & Oswald A (1995). Age differences in three components of employee well-being. *Applied Psychology: An International Review*, **44**, 345–373.

Bond F & Bunce D (2003). The role of acceptance and job control in mental health, job satisfaction and work performance. *Journal of Applied Psychology*, **88**, 1057–1067.

Borrill CS, Wall TD, West MA et al. (1998). *Stress Among Staff in NHS Trusts*. Final Report to NHS Executive. University of Sheffield, Institute of Work Psychology.

Buchanan B (1974). Building organizational commitment: The socialization of managers in organizations. *Administrative Science Quarterly*, **19**, 533–546.

Clegg CW, Wall TD & Kemp NJ (1987). Women on the assembly line: A comparison of main and interactive explanations of job satisfaction, absence and mental health. *Journal of Occupational Psychology*, **60**, 273–287.

Cook J & Wall TD (1980). New work attitude measures of trust, organizational commitment and personal need non-fulfilment. *Journal of Occupational Psychology*, **53**, 39–52.

Cooksey RW & Soutar GN (2006). Coefficient Beta and hierarchical item clustering. *Organizational Research Methods*, **9**, 78–98.

Cooper CL & Bramwell RS (1992). A comparative analysis of occupational stress in managerial and shopfloor workers in the brewing industry – mental-health, job satisfaction and sickness. *Work and Stress*, **6**, 127–138.

Cooper CL & Kelly M (1993). Occupational stress in head teachers – A national UK study. *British Journal of Educational Psychology*, **63**, 13–143.

Corbett JM, Martin R, Wall TD & Clegg CW (1989). Technological coupling as a predictor of intrinsic job satisfaction – a replication study. *Journal of Organizational Behavior*, **10**, 91–95.

Cordery J, Sevastos P, Mueller W & Parker SK (1993). Correlates of employee attitudes toward functional flexibility. *Human Relations*, **46**, 705–723.

Cronbach LJ (1951). Coefficient alpha and the internal structure of tests. *Psychometrika*, **16**, 297–334.

Daniels K, Brough P, Guppy A et al. (1997). A note on a modification to Warr's measures of affective well-being at work. *Journal of Occupational and Organizational Psychology*, **70**, 129–138.

Daniels K & Guppy A (1997). Stressors, locus of control, and social support as consequences of affective psychological well-being. *Journal of Occupational Health Psychology*, **2**, 156–174.

De Cuyper N & De Witte H (2006). The impact of job insecurity and contract type on attitudes, well-being and behavioural reports: A psychological contract perspective. *Journal of Occupational and Organizational Psychology*, **79**, 395–409.

Dollard MF & Winefield AH (1995). Trait anxiety, work demand, social support and psychological distress in correctional officers. *Anxiety Stress and Coping*, **8**, 25–35.

Epitropaki O & Martin R (2005). From ideal to real: A longitudinal study of the role of implicit leadership theories on leader-member exchanges and employee outcomes. *Journal of Applied Psychology*, **90**, 659–676.

Evans S, Huxley P, Gately C et al. (2006). Mental health, burnout and job satisfaction among mental health social workers in England and Wales. *British Journal of Psychiatry*, **188**, 75–80.

Fenton-O'Creevy MP, Winfrow P, Lydka H & Morris T (1997). Company prospects and employee commitment: An analysis of the dimensionality of the BOCS and the influences of external events on those dimensions. *British Journal of Industrial Relations*, **35**, 593–608.

Goldberg, D.P. (1972). *The detection of psychiatric illness by questionnaire.* Oxford, Oxford University Press.

Goldberg DP & Hillier V (1979). A scaled version of the General Health Questionnaire. *Psychological Medicine*, **9**, 139–145.

Goldberg DP & Williams P (1988). *A User's Guide to the General Health Questionnaire.* Windsor, NFER-Nelson.

Goldberg DP, Gater R, Sartorius N et al. (1997). The validity of two versions of the GHQ in the WHO study of mental illness in general health care. *Psychological Medicine*, **27**, 191–197.

Gould-Williams J (2003). The importance of HR practices and workplace trust in achieving superior performance: a study of public-sector organizations. *International Journal of Human Resource Management*, **14**, 28–54.

Gould-Williams J (2004). The effects of 'high commitment' HRM on employee attitudes: The views of public sector workers. *Public Administration*, **82**, 63–81.

Government Statistical Service (1990). *Standard Occupational Classification.* London, HMSO.

Hardy GE, Haynes CE, Rick JE & Shapiro DA (1999). Validation of the General Health Questionnaire-12 using a sample of employees from the Health Care Services. *Psychological Assessment*, **11**, 159–165.

Hardy GE, Woods D & Wall TD (2003). The impact of psychological distress on absence from work. *Journal of Applied Psychology*, **88**, 306–314.

Hicks-Clarke D & Iles P (2000). Climate for diversity and its effects on career and organizational attitudes and perceptions. *Personnel Review*, **29**, 324–345.

Holman D, Chiswick E & Totterdell P (2002). The effect of performance monitoring on emotional labor and well-being in call centres. *Motivation and Emotion*, **26**, 57–81.

Kemp NJ, Wall TD, Clegg CW & Cordery JL (1983). Autonomous work groups in a greenfield site: A comparative study. *Journal of Occupational Psychology*, **56**, 271–288.

Martin R, Thomas G, Charles K et al. (2005). The role of leader-member exchanges in mediating the relationship between locus of control and work reactions. *Journal of Occupational Psychology*, **78**, 141–147.

Matthews BP & Shepherd JL (2002). Dimensionality of Cook and Wall's (1980) British Organisational Commitment Scale revisited. *Journal of Occupational and Organizational Psychology*, **75**, 369–375.

Meyer J & Allen N (1991). A three-component conceptualization of organizational commitment. *Human Resource Management Review*, **1**, 61–90.

Mullarkey S, Jackson PR & Parker S (1995). Employee reactions to JIT manufacturing practices: A two phase investigation. *International Journal of Operations and Production Management*, **15**, 62–79.

Mullarkey S, Jackson PR, Wall TD et al. (1997). The impact of technology characteristics and job control on worker mental health. *Journal of Organizational Behavior*, **18**, 471–489.

Noblet AJ, McWilliams J, Teo STT & Rodwell JJ (2006). Work characteristics and employee outcomes in local government. *International Journal of Human Resource Management*, **17**, 1804–1818.

O'Driscoll MP & Beehr TA (1994). Supervisor behaviours, role stressors and uncertainty as predictors of personal outcomes for subordinates. *Journal of Organizational Behavior*, **15**, 141–155.

Office for National Statistics (2000). *Standard occupational classification 2000*. London, The Stationary Office.

Parker SK (2003). Longitudinal effects of lean production on employee outcomes and the mediating role of work characteristics. *Journal of Applied Psychology*, **88**, 620–634.

Parker SK, Williams HM & Turner N (2006). Modeling the antecedents of proactive behaviour at work. *Journal of Applied Psychology*, **91**, 636–652.

Patterson M, Warr P & West M (2004). Organizational climate and company productivity: The role of employee affect and employee level. *Journal of Occupational and Organizational Psychology*, **77**, 193–216.

Pernice R & Long N (1996). Long-term unemployment, employment attitudes and mental health. *Australian Journal of Social Issues*, **31**, 311–326.

Petrides KV & Furnham A (2006). The role of trait emotional intelligence in a gender-specific model of organizational variables. *Journal of Applied Social Psychology*, **36**, 552–569.

Porter L, Steers R, Mowday R & Boulian P (1974). Organizational commitment, job satisfaction and turnover among psychiatric technicians. *Journal of Applied Psychology*, **50**, 603–609.

Prosser D, Johnson S, Kuipers E, Szmukler G, Bebbington P & Thornicroft G (1996). Mental health, burnout and job satisfaction among hospital and community-based mental-health staff. *British Journal of Psychiatry*, **169**, 334–337.

Rogelberg SG, Leach DJ, Warr PB & Burnfield JL (2006). 'Not another meeting!' Are meeting time demands related to employee well-being? *Journal of Applied Psychology*, **91**, 83–96.

Schalk R, Keunen A & Meijer T (1995). Warr's schalen voor welzin en mentale gezondheid: Factorstructuur en betrouwbaarheid. *Gedrag en Organisatie*, **8**, 116–127.

Sevastos P, Smith L & Cordery JL (1992). Evidence on the reliability and construct validity of Warr's (1990) well-being and mental health measures. *Journal of Occupational and Organizational Psychology*, **65**, 33–49.

Sprigg CA & Jackson PR (2006). Call centres as lean service environments: Job-related strain and the mediating role of work design. *Journal of Occupational Health Psychology*, **11**, 197–212.

Sutherland VJ & Cooper CL (1992). Job stress, satisfaction and mental health among general practitioners before and after the introduction of the new contract. *British Medical Journal*, **304**, 1545–1548.

Sutherland VJ & Davidson MJ (1993). Using a stress audit – the construction site manager experience. *Work and Stress*, **7**, 273–286.

Sutherland VJ & Flin RH (1989). Stress at sea – a review of working conditions in the off-shore oil and fishing industries. *Work and Stress*, **3**, 269–285.

Thayer RE (1989). *The Biopsychology of Mood and Arousal*. Oxford, Oxford University Press.

Totterdell P, Wood SJ & Wall TD (2006). An intra-individual test of the demand-control model: A weekly diary study of psychological strain in portfolio workers. *Journal of Occupational and Organizational Psychology*, **79**, 63–84.

Travers CJ & Cooper CL (1993). Mental health, job satisfaction and occupational stress among UK teachers. *Work and Stress*, **7**, 203–219.

Van Dierendonck D, Haynes C, Borrill C & Stride CB (2004). Leadership behaviour and subordinate well-being. *Journal of Occupational Health Psychology*, **9**, 165–175.

Viinamaki H, Koskela K, Niskanen L et al. (1993). Unemployment and mental well-being – a factory closure study in Finland. *Acta Psychiatrica Scandinavica*, **88**, 429–433.

Wall TD & Clegg CW (1980). A longitudinal field study of group work redesign. *Journal of Occupational Behaviour*, **2**, 31–49.

Wall TD & Clegg CW (1981). Individual strain and organisational functioning. *British Journal of Clinical Psychology*, **20**, 135–136.

Wall TD, Clegg CW, Davies RT et al. (1987). Advanced manufacturing technology and work simplification: An empirical study. *Journal of Occupational Behaviour*, **8**, 233–250.

Wall TD, Corbett JM, Martin R et al. (1990). Advanced manufacturing technology, work design and performance: A change study. *Journal of Applied Psychology*, **75**, 691–697.

Wall TD, Bolden RI, Borrill CS et al. (1997). Minor psychiatric disorder in NHS trust staff: Occupational and gender differences. *British Journal of Psychiatry*, **171**, 519–523.

Warr PB (1987). *Work, Unemployment, and Mental Health*. Oxford, Oxford University Press.

Warr PB (1990a). The measurement of well-being and other aspects of mental health. *Journal of Occupational Psychology*, **63**, 193–210.

Warr PB (1990b). Decision latitude, job demands, and employee well-being. *Work and Stress*, **4**, 285–294.

Warr PB (1994). A conceptual framework for the study of work and mental health. *Work and Stress*, **8**, 84–97.

Warr PB (1996). Employee well-being. In PB Warr (ed.), *Psychology at work*, 4th edn. Harmondsworth, Penguin.

Warr PB, Cook JD & Wall TD (1979). Scales for the measurement of some work attitudes and aspects of psychological well-being. *Journal of Occupational Psychology*, **52**, 129–148.

Watson D, Clark LA & Tellegen A (1988). Development and validation of brief measures of positive and negative affect: The PANAS scales. *Journal of Personality and Social Psychology*, **54**, 1063–1070.

Williams P, Goldberg DP & Mari J (1987). *The Validity of the General Health Questionnaire*. Unpublished Research Report, cited in Goldberg & Williams, 1988, p. 54.

Sourcing Prehistoric Ceramics at Chodistaas Pueblo, Arizona

The Circulation of People and Pots in the Grasshopper Region

ANTHROPOLOGICAL PAPERS OF
THE UNIVERSITY OF ARIZONA
NUMBER 58

Sourcing Prehistoric Ceramics at Chodistaas Pueblo, Arizona

The Circulation of People and Pots in the Grasshopper Region

María Nieves Zedeño

THE UNIVERSITY OF ARIZONA PRESS
TUCSON
1994

About the Author

MARIÁ NIEVES ZEDEÑO was born in Quito, Ecuador, and she completed her undergraduate education at the Escuela Superior Politécnica del Litoral. She received her Master's degree in 1987 and her Doctoral degree in Anthropology in 1991, both from Southern Methodist University, Dallas, Texas. From 1988 through 1991, Dr. Zedeño was a staff member of the University of Arizona Archaeological Field School at Grasshopper, Arizona, and subsequently she supervised the analysis of ceramic artifacts recovered from the ENRON Transwestern Pipeline Expansion Project. Her major professional work remains focused on Southwestern prehistory, but her broad experience also includes participation in archaeological research in the Eastern Sahara as a member of the Combined Prehistoric Expedition in Egypt (1990, 1991) and in northwestern Argentina as Field Supervisor of the Omahuaca Archaeological Project, Earthwatch (1992). Dr. Zedeño was named an Archaeology Research Specialist in the Bureau of Applied Research in Anthropology at the University of Arizona, Tucson, in 1993 and she was appointed to the Adjunct Faculty at Pima County Community College in Tucson in 1994.

Cover: Map of Arizona showing the location of the Grasshopper region near Cibecue Creek and Cibola White Ware vessels from Chodistaas Pueblo (*see* Figs. 1.1, 8.6, 8.15).

THE UNIVERSITY OF ARIZONA PRESS

Copyright © 1994

The Arizona Board of Regents
All Rights Reserved

This book was set in 10.7/12 CG Times
♾ This book is printed on acid-free, archival-quality paper.
Manufactured in the United States of America.

98 97 96 95 94   5 4 3 2 1

Library of Congress Cataloging-in-Publication Data

Zedeño, María Nieves
  Sourcing prehistoric ceramics at Chodistaas Pueblo, Arizona : the circulation of people and pots in the Grasshopper region / María Nieves Zedeño.
    p. cm. -- (Anthropological papers of the University of Arizona; no. 58)
    Includes bibliographic references and index.
  ISBN 0–8165–1455–0 (acid-free paper)
    1. Chodistaas Pueblo (Ariz.). 2. Mogollon culture. 3. Pueblo pottery-- Arizona. 4. Pueblo Indians--Commerce. 5. Pueblo Indians--Antiquities. I. Series.
E99.M76N54 1994
738.3'
09791'35--dc20   94–17545
                                      CIP

Contents

FIGURES

TABLES

Foreword

If Southwestern archaeologists agree on anything, it is that their exceptional pottery encodes more information on prehistoric village farmers than any single material category of the archeological record. In fact, outsiders struggling with plain brown pottery manufactured seemingly unchanged for centuries gaze longingly at the highly decorated, multicolored pottery of the Southwest. Inured to their ceramics and indifferent, perhaps, to the outside world of plain ware, Southwesterners pick away at the alleged excesses of forbears and contemporaries alike. Traditionalists are routinely castigated for their slavish concern with taxonomy and chronology while processualists are derided by some for jumping too quickly to conclusions of prehistory's nonmaterial features and by others for not delving deeply enough into the recesses of the prehistoric mind. To an outside world still worrying with brown plain sherds, this squabbling resembles the bickering of wealthy relatives on a weekend in the country.

Regardless of superficial appearances and doctrinal posturings, the fact is that much "old-time" ceramic analysis remains to be done on the already much studied pottery of the American Southwest. And it is here that Nieves Zedeño's study makes a signal contribution by setting out clearly the contemporary analytical procedures for answering one of the long-standing questions of ceramic-based inference: "Was the pot made locally or nonlocally?" Determining the place of production is, of course, critical to reliable inferences of ceramic circulation involving trade, exchange, or reciprocity; of teaching frameworks underlying reconstructions of organizational principles; and of the semantic content of designs and symbols. In this last regard, for example, it is improbable, when producers and users of a vessel come from different places and cultural backgrounds, that the meaning of the producers' designs will be shared by the users. The present study, therefore, establishes the criteria against which identifications of production locale may be judged and the supporting analysis may be evaluated.

Zedeño's study is also one piece in a large analytical program being put together at Grasshopper, which is in turn an outgrowth of a long research tradition at the University of Arizona. Whereas Zedeño's research focuses on determining where pots were made and how they got to Chodistaas Pueblo, Barbara Montgomery's (1992) research begins at Chodistaas with the movement of pots within the village, from use to discard, and ends with the recovery of whole pots and broken pieces by the archaeologist. Furthermore, the ceramic analyses of Zedeño and Montgomery refine and enlarge the preliminary study of Chodistaas ceramics recovered in the late 1970s by Patricia Crown (1981). Thus, it has taken over 15 years and three major dissertation studies on the ceramics from an 18-room pueblo to establish a framework for the investigation of ceramics from the neighboring 500-room Grasshopper Pueblo, where Daniela Triadan is studying the production of Fourmile Polychrome for her doctoral dissertation. If the ratio of dissertations to rooms at Chodistaas Pueblo holds at nearby sites, then we look with horror at the prospect of 80 dissertations on Grasshopper ceramics. Although this figure is unrealistic, it serves to convey a sense of scale in the ceramic analyses that have characterized University of Arizona archaeological field schools. As far back as Emil Haury's first field school in the Forestdale Valley, we see the critical role of ceramics in authenticating the Mogollon concept, establishing Mogollon pottery as earlier than Anasazi pottery, and supporting Haury's view of the eventual merging of the Mogollon and Anasazi.

It was while the field school was at Point of Pines that refinements to ceramic taxonomy became a dominant theme. Out of that intellectual environment came the type-variety method of classification by Joe Ben Wheat, James Gifford, and William Wasley (1958) and David Breternitz's (1966) classic synthesis of ceramic cross dating. Little wonder, then, that Raymond Thompson's move to Grasshopper was in part to solve questions whose answers lay in ceramic analysis (Thompson and Longacre 1966). When William Longacre took over as director in 1966, traditional concerns with taxonomy, population movement, and trade were augmented by processual archaeology's dual emphasis on ecology and social organization (Longacre and Reid 1974). Clearly, many of these questions about past culture and behavior have been around for some time. What is new are the powerful techniques of analysis to establish credible answers.

It may seem hackneyed to speak of merging traditional questions with contemporary analytical techniques, but such is the practical world of prehistoric archaeology. It is difficult to imagine many questions about the past that have not already been posed in some form by Kidder or Haury. It is equally difficult to pre-

dict where future analytical techniques will take us. The major contribution of Zedeño's study, then, is the structure of the research in combining compositional, technological, and design analysis into a coherent package. Thus, it is not so much the question that drives our research, but the solution, and herein Zedeño demonstrates how solutions are to be achieved and clearly presented. This study will become a standard reference for archaeologists seeking multiple analytical pathways to the identification of local or nonlocal ceramic manufacture and the interpretation of its meaning in prehistory.

J. Jefferson Reid
April 18, 1994

Preface

One feature that distinguishes contemporary ceramic research from traditional and early processual studies of pottery from archaeological sites in the American Southwest is the increasing use of chemical and petrographic characterization of ceramic pastes for reconstructing prehistoric ceramic manufacture and circulation. Petrography, or temper analysis, has been applied to Southwestern ceramic materials since the 1930s, when Anna Shepard conducted a study of pottery from Pecos Pueblo. However, it is only during the last ten years that archaeologists have begun to realize the importance of incorporating sourcing techniques in the identification of local and nonlocal ceramics.

The wealth of information on prehistoric Pueblo peoples that has been gathered through recent ceramic studies invites archaeologists to rethink the conceptual basis for reconstructing behavior from the patterning of ceramic variation. I suggest that the process of rethinking ceramics requires not just the development of new theoretical models for reconstructing prehistoric behavior, but a careful reevaluation and consideration of previous frameworks that have successfully shaped archaeological research in the American Southwest for almost a century.

Complex information on ceramic paste composition can be most cogently interpreted when an approach is followed that integrates all aspects of variability relevant for isolating the behaviors involved in ceramic production and distribution. This integration, too, implies a reevaluation of the dimensions as well as the units of observation and analysis used for partitioning ceramic variation according to the locus of manufacture.

This monograph presents an analytical case where the source of prehistoric ceramics and the possible mechanisms of ceramic circulation were reconstructed using data on manufacturing technology, style, and paste composition. An analytical case in prehistory is one that the archaeologist not simply discovers but builds through analysis and argument, one that is considered the most appropriate for investigating a specific problem (Montgomery and Reid 1990: 89). Chodistaas Pueblo in east-central Arizona, an 18-room masonry ruin occupied for no more than 40 years (from A.D. 1263 to about 1300), presents ideal conditions for building a strong analytical case for identifying local and nonlocal pottery and for inferring behavioral mechanisms of ceramic circulation.

The value of the Chodistaas ceramic assemblage for undertaking this research is that it comprises a range of variability that one would expect to find in much larger sites, where temporal and contextual associations are often ambiguous and where the acquisition of a sample of ceramics representative of the whole site would require an unrealistic amount of excavation. At Chodistaas Pueblo, temporal and contextual associations are controlled, and the whole-vessel assemblage is representative of virtually the entire settlement. These unusual conditions allow the archaeologist to concentrate on the investigation of specific methodological problems such as the identification of local and nonlocal ceramics where direct evidence of ceramic manufacture is absent in the archaeological record. This broadly applicable methodology for making such identifications has been developed in a highly controlled archaeological record where: (1) absolute chronology was available and the ceramics represented a chronologically limited period of time, (2) sample size was adequate, (3) ceramics represented a wide range of stylistic and technological variation, (4) provenience and contextual associations were well-defined, and (5) formation processes were properly controlled. Under these conditions, a strong analytical case for identifying local and nonlocal ceramics has been built.

The study of ceramics from Chodistaas Pueblo underscores the usefulness of analyzing small, single component but well-dated and controlled archaeological sites for isolating ceramic-manufacturing and ceramic-circulating behaviors. A single case, archaeological or ethnographic, cannot be projected uncritically to other times, peoples, or places, but this particular case in prehistory does provide insights into the conceptualization, methodology, and empirical evidence of ceramic manufacture and circulation in neolithic-level communities of the American Southwest.

This book begins with a critical history of ceramic studies in the Southwest and the ways in which the evolution of archaeological theory and method shaped and continue to shape such studies, in particular those addressing ceramic manufacture and circulation. Chapter 2 offers a tridimensional framework for identifying local and nonlocal ceramics. A definition of local manufacture and the necessary evidence for determining locally manufactured ceramics are presented in Chapter 3, and archaeological and ethnographic information is used to delineate behavioral mechanisms involved in the circulation of ceramics (movement of pots, movement of people, and movement of raw materials) and their material correlates. Chapter 4 places the site of Chodistaas in time and space and introduces formal descriptions of decorated and undecorated wares represented in the whole-vessel assemblage at the site.

The next four chapters describe methodological approaches to the study of ceramic style, technology, and provenience as indicators of ceramic manufacture and circulation; evaluate local sources of raw materials; present data on stylistic, technological, and compositional variation of corrugated and plain wares and of polished-painted wares; and discuss the possible mechanisms of circulation of nonlocal wares. The volume concludes with observations about the theoretical and methodological implications of this study and their usefulness for reconstructing the prehistoric behaviors involved in the manufacture and circulation of ceramics in the Grasshopper Plateau and adjacent regions.

Acknowledgements

Many people have contributed their knowledge to this study and several institutions have provided essential financial support and facilities for undertaking it. This research received funding from the National Science Foundation (BNS-27157); the Institute for the Study of Earth and Man, the Department of Anthropology, and the Graduate Student Assembly of Southern Methodist University; the Agnese N. Lindley Foundation; and the Sigma Chi Scientific Society. Publication funds were furnished by the Department of Anthropology and the Southwest Center of the University of Arizona and by an anonymous donor. Field research on the Grasshopper Plateau would not have been possible without the cooperation of the White Mountain Apache and the permission of the Tribal Council. David Meltzer and Fred Wendorf were especially supportive during my years at Southern Methodist University and helped me develop a broad perspective from which to view the archaeological record.

Patricia L. Crown offered me a unique opportunity to work in the American Southwest and entrusted me with the task of continuing her research at Chodistaas Pueblo. At the time of her study she was unable to obtain complete compositional analyses for the ceramics from Chodistaas (Crown 1981), so that many questions remained concerning the loci of production for this pottery. To address these questions, Dr. Crown submitted a proposal to the Conservation Analytical Laboratory of the Smithsonian Institution for instrumental neutron activation analysis of the Chodistaas ceramics in 1986. The proposal was accepted. Recognizing that other commitments would not permit her to conduct this study, she encouraged me to explore the manufacture of this assemblage for my own research.

J. Jefferson Reid not only provided access to the Chodistaas materials, but guided me in the formulation of crucial research questions that developed into this work. Jeff contributed his expertise, advice, and data throughout the preparation of this material.

This project could not have been accomplished without the cooperation of many faculty, staff, and students of the Anthropology Department at the University of Arizona. The staff of the Archaeological Field School at Grasshopper was always ready to exchange information and give useful suggestions to improve the quality of this research. Barbara K. Montgomery and Daniela Triadan worked side-by-side with me, generously sharing their own data and providing valuable insights into the Chodistaas ceramic record. John R. Welch and Daniela Triadan collaborated in the clay survey and experimental clay testing, respectively. Mark Neupert contributed information on ceramic strength experiments, and Leon Lorentzen kindly reviewed sections of this text. Michael B. Schiffer provided access to the equipment of the Laboratory of Traditional Technology (University of Arizona) to conduct experimental tests, and Walter Birkby allowed me to use the facilities of the Human Identification Laboratory (University of Arizona) for sample preparation.

Special thanks are expressed to the members of the Department of Anthropology Writers Group (University of Arizona), including Cathy Cameron, Kelley Hays, Masashi Kobayashi, Laura Levi, Jonathan Mabry, Barbara Montgomery, Barbara Roth, Jim Skibo, Miriam Stark, Chris Szuter, Masakasu Tani, John Welch, and Lisa Young, who reviewed in detail six chapters of the original manuscript and provided excellent comments on its content and style. Other archaeologists and anthropologists shared their knowledge with me, notably Chris Downum, Emil Haury, David Killick, Barbara Mills, Tom McGuire, Michael Schiffer, Emory Sekaquaptewa, Raymond Thompson, and David Tuggle. Two anonymous reviewers offered valuable suggestions for presentation of portions of the chemical characterizations.

Information on ceramic composition presented in this research results from the combined efforts of many individuals and institutions. Ronald Bishop, of the Conservation Analytical Laboratory at the Smithsonian Institution, not only conducted instrumental neutron activation analysis of the Chodistaas Pueblo samples, but also assisted me in the process of data interpretation. James Burton, of the Laboratory of Archaeology at the University of Wisconsin-Madison, ran the ICP spectroscopy analysis promptly and efficiently. The temper analysis was conducted with the collaboration of Lawrence Anovitz and Beth Miksa of the Department of Geosciences at the University of Arizona.

Technical assistance was provided by many individuals. I thank Carol Gifford for her invaluable editorial skills and for providing camera-ready copy for the University of Arizona Press. Ron Beckwith drafted Figure 9.1 and assembled in final form the cover, Figure 1.1, and illustrations in Chapter 8. Barbara K. Montgomery drafted Figures 2.1; 3.1; 4.1; 6.1; 7.2–7.5; 8.6; 8.7*c*; 8.8*a–d*; 8.9*h*; 8.10*a–d, f*; 8.12*b–c*; 8.13*b–c*; 8.14; and 8.15*d, f, h*. The remaining design elements in Figures 8.7 through 8.17 were reproduced from Figure B–1 in the doctoral dissertation of Patricia Crown (Crown 1981a). Figures 4.2 and 4.3 are Arizona State Museum photographs taken by staff members of the University of Arizona Archaeological Field School at Grasshopper. John Johnson, Steve Flora, and the late Walter Allen assisted me in the use of several computer programs.

It is with deep gratitude that I acknowledge the financial and moral support received from my family throughout my university years.

CHAPTER ONE

The Provenience of Prehistoric Ceramics

For decades archaeologists have used prehistoric pottery to infer economic, social, and political activities of the people who made and used it. These durable ceramic bits and pieces have formed the core of investigations aimed at reconstructing the lifeways of prehistoric populations. Aspects of cultural-ethnic affiliation, population movement, community organization, intersite economic and political interaction, exchange of information and goods, and sociopolitical complexity may be discerned from the patterning of ceramic variation. To make such inferences, however, pottery made locally and vessels manufactured elsewhere must first be identified, for no interpretation of the behaviors conveyed in archaeological ceramics can be approached without prior indication as to whether those who crafted the pots were the same as those who discarded them.

Our theoretical and methodological perspectives on the manufacture and circulation of prehistoric ceramics have a century-old history in the American Southwest, where travelers, archaeologists, ethnographers, and art historians have contributed their knowledge to our understanding of the development of American Indian ceramic traditions. In this review of the historical background of research in prehistoric Southwestern ceramics, I focus specifically on those studies that involved, directly or indirectly, the use of assumptions about ceramic manufacture and provenience, on the potential and limitations of traditional and contemporary ceramic studies, and on an evaluation of the aspects of those studies that are useful for reconstructing ceramic manufacture and circulation.

CERAMICS AND CULTURE HISTORY

Ceramic description and classification in the American Southwest began to develop toward the end of the nineteenth century (Dunnell 1986). It was Holmes (1886) who formally introduced the concept that vessels and their properties were attributes useful for constructing pottery groups. Holmes undertook extensive research into ethnographic accounts of pottery manufacture and use, and he advanced suggestions about the evolutionary significance of variability in ceramic technology, form, and ornamentation that he observed throughout the American Southwest. Although his attempts to construct pottery classifications did not go beyond the gross division of ceramics into wares based on surface treatment, he saw classification as an analytic tool potentially capable of both spatial and temporal measurement, and his analysis provided the initial step toward this objective (Dunnell 1986: 163). It was not until the chronological work of Kroeber (1916), Nelson (1916), and Spier (1917) was published that Southwestern archaeologists began to focus more consistently on the potential of ceramic classification for reconstructing culture history.

TRADITIONAL ASSUMPTIONS

Between the late 1920s and 1950s, archaeologists working in the Southwest were concerned mostly with delineating cultural boundaries, establishing regional chronologies through ceramic typology, and inferring ethnic affiliation and cultural relationships (Kidder 1924). A number of ceramic surveys in Arizona and New Mexico sought to define the origins and spatial limits of prehistoric Southwestern cultures. For example, the Gladwins organized extensive surveys with the Gila Pueblo Archaeological Foundation to define the extent of the "Red-on-buff Culture" (Gladwin and Gladwin 1934, 1935). Stratigraphic excavations, and later tree-ring dating, were used to monitor the temporal changes in ceramic assemblages that were crucial for building regional chronologies. It was during the 1930s that the Southwestern typological system of ceramic classification was formalized. Colton and Hargrave (1937) produced a regional synthesis of typological description, chronology, and geographic distribution of ceramics in northern Arizona. Haury's work in the Forestdale Valley of east-central Arizona (Fig. 1.1) contributed to the formalization of Mogollon ceramic typology as a tool for reconstructing regional chronologies and intercultural relationships (Haury 1936, 1940).

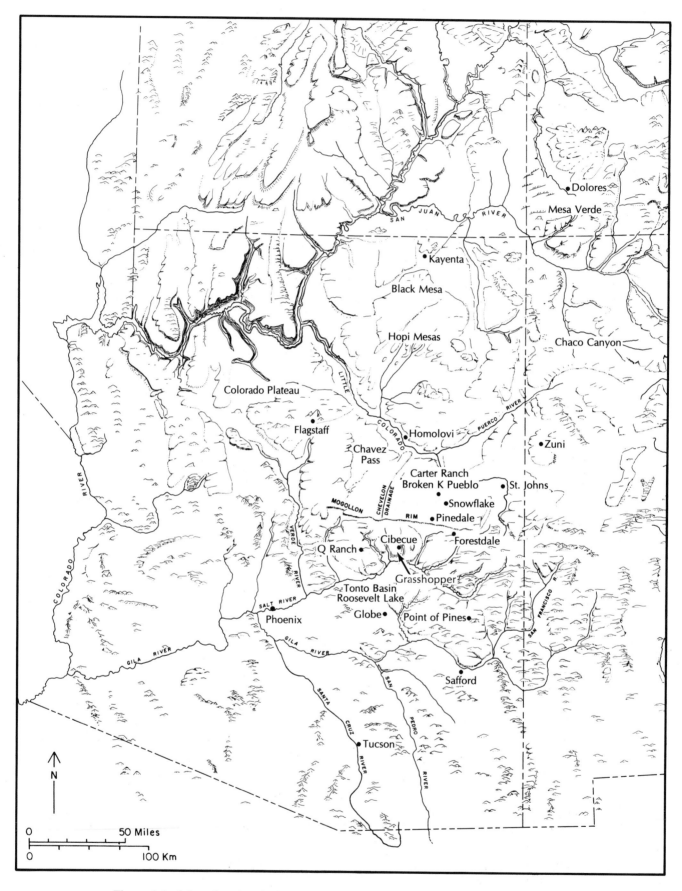

Figure 1.1. Selected archaeological sites and regions in the American Southwest. (Base map courtesy of the Laboratory of Tree-Ring Research, University of Arizona, Tucson.)

[2]

Temporal and spatial reconstructions of discrete cultural entities based on ceramic traits rested on two fundamental assumptions: one, that prehistoric communities of the Southwest were autonomous and self-sufficient and that ceramic manufacture was a household activity practiced in all ceramic-using communities (Braun and S. Plog 1982; Cordell 1991; Gladwin 1943; Judd 1954; Kidder 1936; Lindsay 1969). "It has always been assumed that potting was one of the regular household tasks of every Pueblo woman, that each town was in this regard self-sufficient," wrote Kidder in 1936 (xxiii). Ethnographic accounts of Southwestern Pueblos had a major bearing on the widespread acceptance of such assumptions by archaeologists reconstructing culture history (Braun and S. Plog 1982; Cordell 1991; De Atley 1991). Among modern Pueblo Indians, pottery manufacture is a household craft, and pots are seldom exchanged outside the village (Beaglehole 1937; Bunzel 1929; Dozier 1970). It was thus assumed that this condition also existed among prehistoric Southwestern communities.

Ceramic traits were frequently used for assigning cultural affiliation to a site, although architecture and burial practices were also taken into consideration. Stylistic traits of ceramic assemblages were thought useful for temporal placement, whereas technological aspects of those assemblages were assumed to characterize cultural differences over broad regions; it was thought that each group practiced consistent techniques in manufacturing pottery that differed from adjacent groups (Crown 1981a). Undecorated or culinary wares were used as "index wares" by Colton (1953: 67), who maintained that "in many cases it [index ware] gives a clue to the branch or prehistoric tribe of Indians to which the makers belonged."

Thus, for example, ceramics from sites in east-central Arizona were assigned to Mogollon or Anasazi traditions on the basis of paste color and firing atmosphere of culinary wares (Colton 1939; Colton and Hargrave 1937; Danson and Wallace 1956; Haury 1936, 1940; Reed 1942; Wheat 1955). Hohokam plain wares were identified by evidence that the paddle-and-anvil technique was used for vessel-wall thinning, as opposed to the coil-scrape technique commonly seen in other ceramic traditions (Haury 1945; Roberts 1937). Relative abundance of ceramics displaying technological characteristics of a formally defined ceramic tradition was thought, therefore, to be a reliable indicator of the cultural affiliation of a settlement with heterogeneous ceramic assemblages (Cordell 1991; Crown 1981a; Whittlesey 1982a).

EARLY PROVENIENCE STUDIES

Colton (1941a, 1953; Colton and Hargrave 1937) was one of the few Southwestern archaeologists of his time who expressed concern with prehistoric ceramic exchange. He estimated that the volume of pottery trade must have been enormous considering the abundance of pottery remains in the area (Colton 1941a: 316). Colton's scientific training led him to undertake systematic research aimed at the identification of ceramic provenience. Sponsored by the Museum of Northern Arizona at Flagstaff, he collected clay, temper, and pigment samples, identified paste constituents of large quantities of sherds under the microscope, and performed numerous and valuable experiments to reconstruct pottery firing techniques and to compare fired clays and sherds by their paste color (Colton 1939, 1953).

Colton cautioned archaeologists against the uncritical use of the criterion of relative abundance (that ceramic types represented by abundant vessels at a site were locally made, whereas few vessels representing rare types were nonlocal) as the most generalized way of assigning locus of manufacture to the ceramic assemblage. He suggested that culinary pottery, usually the heaviest and most difficult to transport over long distances, was locally produced in most settlements, and that painted ceramics, especially bowls, were probably traded over long distances (Colton 1941a: 317; Colton and Hargrave 1937). Colton strongly emphasized the need to introduce accurate methods for identifying ceramic provenience; in fact, he urged the development of simple methods of temper identification that could be used in the field. Although his cautionary advice was often ignored (for example, Gladwin 1943: 53), a small number of archaeologists attempted to identify the provenience of ceramics by petrographic analysis (Danson and Wallace 1956; N. Gladwin in Gladwin and others 1937; Martin and others 1961; Shepard 1936, 1942, 1965; Shepard in Judd 1954; Shepard in Smith 1971; Shepard in Wendorf 1953). Other methods of analyzing raw materials, such as glaze and pigment chemistry (Haury 1932; Hawley 1929, 1938), were thought useful for tracing spatial distribution of decorated wares.

Pioneer research in the identification of local and nonlocal ceramics by petrographic analysis can be dated back to 1936, when Shepard analyzed samples of Rio Grande Glaze Paint Ware from Pecos Pueblo (Shepard 1936) and other sites in the Rio Grande area (Shepard 1942). Shepard's studies not only indicated that pottery types thought to be temporally sequential (for example, Glaze IV and Glaze V) had been produced at the same time in different geographic areas, but that quantities of pottery found at Pecos had not been made there. According to Shepard, the technique used for producing Glaze Paint Ware was first introduced from the west, presumably from the Zuni area, and adopted by a few production centers, such as the Galisteo Basin, from where this ware was exchanged. In time, Rio Grande Glaze Paint Ware was manufactured in several independent centers of production and distribution, including Pecos (Shepard 1965). Shepard's general conclusions regarding exchange as one activity commonly practiced by prehistoric Pueblo communities were supported later by Warren's (1969: 36) petrographic, stylistic, and distributional analysis of Rio Grande Glaze Paint Ware, which indicated that Glazes III and IV were manufactured in Tonque Pueblo and extensively traded throughout the Rio Grande Valley and into the Zuni area and the Plains. Shepard's hypothesis of specialized production of this ware, however, was not corroborated by later research (Cordell 1991 reviews this study).

Petrographic analysis of pottery from stratigraphic tests II and IV at Pueblo Bonito in Chaco Canyon (Fig. 1.1) revealed that large quantities of corrugated pottery at the site were manufactured elsewhere (Shepard 1954). In her petrographic analysis, Shepard identified two kinds of temper: sanidine basalt, for which the nearest known source is 80 km (50 miles) west of Chaco Canyon in the Chuska Mountains, and andesite, for which the nearest source is 24 km (15 miles) from Pueblo Bonito. Shepard (1954: 237) felt that the andesite-tempered pottery may have been imported from the La Plata District, which was likely, because the other occurrence of andesite in pottery was found in Mesa Verde Black-on-white, considered intrusive to Chaco Canyon on the grounds of lack of abundance and design style (S. Plog 1980: 59). In contrast, sanidine basalt-tempered pottery occurred in large quantities that continued to increase through time (Judd 1954: 182). Subsequent research in Chaco Canyon and surrounding areas reinforced Shepard's discovery. Toll (1985; Toll and others 1980), Warren (1967), and Windes (1977, 1984) estimated that thousands of these ceramic vessels had been brought into the canyon, probably from the Chuska Valley.

In spite of these outstanding but isolated discoveries concerning the provenience of ceramics in a site or region, archaeologists largely disregarded the possibility that circulation of ceramics was indeed a quite regular activity among prehistoric Southwestern communities. Perhaps the most illustrative example of how widespread this conception was in the practice of archaeology is the skepticism of Judd (1954: 235), who

thought of Shepard's findings of imported culinary pottery in Pueblo Bonito as being "something of archaeological heresy."

The introduction of analytical methods in ceramic analysis seriously questioned the most cherished criteria and assumptions used by Southwestern archaeologists to distinguish between local and nonlocal ceramics (Cordell 1991; S. Plog 1980). First, decoration is not an unambiguous indicator of spatial and temporal placement of pottery types, because vessels that are stylistically identical might be technologically different. Second, relative abundance of undecorated or culinary wares does not warrant the identification of local pottery manufacture. Third, vessel shape, size, and presence of decoration are not clear-cut indicators of what kind of ceramics were most likely to have been traded; not only decorated bowls but large ollas and heavy corrugated jars were transported over long distances and through rugged terrain. Fourth, and especially important, traditional ethnographic models of ceramic manufacture and exchange among modern Pueblo Indians do not provide a direct analogue to prehistoric Southwestern communities.

Nevertheless, provenience studies were not popular among culture historians (Thompson 1991), mainly because they were not crucial for the reconstruction of regional chronologies. The Southwestern system of ceramic classification, best exemplified by the work of Colton and Hargrave (1937), was given temporal depth by cross-dating styles of decoration and tree-ring dates wherever available. Information on variability relative to manufacturing loci did not affect in any significant way the major goal of culture history, and few archaeologists addressed issues that involved the investigation of ceramic manufacturing loci. Furthermore, petrographic analysis such as the one carried out by Shepard required the aid of a specialist, and in many instances successful identifications were not possible (Shepard in Wendorf 1953). Thus, traditional assumptions and criteria for identifying local and nonlocal ceramics continued in use until relatively recently.

CERAMICS AND PROCESSUAL ARCHAEOLOGY

Perhaps the most controversial ceramic studies in the American Southwest were produced by some processual archaeologists during the 1960s and 1970s. Many archaeologists conducted intrasettlement and intersettlement studies of stylistic variation in ceramics, following the premise that aspects of prehistoric societies such as social demography, social organization, and community interaction are reflected in the material system (Binford 1962, 1963, 1965). They thought stylistic variation in prehistoric ceramics could be useful for making inferences about prehistoric Southwestern communities.

Intrasettlement analyses of design variation conducted at Broken K Pueblo (Hill 1965, 1970) and Carter Ranch (Longacre 1964, 1970) in east-central Arizona and at sites in the Cibola area (Kintigh 1979, 1985) and in the Upper Gila area of New Mexico (Washburn 1977, 1978) sought to determine whether nonrandom spatial clusters of ceramic designs were present within contemporaneous areas of a given site. All but Washburn claimed to have demonstrated the existence of such patterning in the archaeological record and, in turn, interpreted it as reflecting residential units, households, or other social groupings.

Because inferences about the significance of stylistic variation were based on the assumption of direct, intergenerational transmission of stylistic information (Binford 1963; Deetz 1965; Hill 1970; Longacre 1970), it was critical that local manufacture of ceramics should be adequately demonstrated. However, as Stephen Plog (1980: 55–62) pointed out, in all but a few of these studies the possibility that the ceramics under analysis were not made locally is not even mentioned; archaeologists did not investigate whether arguments about types of residence units or other social groups were based on pottery not even made in the community in question.

Intrasite studies on stylistic variation assumed that ceramics were made and used by women inhabiting the residential units where the sherds were recovered archaeologically. This assumption is also questionable. For example, refitting experiments on ceramic materials from Broken K Pueblo indicated that contexts of use and discard of ceramics were not adequately isolated (Skibo, Schiffer, and Kowalski 1989). Because of these and other methodological problems (Allen and Richardson 1971; S. Plog 1978, 1980; Redman 1978), it was never effectually demonstrated that nonrandom variation due to social organization occurred within a settlement.

Intersettlement studies of stylistic variation, on the other hand, were based on the assumption that the degree of similarity in ceramic designs over a given region is a direct measure of the intensity of interaction among prehistoric communities and an inverse measure of distance between those communities (Cronin 1962; Leone 1968; Longacre 1964; Tuggle 1970; Washburn 1978). Except for Tuggle's (1970) work, none of these studies discussed the possibility that spatial patterning of

ceramic designs could have been a product of ceramic exchange. Later, Tuggle (in Tuggle and others 1982) conducted one of the first chemical analyses of pottery from the Grasshopper and Q Ranch regions of east-central Arizona (Fig. 1.1).

Stephen Plog's (1977, 1980) stylistic analysis of black-on-white ceramics from the Chevelon drainage is one of the few during this period that included a systematic reevaluation of untested and often incorrect assumptions about manufacture and circulation of ceramics, and he used extensive ceramic sourcing to test whether spatial distributions of design styles were a consequence of exchange, patterns of social interaction, or other processes. Plog argued that ceramics circulated between households and villages primarily through reciprocal exchange ties. This type of exchange, in turn, produced closely integrated social networks through which information and goods flowed freely (Braun and S. Plog 1982; Hantman and S. Plog 1982). The results of his analysis challenged the implicit assumption underlying most of the earlier stylistic studies that the context of manufacture, use, and discard of ceramics was one and the same and that, therefore, patterned stylistic variation observed in the archaeological record directly reflected social interaction of prehistoric communities.

CONTEMPORARY VIEWS

Reconsideration of the dynamics of ceramic production and exchange has become one of the major concerns in contemporary Southwestern archaeology. It has been hypothesized that prehistoric Pueblo communities developed complex sociopolitical organization as a "buffering" response of growing populations to unpredictable environments and unequal spatial distribution of foodstuffs and raw materials. Integrative strategies were incorporated into Pueblo societies as part of a concern with strengthening and maintaining social connections with distant communities (Cordell and F. Plog 1979; Judge 1979; F. Plog 1983; Upham 1982).

Ceramics and Sociopolitical Complexity

The spatial distribution of certain decorated wares has been interpreted as indicating the existence of sociopolitical alliances in the Colorado Plateau, which began to develop around the eleventh century and bloomed during the fourteenth century (Upham 1982). Ceramic production, according to this hypothesis, was hierarchically controlled by an overarching political and religious structure, as suggested by the observed concentration of such ceramics in major political and religious centers and in "high status" burials (Upham and F. Plog 1986). Access to ceramics of high production costs (Feinman and others 1981) was thus probably restricted to influential leaders and their families (Cordell and F. Plog 1979; Hantman and others 1984; Lightfoot and Jewett 1984).

Upham (1982) postulated the existence of two opposite polities north and south of the Mogollon Rim, whose managerial elites were involved in the exchange of Jeddito Yellow Ware and Roosevelt ("Salado") Red Ware, respectively. An intermediate or "buffering" polity located around Silver Creek in east-central Arizona interacted with both north and south, producing and exchanging White Mountain Red Ware. This hypothesis is based on the assumption that decorated vessels are "high production cost" items, produced in specialized loci in restricted areas of the Southwest. "High production cost" is estimated on the basis of the production step measure devised by Feinman and others (1981), which counts the number of manufacturing steps necessary to produce each decorated ware. Because the ceramic data used to support differential production and distribution come mainly from surface collections (Upham and others 1981: 826), the production step measure constitutes a handy method to generate quantifiable differences between wares when contextual and analytical evidence for ceramic manufacture is not available. Upham (1982: 128–132) used petrographic data from 45 polychrome sherds to build his hypothesis of a politically oriented exchange of 4 polychrome wares from 67 sites distributed across the Colorado Plateau. Neutron activation analyses of Hopi yellow-firing ware (Bishop and others 1988) and Gila Polychrome (Crown and Bishop 1987) do not support Upham's hypothesis.

ALTERNATIVE VIEWS OF CERAMIC DISTRIBUTION

In 1988 Bishop and his colleagues published the preliminary results of neutron activation and stylistic analyses of Jeddito Yellow Ware and other yellow-firing pottery from the Hopi Mesas. Since Upham's model of the Jeddito Alliance rested mainly on data from outside the Hopi country, Bishop and his colleagues (1988: 317) considered it important to evaluate the Hopi participation in the proposed alliance and its structure and operation both on and off the Hopi Mesas. To monitor the

development of production and exchange of Hopi yellow-firing pottery through time, 650 sherd samples representing a time span from about A.D. 1300 to 1600 were submitted to instrumental neutron activation analysis (INAA). In addition, 130 clay samples from the Hopi mesas were analyzed by the same method.

The combined results of stylistic and compositional analyses revealed source and design size differences between villages, suggesting that potters worked closely together within a village without sharing knowledge of resources or techniques with nonresidential groups (Bishop and others 1988: 332). No evidence of centrally controlled resources within major Hopi villages was found; each village apparently exploited several clay sources simultaneously, and the decorative evidence suggested preferential but not exclusive use of these clay sources (Bishop and others 1988: 332). Spatial distribution of production loci on Antelope Mesa, for example, indicated that between A.D. 1300 and 1600 Hopi villagers at each community had equal access to resources and manufactured ceramics that were used in that community. The authors concluded that there was little direct evidence to support intervillage alliances of potter groups, kin groups, or elites.

Regarding exchange outside the Hopi country, several vessels apparently produced on Antelope Mesa were recovered at Homolovi II near the Middle Little Colorado River and at Pottery Mound on the Puerco River (Fig. 1.1). Bishop and his colleagues (1988: 334) observed that Homolovi sites have strong ancestral connotations in the oral traditions of the Hopi, whereas Pottery Mound is located east of an area with strong historic Hopi-Zuni interaction identifiable from the fifteenth century. Adams, Dosh, and Stark (1987) comment that, if one were to believe in the veracity of the elite alliance model, the high frequency of imported Jeddito Yellow Ware at Homolovi II could be interpreted as indicating that the majority of its inhabitants were indeed elite.

Neutron activation analysis applied to 187 samples of Gila Polychrome ceramics from 21 sites supports local manufacture of this type at least at the regional level during the fourteenth century (Crown and Bishop 1987; Crown 1994). Although previous petrographic analysis of Gila Polychrome suggested local manufacture in different settlements (Danson and Wallace 1956), alternative explanations for its widespread distribution in the Southwest, such as migration (Franklin and Masse 1976; LeBlanc and Nelson 1976) and exchange (Doyel 1976; Grebinger 1976; Haury 1945, 1976; Lindsay and Jennings 1968, among others) were advanced.

Current research conducted by the Roosevelt Platform Mound Study (Redman 1992) aims at defining the nature of sociopolitical complexity of prehistoric "Salado" communities that inhabited the Roosevelt Lake area in east-central Arizona. The analysis of ceramic materials from Roosevelt sites attempts to measure complexity from the patterns of production and distribution of "Salado" wares, including Roosevelt Red Ware, Salado Red Obliterated Corrugated, and plain and red utility wares (Simon and others 1992). Variation in vessel morphology, manufacturing technology and performance, and provenience of these wares across several large and small sites has been initially interpreted by Simon and her colleagues (1992: 74) as indicating specialization in ceramic production at certain compound villages during the Roosevelt phase (mid to late 1200s). They observe that a production shift to the platform mound communities occurred during the Gila phase (the 1300s).

Although their study may eventually confirm that craft specialization developed during that time, it has yet to reveal evidence in support of sociopolitical complexity of the "Salado" groups. Rather, the manufacture of Gila Polychrome in several regions appears to indicate that a number of processes (local manufacture, exchange, spread of technological knowledge and stylistic information through migration) were involved, perhaps simultaneously, in the development and widespread adoption of this and probably other ceramic traditions (Carlson 1982; Crown 1990, 1994; Doyel and Haury 1976; Montgomery and Reid 1990; Reid and others 1992). It is likely that population movement at the end of the thirteenth century stimulated the spread of ceramic traditions and, at the same time, formalized long distance relationships among formerly mobile groups who shared a common, even if fictive, ancestry (Johnson 1989).

The widespread distribution of decorated ceramics does not seem to be the result of exchange networks exclusively, as Upham's hypothesis implies. Nevertheless, Douglass' (1987) study of the system of production and distribution of Little Colorado White Ware revealed that exchange networks that developed during the late twelfth and early thirteenth centuries produced patterns of ceramic distribution similar to those plotted by Upham (1982) for the later decorated wares. Douglass (1987) conducted an extensive petrographic and heavy mineral analysis of Little Colorado White Ware sherds and clays from sites located around the Hopi Buttes, San Francisco Mountains, and Lower Little Colorado River Valley in northern Arizona. Her study focused on

documenting whether this ware was produced in one or several centers of manufacture and if there was any degree of centralization in its distribution.

Compositional, distributional, and stylistic evidence led Douglass (1987: 295–298) to the conclusion that Little Colorado White Ware was produced in a geographically restricted area and that there was directionality in the exchange of this ware, but that no evidence existed for centralized control and specialized production. Although the distribution of Little Colorado White Ware closely matched the distribution patterns of later decorated wares, there was no evidence to suggest that it functioned as a prestige item. Additionally, Douglass (1987: 351-353) demonstrated that although style is a valid temporal and perhaps functional tool, spatial distributions of individual styles do not demarcate separate interaction networks.

Contemporary research on Southwestern ceramics is now widening our perspectives on the mechanisms of ceramic circulation. Some archaeologists are moving away from exchange networks as the only explanation for nonlocal ceramic distributions in the archaeological record and are considering population movement (Crown 1990, 1994; Lindsay 1987; Reid 1984; Reid and others 1992) or seasonality (Lekson 1988) as important alternative mechanisms for the movement of pottery and the movement of information on pottery manufacture. There is a strong emphasis on ceramic provenience and on reevaluating long-established regional typologies as well as traditional analytical units.

RETROSPECTION

Current reconstructions of Southwestern prehistory that are mainly based on ceramic attributes are increasingly dependent on accurate methods of compositional analysis for identifying local and nonlocal ceramics. These methods alone are insufficient for interpreting behavior from the ceramic record, for they address but one aspect of ceramic variation. The sources of variation of design style and technology, as well as the mechanisms of stylistic and technological transfer must first be understood in conjunction with compositional data. The legacy of Southwestern culture history for contemporary ceramic studies is precisely a clear understanding of the nature of stylistic and technological variability observed in prehistoric ceramics. Early processual archaeologists, for example, were unsuccessful in their attempts to interpret stylistic variation, partly because their assumptions about design style were borrowed uncritically from ethnographic situations. Their models and hypotheses ignored accurate observations made by culture historians on how design style was transferred in prehistoric Southwestern ceramic manufacture.

Uncritical borrowing of models and assumptions is also exemplified in contemporary attempts to demonstrate the existence of restricted, specialized ceramic production and complex exchange networks. These attempts have only replaced previous untested assumptions of self-sufficiency and autonomy, without an adequate understanding of the structure and organization of prehistoric Southwestern populations (Johnson 1989) and, more specifically, without adequate ceramic data. It is only through recent research on ceramic provenience and the context of circulation that Southwestern archaeologists are beginning to expand their knowledge about how population movement, increase in sedentism, agricultural intensification with concomitant demand for storage facilities, and population aggregation affected ceramic manufacture and circulation (Crown 1994; Reid and others 1992; Toll 1985).

Technology and the mechanisms of technological transfer are aspects that have been neglected in ceramic studies during the last three decades, except for research on vessel function. The potential and limitations of technological variation as a reliable indicator of the cultural-ethnic identity of ceramic-producing groups has not been consistently reevaluated since early observations about group differences in pottery technology were made (Whittlesey 1982a). Compositional analysis alone is often insufficient to identify loci of ceramic manufacture; therefore, proper interpretation of data on ceramic composition must include a detailed analysis of manufacturing technology. It is only by observing ceramic variation as a whole (style, technology, and provenience) that aspects of such variation relevant for

inferring where pottery was made and how it was circulated may be isolated.

Ceramic variation, however, cannot be interpreted without a consideration of the formation of the ceramic record and the distortions introduced by behavioral and natural processes (Schiffer 1987). It is unfortunate that a large number of studies of ceramic production and distribution have been based on assemblages from large pueblos with complex and often uncontrolled formation processes, from surface collections from undated sites, and from museum collections that in many cases lack adequate information on provenience. Although regional studies provide a broad frame of reference for ceramic production and distribution, the kind of archaeological contexts they often include make it difficult to monitor how well the sample under study represents variation in time, manufacture, use, or discard of ceramics. In other words, the behaviors involved in ceramic manufacture and circulation will not be accessible to our understanding unless the sources of ceramic variation in archaeological contexts are properly identified (Montgomery and Reid 1990; Reid 1985; Reid and others 1992).

In summary, contemporary research on prehistoric Southwestern ceramics would benefit from a constructive reevaluation of both traditional and processual archaeological studies and their assumptions, methods, and interpretations, extracting valuable observations and information provided by earlier archaeologists and overcoming past limitations. We must build our knowledge on previous contributions that have stood the test of time, for the mere replacement of one model by another, or of one set of assumptions by another, will not increase our understanding of prehistoric behavior. This is the convergence I seek in this study, and the following brief chapter outlines a tridimensional approach to ceramic analysis that I believe will clarify our perception of that prehistoric behavior.

A Tridimensional Approach to Identifying Ceramic Variation and Manufacturing Loci

Pottery is one of the most complex materials of the archaeological record, both compositionally and culturally. Many different behaviors, traditions, and choices are responsible for selecting raw materials, combining them to obtain a paste, and forming and decorating vessels. Ecological, technological, and cultural variables such as climate, degree of sedentism, agricultural activities, demographic growth, and technological innovations all interact in the production of ceramics (Arnold 1975, 1985).

Archaeologists perceive ceramic expression as one of almost limitless malleability and behavioral sensitivity. Pottery produced in emergent village farming communities such as pueblos of the American Southwest is loaded with cultural and behavioral information (Reid and others 1989). The complexity of ceramic-producing behavior found in neolithic-level communities provides the archaeologist with an enormous number of attributes from which to select those most likely to encode the behavioral signals of interest. Not all attributes, however, are equally useful for identifying local and non-local ceramics.

Archaeologists generally divide ceramic variation into two independent but complementary categories: design style and technology. A common view is that style is more susceptible to temporal change than technology, because technology is directly affected by adaptive constraints (Dunnell 1978; Rice 1984); in fact, most chronologically oriented ceramic taxonomies, such as the Southwestern typological system, are constructed largely on the basis of stylistic variation. When viewed within a particular time period, design style is often thought to be a culturally bounded manifestation that signals geographic, cultural, ethnic, and social distinctions between social units, communities, or even regions, whereas technology may crosscut such boundaries (Wright 1984).

For decades, spatial stylistic similarities and differences have been equated with group membership; traditionally, this equation was widely used in defining culture areas. More recent approaches have interpreted stylistic variation as signaling aspects of: (1) social organization (Hill 1965, 1970; Longacre 1964, 1970), (2) village autonomy (Leone 1968), (3) degree of interaction (Tuggle 1970; Washburn 1978; Whallon 1968), (4) information exchange and social distance (Braun and S. Plog 1982; Hantman and S. Plog 1982; S. Plog 1980; Wobst 1977), and (5) symbolization of relationships of power among interest groups (Hodder 1982a, 1982b, 1985, 1986; Shanks and Tilley 1987a, 1987b).

Several assumptions underlie these interpretations. First, people consciously or unconsciously generated and used design styles on pottery for signaling identity, social distance, communication, interaction, and power negotiation. Second, style was transmitted through direct learning channels such as mother-to-daughter. Third, the stylistic patterning observed in prehistoric pottery directly corresponds to the social units who made and used the pottery (S. Plog 1980).

Defining the relationships between stylistic variation of prehistoric pottery and past behavior requires that the archaeologist investigate the social contexts of the manufacture and use of ceramics (Binford 1965). A number of archaeological studies have repeatedly demonstrated that there exists a complex relationship among stylistic patterns, the nature of craft production, and the degree of exchange (S. Plog 1983). In this regard, ethnographic evidence suggests that, even if stylistic variation generated by potters who interact face-to-face could, in principle, signal identity, boundaries, or social roles, our lack of understanding of the mechanisms of transfer of stylistic information and of ceramic circulation precludes any direct interpretation of design styles and their distributions as we may observe them in archaeological situations (Graves 1981; Lathrap 1983; Herbich 1987; Stanislawski 1973). Therefore, style *alone* may not be a useful indicator of the loci of ceramic manufacture. In the American Southwest, where decorated perishable items such as baskets and textiles are occasionally preserved in the archaeological record (Hays 1990), it is readily apparent that design information can be carried on any medium suited to decoration and that design may be transferred to another potter by observation. Decorated items, including pots, may have been obtained through a number of processes, most commonly exchange (Reid 1984: 145).

In contrast to design, the transmission of information on ceramic technology involves a "teaching framework" (Schiffer and Skibo 1987: 597). Technological knowledge may be conceived as an information system, which contains the rules that underlie the processing of raw materials into finished products. Although the basic physical and chemical principles for the transformation of clay into pottery are universal, every technological process involves a sequence of behaviors that results from specific technical and cultural choices (Schiffer and Skibo 1987) or technological "styles" (Lechtman 1977). The intergenerational transmission of specific technological knowledge leads to the development of a tradition (Shepard 1985).

The adoption of a ceramic technology requires not only the acquisition of an innovative idea but also the development of manipulative practice, the formation of motor habits, and most important, the existence of a receptive social and cultural setting for the innovation to be accepted (Arnold 1981; Kroeber 1963; Schiffer and Skibo 1987; Wright 1984). Hence, archaeological recovery of evidence for the transfer of technological knowledge often implies direct contact with the product *and its producer*, regardless of whether such contact crosscuts stylistic boundaries. The patterning of technological variation in prehistoric pottery has more potential than style for identifying local and nonlocal ceramics, because it signals more precisely face-to-face interaction among potters who produced ceramic vessels under a common "mental template" or shared technological knowledge (Rice 1980). Furthermore, the transmission of this critical knowledge is more restricted by adaptive constraints and cultural factors than the transmission of stylistic information.

The mechanisms of transfer of stylistic and technological information must not be assumed uncritically, but inferred from the broad patterns of archaeological ceramic variation. For example, in the American Southwest, archaeologists traditionally recognized ceramic technology rather than style as a diagnostic aspect of archaeological cultures (Colton 1941a, 1953; Colton and Hargrave 1937; Gladwin and Gladwin 1934, 1935; Haury 1945; Hawley 1929; Reed 1942). Even though the parameters with which archaeological cultures were defined have undergone significant changes in the last thirty years, the basic observations of the usefulness of style as a temporal rather than "cultural" marker and of

technology as a "manufacturing loci" marker are reasonable and demonstrable (Crown 1981b; Douglass 1987; Downum and Sullivan 1990; Doyel 1984; Reid 1984; Rugge and Doyel 1980).

It is possible, in principle, to distinguish between the locality in which a pot is recovered and the place of its manufacture by taking into account the interplay of availability and exploitation of resources on the one hand and the technology used to manufacture ceramics on the other (Arnold 1981, 1985; Bishop 1980; Bishop, Rands, and Holley 1982; Rice 1982, 1987; Shepard 1985). Compositional or provenience studies, which constitute the third analytical approach, address two inseparable aspects in the identification of resources for ceramic manufacture. These are: (1) physical and chemical analyses of the ceramic fabric, for which many techniques of varying degrees of precision and accuracy are available (Bishop, Rands, and Holley 1982; Neff 1992; Rice 1987), and (2) evaluation of resource potential (clay, temper, pigments, and fuel) in the study area (Arnold 1985; Howard 1982; Nicklin 1979).

Correlating archaeological materials with resources is a complex process that requires not only knowledge of the specific geological environment surrounding the area in question, but also the extent to which distinct raw materials used in the manufacture of a given assemblage represent more than one locus of manufacture. An extensive review of ethnographic and archaeological cases for which the distance from the manufacturing locus to the resources was known (Arnold 1985) indicates that "catchment areas" for clays do not extend beyond 7 km (about 4.4 miles) from the manufacturing loci in 82 percent of the cases analyzed. Temper and pigments, on the other hand, may be obtained from more distant sources (Arnold 1985: 36). In addition to immediate availability of raw materials, other factors must be considered, such as accessibility, presence or absence of other contemporaneous communities near potential sources, exhaustion of clay sources in the immediate vicinity of the settlement or region in question, and adequacy of known clay sources for pottery manufacture.

THE UNIT OF ANALYSIS

Because manufacturing technology and composition may be more useful for determining the production loci of Southwestern ceramics than is design style, I use *ware* as the unit of observation and analysis for this research. Ware is perhaps the earliest defined unit of ceramic classification still in use in the American Southwest. As Colton and Hargrave (1937: 2) noted, ware was first used by Stevenson in 1883; Holmes (1886), and later Fewkes (1904), followed Stevenson and defined wares on the basis of surface finish and paste color (see also Guthe 1934). It was Colton, however, who formalized the use of ware as the key unit in ceramic classification. Colton (1953: 51, 55) defined ware as a "group of pottery types which consistently show the same methods of manufacture. . . . which are passed on from mother to daughter." He identified five criteria to separate one ware from another: (1) selection of the clay, high or low in iron; (2) selection of temper; (3) method of thinning pottery by paddle and anvil or by scraping; (4) consistent use of certain kinds of slips, paint, and forms; and (5) final firing atmosphere, oxidizing or reducing (Colton 1953: 55).

A brief statement about Colton's definition of ware by Wheat, Gifford, and Wasley (1958: 34–35) noted that it "has little temporal or spatial implications." When discussing the use of ware in Maya ceramic classification, Rice (1976: 541) proposed a redefinition of ware restricted to attributes of surface treatment. Rice argued that paste composition and surface treatment were two independent attributes, the former being influenced by resource availability; therefore, paste composition should be considered a single modal or analytic unit that crosscut types and wares (Rice 1976: 541). In more recent statements (Rice 1982: 52), however, she advocated the use of attributes of paste composition in the definition of wares, because they related more closely to problems of pottery production and distribution addressed through physical and chemical analyses. In my research I have followed closely Colton's original definition of ware for several reasons. First, his all-inclusive ware is the only taxonomic unit that approximates the actual behaviors involved in ceramic manufacture. The five criteria he used to separate one ware from another correspond to the major stages of the manufacturing process (Rice 1987; Rye 1981; Shepard 1985). Furthermore, Colton's definition includes the transfer of technological knowledge, which is not only a fundamental mechanism in the evolution of ceramic manufacturing traditions, but also a useful conceptual tool for identifying local and nonlocal ceramics.

Second, the lack of temporal and spatial connotations in Colton's ware concept is irrelevant, because ware includes types and series of types that are chronologically and geographically bounded, respectively. Types alone, on the other hand, are not nearly as useful for identifying manufacturing loci because they are defined mainly by attributes of surface treatment and

decoration, which are sensitive to temporal variation but do not necessarily indicate provenience. Moreover, the fact that wares as defined by Colton have almost no temporal restrictions facilitates, in principle, tracing technological transfer through time by identifying continuity in manufacturing technology.

Third, although I basically agree with Rice's (1976) observation that attributes of paste composition depend on local resource availability, including these attributes in ware identifications together with all other technological characteristics permits the recognition of *within-ware* variations; these, for instance, may in turn indicate manufacture of a given kind of pottery in different regions. Similarly, an all-inclusive ware concept allows the identification and comparison of aspects of ceramic manufacture common to more than one ware as well as those restricted to a single ware.

In sum, identification of technological relationships among wares permits the isolation of technological attributes that may be useful for elucidating whether variations between or within wares indicate distinct loci of manufacture. Because not all attributes are equally sensitive to variation due to specific processes of ceramic manufacture, it is only through a comparison of complete sets of attributes observable in each ware that similarities and differences of significance can be elicited. Conversely, a priori selection of one or two attributes for defining wares decreases the probabilities of identifying the range of variation associated with a given ceramic tradition.

ANALYTICAL PROCEDURES

In this tridimensional approach, style, technology, and provenience of ceramics provide independent but complementary lines of evidence for distinguishing local from nonlocal ceramics in the archaeological record. The methodological value that each of these variables has for making this identification depends largely on the broad patterns of ceramic variability as well as on the variation encountered in the geological environment of the region under study. Summarized below are the general procedures followed in this research to distinguish local from nonlocal wares at Chodistaas Pueblo (Fig. 2.1), a well-dated and short-lived settlement (A.D. 1263 to about 1290) in the Grasshopper region of east-central Arizona.

Chemical and mineralogical analyses were conducted on a large sample of complete and partial vessels, representing both decorated and undecorated wares, to identify distinct sources of the raw materials employed

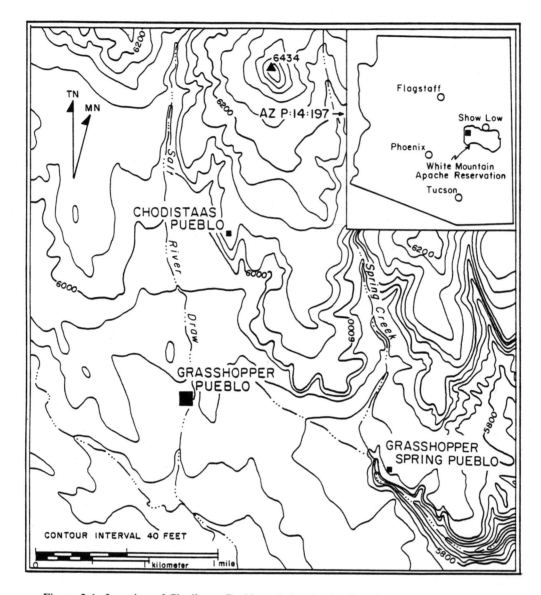

Figure 2.1. Location of Chodistaas Pueblo and sites in the Grasshopper region, Arizona.

in the manufacture of these vessels. Chemical analysis by instrumental neutron activation (INAA) and by inductively coupled plasma emission spectroscopy (ICP) provided fine-grained criteria for isolating different paste fabrics within each formally defined ware. Temper observations complemented the identification of clay sources by providing information that could be compared with the geology of the Grasshopper Plateau. A clay survey within a 7–km (about a 4–mile) radius from Chodistaas Pueblo yielded comparative data on the availability and potential of clay sources in the region.

The technological analysis involved reconstructing step-by-step the manufacturing process of each of the wares present in the assemblage. Proceeding in this

manner made it possible to record technological similarities across formally defined wares as well as differences within a single ware. Correlation between technological attributes and vessel shape (jars, bowls, pitchers) was recorded to evaluate variation due to factors other than manufacturing loci, such as functional differences.

The limitations of stylistic variability for tracing ceramic provenience would be greatly reduced if at least a few patterns of covariation between specific technological or compositional characteristics and stylistic attributes could be determined. The stylistic classification originally used by Crown (1981a) in her analysis of the Chodistaas pottery is specific to the design configurations observable in whole vessels rather than in sherds, and includes Red Mesa, Puerco, Roosevelt, Snowflake, Tularosa, Kayenta-Tusayan, Pinedale, and Cibicue styles. Thus, in my research an additional 84 decorated vessels were incorporated into Crown's (1981a) stylistic classification and contrasted with data on compositional and technological variability to examine the extent to which design styles present in the Chodistaas assemblage could be used as indicators of loci of ceramic manufacture.

Data on pottery from excavated sites on the Grasshopper Plateau (Grasshopper Spring, Grasshopper Pueblo, and AZ P:14:197 ASM; Fig. 2.1) were also incorporated in the analysis to expand spatial and temporal perspectives on ceramic variability. The study of surface ceramics from sites on the Grasshopper Plateau, in the Cibecue and Forestdale valleys, and from other mountain sites to the east and west was useful for understanding the distribution of decorated and undecorated wares beyond Chodistaas. Similarly, information on ceramic provenience, technology, and style from several regions of the Arizona mountains as well as of the Colorado Plateau was valuable for constructing arguments and making inferences about possible mechanisms of circulation of decorated and undecorated wares present at Chodistaas Pueblo. The behaviors involved in ceramic circulation and their role in the formation of non-local ceramic assemblages are discussed in Chapter 3.

CHAPTER THREE

Ceramic Circulation
Behavioral Mechanisms and
Archaeological Correlates

The variability observed in archaeological ceramics is partially the result of mechanisms of circulation acting over restricted as well as extensive areas. Almost every assemblage includes pottery of obvious nonlocal origin, namely, "rare" decorated or plain vessels often manufactured in distant regions. Almost every assemblage also includes nonlocal pottery that may not be readily distinguishable from that locally made. A number of assemblages, particularly from sites located in boundary or transitional areas, contain equal amounts of local and nonlocal pottery.

Increasingly, research aimed at the identification of locus of production of prehistoric Southwestern ceramics has suggested that pottery vessels circulated regularly among proximate as well as distant communities since at least A.D. 800 (Blinman and Wilson 1992; Hegmon and others 1992). In numerous cases, the frequency of nonlocal pottery found in a given site may be almost as high as that of locally made pottery (Blinman and Wilson 1992; Franklin 1982; Toll 1985; Windes 1984). These and other studies have demonstrated that a priori criteria for identifying nonlocal ceramics are inadequate for addressing issues of past behavior that require the establishment of connections between ceramic artifacts and the people who manufactured them.

The following paragraphs offer a working definition of local manufacture that takes into account the specific case of Chodistaas Pueblo and provides an introductory framework against which circulation of ceramics can be evaluated. The behavioral mechanisms of circulation (movement of pots, movement of people, and movement of raw materials) are examined, and the potential and limitations for differentiating them in the archaeological record are discussed.

DEFINING LOCAL CERAMICS

Local manufacture of ceramics can be conceptualized at two inclusive levels: settlement and region. In the most restricted sense, local manufacture refers to the production of pottery within a given settlement. On the other hand, regional manufacture implies ceramic production by a number of communities among which common resources were exploited, by-products were circulated, and technological knowledge was shared. In this sense, ceramics may be considered local if it can be reasonably demonstrated that they were manufactured within a specific region. In this study, I use regional manufacture as a concept equivalent to local manufacture for a number of reasons.

First, all the decorated and undecorated wares in the Chodistaas Pueblo assemblage are also represented in whole and partial vessels from rooms excavated at Grasshopper Spring, the second largest contemporaneous community (9 rooms) in the region, located 1.5 km (1 mile) south of Chodistaas (Fig. 2.1). The assemblage similarities between the two sites suggest that Chodistaas inhabitants shared raw material sources and technological and stylistic information with their neighbors, or that perhaps both pueblos obtained vessels from neighboring as well as from distant communities.

Second, the potential for distinguishing between the products of each community through analysis of paste composition would depend on whether each used compositionally distinct raw materials (Bishop 1980; Bishop, Rands, and Holley 1982). The sites in question are located in a relatively homogeneous geological setting (mainly formed of sandstone and limestone deposits), a situation that decreases the likelihood of successful discrimination between ceramics manufactured in each settlement. Furthermore, even if geologically or compositionally distinct sources in the region were exploited, it is likely that nearby communities shared procurement areas.

Arnold (1980: 148–149) compares 61 ethnographic cases where distance to ceramic raw material sources is known. He observes that, although 91 percent of the communities obtain their clay and temper resources from a distance of 7 km (4.4 miles) or less, communities separated by less than 10 to 14 km (8.7 miles) often have overlapping resource areas (Arnold 1985: 35–60). One of the most significant implications of Arnold's study for archaeological interpretation is that behavioral as well as environmental variables may obscure the processes of intraregional exchange of ceramics.

Third, Chodistaas and Grasshopper Spring pueblos lack direct evidence of on-site pottery manufacture, namely, artifacts associated with vessel formation clustered around pottery-making and pottery-firing facilities (Sullivan 1988: 24). The recovery of raw materials and tools provides especially good evidence for on-site manufacture when raw materials can be matched with the end product (Triadan 1989: 9). Unfortunately, only a few tools of ambiguous function and small quantities of pigments and clays were preserved in the rooms at Chodistaas (Crown 1981a: 49). Nevertheless, it is entirely possible, if not demonstrable, that both Chodistaas and Grasshopper Spring inhabitants were manufacturing ceramics somewhere in the vicinity of the pueblos or even at the location of their preferred clay sources (Nicklin 1979; Reid 1989: 79).

To summarize, ceramics that have the highest probability for manufacture by the settlers of Chodistaas Pueblo and contemporary communities of the Grasshopper Plateau are considered, for the purposes of this research, *local* ceramics. The uplands of the Grasshopper Plateau are roughly bounded by Chediski Peak on the north, the Salt River on the south, Spring Ridge-Spring Creek on the east, and the Canyon Creek escarpment on the west (Fig. 3.1).

NONLOCAL CERAMICS: BEHAVIORAL MECHANISMS

Delineation of the probable behaviors involved in the circulation of ceramics into Chodistaas Pueblo requires, first of all, an appraisal of the pueblo's location in relation to its neighbors. As described in Chapter 4, the late Pueblo III period settlement pattern on the Grasshopper Plateau consisted of dispersed, small homesteads (2 to 5 rooms) loosely clustered around a focal community of no more than 20 rooms. Chodistaas, the largest of these settlements and the only one with an enclosed plaza, was a focal community in the region (Montgomery 1992; Reid 1989). Similar patterns were observed in contemporaneous settlement groups of adjacent regions, Q Ranch to the west (Whittlesey 1982b) and Cibecue Valley to the east (Reid and others 1993).

No contemporaneous settlements larger than 30 or 40 rooms have been found within a 45–km (28-mile) radius from Chodistaas; late Pueblo III period mountain communities in the Grasshopper Plateau were geographically isolated from major population centers, such as

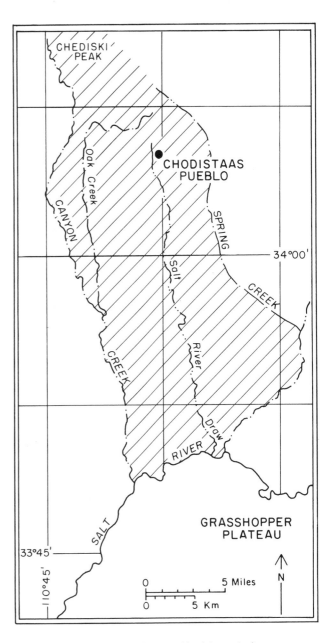

Figure 3.1. Geographical boundaries of the Grasshopper Plateau.

Point of Pines or Pinedale. Where and how did these small communities, located in a backwoods area, obtain their ceramics? Possibly they produced all their own pottery, or they obtained vessels from nearby communities. However, the presence of Cibola White Ware and other decorated wares at Chodistaas, Grasshopper Spring, and site AZ P:14:197, the neighboring late Pueblo III period sites that have been excavated, leads to the hypothesis that a substantial quantity of pottery came from outside the Grasshopper Plateau.

By giving local manufacture a regional perspective, the archaeologist precludes the identification of community relationships within the Grasshopper Plateau. Nonetheless, three alternatives through which nonlocal ceramics could have entered the systemic assemblages at Chodistaas Pueblo and other communities on the Grasshopper Plateau can be inspected: movement of pots, movement of people, and movement of nonlocal raw materials for local ceramic manufacture. These alternatives are by no means exclusive and, in principle, could combine to generate any specific ceramic assemblage.

Movement of Pots

Vessels could have entered Chodistaas Pueblo through formal trade networks or through other, less complex, modes of material exchange, including economic, social, and ceremonial reciprocity (Bennett 1968; Cheal 1988; Earle and Ericson 1977; Ericson 1977; Frisbie 1982; Neale 1977; Orlove 1977; Plog 1977; Polanyi 1957; Renfrew 1975; Sahlins 1965). Trade and exchange are often used interchangeably (Renfrew 1975: 4), but here I refer to them as separate concepts to differentiate between *trade*, or organized, large-scale material transactions that took place regularly over relatively long periods of time and involved the flow of significant volumes of goods (Plog 1977: 129), and *reciprocal exchange*, or recurrent, independent, symmetrical, and small-scale material transactions that did not have the organizational requirements nor the economic impact of trade networks, but that served to reinforce intercommunity relationships. Reciprocal exchange may have involved two or more mutually supporting communities in a system that opened access to resources from different environments as well as to nonlocal goods, maintained social and political ties through marriage, and fostered community identity by transcending cultural and ethnolinguistic boundaries (Cheal 1988: 58, 86, 91; Ericson 1977: 118; Frisbie 1982: 21).

In modern Pueblo societies, reciprocal exchange far more commonly circulates pottery than does trade (Frisbie 1982: 21). For example, Hopi who live on First Mesa, a ceramic-manufacturing community, circulate ceramic bowls during Katsina ceremonies, when children receive bowls containing small presents. The family of a First Mesa groom often includes ceramic bowls in the wedding gifts given to the bride and her family, particularly if the bride lives outside of First Mesa. As Emory Sekaquaptewa told me in 1990, acknowledgment of clan affiliation among the mesas stimulates material transactions embedded in ceremonial and social relationships.

Trade networks seem to have developed early in the San Juan Basin and the Colorado Plateau (Douglass 1987; Toll 1981; Toll and others 1980; Warren 1967; Windes 1977, 1984). Apparently, however, this was not the case in the Arizona mountains, where extensive ceramic trade developed only after A.D. 1300. Chodistaas Pueblo and other communities in the Grasshopper and Q Ranch regions did not participate in the network that presumably distributed St. Johns Polychrome throughout Arizona and New Mexico during the thirteenth century (Carlson 1970, 1982; Graves 1982). Only four bowls of this type have been recovered from room floors at Chodistaas and Grasshopper Spring pueblos, and only a few sherds came from surface and room fill. The absence of large population centers in the area and the topographical barrier of the Mogollon Rim may have discouraged other groups from establishing regular trade networks with mountain settlers.

It has been argued that Chodistaas Pueblo and other contemporaneous settlements in the Grasshopper and Q Ranch regions lacked the residential stability and the population mass needed to attract a large flow of goods from distant sources on a regular basis (Reid 1989: 79). A few obsidian flakes, shell and turquoise ornaments, two Hohokam-like palettes, and two St. Johns Polychrome bowls are the only commodities found at Chodistaas that could be traded items. A low magnitude but recurrent flow of pots through reciprocal ties established with communities outside the region, possibly with those located in different ecological settings or even with those of different ethnolinguistic affiliation (Ericson 1977: 118), may account for the presence of nonlocal ceramics in the Grasshopper Plateau area during the late 1200s.

Movement of People

If reciprocal exchange was the most probable kind of transaction by which inhabitants of Chodistaas Pueblo acquired some of their pots, then movement of people perhaps constituted a common mode of bringing them into the settlement. On the basis of a pervasive pattern observed in Pueblo III period settlements of the Arizona mountains and in most areas of the northern Southwest (LeBlanc 1989; Neily 1988; F. Plog 1989), it has been suggested that Chodistaas was occupied part time, at least initially (Reid 1989: 77). For small, short-lived communities that practiced cultivation as well as hunting and gathering, mobility was probably an adaptive strategy that helped them to survive in a marginal environment (Johnson 1989: 372). Settlements were not necessarily abandoned for long periods of time; seasonal, temporary, or short-term mobility would have facilitated the acquisition of pots and other goods from distant communities and at the same time reinforced social and political relationships through marriage and other alliances.

Aside from seasonal, temporary, or short-term mobility away from small mountain settlements, migration of small social units into the mountains could have contributed to an increase in the inventory of nonlocal pots. Migrations of varying magnitude are known to have occurred during the late 1200s. The best documented case of such events in Southwestern prehistory is the Kayenta migration into Point of Pines (Maverick Mountain phase), supported by architectural, botanical, ceramic, and other lines of evidence (Haury 1958). This migration was relatively large, involving approximately 50 to 60 families who lived with the Point of Pines natives for at least 20 years (Haury 1958: 6). Other Kayenta-Tusayan-related migrations into the Safford area (Brown 1973) and into the San Pedro Valley (Di Peso 1958; Franklin and Masse 1976; Lindsay 1987) are documented in the ceramic record, indicating that a trend of southward population movement began sometime in the second half of the thirteenth century. In relation to Haury's reconstruction of the Maverick Mountain phase, Reed (1958: 7) noted that the movement of Kayenta people across 320 km (nearly 200 miles), bypassing populated areas such as Hopi, Chavez Pass, or the White Mountains to reach the country of the upper Salt River drainage and beyond, suggested that Kayenta populations maintained previous contact and were acquainted, directly or indirectly, with the people living at Point of Pines. Long-term, long-distance relationships maintained among groups inhabiting different territories, and perhaps belonging to distinct cultural, ethnic, and linguistic traditions, thus influenced the choice of destination of migrating groups.

Ethnic coresidence on a smaller scale than that seen at Point of Pines, however, could have involved the immigration of a single social unit, perhaps from one of the numerous homesteads containing a couple of households that were scattered throughout the Southwest (Johnson 1989: 381; Reid 1989: 79). Wilson (1988) reported a case of a small-scale Mogollon migration into the Dolores area, southwestern Colorado. Small-scale migrations may have been a prelude to larger

population movements, resulting from demographic shifts on the Colorado Plateau that brought Anasazi people into the mountains to live in pueblos such as Grasshopper or to establish separate pueblo communities (Reid 1989: 80; see Crown-Robertson 1978 for a detailed review of prehistoric migration in the American Southwest). The archaeological record, in most cases, does not lend itself to a clear identification of large-scale, not to mention small-scale, migrations. But, as Reed (1958: 7) observed, the introduction of nonlocal pots and nonlocal ceramic-manufacturing technologies into a settlement or region did not necessarily imply mass migration, for the movement of individuals or families, as well as exchange, travel, and intermarriage, would have sufficed to spread pottery and techniques over wide territories.

Movement of Raw Materials

The use of nonlocal raw materials for local ceramic manufacture (clay, temper, pigments, and fuel) is a potential source of error when attempting to identify imported ceramics. If mobility favored the acquisition of pots made in regions far from the one in question, it could have facilitated as well the exploitation of high quality raw materials unavailable locally. Thus, the likelihood that raw materials rather than pots were imported into Chodistaas Pueblo needs to be examined.

There is a close relationship between the ability of a population to exploit profitably a given resource and the energy expenditure required for this exploitation. Because energy expenditure is in turn closely related to resource distance, a population can efficiently exploit only those resources which are located within a certain distance (Jarman 1972 as quoted by Arnold 1985: 32). Using Browman's (1976) model of exploitable territory threshold, Arnold (1985: 33) mentioned four major components associated with distance/returns in resource exploitation: geodesic distance, pheric (topographic) distance, transport costs, and social and psychological costs. A range exists where resource exploitation can be maximized at minimum cost: this is the preferred range of exploitation. Beyond a certain limit, exploitation becomes uneconomical.

Although the distance that a potter would travel to acquire good quality raw materials varies cross-culturally, there is a strong tendency in ethnographic pottery-making communities to exploit resources that can be reached within a day's walking distance (Nicklin 1979: 439). This is particularly true for clay and to a large extent for temper, both of which are needed in large quantities, are heavy, and are difficult to transport. Slips and pigments of desired color, on the other hand, can be hard to obtain nearby and are often acquired from greater distances (Arnold 1985: 36). Because water and fuel are needed for subsistence activities, a regular supply of both is usually available in the immediate vicinity of a pottery-making community. Resource threshold distances, however, may vary according to the degree of sedentism of the community in question; clay source locations used occasionally by mobile groups may be well beyond the preferred range of exploitation. These occasional sources could even be located and exploited while carrying out activities unrelated to ceramic manufacture (Gould 1980). Nevertheless, a narrow range of resource exploitation is common in semisedentary communities (Arnold 1985: 36).

The pheric or topographic distance to a resource also affects significantly the use of nonlocal raw materials. River navigation and availability of pack animals facilitates long-distance procurement of raw materials. Conversely, in areas of rough topography potters may be more limited in their travel distances (Arnold 1985: 37; DeBoer 1984; DeBoer and Lathrap 1979). But even when transportation facilities are at hand, potters usually procure the necessary raw materials in conformity with the principle of "least effort" (DeBoer 1984: 545; Zipf 1949), or the notion that humans tend to exploit proximate resources in preference to more distant ones. Sociocultural factors such as restricted access to a specific source, presence of other groups in an area rich in raw materials, or convenience in acquiring pots rather than transporting raw materials from distant sources are equally important when considering ceramic resource exploitation.

Information on the use of nonlocal clays and temper for ceramic manufacture in the American Southwest is especially meager. This is in part due to infrequent sourcing of ceramics and to the readiness with which archaeologists apply the "trade" label to ceramics of presumably nonlocal origin. Shepard (1936: 451) observed that only a few instances of trade in body clays were recorded from historic pueblos, but that there was considerable documentation of trade in slip clays, suggesting that fine-textured clays of pleasing color were relatively scarce. Today's Zia people must obtain hematite pigments through trade with the Hopi and, therefore, they are willing to travel as far as Chaco Canyon to collect it (Stoffle and others 1994). On the Grasshopper Plateau, a variety of brown-red firing clays and hematite pigments are locally available (Triadan

1989), whereas white-firing clays and pigments, which are not common in the area, must have been acquired elsewhere in prehistoric times.

Transporting large quantities of clays and temper from distant sources might have been less convenient than transporting pots, even when risk of loss by breakage is considered, partly because clays and temper weigh more than finished vessels (Arnold 1985: 36) and because exchange of ceramics may be chosen over local manufacture in situations where intercommunity relationships need to be constantly reinforced (Chagnon 1968). It is more likely, then, that movement of raw materials in any significant quantity was confined to the Grasshopper Plateau or perhaps to the adjacent Q Ranch and Cibecue Valley regions.

CIRCULATION OF CERAMICS AND ARCHAEOLOGICAL CORRELATES

Much of the variability observed in the ceramic record, specifically in assemblages from Southwestern sites, is likely the result of multiple residential associations of the people who used and discarded those vessels as well as of exchange with more or less spatially distant relations (Johnson 1989: 384). Unfortunately, the isolation of archaeological correlates for these mechanisms is seriously limited because they often produce similar material outcomes and distributional patterns.

A number of years ago, Shepard (1985) emphasized the risks of incurring erroneous identifications of nonlocal ceramics precisely because many different past behaviors (ceramic exchange, raw materials exchange, ethnic coresidence, imitative behavior, among others) tended to produce the same range of variability. Shepard (1985: 339) provided a summary of those behaviors and the possible material outcomes that archaeologists may isolate and use to infer mechanisms of pottery circulation. In Table 3.1, I have adapted Shepard's summary to the previous discussion, emphasizing those situations likely to be encountered in the archaeological record. The identification of such situations depends not only on the extent to which compositional, technological and stylistic differences between local and nonlocal ceramics are recognizable, but also on the ability to isolate particularities of the appearance or occurrence of a specific ware in a given assemblage.

A strong indicator of change in the nature of ceramic exchange and socioeconomic impact thereof is the appearance of production for exchange, with the subsequent increase in standardization and development of

Table 3.1. Nonlocal Ceramics

Behavioral Mechanisms	Material Correlates
I. *Movement of Pots*	
Trade or exchange	Distinctive raw materials, techniques, and styles
II. *Movement of People*	
A. Foreign people bringing nonlocal pots	Indistinguishable from I, unless rate and timing of occurrence and contextual associations are controlled
B. Foreign people making pots in their own tradition with imported raw materials	Same as above
C. Foreign people making pots in their own tradition with local raw materials	Identified on the basis of raw materials
D. Foreign people making pots in the local tradition with local raw materials	Indistinguishable from pots made by local people if imitation of local tradition is good
E. Foreign people combining both traditions and using local raw materials	Identified on the basis of raw materials and elements of the local tradition
F. Foreign people combining both traditions and using imported raw materials	Identified on the basis of raw materials
III. *Movement of Raw Materials*	
A. Local people making pots in the local tradition with imported raw materials	Identified on the basis of raw materials
B. Local people making pots in the foreign tradition with imported raw materials	Distinction from imported pots depends on the quality of the imitation
C. Local people combining their own and foreign traditions and using imported raw materials	Indistinguishable from IIF

Note. In most cases, potters import only one kind of raw material (commonly slips, pigments, or glazes) and combine it with local raw materials (clays, temper, or both; Arnold 1985; Shepard 1985).

productive specialization (Costin 1991). The presence of large quantities of local as well as nonlocal White Mountain and Roosevelt Red wares at Grasshopper Pueblo indicate that, during the fourteenth century, the Grasshopper Plateau communities became involved in the extensive trade network that distributed these wares throughout the Southwest (Mayro and others 1976; Reid and Whittlesey 1992; Triadan 1994). Whittlesey (1974) noted that decorated bowls from Grasshopper Pueblo were made proportionally so they could "nest" for easy transportation. Specialized workshops where abundant raw materials (tempered and untempered clays, pigments) and manufacturing tools (pukis, pigment-stained ground stone, bone tools) were recovered have been identified at this site (Triadan 1989).

Volume and directionality of exchange are additional indicators of extensive trade (F. Plog 1977). At Homolovi II more than one-half of the pottery was imported from the Hopi Mesas, where ceramic production for exchange developed after A.D. 1300. Adams (1991: 119a)

hypothesizes that because fuel for pottery-making was scarce, Homolovi people were probably trading cotton for yellow wares. Moreover, the nonlocal ceramic assemblage at Homolovi suggests that the inhabitants may have been acting as intermediaries in the network that distributed yellow wares as far as Zuni, the Tonto Basin, and the Verde Valley in Arizona.

The nature of the ceramic evidence for movement of people is best exemplified in the Kayenta migration events outlined above. Haury (1958: 2) noted that Tsegi Orange Ware, which was associated with the Kayenta migration into Point of Pines, was manufactured with nonlocal raw materials as well as with local materials but in a foreign style (Maverick Mountain Polychrome of Kiet Siel Polychrome style) consistent with the imported Tsegi vessels. Haury also observed a tendency to incorporate elements of the native decorative style into the local version of Tsegi Orange Ware. Maverick Mountain pottery was not made after the immigrants left Point of Pines, further suggesting it was made by foreign potters. Nonlocal Tsegi Orange Ware, on the other hand, could have been either brought into Point of Pines by the Kayenta or acquired through exchange. Although the uneven distribution of Kayenta-related ceramics across the settlement indicates that the pottery was predominantly used by the immigrants (Haury 1958: 3), the occurrence of minor ceramic exchange with the locals is indicated by low frequencies of native ceramics in Kayenta rooms, and vice versa.

Another situation where movement of people visibly influenced the ceramic record is documented by Lindsay, who suggested that the development of local polychrome ceramics (Tucson Polychrome) in the San Pedro Valley was stimulated by the presence of Kayenta-Tusayan people in the region around A.D. 1300. According to Lindsay (1987: 196), Tucson Polychrome has "an affinity to both Gila Polychrome and Maverick Mountain Polychrome, but ultimately has its roots in the northern polychrome tradition." The Kayenta-Tusayan influence in the ceramic materials of the San Pedro settlements extended to the undecorated assemblage, where large-mouthed globular jars (a form similar to Kiet Siel Gray), perforated rim plates, and a few vessels with corrugated surface finish are present (Lindsay 1987: 196). Brown (1973: 139), too, noted the presence of a Kayenta-Maverick Mountain "cultural unit" in the Pueblo Viejo portion of the Safford Valley on the basis of nonlocal as well as locally made Maverick Mountain pottery. Brown (1973: 127) suggested that a short-range migration from the Point of Pines-Reserve area may have introduced the Kayenta-related trait complexes into the Safford Valley.

Small-scale movement of people, such as inter-marriage, may not be evident at all in the ceramic record. A common assumption among Southwestern archaeologists has been that a woman who came to live in her husband's community continued to practice her own ceramic traditions, thus introducing a foreign element in the native ceramic assemblage (Hill 1965, 1970; Longacre 1964, 1970). Ethnographic evidence, however, shows that in many instances women adopt the local ceramic tradition soon after they move into their husbands' villages (Graves 1981; Herbich 1987). Nonetheless, careful analysis of the ceramic record may provide information on small-scale migrations. Wilson (1988: 431), for example, examined Mogollon smudged pottery recovered from Pueblo I period sites in Dolores, southwestern Colorado, and found not only a small number of imported smudged vessels but also locally produced wares with smudged surfaces. Smudging technology is not part of the Mesa Verde ceramic tradition,

nor is it a practice that can be copied by visual inspection. This type of evidence is circumstantial, but it stimulates the search for additional evidence of the movement of people. At Chodistaas Pueblo, differences in spatial arrangement and construction dates between the northern and southern room blocks (see Chapter 4) may well be the product of immigration of a "family unit" into the settlement during the A.D. 1280s when the southern room block was built.

Information on the movement of nonlocal clays for the manufacture of local ceramics is primarily restricted to the ethnographic record. Such situations often involve the acquisition of clays from distant sources either forced by exhaustion of local beds or facilitated by traditional or modern transportation (DeBoer 1984; Thompson 1958). Movement of other kinds of raw materials, on the other hand, is occasionally identifiable in the archaeological record. Small amounts of yellow and white pigments were recovered from Room 113, a storage-manufacturing room at Grasshopper Pueblo. After conducting X-ray diffraction and firing experiments on a large sample of clays, pigments, and sherds, Triadan (1989: 71) suggested that both pigment clays were probably imported for the manufacture of Fourmile Polychrome at the pueblo.

Shepard (1936: 451) mentioned that historic potters of San Ildefonso obtained red clay for black ware slip from beds in the Valle Grande of the Jemez range, a one-day trip on horseback. The white slip of the Laguna Indians was obtained in trade by the Zuni, and San Ildefonso potters used the fine-textured, cream-colored slip of Santo Domingo, traded from either Cochiti or Santo Domingo. Elson and Doelle (1986) suggested the movement of micaceous schist, a mineral widely used as temper for the manufacture of decorated and undecorated ceramics in the Tucson Basin. The only known source of micaceous schist is located in the Rincon Mountains, and it may have been transported to the Santa Cruz Valley, approximately 30 km (18 miles) to the west. It seems likely that potters restricted the movement of raw materials to the scarce but more transportable slips, pigments, and glazes, using readily available clays and temper to manufacture the bulk of their ceramics.

Identification of the patterns of pottery circulation depends on the extent to which technological and stylistic differences between local and nonlocal ceramics are recognizable in the archaeological record and on the ability to discriminate local from nonlocal raw materials and to relate them, at least in a general way, to the local geology. However, deciding which of the many possible mechanisms of circulation served to introduce presumed nonlocal ware to the ceramic assemblage in question may not be possible without knowledge of the circumstances surrounding the appearance or occurrence of each ware. Knowing the patterns of distribution of a given ware over wide regions (magnitude, direction) may be helpful in inferring the participation of a community in trade networks.

Haury's (1958) identification of the Kayenta migration to Point of Pines is a strong case in prehistory that suggests the movement of people may be identified by the sudden appearance of a nonlocal ware in a settlement or region, particularly if it is followed by manufacture of foreign ceramics with local raw materials. Conversely, the recurrence of a presumed nonlocal ware throughout the occupation sequence of a settlement suggests continued reciprocal relationships among producers and consumers of that ware. Changes in nonceramic aspects of the archaeological record, such as the addition of room blocks, appearance of distinctive architecture and portable items, and identification of physically distinct individuals in burials, may be related to movement of people and consequent ethnic coresidence.

The subtle nature of the evidence for ceramic circulation requires a tight control of timing in the occurrence of a nonlocal ware and of formation processes responsible for its presence in the archaeological record. Chodistaas Pueblo is a site where exceptional recovery conditions combine with high technological and stylistic variability of the ceramic assemblage to provide a fertile ground for refining inferences about circulation of ceramics. Although the identification of nonlocal wares is based on their compositional and technological characteristics, the mechanisms of circulation of those wares into the pueblo are suggested by broad patterns of distribution on the Grasshopper Plateau and in other regions, by the frequency of their occurrence in surface and floor assemblages, by the rate and timing of their occurrence, and by other visible changes temporally associated with their occurrence. In addition, the temporal perspective gained from the later ceramics at near-by Grasshopper Pueblo provides a comparative situation that helps to evaluate the connections between a nonlocal ware and its probable mechanism of circulation.

The following chapters present and justify the methods followed in the analysis of ceramic variability at Chodistaas Pueblo. Results of this analysis are integrated with additional archaeological evidence from Chodistaas and neighboring communities to propose probabilities for local manufacture and to infer the specific mechanisms of ceramic circulation of nonlocal wares.

CHAPTER FOUR

The Ceramic Assemblage at Chodistaas Pueblo

Chodistaas Pueblo is located 1.6 km (1 mile) north of Grasshopper Pueblo on the White Mountain Apache Reservation in east-central Arizona (Fig. 2.1). It was built on the south end of a northwest-southeast trending bluff rising 24.4 m (80 feet) above a minor drainage of Spring Creek, which parallels the bluff to the west. The elevation of the site is 1,853 m (6,078 feet) above sea level.

Geologically, Chodistaas Pueblo rests on an outcrop of the Permian Supai Formation, Cibeque Member, which is composed of reddish brown and light gray sandstone and shale. The sandstone unit predominates on the Grasshopper Plateau, and it is nonfossiliferous, cross-bedded, calcareously cemented, and fills channels in the underlying units. Nodular limestone and chert pebbles are locally present at various stratigraphic positions (Finnell 1966; Winters 1963). Surface red clayey soils and clay beds of secondary deposition are common in the region, and the sterile stratum underlying the room floors at Chodistaas is red clay.

This geological environment surrounds the site in a radius of at least 4.8 km (3 miles) to the north and east. An isolated outcrop of Tertiary Younger Gravel is located within 2.4 km (1.5 miles) to the southeast. This outcrop is characterized by large pebbles of quartzite, limestone, chert, diabase, and granite, and light gray to pinkish gray and grayish red coarse sands composed mainly of feldspar, chert, and claystone. The outcrop is locally cemented by calcite (Finnell 1966). Naco Limestone extends to the west and south of Salt River Draw.

ENVIRONMENT

The Grasshopper Plateau is located within the physiographic subprovince designated by Moore (1968) as the "Carrizo Slope," a plain of gently sloping sedimentary rocks cut by numerous canyons that have been carved by generally south-flowing streams. Differential erosion has modified the surface of the slope, forming cliffs and benches (Moore 1968: 6–8). This plain slopes southward from the Mogollon Rim to the Salt River. It characterizes the Transition Zone, a broad diagonal band of uplands that is geographically, geologically, and ecologically intermediate between the southern edge of the Colorado Plateau and the Basin-and-Range Province (Peirce 1985).

The differences in elevation within the Transition Zone make the Grasshopper region an ecotone with high biotic diversity. Species characteristic of lower elevations such as ocotillo, agave, and members of the *Opuntia* family are present, as well as mixed piñon-juniper-oak woodlands, ponderosa pine, and stands of Douglas Fir, which occur in the higher elevations (Holbrook and Graves 1982: 5). Both the Upper Sonoran and the Evergreen Woodland biotic communities (Lowe 1964) are well represented.

Even though the environment of the Grasshopper region has been altered by range expansion programs conducted in the 1960s, it appears that modern climate, topography, soils, and biotic resources remain roughly similar to late prehistoric conditions (Bohrer 1982; Dean and Robinson 1982; Kelso 1982; Sullivan 1980; Welch 1991). Compared with most other Southwestern uplands, agricultural potential is high in the Grasshopper region; 40.1 cm to 50.1 cm (16 to 20 inches) annual rainfall, 120 to 160 frost-free days, and abundant meadows with relatively high quality soil indicate the region's suitability for agriculture (Tuggle and others 1984: 102–104). Furthermore, the entire region below the rim slopes southward, maximizing exposure to solar radiation (Welch 1991).

Paleoclimatological information derived from tree-ring samples from Grasshopper Pueblo indicate that during the period of the Great Drought (from A.D. 1276 to 1299) the Grasshopper Plateau was characterized by a thinning of the forest and a lowering of the water table, producing conditions amenable for agriculture (Dean and Robinson 1982: 59). These factors may have attracted populations from areas ravaged by the Great Drought, who established small, stone-walled pueblos (Graves and others 1982).

Today, shallow deposits of native soil (Jacks Gravelly Clay Loam) support an open woodland of piñon, ponderosa pine, juniper and scattered manzanita, which provide a visible and accessible ground surface. A layer of forest litter and sheet debris surround the site, covering the soil deposits. Immediately below, there is bedrock (Crown 1981a).

SETTLEMENT PATTERNS

The expansion of above-ground masonry pueblos on the Grasshopper Plateau can be dated to the second half of the thirteenth century, a time of organizational changes in the Arizona mountains. These changes were brought about by two factors: an increase in contact with people to the north, and local experimental adjustments to diverse mountain environments in both subsistence and social organization (Graves and others 1982; Reid 1982, 1989; Reid and Tuggle 1988; Reid and Whittlesey 1982; Tuggle 1970; Whittlesey 1982b; Whittlesey and Reid 1982a). In other regions of the Mogollon mountains, such as Point of Pines, processes similar to those in the Grasshopper region were underway before the mid 1200s, largely because of sustained contact with people to both the north and south (Haury 1958; Johnson 1965).

Reconstruction of the settlement patterns and subsistence strategies on the Grasshopper Plateau and in the Q Ranch region to the west reveals that small hamlets (2 to 5 rooms) clustered around focal communities of no more than 20, low-walled surface rooms that served a dispersed, local population (Whittlesey and Reid 1982a). During most of the thirteen century, the loosely clustered settlements were linked through residential moves; full-time occupation of a settlement was infrequent. Residential mobility, however, appears to have been bound to specific regions: in the Chevelon drainage, for example, the settlement system centered on small communities with nearly full-time occupations (Whittlesey and Reid 1982a). In the Q Ranch region, many small settlements were oriented toward special tasks such as plant procurement and processing on a seasonal basis (Whittlesey 1982b).

The late Pueblo III period settlement pattern on the Grasshopper Plateau consisted of at least two, or perhaps three, settlement clusters. Chodistaas, the only pueblo of this period that had an enclosed plaza, was the focal community of one of the largest clusters. Architectural features such as wall height and roof construction at Chodistaas and Grasshopper Spring pueblos (Fig. 2.1) are in accord with the idea that these pueblos may have been occupied seasonally (Lorentzen 1988; Montgomery 1992; although see Crown 1981a for a contrasting view), thus fitting into the general pattern of seasonal occupations throughout the Arizona mountains during the late 1200s. Reid (1989: 77) contends that full-time occupation of Chodistaas may not have occurred until the mid 1280s, during the height of the Great Drought when the latest four rooms were built, probably to expand habitation-storage facilities.

The last decade of the thirteenth century witnessed an increasing dependency on the cultivation of corn and beans with dry farming techniques that probably favored residential stability and full habitation, although hunting and gathering continued to be a prominent component of the subsistence economy (Welch 1991). During the period of the Great Drought (A.D. 1276–1299), population grew in the Grasshopper region as a result of immigration from the north and increased residential stability (Reid 1989: 77). This increase may have restricted access to wild resources, and toward the end of the thirteenth century settlements clustered near agricultural land. It was not until after A.D. 1300 that population aggregation and full agricultural commitment (Welch 1991) brought about organizational changes that characterized the Pueblo IV occupation in the region.

ARCHAEOLOGY

Chodistaas Pueblo was first recorded in 1966 and a surface collection was made in 1969 (Tuggle 1970). The initial goal was to examine a preaggregation site in order to understand further the processes of Pueblo IV aggregation in the region (Crown 1981a; Reid 1973). Prior to 1976, systematic excavations in the Grasshopper region were limited to Grasshopper Pueblo (Hough 1935; Longacre and Reid 1974; Thompson and Longacre 1966) and to Canyon Creek Ruin (Haury 1934).

Chodistaas Pueblo was selected for investigating preaggregation processes because its estimated dates of occupation had been placed between A.D. 1100 and 1250 on the basis of surface ceramics (Tuggle 1970). Architecturally, Chodistaas suggested a date late in this period and a complexity more directly antecedent to that at Grasshopper than other, roughly contemporaneous sites in the region (Crown 1981a: 19).

Four phases of field research (1976–1979; 1982–1985; 1988; 1991) included excavation of 17 of 18 masonry rooms at Chodistaas Pueblo and excavation of test units in the plazas and outside the pueblo walls. Excavation of the pueblo rooms revealed the site's unique research potential: 136 tree-ring dates indicated

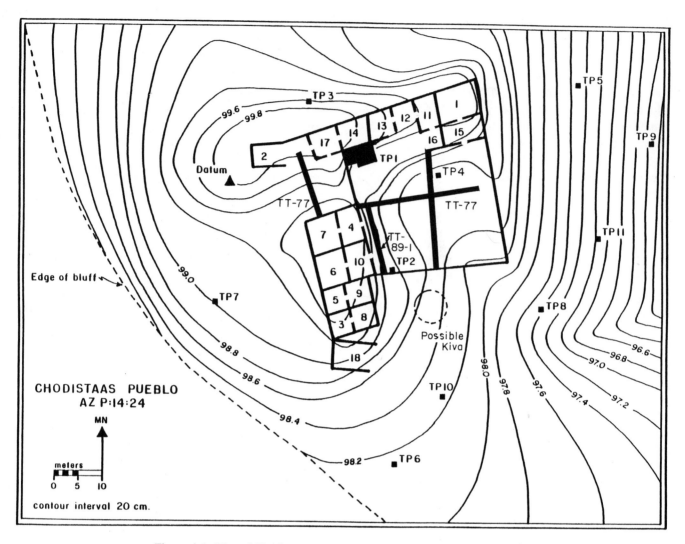

Figure 4.1. Plan of Chodistaas Pueblo, showing excavated rooms, test pits (TP) and test trenches (TT).

that Chodistaas was occupied for no more than 40 years, with less than 30 years of building activity (A.D. 1263 to about 1290). Charred beams and debris covered what has been interpreted as a "complete non-perishable artifact inventory" (Crown 1981a; Montgomery and Reid 1990), which represented both indoor and outdoor activities. The inventory also included small quantities of exotic materials such as obsidian, turquoise, shell, and two Hohokam-like palettes. The end of the occupation at Chodistaas came with a complete burning of the pueblo. This event is estimated to have occurred in the 1290s, on the basis of the latest tree-ring date of A.D. 1288 (noncutting), the absence of fourteenth-century White Mountain Red Ware ceramics on room floors, and the aggregation at nearby Grasshopper Pueblo beginning around A.D. 1300 (Crown 1981a: 31; Montgomery and Reid: 1990: 89). In addition, archaeomagnetic samples from a firepit and jacal wall in Room 2a dated at A.D. 1255 ± 40 and 1265 ± 80, and a firepit

in Room 9 dated at 1240 ± 40 (Crown 1981a: 31). These dates are consistent with the estimated time of abandonment of the pueblo. However, standard deviations of these dates cover the entire occupation of the pueblo and thus cannot be adequately interpreted in the absence of ceramic and tree-ring data.

Excavation Sequence

A detailed description of excavation procedures and results of the first phase of research (1976–1979) has been provided by Crown (1981a). Nine masonry rooms (1, 2, 3, 5, 8, 9, 11, 15, and 16) were excavated during this period in order to define the site occupation span, construction sequence, and residential unit size. In addition, strata below the floors of several rooms were excavated, and sections of Plazas 1 and 2 were trenched in an attempt to obtain information on outdoor activity areas (Fig. 4.1).

[24]

Rooms revealed four geological or cultural strata: (1) surface, consisting of humus and loosely packed material covering the structures; (2) wall fall, a stratum comprised of large masonry rocks, trash, and dirt fill; (3) roof fall, a stratum formed by one or more layers of charred roof beams and daub, the lowest lying directly on the floor; and (4) floor, or occupational surface. Room floors usually did not present any clear change in soil texture, color, or compaction. Therefore, Crown (1981a: 26) defined occupational surfaces or "floors" for each room on the basis of features, flat-lying paving stones, artifacts, and roof beams that lay directly on those surfaces.

After a careful consideration of artifacts in the room assemblages (ceramic vessels, ground stone, polished stone, chipped stone, shell, bone, turquoise, pigments, palette, and other items), floor features (slab-lined hearths, firepits, mealing bins, ventilators, and platforms), and architectural data (masonry types, room sizes, access, and roofing species), Crown divided the rooms into four functional classes: (1) habitation (Rooms 8, 9, 11, and 1), with artifacts and features associated with cooking and heating activities, grinding and food preparation, and perhaps some manufacturing activities; (2) storage (Rooms 3 and 5), which lacked the major features characteristic of habitation rooms but had large quantities of jars compared to the total assemblage of other rooms; (3) community-secular (Rooms 2c and 16 and two three-walled structures opening to Plazas 2 and 1 respectively), with artifactual and architectural evidence to suggest activities associated with food preparation and storage; and (4) community-ceremonial (Rooms 2a, 2b, and 15), with features such as centralized firepits, well-plastered walls and floors, benches, and exotic artifacts. The habitation and storage rooms were further classified into four households: 1, 11, 5 and 9, and 3 and 8 (Crown 1981a: 40–65). In her recent interpretation of Chodistaas floor assemblages and room function, Montgomery (1992) classified Rooms 3, 5, 8, and 9 as storage rooms that likely belonged to two households in the southern room block.

The first phase of research at Chodistaas Pueblo suggested that late Pueblo III period occupations in the Grasshopper region contained information useful for elucidating organizational changes in this area of the mountains at the end of the thirteenth century. In fact, a more complete sample of excavated rooms was necessary in order to contrast household organization at Chodistaas with that at Grasshopper Pueblo, to refine criteria for interpreting room function, and to clarify temporal differences in the composition of ceramic assemblages from Pueblo III and Pueblo IV periods (Ciolek-Torello 1978, 1985). The second phase of field research at Chodistaas (1982–1984) was thus planned to address these problems. This phase included the excavation of five rooms, three in the north room block (Rooms 13, 14, 17; Fig. 4.2) and a pair in the south room block (Rooms 7 and 4; Fig. 4.3). In addition, test pits were excavated along the walls in Plaza 2 to obtain more information about outdoor activities (Montgomery 1992).

Excavation of the southern room block continued in 1988. The third phase of field research focused on the reconstruction of formation processes, which was crucial not only for evaluating the data obtained from previous excavations but also for further understanding the events that took place just prior to the abandonment of Chodistaas. In addition to excavating Rooms 6 and 10, a final exploration of outdoor areas involved the excavation of: (1) 12 test pits located in the surroundings of the site to plot the depth, density, and extension of debris deposition; (2) a 3-m by 7-m test pit in the northwest corner of Plaza 1; and (3) a semicircle of stones that was thought to be part of a ceremonial structure. The excavation of Room 18, a ceremonial structure in the southern room block, was completed in 1991.

Architectural features (bond-abut relationships, access, wall masonry) and tree-ring dates recovered between 1976 and 1991 show that Chodistaas Pueblo was constructed in several episodes of building activity. Crown had already advanced a tentative four-phase construction based on the rooms excavated through 1979 (Crown 1981a: 35–39, Fig. 5). According to a sequence proposed to me in 1991 by Barbara Montgomery, the first episode involved the construction of Rooms 13 (A.D. 1263r) and 12 (unexcavated), which abutted the north wall of Plaza 1. Room 14 (A.D. 1268r) and perhaps Room 17 were added shortly after, and by 1270, Rooms 1 and 11 had been built against the northeast corner of the plaza. Two years later, Rooms 15 and 16 were added to the pueblo, abutting Rooms 11 and 1, respectively. Room 2 (a, b, and c) was probably constructed around 1272; it has dates no later than 1271.

Construction of the southern room block took place between A.D. 1280 and 1286. A single cutting date for Room 7 suggests that this and probably Rooms 4, 6, and 10 were built during 1280. Because Rooms 4 and 10 were not bonded to the west wall of the plaza, the construction sequence of these rooms and the plaza is unclear. Montgomery (1992) provides two alternative sequences: (1) Plaza 1 was expanded by moving the wall farther south in order to include additional rooms, or (2) sections of the west wall of Plaza 1 were broken

Figure 4.2. Field crew excavating Room 13 at Chodistaas Pueblo in 1984.
(Arizona State Museum photograph 65412, University of Arizona.)

when Rooms 4 and 10 were added to the pueblo. Origi-nally, the southern room block may have consisted of two three-walled structures that were further divided into four rooms.

Both alternatives are equally plausible and would explain the absence of a continuous west wall. Both pairs of rooms (4 and 7, 10 and 6) are similar in layout and appear to have been built almost contemporane-ously, even though Rooms 6 and 10 abut onto Rooms 7 and 4 (Montgomery 1992). No cutting dates were obtained from Rooms 6 and 10.

Around A.D. 1285, the southernmost rooms (Rooms 3, 5, 8, and 9) were added to the pueblo. They were built as a single large square abutted to Rooms 6 and 10, and then divided into four rooms (Crown 1981a). Tree-ring dates cluster around A.D. 1285, supporting this sequence. Room 18 (a and b), a three-walled cere-monial structure that, like Room 2, opens to the east, was probably built soon afterward, since its northwest corner rests against the southwest corner of Room 3.

The remarkable difference in spatial arrangement of the north and south room blocks is one characteristic that supports the late construction date for Rooms 4, 7,

6, and 10. These rooms parallel the symmetrical ar-rangement of the southern room block, suggesting that all of them were built under similar architectural, func-tional, or residential criteria. The number and distribu-tion of artifacts and features indicate that Rooms 4 and 10 served similar functions, possibly habitation. This inference is based on the presence of a mealing bin and two slab-lined hearths in each of these structures and on the low number of storage vessels and other artifacts on the floor. Rooms 6 and 7 have a high number of vessels and artifacts that generally indicate storage-manufactur-ing activities (Montgomery 1992, Chapter 7). In con-trast, the rooms in the northern room block were not built in pairs as were those in the southern room block; however, connecting rooms may have had complemen-tary functions.

The pueblo, then, could have been organized in two major residential units, namely, northern and southern room blocks. The fact that each room block had its own ceremonial room (Room 2 in the north and Room 18 in the south) supports this tentative reconstruction of the residential organization at Chodistaas Pueblo. It is unclear how Room 15, identified by Crown (1981a: 61)

Figure 4.3. Room 7 at Chodistaas Pueblo, showing artifacts on Floor 1.
(Arizona State Museum photograph 62618, University of Arizona.)

as a ceremonial activity room, fits into this reconstruction. Two exotic artifacts were on the floor of
Room 15, a Hohokam-like palette and a St. Johns Polychrome bowl, but similar items were also found on the
floors of two storage-manufacturing rooms, 7 and 14,
respectively. The access to the plaza and the bench,
however, confirm the unusual character of Room 15.

Evidence of outdoor activities was recovered from
Test Pit 88–1, located along the south wall of Room 14.
Here, a firepit and a slab-lined hearth were associated
with high concentrations of manufacturing tools (for
example, a shaft straightener), grinding implements,
raw clay, and at least one complete jar. Slab-lined
hearths are usually indoor features, but there is no indication that this area was part of an enclosed structure.
These investigations demonstrated the use of open areas
for a wide range of activities. Unfortunately, no information of similar significance was recorded from previous excavations of Plazas 1 and 2.

A detailed analysis of construction, household organization, and room function at Chodistaas Pueblo is provided by Montgomery (1992). It is important to stress
that there are similarities as well as differences in the
organization of domestic space between Chodistaas and
Grasshopper Pueblo. As Reid (1989: 78) notes, Chodistaas had larger rooms than Grasshopper (29 square
meters versus 16 square meters, on average), the late
rooms at Chodistaas were arranged in complementary
pairs, and room functions (habitation, storage, and manufacturing activities) were less rigidly assigned at Chodistaas. Organizationally, however, the southern rooms,
built after A.D. 1280, resemble Grasshopper Pueblo
households more closely than rooms built during the
first decades of occupation at Chodistaas, suggesting
continuity between both pueblos. Furthermore Room 18
appeared to be a transitional architectural form between
late Pueblo III period ceremonial rooms and the kivas
at Grasshopper Pueblo (Reid and Montgomery 1993).

FORMATION PROCESSES AT
CHODISTAAS PUEBLO

Montgomery's (1992) research at Chodistaas Pueblo
includes detailed observations of the effect that natural
and cultural processes had in the actual deposition of

artifacts on the site surface and in the rooms (Montgomery 1990; Montgomery and Reid 1990). According to Montgomery, two independent surface collections and excavation of 12 test pits provide a well-documented record of distribution, density, and depth of cultural remains that litter the pueblo surroundings. Deposits that contain cultural material are shallow (7 cm to 36 cm); no soil build-up has occurred in areas around the room blocks, because they are located in an erosional setting. High densities of cultural material are found almost exclusively on the eastern slope of the bluff, and artifactual density is low in test pits excavated in areas north, south, and west of the pueblo. There is little evidence of the distorting effects of vegetation, small and large mammals, and insects on the surface materials. Likewise, no vandalism has introduced room fill or burial assemblage sherds on the surface.

Excavation of 17 masonry rooms at Chodistaas has produced 340 complete and partial vessels. The integrity of the ceramic assemblage in these rooms is a good indicator of the minimal effect that environmental processes had in incidence and location of vessels. Even though tree roots have affected pueblo masonry, they have not severely altered the location of the pots (Montgomery and Reid 1990). On the other hand, a number of behavioral processes were responsible for the presence of whole and nearly complete pots in the rooms at Chodistaas Pueblo. The conditions of Chodistaas abandonment and burning argue against curation and scavenging as a significant factor for modifying room ceramic assemblages (Montgomery 1990; Montgomery and Reid 1990). Costly items such as metates and rare items such as Hohokam-like palettes were not removed from the floors. It seems highly probable that the pueblo was occupied until shortly before it burned.

Montgomery and Reid (1990; Montgomery 1990, 1992) observe that the intentional filling-in of rooms with dirt and trash immediately after the burning of the pueblo contributed greatly to preserving room assemblages from postoccupational scavenging. The authors mention three facts that support this inference: (1) above-ground, masonry rooms on a bluff top characterized by erosion were quickly filled; (2) the relatively rapid filling of at least three rooms (10, 14, and 17) is indicated by a brief reoccupation that left two prehistoric hearths and one stone wall above the trash fill level; and (3) sherd density in the room fill is unusually high. Additionally, Lorentzen (1988) estimates that Room 10 was filled immediately after the burning, as suggested by the high number (66 out of 76) of dis-

carded projectile points found in the fill that suffered the discoloration effects produced by exposure to intense heat. The extremely good preservation of charred roof beams definitely indicates that they were covered within a short time and were well protected from the ravages of the environment (Montgomery 1993).

The intentional burial of household belongings at Chodistaas Pueblo was not observed in the rooms excavated at Grasshopper Spring Pueblo, which also have pots left on the floors. Montgomery (1993) reports that this unusual case of abandonment may well be related to the pivotal role of Chodistaas, the only pueblo in the region that has an enclosed plaza, as a focal community in the area. She suggests the initial interpretation that these rooms were intentionally buried as part of ritual activity associated with the burning and abandonment of the pueblo.

The circumstances surrounding the abandonment of Chodistaas Pueblo remain unknown. However, the timing of abandonment, about A.D. 1300, coincides with the founding of Grasshopper Pueblo, which, in turn, seems to have been partially related to population movement onto the Grasshopper Plateau at the end of the thirteenth century (Crown-Robertson 1978; Graves and others 1982; Reid 1989; Whittlesey 1978). Burning and abandonment of small settlements followed by population aggregation at a large pueblo may be signaling some sort of conflict between local settlers and immigrants, an idea that cannot be substantiated at this time.

Thus far, there is insufficient evidence to infer that Chodistaas rooms changed in function, were abandoned early, or were filled with trash before the pueblo burned. Although traces of an earlier Mogollon pit house occupation located under the floors of Rooms 15, 7, and Plaza 2, and of a later (after A.D. 1300) prehistoric occupation on top of the already filled Rooms 10, 14, and 17 were identified, these occupations did not alter room floor assemblages.

To summarize, the site of Chodistaas provides the most complete set of data known for Pueblo III period occupations in the Arizona mountains. The exceptional chronological control of its construction sequence, the wealth of information on room assemblage composition, and the detailed reconstruction of formation processes allow the archaeologist to address a variety of issues, such as room function and household organization, architecture, abandonment processes, and more specific problems regarding artifactual variability. The particular time period during which Chodistaas Pueblo was occupied, and the conditions surrounding its abandonment, underscore the significance of this site for tracing the series of events that occurred just prior to aggregation at Grasshopper Pueblo. The whole-vessel assemblage is one of the most informative aspects of the archaeological record at Chodistaas, and it is described below.

CERAMIC WARES

The ceramic assemblage from Chodistaas Pueblo consists of 340 whole and partial vessels, 115 of which are decorated. Because 10 of those vessels were recovered from the floor of Room 18 after this study was completed (Montgomery 1992), only 330 of the pots are included in this analysis. All but 6 partial vessels came from room contexts at Chodistaas (Appendix A). Portions of five undecorated jars and one decorated bowl were found in association with outdoor activity areas in Plaza 1 (Tp–88–1). Most of the vessels were part of household assemblages probably in use until shortly before the pueblo was abandoned.

When excavated, most large vessels were sitting upright along the walls on the floor of storage and habitation rooms and near room features. The broken pots atop roof beams above the floor surface indicate that they were sitting on the roof when the roofs collapsed during or after the fire (Crown 1981a: 74). Roofs were not used as working or heavy storage surfaces, however, as they were constructed entirely with secondary beams that could not have supported much weight (Montgomery 1992: 214). Vessels outside Room 14 in the northwest corner of Plaza 1 were also associated with features and working implements; because they were incomplete, it is less clear whether or not they may have been discarded vessels. Careful sorting and refitting of fill sherds and broken pots was conducted throughout the field research at Chodistaas Pueblo in order to avoid spurious estimates of vessel completeness (but see Montgomery 1992: 220).

Most rooms included at least one decorated bowl and one decorated jar. Even though the number of vessels and the percentages of decorated and undecorated jars and bowls varied from room to room in relation to function, all wares represented in the pueblo were present in each of the two room blocks, indicating that these wares were *equally* accessible to residents of both the northern and southern room blocks throughout the occupation of the pueblo (Table 4.1). In other words, no temporal differences between the ceramics of each room block were detected.

Crown (1981a) wrote the first complete description of the 197 vessels from 9 rooms excavated from 1976 to 1979. Her classification of decorated vessels followed previously published formal types. Undecorated vessels were given a descriptive label without the geographical component of type names. Although traditional decorated type labels are often useful, I have regrouped the already analyzed vessels into wares. As stated above, ware is a parsimonious and flexible analytic category for partitioning an assemblage into units that facilitate identification of local and nonlocal ceramics. The general description of the Chodistaas Pueblo ceramic assemblage introduced here emphasizes the use of ware rather than type as the unit of classification and analysis.

Decorated Wares

The decorated assemblage at Chodistaas Pueblo is dominated by Cibola White Ware and Roosevelt Red Ware. White Mountain Red Ware and painted corrugated wares are present in small numbers (Table 4.1).

Cibola White Ware

Cibola White Ware is a mineral-painted, generally white-slipped pottery. Vessels are characterized by white to gray paste (Munsell Color 2.5YR 8/0, 7.5YR 8/0) finely tempered with quartz sand and often crushed sherds. Commonly these vessels display smooth, polished and slipped surfaces, and they were fired in a moderately high-temperature, nonoxidizing atmosphere (Colton 1956; Colton and Hargrave 1937; Fowler 1989; Plog 1980).

The design layout of jars and pitchers conforms to Haury's (1931) description of Pinedale Black-on-white: they have two zones of decoration, body and neck, the body decoration consisting of a single broad field defined by two framing lines, one located a few centimeters below the neck and the other near the base, which is always left unpainted. The neck decoration, as described by Colton and Hargrave (1937: 242), usually displays solid stepped elements, triangles, vertical bars or short lines pendant from the rim. The body designs themselves, however, are not "Pinedale" and, therefore, these vessels should not be typed as such (but see Crown 1981a: 67).

Black-on-white bowls in the Chodistaas assemblage do not fit the defined description for Pinedale Black-on-white given by Colton and Hargrave (1937: 242). Only two of ten bowls exhibit the quartered layout often seen in Pinedale Black-on-white bowls (Crown 1981a: 68), and a third one is Snowflake Black-on-white. It is difficult to assign the remaining bowls to a well-defined type. All of them are, nevertheless, Cibola White Ware.

Table 4.1. Decorated Vessels by Room and Ware

Room No.	Cibola White Ware	Roosevelt Red Ware	White Mtn. Red Ware	Painted Corrugated	Total	Percent
1	2			2	4	3.5
2	1	3		1	5	4.4
3	6	3		3	12	10.6
4	2	3		2	7	6.2
5	5	3		2	11	9.8
6	6	5		2	13	11.5
7	4	6	1	1	12	10.6
8	5	7		2	13	11.5
9	7				7	6.2
10						
11	2	3		2	7	6.2
13	2	3		1	6	5.3
14	4	1		2	7	6.2
15	3	2	1		6	5.3
16	2				2	1.8
17						
Tp 1		1			1	0.9
Total	51	40	2	20	113	
Percent	45.1	35.4	1.8	17.7		

Crown (1981a: 298, Fig.14) identified seven design styles for jars, bowls, and pitchers: Red Mesa, Puerco, Roosevelt, Kayenta, Snowflake, Tularosa, and Pinedale.

Roosevelt Red Ware

Bowls of Roosevelt Red Ware are Pinto Black-on-red and Pinto Polychrome, both constructed by the coil-and-scrape technique. Paste is gray-brown to orange (Munsell 10YR 5/1 to 10YR 5/6), tempered with fine water worn sand, crushed white sherds, or both. Pinto Black-on-red has orange to red slip (Munsell 5YR 4/6 to 2.5YR 4/6) on the interior and orange slip on exterior surfaces. Pinto Polychrome has white slip on interior surfaces. Organic substances, or a mixture of organic and black mineral pigments, were used to paint designs in bowl interiors (Colton and Hargrave 1937: 86; Gifford 1957; Gladwin and Gladwin 1930; Lindsay and Jennings 1968; Young 1967). Refiring of sherds from Chodistaas Pueblo vessels indicated the presence of organic pigment with no mineral admixture, according to Patricia Crown in 1990.

Design styles are mostly Pinedale and often show offset quartered layouts or threefold layouts filled with solid and hachured stripes, scrolls, scrolls with scalloped or serrated edges, steps, keys, squares, and triangles (Colton and Hargrave 1937: 86). Uncommon variations seen at Chodistaas and Grasshopper Spring pueblos consist of white or black designs on the exterior

that are similar to St. Johns Polychrome (Mera 1934: 15), and interior black *and* red designs over white slip (Crown 1981a).

White Mountain Red Ware

White Mountain Red Ware is represented in the assemblage by only two St. Johns Polychrome bowls (Carlson 1970, 1982; Gladwin and Gladwin 1931; Graves 1982). Both of them have light buff paste tempered with quartz sand and crushed sherds. Surfaces have a thick layer of orange-red slip unevenly smoothed to lightly polished. Designs are painted with black mineral paint on the interior and white paint on the exterior surfaces.

Painted Corrugated

Vessels that display painted designs over indented-corrugated surfaces were assigned to Salado White-on-red Corrugated, Cibicue Painted Corrugated (a renaming of the corrugated variant of Cibicue Polychrome), and McDonald Painted Corrugated (Crown 1981a: 71). These types share several characteristics. Bowls are made of gray-brown to orange paste (same color range as in Roosevelt Red Ware), tempered with fine to medium quartz sand and sometimes with diabase (a rock of basaltic composition). They have polished and smudged

Table 4.2. Undecorated Vessels by Room and Ware

Room No.	Plain		Corrugated				Total	Percent
	Red	Brown	Brown	Gray-orange	Unidentified	Salado Red		
1			1	1			2	0.9
2	3	1	7	3	2		16	7.4
3	3	2	12	3		2	22	10.1
4			3	3	1	1	8	3.7
5	3	1	12	8	1		25	11.5
6	5	2	8	3	3	2	23	10.5
7	4		4	6	2	2	18	8.3
8	7	1	7	6		3	24	11.1
9	7		2	5	1		15	6.9
10			2	2			4	1.8
11			6	1		1	8	3.7
13	1			3			4	1.8
14	1		5	2	1		9	4.2
15	2	1	2	2		2	9	4.2
16	2	1	5	1			9	4.2
17	2		11	1	1	1	16	7.4
Tp 1		2	2	1			5	2.3
Total	40	11	89	51	12	14	217	
Percent	18.4	5.1	41.0	23.5	5.5	6.5		

interior surfaces and obliterated corrugations with fairly regular indentations. Salado White-on-red Corrugated has exterior raspberry red slip (Munsell 2.5YR 4/4). This type and McDonald Painted Corrugated have exterior designs painted with fugitive white pigment (Colton and Hargrave 1937; Gladwin and Gladwin 1930;). The two Cibicue Painted Corrugated bowls that occur in this assemblage are of the obliterated-corrugated variety (Mauer 1970: 9), with dark red and white fugitive designs on the exterior surface.

Although exterior designs have almost disappeared on most McDonald bowls, when visible they are similar to the white-striped designs displayed on Salado White-on-red Corrugated bowls; however, they do not have the horizontal band just below the rim that is characteristic of McDonald Painted Corrugated. At Chodistaas, Salado White-on-red Corrugated also occurs in jar form, but these vessels are more similar in paste texture to undecorated corrugated jars and bowls than to painted corrugated bowls.

Undecorated Wares

Corrugated and plain wares are the two broad categories of undecorated vessels in the assemblage (Table 4.2), and both are further divided by the presence or absence of red slip.

Crown (1981a) provided a detailed description of brown corrugated vessels, most of which she grouped under brown indented obliterated corrugated, a type "class" of vessels present in mountain sites dated to the thirteenth and fourteenth centuries. Crown did not designate gray corrugated wares as a separate group in the assemblage, but recent work indicates a partition between brown and gray corrugated pottery is useful.

Brown Corrugated

These indented obliterated corrugated vessels are commonly characterized by a brown-red paste (Munsell 5YR 4/3, 4/4, 4/6) of medium or coarse texture with abundant temper that often includes particles of diabase and muscovite, with wide coils and indentations. The exterior surfaces exhibit varying degrees of obliteration of the coils and indentations caused by wiping (Crown 1981a: 71). A few vessels were classified into different descriptive types according to variations of surface manipulation, although they are generally similar to brown indented obliterated corrugated (Crown 1981a: 73).

Gray-orange Corrugated

The gray corrugated vessels (also called gray-orange to distinguish them from "plateau" Cibola Gray Ware) are also indented obliterated, but differ from brown corrugated vessels in a number of attributes. They have gray-to-reddish yellow paste (Munsell 7.5YR 5/0 to 7.5YR 6/6) tempered with medium to coarse quartz sand or weathered quartzite, usually thin walls, narrow coils and small, slightly obliterated indentations.

Unidentified Corrugated

Several vessels were not visually classified as either brown or gray corrugated; they had dark brown paste and unidentified temper. Refiring of sherds from these corrugated vessels was useful for refining this initial classification.

Salado Red Corrugated

These indented obliterated corrugated vessels have raspberry red slip (Munsell 2.5YR 4/4) on the exterior surface (Colton and Hargrave 1937; Gladwin and Gladwin 1930; Lindsay and Jennings 1968). The type is represented in bowls and jars whose interior surfaces are often smudged and slightly polished. Variations of interior surface treatment include smoothing in jars and raspberry slip in bowls. Overall, jars and large bowls of this type are similar to brown corrugated wares in all technological attributes but red slip. Small bowls, however, resemble the paste texture and color, vessel shape, and size of corrugation present in McDonald Painted Corrugated and Salado White-on-red Corrugated bowls.

Plain Wares

At Chodistaas Pueblo plain wares include mainly red-slipped and polished vessels. Brown, unslipped plain wares are rare and mostly limited to miniature vessels. Red plain ware jars and bowls are made of a coarse brown to red paste (same color range as in brown corrugated), generally tempered with coarse quartz sand, rarely with diabase. Vessel wall thickness varies but it is usually thinner than in brown corrugated vessels; walls have paddle and anvil marks. Exterior surfaces of jars and bowls are slipped and have polishing striations. Interior surfaces are smudged, although variations, including smoothing in jars and red slip in bowls, are also present. Jars occasionally have long necks with small apertures and sharp-angled shoulders; ellipsoidal vessels also occur at the site.

WARES AND CERAMIC TRADITIONS

The wares I outlined above have been commonly associated with distinct ceramic traditions of prehistoric groups in the Southwest. Gray Corrugated Ware, Cibola White Ware and White Mountain Red Ware are recognized as diagnostic of groups who inhabited eastern Arizona and western New Mexico to the north of the Mogollon Rim (Cibola White Ware Conference 1958; Carlson 1970, 1982; Crown 1981b; Graves 1982; Rugge and Doyel 1981; Sullivan and Hantman 1984). Roosevelt Red Ware and Salado Red Corrugated are thought to characterize assemblages of the loosely defined Salado groups who presumably inhabited east-central and central Arizona (Doyel and Haury 1976; Gladwin and Gladwin 1934; Wood and McAllister 1982). Brown Corrugated, Gray-orange Corrugated, Red Plain, and Painted Corrugated vessels belong to what are considered long-standing ceramic traditions in the Arizona mountains and other areas occupied by Mogollon groups (Reed 1942; Haury 1945).

That all of these ceramic traditions are represented in the assemblage of a small pueblo situated in an isolated backwoods area raises questions as to whether these traditions belong to distinct groups each manufacturing their own characteristic ceramics and circulating them among other communities, including Chodistaas Pueblo, or each producing technologically and stylistically diverse ceramics. These questions are of crucial importance to Southwestern archaeologists because they address deeply rooted concepts of ethnic-cultural affiliation of prehistoric groups that are based to a large extent on ceramic variation. It is most probable, however, that ceramic variability at Chodistaas Pueblo was generated not by a single behavior but by a combination of different behaviors, such as local manufacture of "indigenous" pottery, circulation of ceramics by different mechanisms, and local manufacture of "foreign" pottery using technological criteria learned through coresidence with immigrants bearing a ceramic tradition different from the indigenous one (Shepard 1985: 339).

The extent to which archaeological correlates of distinct pottery-producing and pottery-circulating behaviors can be isolated in the ceramic record is partially a function of the actual characteristics of a particular assemblage, the degree of temporal and contextual controls that can be achieved over the assemblage, and the specific methodology used for isolating the correlates. Although much of past behavior involved in the generation of highly varied ceramic assemblages will remain beyond the reach of archaeological inquiry, an attempt can be made to refine inferences of pottery manufacture and circulation at Chodistaas Pueblo through the identification of local and nonlocal ceramics.

CHAPTER FIVE

Ceramic Design Style and Technology
Methods of Analysis

The analyses of technology and design style provide two complementary lines of evidence for the identification of local and nonlocal ceramics, because both dimensions may vary independently and may be transmitted at different rates and through different information channels. Although design style information can be transferred from any design-bearing item to pottery by visual inspection, the transmission of technological knowledge involves a "teaching framework" (Schiffer and Skibo 1987: 597). Hence, the recovery of archaeological evidence of technology transfer often implies direct contact with the product and its producer, whereas evidence for the transfer of stylistic information does not.

The degree to which raw material selection is affected by technical and stylistic behaviors involved in pottery manufacture varies from one social context to another (Arnold 1981; Bishop and others 1988). Therefore, it is essential that the degree of covariation between technology, design style, and paste composition of archaeological ceramics be determined to further understand those behaviors.

The following paragraphs briefly summarize current perspectives on the analyses of technology and design style of Southwestern ceramics and describe the approach taken for selecting and recording technological and stylistic attributes of the vessels from Chodistaas Pueblo. The procedure for identifying attributes diagnostic of ceramic manufacturing loci is then presented.

DESIGN STYLE AND SOUTHWESTERN CERAMICS

By "design styles" I refer strictly to painted patterns on ceramic vessels that occur repeatedly in time, space, or both. The analysis of design styles has a long history in the American Southwest. Several classic reports contain detailed descriptions of design layouts. In 1929, Bunzel discussed the ceramic decorative style of four contemporary pueblos (Zuni, Hopi, Acoma, and San Ildefonso) in terms of layout arrangement. Amsden (1936) attempted to characterize the design variability

of Hohokam vessels, and Kidder (1936) was interested in the evolution of Pecos pottery designs through time. Similar layout analyses were completed by Morris (1939) on La Plata ceramics; by Beals, Brainerd, and Smith (1945) on pottery from northeastern Arizona; by Brew (1946) on material from Alkali Ridge; and by Smith (1971) on ceramics from the Western Mound of Awatovi.

It was Amsden (1936) who first introduced the traditional "layout-and-filler" hierarchical approach for characterizing design configurations on Hohokam vessels, and he thought that this approach could be used to compare ceramics from different cultures (Jernigan 1986: 5). Colton and Hargrave (1937) elaborated on the notion of hierarchical levels of design, but used elements and motifs arranged in patterned ways instead of layout and fillers as did Amsden. Their method of characterizing design styles was practical in the sense that it was conceived for classifying thousands of sherds where layout would not be observable. Colton and Hargrave (1937: 17) considered that design styles were important time correlation criteria, and that they could be used "in a manner similar to the use of index fossils in paleontology." They named formal styles only after a particular style was observed on more than one type and claimed that the widespread distribution of stylistic trends in the Southwest was the product of "acculturation," that is, "the acceptance of ideas by one group of people from people of a different line" (Colton and Hargrave 1937: 14). Thus, grouping types by design style could lead to understanding the patterns of diffusion of ideas. Formal styles defined by particular combinations of elements and motifs, such as Lino, Walnut, or Sosi, were, therefore, treated independently of type series. This way of defining formal styles became established in the Southwest, and archaeologists continue to define and use styles to characterize ceramic traditions, as did Carlson (1970) in his study of White Mountain Red Ware.

During the 1960s, the focus on design style shifted from spatial-temporal frameworks to social interpretations of ceramic design variation. A number of studies sought to isolate spatial clusters of design attributes, at the intrasettlement, intersettlement, and interregional levels, that could have been the result of residence groups, lineages, marriage networks, or clusters of communities cooperating in economic, social, and political activities (Cronin 1962; Hill 1965, 1970; Kintigh 1985; Leone 1968; Longacre 1964, 1970; S. Plog 1978, 1980; Tuggle 1970; Washburn 1977, 1978; Zaslow 1977; Zaslow and Dittert 1977, among others).

Working under the assumption that the archaeological distributions of designs directly corresponded to the social units who made and used decorated pots, many researchers (Hill 1970; Longacre 1970; Tuggle 1970) adopted the "design element" approach in an attempt to isolate the individual elements of pottery design and explain their spatial occurrence in terms of degree of interaction, or group membership. The "design element" approach consisted of recording all the design elements appearing on the pottery under study, calculating the frequency of occurrence of each element in the pottery assemblage associated with each group or subgroup, and comparing frequencies directly or statistically (Rice 1987: 253). This approach has been criticized from a variety of perspectives, but most often for its lack of replicability and lack of equivalency between units of analysis or elements (S. Plog 1983: 129; Tuggle 1970; Washburn and Ahlstrom 1982; Watson 1977).

Washburn (1977, 1978), Zaslow (1977), and Dittert (Zaslow and Dittert 1977) used symmetry analysis as an alternative to the design element approach to test the social interaction theory. This type of analysis was first advocated by Shepard (1956). It involved defining a basic or fundamental part of the design (element or motif) that is repeated at regular intervals and recording the motions by which this part is repeated or the transformation by which it is moved and superimposed upon itself around a real or imaginary point or line to form the design (Rice 1987: 261). The four types of symmetry so defined, translation, reflection, rotation, and slide reflection, were considered by Washburn (1978) universals, in that all patterns are reducible to these categories and thus could be replicated in any study.

Stephen Plog (1978, 1980, 1983) and Redman (1977, 1978) utilized a hierarchical method for analyzing designs. Using many ideas from Friedrich's (1970) stylistic analysis of Tarascan pottery, these researchers discriminated between primary and secondary units or elements: primary units occurred in isolation or in combination with other units, whereas secondary units occurred only in combination with other units (S. Plog 1980: 49). Redman (1978) used this approach for testing the social interaction hypothesis. Stephen Plog

(1980) was concerned with the use of ceramic designs to signal or communicate information and to demarcate social distance among prehistoric groups (Braun and S. Plog 1982; Hantman and S. Plog 1982), and he was the first to test systematically the relationship between ceramic design variation and manufacturing loci. He concluded that many of the design distributions observed in the archaeological record were the result of ceramic exchange.

More recently, Jernigan (1982, 1986) used formal styles of White Mound, Kiatuthlanna, and Red Mesa black-on-whites to review the hierarchical approach to stylistic analysis. He contended that the segmentation of designs into hierarchical units, such as motif, element, and layout, presents a methodological problem in the American Southwest in which the need to encompass the observed variability causes the proliferation of stylistic units and complicates any analysis. Jernigan's alternative method involves identifying design units at a single level, that is, configuration or *schema*, and looking at how these units are used in a corpus of designs executed in a single style. He defines *schema* as "a configuration or pattern of configurations for which there is evidence that the configuration or pattern was conceived as a distinct unit by the makers of the style" (Jernigan 1986: 9). A *schema* can be defined by the manner in which it is used across a number of vessels or design contexts. In Wasley's words (1959: 234, as quoted by Jernigan 1986), such a stylistic unit may be an element, a motif, or a combination thereof that is complete in itself and can be used to create a whole design by simply repeating that unit without adding anything new (DeGarmo 1975 discusses a similar concept of stylistic units).

Jernigan's nonhierarchical model has been criticized by Douglass and Lindauer (1988), in particular because he considers his units as "emic," or the ones that best reflect the original concept of the makers of the style, and because of the ambiguous terms in which he defines configurations or *schemata*. One problem regarding his ambiguity in defining configurations is that a large number of vessels of a single style is needed to provide unequivocal evidence for the repeated use of a configuration in that style. The full range of variation in the symmetry of a configuration, or in the relationship between configurations, cannot be observed in a single assemblage. However, the concept of a stylistic unit, configuration, or *schema* that is complete within itself may be flexible enough to allow one to extract the most distinctive features of a corpus of designs in a given assemblage by simple observation.

Design Style Variation and the Circulation of Ceramics

The methodological perspectives on the analysis and interpretation of design variation summarized above have been the subject of much criticism (Allen and Richardson 1971; Crown 1981a; S. Plog 1976, 1978, 1980; Skibo, Schiffer and Kowalski 1989). Perhaps the most fundamental flaws of these studies were to assume uncritically that archaeological distributions of ceramic designs directly corresponded to the people or social units who made and used them and that styles were transmitted through direct learning channels.

In the context of prehistoric Southwestern ceramics, there are two related processes that must be considered when interpreting the distribution patterns of designs: circulation of ceramics and transfer of stylistic information. On the one hand, decorated ceramics were widely moved over long distances in different time periods. The movement of pots and other decorated items facilitated the diffusion of designs that were readily transferred to the local decorated wares. On the other hand, throughout prehistory people moved across the Southwest; ethnic coresidence likely fostered direct interaction between local and immigrant potters and stimulated the adoption of new criteria for decorating pots. These two mechanisms of ceramics circulation, movement of pots and movement of people, had a pervasive effect in the transfer of stylistic information in the prehistoric Southwest, obscuring the relationships between the distributions of design variation in prehistory and the context of ceramic manufacture.

From this perspective, it seems improbable that the actual distribution patterns of ceramic designs would provide significant information for making inferences about interaction, group membership, or social distance without prior indication of where the decorated pots were produced. Furthermore, if one considers that potters in the Southwest readily incorporated design information from "foreign" pots and other decorated items into their own repertoire, then one could ask whether designs had indeed the functions (identity, membership, social distance, to name a few) that archaeologists are willing to assign to them. To date, for example, no one has demonstrated adequately that vessels with certain designs cluster nonrandomly within areas of a site or that designs on vessels within a site are more similar than designs on vessels at sites less than 50 km to 80 km (30 to 50 miles) apart (S. Plog 1980: 124).

Only recently have Southwestern archaeologists attempted to determine whether the decorated ceramics under study were locally made in the first place (Crown 1994; Deutchman 1980; Douglass 1987; Neitzel and Bishop 1990; S. Plog 1980; Triadan 1994; Tuggle and others 1982; Whittlesey and others 1992; Zedeño 1992). Lack of information on the relationships between ceramic design variation and the context of manufacture prevents archaeologists from using such variation to further understand the archaeological record. One starting point for gaining insights to those relationships is to determine the extent of design variability generated by a single manufacturing source and the existence of covariation between design styles and sources.

Most of the recent studies oriented toward the reconstruction of exchange systems of decorated ceramics encompass design style distributions over broad regions. These studies attempt to determine whether formal design styles cluster nonrandomly as a result of ceramic exchange by observing the degree of covariation between styles and paste composition. Deutchman (1980) used this approach to investigate the exchange of Tusayan White Ware bowls and jars of Sosi and Dogoszhi styles between several sites on Black Mesa. Douglass (1987), in her reconstruction of the production and distribution system of Little Colorado White Ware, used six design styles (Black Mesa, Sosi, Flagstaff, Walnut, Padre, and Leupp) to test whether the distribution of these styles throughout the Little Colorado River drainage corresponded to specific exchange spheres. Regional studies provide a broad perspective on the relationships between ceramic design variation observed in the archaeological record and manufacturing loci. However, because of their scope, these studies are often restricted to the analysis of sherd samples from surface collections and limited excavations, where contextual and temporal associations may be difficult to determine.

Assemblages such as the one recovered at Chodistaas Pueblo offer the opportunity to observe design variation from a narrower but better controlled perspective than do assemblages from regional studies: that is, to observe the amount of variability in a settlement occupied for a short period of time and to determine the extent of variability generated by a single manufacturing source. Analysis of designs on whole vessels gives a more accurate idea of the range of variation in a formal style than does analysis of large sherd collections. Eight design styles (Red Mesa, Puerco, Roosevelt, Kayenta, Snowflake, Tularosa, Pinedale, and Cibicue) were identified at Chodistaas (Crown 1981a). Seven of these styles appear in Cibola White Ware vessels, for which complete data on chemical composition are available. Thus, it is possible to determine how many of these styles were produced from a single compositional source and whether or not they can be used to discriminate between manufacturing sources. The one exception is the Kayenta-Tusayan style. This style, and its corresponding type, was defined originally for Tusayan White Ware (Beals and others 1945), and it has no typological equivalent in the Cibola series. Generally, Cibola White Ware sherds decorated in this style are included within Pinedale Black-on-white.

Analysis of Design Styles at Chodistaas Pueblo

Crown (1981a) conducted a complete element-motif-layout and symmetry analysis of decorated vessels from nine rooms at Chodistaas Pueblo. Her goal was not to test any set explanatory models of ceramic design variation, but rather to document the amount of variation as completely as possible and to search for patterns in that variability (Crown 1981a: 216). Moving from the least to the most comprehensive analytical units, Crown defined elements, elaborations, motifs, fillers, and layouts and calculated the frequencies of each of these units by type, form, and room. Furthermore, she recorded types of symmetry, dimensional categories, counterchange, and focus of decoration and measured continuous variables such as design width, distance from the rim, and width of framing bands. Crown identified formal design styles based on available style descriptions and calculated the frequencies of each style by ceramic type and by room. Unfortunately, the inconclusive results of the petrographic analysis prevented Crown (1981a: 161) from testing whether the high variability present in the designs of Chodistaas vessels was, in part, a result of ceramics circulation. Thus, her conclusions regarding the nature of ceramic design variation at the site were based on the tentative assumption that the vessels were locally manufactured (Crown 1981a: 307).

Now that the number of decorated vessels recovered from the site has increased to 113, and that information on paste composition (INAA) is available for most of them, it is possible to reevaluate the relationship between design variation and sources of manufacture. To complete this reevaluation, I considered known, formal design styles as units of analysis, which in turn were recorded by ware. Using ware as the discriminating category facilitated the observation of correlations between styles and form, because the majority of decorated jars are Cibola White Ware and almost all decorated bowls are Roosevelt Red Ware.

Formal design styles provide combinations of elements and motifs that have been identified previously and that are known to recur in time and space. In contrast, recording elements and motifs as independent units of a design may mask variation associated with manufacturing loci, because those units occur independently across design styles from different archaeological areas. Colton and Hargrave (1937: 18) observed that elements and motifs were repeatedly used and recombined in different prehistoric ceramic traditions throughout the Southwest, and that potters were conservative when adding new motifs and patterns to their repertoire. Conversely, as Colton and Hargrave pointed out, the combining of elements, motifs, and patterns into a complete design varies to a considerable degree; this variation is quite remarkable in whole vessel assemblages such as the one at Chodistaas Pueblo. Recording formal style on whole vessels, therefore, allows us to understand the "grammar" of a design: as words acquire specific meaning only when they are integrated in a complete sentence, so do stylistic units express some cultural value when observed in relationship to one another and to the whole design.

The analysis concentrated on Cibola White Ware designs, because they display the highest amount of variability. General comparisons between Cibola and other decorated wares were also investigated. The following procedures were used to test the degree of covariation between design styles and paste composition, and the results of this analysis are presented in Chapter 8.

1. The formal design style classification initiated by Crown (1981a) was completed with the addition of vessels recovered after 1979.

2. The formal design styles recorded were partitioned according to paste composition groups.

3. By looking at a number of vessels decorated in different styles, such as the Cibola black-on-white vessels from Chodistaas Pueblo, I was able to identify stylistic units (following Wasley 1959: 234), such as interlocked rectangular scrolls, that crosscut formal styles and that were used alone or in combination with other units. Presence or absence of such stylistic units within a style and across styles, as well as the relationship between such units and the whole design (focus vs. filler) was recorded. Presence or absence of those stylistic units within a given compositional group was also recorded to determine whether there was a relationship between stylistic units and analytical sources.

CERAMIC TECHNOLOGY IN THE AMERICAN SOUTHWEST

Ceramic technology refers to the body of knowledge about materials and practices to manipulate them that prehistoric potters used to manufacture vessels with specific physical properties and aesthetic effects (after De Atley 1991). Technological practices include selection of particular raw material sources, paste preparation, and forming, finishing, and firing of vessels. Raw material selection and paste preparation are generally dependent on the availability, variability, and quality of raw material sources. In addition, technical choices may be affected by social and cultural constraints and by functional considerations such as the performance characteristics needed for specific vessels. Thus, whereas raw material selection and paste preparation involve a potter's choice, raw material composition (chemical and mineralogical) is geographically and geologically determined and, thus, it constitutes a dimension of variation independent of ceramic technology.

The interest in ceramic technology in the American Southwest is rooted in early ethnographic studies that sought to classify ethnic groups in evolutionary stages according to their technological advancements (Bernard and Pelto 1987; De Atley 1991). Detailed descriptions of the process of ceramic manufacture included Fewkes' (1898) account of Hopi pottery and Stevenson's (1904) study of Zuni pottery. Even though Holmes recognized the paramount importance of chronological issues at the turn of the century, in practice his accounts of prehistoric Southwestern ceramics were largely geographic (Dunnell 1986: 162). His gross division of wares (coil-made or corrugated, painted, plain, and white) was based on surface treatment and became the foundation of later classificatory efforts. Cushing (1886) combined ethnographic and linguistic accounts of ceramic manufacture with archaeological information in an attempt to understand the evolution of pottery manufacture in the Southwest. Although early studies were limited to observations on the different stages of the process of pottery manufacture, an occasional study of a more technical nature appeared, such as Nordenskiöld's (1893) analysis of raw materials and pottery mineralogy.

Later ethnographic accounts of pottery manufacture, such as Mary Colton's (1931) and Gifford's (1928) descriptions of Hopi pottery, Chapman's (1936) study of Santo Domingo pottery, Guthe's (1925) study of San Ildefonso pottery, Roger's (1936) account of Yuman pottery, and Shepard's (1936) observations on pueblo pottery manufacture, were strongly oriented toward tracing historical trajectories of the pottery craft in the Southwest. By this time, the link between ceramic technology and ethnicity suggested in earlier studies had been established as a primary methodological tool for identifying prehistoric cultures.

Colton (1939, 1941a, 1953; Colton and Hargrave 1937) thought that the basic techniques of pottery manufacture were transmitted from mother to daughter in a manner analogous to a "biological line" (Colton and Hargrave 1937: 14) and were unchanged over long periods of time. Thus, technological aspects of a ceramic ware were important in archaeological synthesis because they contained information about the cultural affiliation of the potters. As a result, Colton focused his methodological efforts on developing practical guidelines to identify and describe technological variability observed in large sherd collections and to formalize typological descriptions. Most of his suggestions for recording temper, hardness, texture, color, forming, surface treatment, paint, and firing could be carried out directly in the field or with the aid of relatively simple laboratory equipment (Colton 1953). In addition, Colton (1939) performed several experiments to replicate firing techniques associated with the Anasazi on the Colorado Plateau.

Hawley (1929, 1930, 1938) performed several chemical analyses of black paints used on white wares. She suggested that spatial distributions of paint types were "valuable to the study of culture areas and influences" (Hawley 1929: 732) and were useful for tracing population movements as well (Hawley 1929: 749). She also conducted a chemical examination of prehistoric smudged wares, which were considered part of the Mogollon ceramic tradition. A 1932 study by Haury of the technology, chronology, and distribution of lead glaze painted pottery in the Southwest suggested contacts among widespread groups in Arizona and New Mexico. Roberts (1937) recorded the occurrence of pottery manufactured with paddle-and-anvil along the Gila River Basin and used this information to delimit the boundaries of the Hohokam culture.

Shepard's (1936, 1942, 1956) approach to the study of ceramic technology had a strong foundation in geology, and, in contrast to Colton's, it required knowledge of specialized techniques such as petrography. Less concerned with chronology building than her contemporaries, Shepard concentrated on the identification of ceramic materials and the locations of their sources and on indications of workmanship. Her aim was: "To trace the [technological] history of the potter's craft and to recover more accurately and in greater detail than is possible by other methods the evidence which pottery preserves of cultural development, contacts, and influences" (Shepard 1936: 389).

Accordingly, Shepard observed in great detail the physical and mineralogical properties of ceramic pastes, as well as the evidence of forming techniques, surface treatment, painting, and firing. Her major contributions to the technological study of Southwestern ceramics include the study of pottery from Cameron Creek Village (in Bradfield 1931), Pecos Pueblo (Shepard 1936, 1942), La Plata (in Morris 1939), Chaco Canyon (in Judd 1954), Petrified Forest National Monument (in Wendorf 1953), and the Western Mound of Awatovi (in Smith 1971).

In spite of Shepard's valuable insights into ceramic technology and provenience, the majority of ceramic reports written during the next twenty years limited technological observations to general descriptions of wares and types (Beals and others 1945; Colton 1955; Dittert 1959; Haury 1940; Martin 1943; Martin and Rinaldo 1940, 1950; Martin and others 1949; Rinaldo and Bluhm 1956; Wasley 1952). Martin, Rinaldo and Longacre's (1961) report of archaeological investigations at Mineral Creek Site and Hooper Ranch Pueblo constitutes perhaps one of the few exceptions, because it included detailed information on ceramic technology and provenience.

Most efforts that included a description of ceramic technology were directed toward systematizing the Southwestern typological system of ceramic classification (Wheat, Gifford, and Wasley 1958), as was evident in regional ceramic conferences such as those organized by Colton at the Museum of Northern Arizona (Colton 1955, 1956) and the Cibola White Ware Conference (1958). These ceramic conferences emphasized pottery types as defined by design and technology, as technology was then conceived; all archaeologists were expected to have a general background knowledge in geology, and all of them carried a hand lens to observe ceramic paste. More recently, revisions of the traditional typological system have involved reevaluations and syntheses of the results of descriptive studies generated by culture historians (Schroeder 1982) and refinements of regional typologies in light of new information on ceramic provenience (Fowler 1989; Sullivan and Hantman 1984).

The late 1950s approach was followed by the New Archaeology emphasis on functional variability. During the 1960s and 1970s, ceramic studies involving technological observations were oriented toward the inference of vessel function, and thus they emphasized vessel morphology, performance characteristics, and use-wear (Braun 1983; De Atley 1973; Ericson and De Atley 1976; Ericson and others 1971; Matson 1965). This kind of research was considered important for reconstructing room function, activity areas, and household organization (Ciolek-Torello 1978; DeGarmo 1975; Hill 1968; Rohn 1971; Turner and Lofgren 1966). Vessel morphology and derived function appeared useful for assigning site function as well (F. Plog and others 1976; S. Plog 1980; Reid and Whittlesey 1982; Stafford and Rice 1980).

Those interested in the organization of ceramic production explored variability in technical standardization (Feinman and others 1981; Graves 1982; Hagstrum 1985; Hantman and others 1979). Although ceramic provenience was not an issue of great concern during this time, a few significant studies used technological attributes and sourcing techniques to address circulation of ceramics. For example, Warren (1967) and Windes (1977) conducted extensive petrographic analyses of ceramics from Chaco Canyon. Whittlesey (1974) measured proportions of decorated bowls from Grasshopper Pueblo and identified nestability in bowls that could have been manufactured for exchange. Subsequent studies in ceramic functional attributes (Neupert 1994; Skibo and Schiffer 1987; Skibo, Schiffer, and Reid 1989; Young and Stone 1990) and technical standardization of production (Bronitsky 1986) involved experimental testing of performance characteristics.

Recently, a strong emphasis on reconstructing ceramic production and distribution and sociopolitical organization at the interregional level has stimulated research in ceramic technology, in particular the selection and processing of raw materials. Such studies have been applied to Hopi Yellow Ware (Bishop and others 1988), Roosevelt Red Ware (Crown 1990, 1994; Crown and Bishop 1987), White Mountain Red Ware (Triadan 1994); Tusayan White Ware (Deutchman 1980; Neitzel and Bishop 1990), Cibola White Ware (S. Plog 1980; Toll and others 1980; Windes 1984; Zedeño and others 1993), Little Colorado White Ware (Douglass 1987; S. Plog 1980; Zedeño and others 1993), and Hohokam wares (Abbot 1993; P. Fish and others 1992; Heidke and Stark 1994).

Current information on ceramic provenience has been generated primarily in large contract projects throughout the Southwest. Much of the research by Arizona State Museum personnel involved technological and provenience analyses, as for example in the Dead Valley, Springerville area (Doyel 1980; Rugge and Doyel 1980) and in the St. Johns area (Crown 1981b).

The Cholla Project included trace-element analysis by neutron activation of white and corrugated wares (Tuggle and others 1982). The Salt-Gila Aqueduct Project (Teague and Crown 1983) conducted an extensive analysis of regional variation in the manufacture of Hohokam ceramics that involved raw material identification (X-ray fluorescence, petrography), refiring experiments, and recording of variation in form and surface treatment. Archaeological research at Las Colinas included X-ray fluorescence and petrography of Hohokam ceramics (Crown and others 1988). The San Javier Bridge Site project in the Tucson Basin (Ravesloot 1987) included technological, petrographic, and neutron activation analyses.

The Institute for American Research (now the Center for Desert Archaeology) incorporated geological reconnaissance, X-ray fluorescence, and petrography in the analysis of Hohokam ceramics from Tanque Verde Wash (Heidke 1986a), West Branch Site (Crown and others 1986; Lombard 1986), and the Valencia site (Lombard 1985). Other aspects of ceramic technology such as surface treatment, paint, and morphology were also recorded in an attempt to refine the regional chronology (Heidke 1986a, 1986b) and to identify functional differences between pottery types (Abbott 1988; Heidke 1986a; Wallace 1986). Investigations in the Dolores area, southwestern Colorado (Blinman and Wilson 1988; Wilson and Blinman 1988; Wilson and others 1988), in the Snowflake–Mesa Redonda area, northeastern Arizona (Neily 1988), and along the San Juan Basin and Transwestern (northern Arizona) pipeline corridors (Zedeño and others 1993) involved technological and compositional analyses of ceramics and clays.

Technology Transfer and the Circulation of Ceramics

Ceramic sourcing is undoubtedly the primary technique for determining ceramic manufacturing loci. Frequently, however, it presents problems of sample size, of resolution of the particular method used in sourcing, or of geological homogeneity in the area where the ceramics were presumably manufactured (Bishop, Rands, and Holley 1982). These limitations may decrease the archaeologist's ability to interpret compositional data in isolation from other aspects of ceramic variation.

The increasingly strong reliance on mineralogical and chemical analyses to identify local and nonlocal ceramics in the American Southwest has obscured the impor-

tance of ceramic technology as an integrated body of information about the people who made the pots. Traditionally Southwestern archaeologists have recognized that the transfer of technological knowledge most likely occurred through direct contact among potters. It is likely that the sequence of behaviors that resulted from specific technical and cultural choices was not learned visually, but through the development of manipulative practice and the formation of motor habits within a receptive social and cultural context. Therefore, there are technological aspects of ceramic manufacture that are particular to a group of people, which, if identified archaeologically, serve to distinguish local and nonlocal ceramics.

An example of the complex nature of technology transfer is the evolution of Mimbres Black-on-white pottery. LeBlanc (1982; Gilman in Leblanc and Whalen 1980) evaluated technological variables involved in the manufacture of white wares to make a strong case against an Anasazi intrusion in the Mimbres area. LeBlanc (1982: 112) pointed out that, although it is not clear how Mimbres Black-on-white was produced, the extreme variation in firing conditions observed in this ware suggested that Mimbres potters never had complete command of a reducing atmosphere. Rather than being the product of an intrusive new technology, Mimbres Black-on-white was a local attempt at copying the color scheme of the Anasazi area. One needs only to look at photographs of Classic Mimbres bowls to realize that defects due to firing accidents were common, not uncommon, and that those bowls did not "fit" the standards of Anasazi firing technology.

In the American Southwest, frequent mobility of small communities may have restricted the transfer of technological knowledge to those potters who were able to maintain direct interaction on a relatively regular basis. Sharing of information on ceramic technology was probably limited to closely related communities, both geographically and socially. The prevalence of a pattern of restricted technology transfer likely had a major bearing in the development of localized technological traditions, even after communities became increasingly sedentary. For example, knowledge of particular clay sources for the manufacture of Jeddito Yellow Ware on the Hopi Mesas was apparently restricted to residential groups (Bishop and others 1988: 332). However, the rapid adoption of specific technological criteria, such as those of the widely manufactured Gila Polychrome, seems to have been the direct result of migration and subsequent ethnic coresidence (Crown 1994; Reid 1989). Instances of small-scale migration may also be inferred by observing technological variables. Wilson (1988) was able to detect a case of individual or small group migration from the Mogollon mountains to the Dolores area during the Basketmaker III to Pueblo I period. This instance was suggested by the presence of Mogollon smudged pottery associated with a small number of local smudged vessels.

These examples show instances in which the wealth of information conveyed in ceramic technology may be useful to (1) isolate the behaviors involved in the selection and manipulation of raw materials as well as in the forming, finishing, and firing of vessels, (2) determine whether particular behavioral choices are a product of localized technological traditions, and (3) infer face-to-face interaction among peoples of different ethnic or cultural backgrounds. There are three distinct ceramic traditions represented in the Chodistaas Pueblo wares (Chapter 4), and through the analysis of the manufacturing technology associated with each tradition, it is possible to evaluate the validity of associating particular wares with localized ceramic traditions.

Technological Analysis of Vessels from Chodistaas Pueblo

Crown (1981a) described in detail the variation in manufacturing technology of whole and partial vessels from Chodistaas Pueblo to determine how they were made and where they were manufactured (Crown 1981a: 121). She recorded construction techniques, wall thickness, surface treatment and finish, and compared their frequencies by pottery type, room, and vessel form. In addition, she recorded "stylistic" aspects of corrugated vessels (number and direction of indentations, and number and direction of corrugations), and compared their frequencies by pottery type. Refiring of sherds facilitated the identification of paints, slips, and clay types used in the manufacture of the vessels. Her analysis included vessel morphology and function.

I reexamined both manufacturing technology and paste composition of the Chodistaas Pueblo vessels to obtain more information on production loci. The macroscopic attributes recorded for each vessel follow the standard steps of the manufacturing process: raw material selection (paste and pigments), construction techniques, surface treatment and finishing, and firing techniques. I was particularly interested in contrasting attributes commonly thought to be diagnostic of specific ceramic traditions against information on paste composition.

Raw Materials

Temper and pigments generally have been considered characteristic of localized ceramic traditions and thus have been used as primary criteria for defining wares (for example, Colton and Hargrave 1937; Hawley 1929, 1938; S. Plog 1980; Rugge and Doyel 1980; Sullivan and Hantman 1984). Even though temper variation is to a large extent a function of resource availability, the consistent use of certain preparation techniques, such as crushing sherds as opposed to crushing rocks, or adding sand instead of crushing other materials, may signal the existence of a localized technological tradition.

Whether temper variation reflects natural availability or cultural choice may only be determined through a careful study of temper sources in the study area. Similarly, the consistent use of mineral versus organic pigments for painting black-on-white, black-on-red, and polychrome vessels indicates not only localized painting technologies but also firing technologies. Manganese paint will remain black regardless of firing atmosphere, but most iron paints will turn red and organic paint will disappear unless fired in a reducing or nonoxidizing atmosphere (Rice 1987; Rye 1981; Shepard 1985).

In many cases both temper preparation and pigment selection may indicate only broad areas of occurrence of different technologies. Thus it is necessary to obtain finer discriminations between and within wares to be able to identify manufacturing sources in a region or adjacent regions.

Chemical characterization of the ceramic paste and petrographic identification of temper constituents provide, in principle, such discriminating criteria. Chemical analysis of slips and pigments, on the other hand, may be deceiving, because pigments are needed in small quantities and thus are likely to be transported for longer distances than clay and temper (Arnold 1985; Shepard 1936, 1985).

Preliminary observations and classification of vessels according to paste texture and temper type were made with the aid of a 10x binocular microscope. The initial temper groups served as sampling strata for detailed qualitative temper analysis. Refiring of sherds from every broken vessel facilitated the identification of black paint types and also served to standardize paste color. Refiring was useful for separating vessels according to paste color; the groups defined by paste color also served as sampling strata for neutron activation and ionic extraction analyses.

The results of these analyses are presented in the following chapters.

Forming Techniques

With the exception of a few small vessels molded entirely by hand, coiling was the generalized technique used to form vessels in the prehistoric Southwest (Colton 1953: 17). Variations in the method of starting a vessel included the use of a round mold to cast the base, on which coils were attached in rings or spirals, and continuous coiling that began at the base (Colton 1953; Fontana and others 1962; Gifford 1928; Guthe 1925; Haury 1945). These variations could have been related to localized technologies. They are difficult to observe even in corrugated vessels, because of coil obliteration or missing base fragments.

The direction of coiling, measured clockwise or counterclockwise (Crown 1981a: 144), could have been the product of handedness or of culturally or linguistically constrained motor habits (Arnold 1981; Rice 1980), but again, it is often impossible to record due to obliteration of coils at the base. This attribute was recorded whenever possible.

The average number of coils per four square centimeters is an attribute often used to separate types of corrugated vessels (Beals and others 1945; Gifford and Smith 1978). Crown (1981b) used this attribute in combination with temper type and other attributes to separate the manufacturing loci of gray corrugated and brown corrugated wares from the St. Johns area. Crown (1981a: 139) observed that in the Chodistaas Pueblo assemblage the number of coils were proportional to vessel size. However, the presence of gray indented corrugated vessels, which could be of an origin distinct from brown indented obliterated corrugated vessels, may also account for the variation in number of coils.

Average wall thickness, however related to vessel size, was considered as a possible diagnostic attribute of manufacturing loci, because gray corrugated jars were consistently thinner than brown corrugated jars of similar size.

Vessel thinning, a secondary forming technique, has been one of the most generalized attributes for assigning cultural affiliation to ceramic assemblages: paddle-and-anvil to Hohokam and coil-and-scrape to Anasazi and Mogollon groups (Doyel 1978; Gladwin and Gladwin 1934, 1935; Haury 1945; McGuire 1975; Wendorf 1953; Wood 1980). Whittlesey (1982a: 18–20), however, noted the occurrence of both vessel thinning techniques within a single ware, type, or even vessel, and the strong association of vessel morphology and thinning technique. Wendorf (1953: 50) recorded paddle-and-anvil finished pottery (Adamana Brown) in Mogollon-Anasazi sites in the Petrified Forest National Monument. Thus, vessel thinning technologies may not be as useful for identifying manufacturing loci of ceramics as previously thought. Nevertheless, the presence of paddle-and-anvil scars was recorded when visible on the interior or exterior surfaces.

Surface Treatment and Finishing

Three aspects of surface treatment and finishing were recorded: slip color, smudging, and shape and average number of indentations per four square centimeters. The occurrence of "raspberry" red slip versus orange-red slip was observed, because the former color seems to have been restricted to wares in the mountains (such as Salado Red Corrugated and Salado White-on-red Corrugated) where raspberry red hematite is abundant, whereas the orange-red slip had a more generalized distribution, both across wares and geographically.

Smudging of bowl interiors is a long-standing technology of the mountain Mogollon ceramic tradition (Haury 1945; Rinaldo and Bluhm 1956). It also appears in Salado Red Corrugated jars and shouldered red plain jars. It was necessary, then, to contrast paste composition against the presence or absence of smudging to test whether smudged vessels were associated with a single manufacturing source.

Indentations have often been considered "stylistic" rather than technological attributes (Brunson 1985; Crown 1981a, 1981b; Gifford and Smith 1978). To avoid the confusion of recording stylistic attributes on undecorated vessels, I included indentations in technology (surface treatment), because the Chodistaas vessels do not display indentations arranged in banded layouts such as those seen in the Point of Pines assemblages. Shape of indentations clearly reflects the tool used to indent coils on wet paste and often is consistent within a ware, although some variation associated with vessel morphology may be observed. Average number of indentations per four square centimeters, although related to number of coils and therefore with vessel size, is also often consistent within a ware. Both attributes were recorded for all corrugated wares.

Firing Techniques

The development of a successful firing technology is the most critical aspect of ceramic technology, for it requires achieving optimum balance between the physical and chemical properties of the raw materials and the atmosphere, temperature, and timing of the firing process (Rice 1987; Rye 1981; Shepard 1985). Firing technology implies a long process of experimentation until the desired finished product is obtained. Colton (1939) and Shepard (1985) conducted a variety of experiments in an attempt to replicate the reducing or nonoxidizing conditions in which black-on-white and yellow wares were presumably fired.

Although the firing technology used for most prehistoric Southwestern ceramics could fit into a generalized model of traditional preindustrial pottery manufacture, certain decorated wares, such as Cibola White Ware, required specific technological knowledge that has no ethnographic analogues (Shepard 1985: 80). Selecting light-firing clays and fuel that burns with a smokeless flame was crucial for achieving flawless, uniformly fired, unsmudged, black-painted, white pots. Pottery similar to Cibola White Ware has been reproduced under experimental juniper fires, which required a careful control of atmosphere in order to avoid soot-ing and smudging (Shepard 1985: 80). This example suggests that specific information on firing technology could not be acquired without direct interaction among potters, although replication of color effects or schemes, as in the case of Mimbres Black-on-white pottery, was always possible. Controlled refiring experiments were made using sherds from every broken vessel at Chodistaas Pueblo. Changes in the color of paint and paste cores were used as indicators of original firing conditions (Shepard 1985).

In summary, the process of manufacture of all wares was reconstructed in an attempt to identify attributes particularly useful for identifying manufacturing loci of each ware and to evaluate the concept of a "technological tradition." The discussion now turns to a detailed description of ceramic sourcing procedures at Chodistaas Pueblo, including clay sourcing and several laboratory experiments designed to test the suitability of raw materials and to compare them with the prehistoric pottery.

CHAPTER SIX

Clay Survey and Compositional Analysis of Vessels from Chodistaas Pueblo

Ceramic materials contain information about the dynamics of the ceramic-manufacturing process in which potters made choices both constricted and enhanced by the material properties, by their technological knowledge, and by the sociocultural environment. Because ceramic paste composition is not only a product of cultural choices but also of natural availability, compositional studies of prehistoric pottery become more relevant when knowledge of the geological environment is incorporated in archaeological research. Assessments of availability and variability of potential raw material sources in a given region, combined with compositional analysis of samples from those sources, provide an ecological, mineralogical, and chemical perspective from which to view variability in ceramics. These concepts are discussed by Adan-Bayewitz and Perlman (1985), Arnold (1981), Bishop (1980), Bishop, Rands, and Holley (1982), Howard (1982), Matson (1965), Neff (1992), Rands and Bishop (1980), Rice (1987), Rye (1981), and Shepard (1985).

The procedures used in the evaluation of resource availability in the vicinity of Chodistaas Pueblo and the information obtained through these procedures are presented below, followed by a description of the methods of analysis of compositional variability of the ceramic vessels from the site. The potential and limitations of these methods and the assumptions that underlie them are discussed.

EVALUATION OF CLAY SOURCES

According to Bishop, Rands, and Holley (1982: 276), identification of distinct sources of raw materials used in the manufacture of ceramics may be done directly, by establishing probable relationships of pottery to geographically localized raw materials, or indirectly, by demonstrating differences in ceramic pastes thought to be sufficient to indicate the existence of geographically isolable resources. Of the two approaches, the former takes the research beyond the identification of compositional similarities and differences in a ceramic

assemblage to the delineation of resource procurement zones (Rands and Bishop 1980: 19). Delineating resource procurement zones is especially critical when analyzing ceramic paste composition, because the raw materials (clay and temper) need not coincide in their place of procurement.

The resource procurement zone is a catchment area that surrounds the settlement where the ceramics under study were or could have been manufactured, the area where prehistoric potters presumably acquired the bulk of their raw materials. This concept closely resembles Browman's (1976) "primary exploitation threshold," where individuals obtain their resources at minimum energy cost and maximum benefit. From an archaeological perspective, however, a resource procurement zone is arbitrarily defined according to the settlement pattern of the region under study and its geologic and topographic characteristics. It may be delimited tentatively using both criteria and then refined and tested by comparing the chemical and mineralogical composition of potential raw materials with that of the prehistoric pottery. Although delimiting and testing "archaeological" resource procurement zones do not imply a direct relationship or "match" between ceramic pastes and geographically localized resources except under the most favorable conditions (Bishop, Rands, and Holley 1982: 280), they do provide additional information on the potential and limitations of local manufacture of ceramics.

In the case of Chodistaas Pueblo, where no direct evidence of ceramic manufacture is available from the site, acquiring detailed information on the availability, quality, and compositional variability of raw materials (in particular, clays) was crucial for isolating local wares. An area to be surveyed for clay sources was arbitrarily delimited using Arnold's (1985: 35–60) cross-cultural estimates of the primary territory of clay exploitation. The clay survey was conducted in three phases.

During the first phase, a preliminary reconnaissance was made within a radius of 7 km to 10 km (about 4 to

6 miles) from Chodistaas Pueblo. This area included exposures of both Upper Supai sandstone (Cibeque Member) to the north and east of Chodistaas and Naco limestone to the west and south. This reconnaissance phase followed general guidelines provided by Rye (1981), Rice (1987), Howard (1982), and Talbot (1984), and it focused on clays rather than on temper, even though potential temper materials such as sand and weathered diabase were collected wherever possible for comparative purposes. As Rye (1981: 13) noted, comparison of tempering materials with local mineral sources may be done with relative ease by petrographic analysis of ceramic thin sections. The area was surveyed according to natural topography, changes in vegetation, and presence of known prehistoric sites. Limitations imposed by low accessibility and poor visibility of forested areas introduced a bias in the overall survey strategy. Because of the dense vegetation coverage and humus deposited on soil surfaces, the extent and thickness of clay deposits were difficult to assess. Road cuts and stream banks presented the most accessible clay exposures, many of which revealed good potting properties when tested in the field (Howard 1982: 146; Rice 1987: 319).

Covered subsurface deposits were not tested, although in a few cases these deposits were located fortuitously. Augering is a recommended survey technique for subsurface soil sampling (Talbot 1984), but it is impractical on the Grasshopper Plateau because the soil is full of cobbles. The usefulness of sampling subsurface clay deposits for this particular research is also questionable, because traditional potters commonly prefer to exploit sources that are easily accessible with simple mining technology (Nicklin 1979). In the American Southwest, borrow pits probably dug to obtain clays were found at large pueblo sites in the Pinedale area, but those pits were usually shallow (Lightfoot and Jewett 1984: 60).

The second phase of the survey involved recording information on known clay sources and sampling them. Even though most geologic and soil maps available for the region are too general to be useful for the location of clay beds, the geological survey of the Fort Apache Indian Reservation (Moore 1968: 73) mapped, sampled, and test-fired 19 clay sources, 13 of which have potting-quality clays. Unfortunately, all of these sources are more than 25 km (15 miles) from the Grasshopper Plateau. Nonetheless, this information proved valuable for comparison with the closer sources. Following Moore's (1968) survey, cretaceous clay deposits situated in the Forestdale Valley and in Hop Canyon, northeast

of Grasshopper Pueblo, were sampled. Although located well beyond the Grasshopper Plateau, these are the closest known deposits of white-firing clays of ceramic quality, and thus they were particularly important for comparisons with Cibola White Ware pastes. The carbonaceous alluvial clay at Tundastusa Ruin in the Forestdale Valley and the red clayey soils of Corduroy Creek were also sampled. In addition, six clay deposits located beyond the preliminary reconnaissance area were also sampled during field trips to Canyon Creek, Pepper Canyon, and Q Ranch. This phase was useful for targeting clay deposits located outside the preliminary survey area. Because this area was delimited arbitrarily, there was a possibility that it might not cover all sources that could have been exploited by the prehistoric potters.

For the third phase, an area of 4.5 km (2.7 miles) in radius from Chodistaas Pueblo was intensively surveyed by foot to complete the survey started in the preliminary reconnaissance. I had noticed that, although clayey soils are abundant in the region, extensive beds of clean clays are not common in the vicinity of Chodistaas. Also, the majority of workable clays collected around Chodistaas were brown-red, whereas light colored clayey deposits were highly contaminated by weathered limestone sediment. A more intensive survey was necessary to double-check the presence or absence of light-colored clays of potting quality. This survey extended along each of the seasonal streams that run north-south on the Grasshopper Plateau. The locations of sampled clay deposits on the Grasshopper Plateau and in adjacent areas are shown in Figure 6.1.

In spite of the limitations mentioned above, 32 clay exposures were sampled (Table 6.1). The samples collected vary in weight from 0.5 kg to 1.0 kg. Larger samples are useful for extensive testing, but for the purposes of this research, which required 300 mg of powdered clay for compositional analysis (INAA and ICP) and 100 grams for test briquettes, about 450 grams (1 pound) proved to be sufficient (Howard 1982). Additional samples were collected by Crown (1981a) and me (1988–1990 seasons) during excavations at Chodistaas and Grasshopper Spring pueblos. Light gray clay was found surrounding a hearth on the floor of Room 10 at Chodistaas; it appeared to have been intentionally deposited there, because the matrix color of the floor was reddish brown. A similar clay was also used to line a mealing bin in Room 4 at Grasshopper Spring. Red clay was collected from the bottom of Test pit 88–5 at Chodistaas; this clay underlies the ruin and is immediately atop bedrock. The clay collection was supplemented by 63 clay samples recovered in Room 113, a storage-manufacturing room at Grasshopper Pueblo (Triadan 1989: 79). This material provided further comparative criteria for the analysis and broadened the perspective on potential raw material sources in the region.

Clay Testing

Field tests conducted by graduate students of the University of Arizona Archaeological Field School and by me measured plasticity, drying shrinkage, and firing properties of the clay samples. These tests provided preliminary criteria to determine which clay samples were suitable for further tests and sourcing. A more detailed assessment of workability and firing performance of the collected clays was necessary to narrow down the potential raw material sources and to compare the color range of fired clays to that of refired sherds from broken vessels. Examination of the clay samples from the survey and from excavations at Chodistaas, Grasshopper Spring, and Room 113 at Grasshopper Pueblo showed that apparent variation in color was limited to four groups: brown to reddish brown, light red to orange, dark to medium gray, and buff to grayish white clays. Fifteen clay samples from these color groups were selected for detailed laboratory testing; five of them came from Room 113 (Triadan 1989).

Workability Tests

Two performance characteristics of the clays were measured to obtain a relative estimate of workability: plasticity and drying shrinkage. Plasticity refers to the ability of a clay body, on the addition of a limited amount of water, to be shaped by pressure and to retain that form when the pressure is relaxed (Rice 1987: 58). Drying shrinkage, on the other hand, refers to the "packing" of clay particles resulting from the loss of water that was mechanically combined with dry clay to develop plasticity. When the clay is wet, a water film surrounds and separates each clay platelet and acts as a lubricant. During drying, the water film is removed and the clay body shrinks as the surface tension of the remaining water draws the particles together (Rice 1987: 64). Test briquettes made of each of the selected clays were used to measure plasticity and drying shrinkage. First, approximately 200 grams of each sample were ground to fine powder in a mortar. The powder was dried and sifted through two fine USA Standard

Testing Sieves (#60–250nm and #120–125nm) to remove coarse particles. Fifty grams of each powdered sample were weighed and used to perform the "water of plasticity" test. This test is commonly used to assess the percentage of water weight required to develop optimum plasticity in a dry clay (Rice 1987: 63). Water from a graduated cylinder was added to the powdered clay until it could be shaped into a coil that would not crack. The amount of added water was recorded. More water was then added until the clay body became sticky and the amount of added water was again recorded. Since 1 cc of purified water at 4°C (39.2°F) is equivalent to 1 gram, for 100 grams of clay the volume of water added equals the percentage of water of plasticity (%WP). Thus, the percentage of water of plasticity for 50 grams of clay can be expressed as 2x cc, where x is the amount of added water. Once converted into percentages, the two water volumes gave the range of workability of each clay sample, from initial plasticity to stickiness. This test eliminated three samples that had high limestone content and were not workable.

A second test to estimate clay plasticity was then performed. This test measures the difference in wet weight and dry weight of a clay specimen. The weight loss caused by the evaporation of film water is equal to the amount of water originally needed to develop plasticity (Rice 1987: 62). The wet clay was shaped into 3-cm by 9-cm by 0.8-cm briquettes. Each briquette was weighed, air-dried for 24 hours between plaster blocks, oven-dried for 6 hours at 105°C (221°F), and weighed again. The percentage of water of plasticity was calculated using the formula:

$$\%WP = \frac{\text{weight (wet) - weight (dry)}}{\text{weight (dry)}} \times 100$$

Overall, the results of these two tests are comparable (Table 6.2). Of the 15 clays initially selected, 12 are suitable for ceramic manufacture, because they reveal the wide range of workability needed for constructing a vessel by coiling (Nelson 1984: 322; Ries 1927: 227). Additionally, samples 907 and 621, both of which are extremely fine-textured, sticky, and very plastic, could have been used as slip clays (Triadan 1989: 71). The results of the plasticity tests, however, must be taken cautiously, because there is an element of individual judgement when deciding whether a clay has achieved plasticity, and, therefore, the initial measurement of water percentage may be biased.

Drying performance of the samples was evaluated by measuring linear drying shrinkage (%LDS) and by observing the development of cracks and deformities in

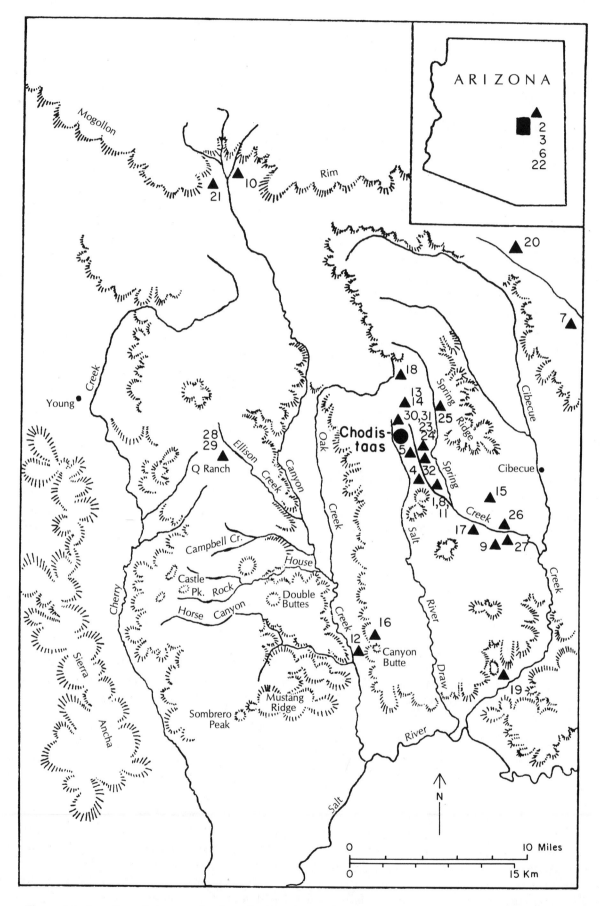

Figure 6.1. Location of clay samples from the Grasshopper Plateau and adjacent regions (see Table 6.1).

[46]

Table 6.1. Location and Description of Clay Samples (1988–1990)

Sample Number	Location	Context	Description	Color	Field Evaluation
1	Grasshopper Spring Creek	Stream bank	Organic clay	5YR 5/1	Workable
2	Corduroy Creek	Road cut	Limestone–clay	10YR 7/2	Unsuitable
3	Corduroy Creek	Large rodent hole	Clayey soil	5YR 4/6	Workable
4	Grasshopper Spring Creek	Stream bank	Weathered claystone	5Y 5/1	Workable
5	Grasshopper Spring Creek	Stream bank	Weathered claystone	2.5YR 6/2	Workable
6	Hop Canyon	Road cut	Shale	10YR 6/1	Workable
7	Carrizo	Road cut	Limestone–clay	10YR 7/2	Unsuitable
8	Grasshopper Spring Creek	Stream bank	Clayey soil below #1	2.5Y 6/4	Workable
9	Cibecue	Road cut	Subsurface clay bed	10YR 6/1	Workable
10	Dazen Canyon	Road cut	Limestone–clay	10YR 7/2	Unsuitable
11	Grasshopper Spring Creek	Stream bank	Mottled clay–silt	10YR 5/3	Unsuitable
12	Canyon Creek Arroyo	Stream bank	Clay–silt bed	2.5YR 6/0	Unsuitable
13	Grasshopper Butte	Road cut	Clayey soil	5YR 4/6	Workable
14	Grasshopper Butte	Road cut	Clay–silt bed	5Y 5/1	Unsuitable
15	Spring Ridge	Road cut	Calcareous clay	10YR 7/1	Workable
16	Canyon Butte	Road cut	Subsurface clay bed	2.5YR 5/2	Workable
17	Spring Creek	Stream bank	Claystone	5YR 5/4	Workable
18	Grasshopper Butte	Road cut	Limestone–clay	10YR 7/2	Unsuitable
19	Spring Creek	Stream bank	Weathered claystone	5Y 6/1	Workable
20	Carrizo Creek	Stream bank	Clay bed	10YR 6/1	Workable
21	Chediski Farms	Road cut	Weathered claystone	10YR 6/1	Workable
22	Forestdale Valley	Stream bank	Organic clay bed	10YR 6/1	Workable
23	Spring Creek	Stream bank	Limestone–clay	5Y 5/1	Unsuitable
24	Spring Creek	Stream bank	Weathered claystone	2.5Y 7/2	Workable
25	Spring Creek	Stream bank	Subsurface clay bed	10YR 6/1	Workable
26	Spring Creek	Stream bank	Subsurface clay bed	10YR 7/1	Workable
27	Spring Creek	Stream bank	Subsurface clay bed	2.5YR 7/2	Workable
28	Q Ranch	Stream bank	Organic clay	5Y 2.5/2	Workable
29	Q Ranch	Stream bank	Organic clay	10YR 4/4	Workable
30	Chodistaas, Room 10	Below mealing bin	Calcareous clay	5Y 5/1	Workable
31	Chodistaas, Test pit 88–5	Atop bedrock	Subsurface clay bed	5YR 3/4	Workable
32	Grasshopper Spring, Room 4	Below mealing bin	Calcareous clay	10YR 6/2	Pigment clay(?)

Table 6.2. Workability Tests on Selected Clays

Sample Number	%WP (Test 1)	Weight Wet (g)	Weight Dry (g)	%WP (Test 2)	% LDS	Comments
621*	35–38	44.34	33.64	31.81	5.0	Pigment clay
802*	25–28	43.05	34.79	23.75	5.0	Good
854*		41.26	30.53	35.16	10.0	Excellent (tempered)
907*	29–32	44.19	34.07	29.70	7.5	Pigment clay; good
1223*	30–32	40.25	31.19	36.89	10.0	Good
30	31–34	44.91	34.35	30.74	6.0	Excellent
31	32–39	43.12	31.85	35.38	2.0	Fair; a little stiff
9	27–30	44.82	35.92	24.77	2.0	Excellent
17	26–30	46.18	37.35	23.64	4.0	Excellent
21	24–26	47.47	39.37	20.57	6.0	Excellent
20	36–42	54.88	35.34	29.82	8.0	Fair; drying cracks
16	33–37	44.89	33.38	34.45	10.0	Fair, drying cracks
6	26–40	43.26	34.35	25.93	10.0	Excellent
22	36–41	42.52	34.61	22.85	6.0	Very Good
2	26–34	40.02	31.82	25.77	2.0	Coarse; drying cracks

*Clays are from Grasshopper Pueblo, Room 113 (Triadan 1989: 61–62).

Table 6.3. Color Changes in Fired Clays

Survey Clays

Centigrade	Sample 9	Sample 17	Sample 21	Sample 20	Sample 16	Sample 6	Sample 22
0°	10YR 6/1	5YR 5/4	10YR 6/1	10YR 6/1	2.5YR 5/2	10YR 6/1	10YR 6/1
500°	5YR 7/2	5YR 6/6	5YR 7/2	10YR 7/2	5YR 6/2	10YR 7/2	2.5YR 7/4
550°	5YR 7/3					7.5YR 8/2	10YR 7/3
600°							
650°			2.5Y 8/2	10YR 7/3			10YR 7/4
700°			10YR 8/3		5YR 6/3		
750°							
800°	5YR 8/3	5YR 7/6		7.5YR 6/6	2.5YR 5/4	7.5YR 7/2	
850°							7.5YR 6.5/6
900°							7.5YR 6/6
950°	10YR 7/3		10YR 8/4	5YR 6/6		7.5YR 8/4	

Clays from Grasshopper Pueblo and Chodistaas Pueblo

Centigrade	Sample 621*	Sample 802*	Sample 854*	Sample 907*	Sample 1223*	Sample 30	Sample 31
0°	10YR 6/6	7.5YR 5/2	7.5YR 5/4	5YR 7/1	10YR 5/2	5Y 5/1	5YR 3/4
500°	2.5YR 5/6	5YR 6/4	7.5YR 5/6	10YR 7/1	7.5YR 6/4	10YR 7/2	2.5YR 4/6
550°							
600°			5YR 5/6	10YR 8/1			
650°		5YR 6/6			7.5YR 6/6		
700°						10YR 8/3	2.5YR 4/8
750°							
800°							
850°	2.5YR 5/8		5YR 5/8		5YR 6/8	7.5YR 8/4	
900°							2.5YR 5/8
950°			2.5YR 5/8			10YR 8/4	

*Clays from Grasshopper Pueblo, Room 113 (Triadan 1989: 61–62).

the briquettes during drying. This test was made on untempered clays, so that linear drying shrinkage would not be artificially reduced. A 5-cm line was marked on each of the wet briquettes and was remeasured after they were completely dry. The length difference was then converted into a percentage. This figure represents the linear drying shrinkage (5 cm = 100%). As shown in Table 6.2, %LDS of the tested clays is relatively low (Ries 1927: 227), indicating a high range of material flexibility. One of the clays showed a tendency to develop drying cracks or deformities.

Firing Performance Test

A firing performance test was conducted to observe how well the selected clays withstood high temperatures and to obtain a color range comparable to that of the prehistoric sherds. The test briquettes were cut into eleven pieces, one of which was left unfired. The remaining pieces were fired in a Neycraft enamel furnace at increments of 50°C from 500°C (932°F) to 950°C (1742°F), piece by piece. Under the assumption that the maximum temperature reached in a traditional open fire or a shallow pit would be held only between 5 and 20 minutes, without necessarily achieving complete oxidation of a vessel (Rye 1981: 98; Shepard 1985: 84), every piece of each briquette was exposed for 30 minutes to a specific temperature in order to avoid incomplete oxidation. After the projected furnace temperature was reached and held for 30 minutes, the pieces were left in the furnace to cool down to approximately 300°C (572°F). Changes in color are recorded in Table 6.3. Samples containing a high percentage of limestone crumbled during firing.

Refiring of Sherds

Color variations on the surface and in the core of a vessel wall are caused by uncontrolled temperature and atmosphere conditions during the original firing process

Table 6.4. Refired Sherds from Chodistaas Pueblo
Changes in Color and Hardness, Estimated Firing Temperature, and Estimated Atmosphere

Centigrade (H = Mohs Hardness)	McDonald Painted Corrug. (H)	Salado White-on-red (H)	Pinto Black-on-red (H)	Pinto Black-on-red (H)	Pinto Black-on-red (H)	Pinto Black-on-red (H)	Pinedale Black-on-white (H)
0°	10YR 5/4 (4)	10YR 5/4 (4)	5Y 4/1 (3)	7.5YR 6/4 (3)	10YR 3/1 (3)	5YR 5/4 (3)	2.5YR 6/0 (5)
500°	(4)	7.5YR 4/4 (5)	(3)	7.5YR 3/4 (3)	10YR 4/1 (3)	(3)	(5)
550°	(4)	(5)	(3)	(3)	5YR 4/6 (3)	(3)	(5)
600°	(5)	(5)	10YR 5/1 (3)	(3)	10YR 4/2 (3)	(3)	(5)
650°	7.5YR 4/5 (5)	10YR 5/3 (5)	(3)	(4)	(4)	5YR 5/6 (4)	(5)
700°	(5)	7.5YR 5.5/6 (5)	10YR 6/3 (4)	(4)	10YR 4/3 (4)	(5)	(5)
750°	(5)	(6)	(5)	(4)	5YR 5/6 (5)	(5)	(6)
800°	(6)	(6)	7.5YR 6/6 (5)	5YR 6/6 (5)	(5)	(5)	(6)
850°	7.5YR 4/5 (6)	(6)	(5)	5YR 5/6 (5)	(5)	(6)	5Y 8/1 (6)
900°	5YR 5/6 (6)	5YR 5/6 (6)	5YR 5/6 (5)	(6)	(6)	(6)	7.5YR 8/2 (6)
950°	(6)	(6)	(6)	(6)	(6)	(6)	10YR 8/3 (7)
EFT[1]	600–700°C	600–650°C	600–700°C	550–650°C	650–700°C	600–700°C	750–800°C
EFA[2]	Incomplete ox.	Incomplete ox.	Incomplete ox.	Incomplete ox.	Incomplete ox.	Incomplete ox.	Nonoxidizing

	Pinedale Black-on-white (H)	Brown Indented Corrugated (H)	Brown Indented Corrug. (H)	Gray Indented Corrug. (H)	Gray Indented Corrug. (H)	Red Plain (H)	Red Plain (H)
0°	2.5Y 8/0 (5)	10YR 4/1	5YR 3/1 (4)	2.5YR 3/1 (5)	10YR 4/1 (5)	10YR 4/1 (4)	7.5YR 3/0 (4)
500°	(5)	(5)	(5)	(5)	(5)	(4)	(4)
550°	(6)	10YR 4/2 (5)	(5)	(5)	(5)	(4)	(5)
600°	(6)	(5)	5YR 3/2 (5)	(5)	(6)	(5)	(5)
650°	(6)	10YR 4/3 (5)	5YR 4/4 (5)	(5)	(6)	(5)	(6)
700°	5Y 8/1 (6)	(5)	(5)	(5)	(6)	10YR 6/4 (6)	(6)
750°	(6)	(5)	(5)	(5)	(6)	(6)	10YR 5/3 (6)
800°	(7)	(5)	(5)	(6)	(6)	(6)	(6)
850°	(7)	(5)	(6)	2.5YR 3/2 (6)	(6)	(6)	10YR 6/6 (6)
900°	10YR 8/1 (7)	(5)	5YR 4/6 (6)	(6)	5YR 6/6 (7)	5YR 5/8 (6)	2.5YR 5/8 (6)
950°	(7)	5YR 4/4 (6)	(7)	2.5YR 6/8 (6)	(7)	(6)	(6)
EFT[1]	800–850°C	650–700°C	600–650°C	750–800°C	600–650°C	650–700°C	600–700°C
EFA[2]	Nonoxidizing	Incomplete ox.	Incomplete ox.	Incomplete ox.	Incomplete ox.	Incomplete ox.	Incomplete ox.

Note: Color was recorded for the darkest section of the sherd cores.
1. EFT = Estimated firing temperature. 2. EFA = Estimated firing atmosphere.

(Rye 1981: 98; Shepard 1985: 105). To achieve color ranges in sherds that are comparable to those obtained in fired clays, it was necessary to standardize color by refiring them. Twenty-five large sherds of different wares were selected from the Chodistaas Pueblo and Grasshopper Pueblo collections. Each sherd was cut into eleven pieces, ten of which were submitted to exactly the same procedure followed for the test briquettes. Changes in color of paste, slip, and paint were recorded for each piece, using a Munsell Color Chart. Changes in surface hardness were recorded using the Mohs Scale (Table 6.4). Sherd and briquette pieces were then arranged by temperature and color to find similarities between clays and refired sherds. The color variability observed in the fired clays covers that observed in the refired sherds, suggesting that most, if not all, of the tested clays could have been used in the manufacture of the wares represented in the sherd sample. Table 6.5 shows color similarities between refired vessel sherds and fired clays.

This test also helped to assess the probable range of original firing temperatures (Shepard 1985: 223), to determine iron, manganese, and carbon in black paints of decorated wares (Hawley 1929; Shepard 1985: 33–43), and to approximate, when possible, the original firing atmosphere (Shepard 1985: 106–107). Color changes can be used with caution to estimate the original firing temperature when compared with the unfired piece of each sherd. The principle is that after a clay has been fired once, its physical and chemical transformations will be fixed at the point of maximum temperature; these properties will remain unaltered unless it is refired at a temperature that exceeds the original maximum temperature. Color changes in the sherd core, in

**Table 6.5. Color Similarities Between
Refired Sherds and Fired Clays**

Refired Sherds	Fired Clay Sample
McDonald Painted Corrugated	20
Salado White-on-red	20
Pinto Black-on-red	17, 802
Pinto Black-on-red	17, 802
Pinto Black-on-red	17, 802
Pinto Black-on-red	17, 802
Pinedale Black-on-white	None
Pinedale Black-on-white	907
Brown indented corrugated	854, 1223
Brown indented corrugated	854, 1223
Gray indented corrugated	22
Gray indented corrugated	None
Red plain	20
Red plain	20, 802

Note: Colors were compared at 950°C.

principle, could occur only after this temperature had been reached (Rice 1987: 427–428; Shepard 1985: 223). In practice, however, ceramics that were originally fired at low temperatures may suffer color changes due to post-depositional processes. Changes in hardness are more problematic to evaluate, because hardness depends not only on firing temperature but on the mineral composition of clays, impurities, microstructural features, and surface treatment (Rice 1987: 357; Shepard 1985: 114). In general, increase in surface hardness tended to correlate with increase in firing temperature, thus providing support for estimates of the original firing temperature.

Changes in core color also provide clues to the approximate original firing atmosphere conditions. Because the atmosphere in an open fire cannot be properly controlled once the firing process has begun, it fluctuates throughout the different stages of this process and the color ranges observable in a vessel are a product of the atmosphere conditions during the last stage only. Nevertheless, general tendencies may be observed (Rice 1987: 345; Rye 1981: 116; Shepard 1985: 106).

Changes in the color of slips and paints added information about firing atmosphere and basic paint constituents. Black paint that turned red when refired indicated that the iron minerals of the paint were not oxidized originally. Well-finished, organic-painted ceramics were probably fired in a low-temperature, oxygen-deficient atmosphere, otherwise the paint would have burned off above 700°C (1292°F), as happened with many carbon-painted sherds. Black paint that did not change in color when oxidized probably contained manganese as its main chemical constituent.

For classificatory purposes, the refiring of sherds enhances greatly the visibility of paste inclusions, facilitating sorting and examination of temper under a low-power binocular microscope. After looking at the promising results obtained by refiring the sherd samples, I decided to refire a small sherd of every broken vessel of the Chodistaas assemblage. The sherds were refired at 950°C (1742°F) for complete oxidation. As expected, this exercise eased the sorting of temper groups, in particular sherd temper in white ware sherds, and uncovered subtle but consistent differences in the paste color of several wares. Again, these differences served as sampling strata for INAA and ICP.

To summarize, determining the range of macroscopic variability in both clay sources and ceramics assisted in evaluating the potential of the local environment for the development of local ceramic manufacture. In this case, workability and firing performance tests suggested that inhabitants of the Grasshopper Plateau had several sources of buff, brown, and red potting clays but practically no white potting clays from which to choose. Furthermore, comparing clay variability with that observed in the prehistoric pottery provided preliminary criteria for establishing probable local and nonlocal paste groups, even within each ware, that served as sampling strata for compositional characterization. Similarly, clays judged to be the closest to the tested wares were also submitted to compositional analysis in the hope that a direct relationship between sources and ceramics would be discerned.

COMPOSITIONAL ANALYSIS

The detailed analysis of ceramic paste composition, aimed at the study of ceramic provenience, requires "a convergence of traditional archaeological interests with techniques of the natural and physical sciences," note Bishop, Rands, and Holley (1982: 276). Formal attribute analysis of ceramics must be integrated with mineralogical and chemical analyses of the ceramic paste in order to determine local and nonlocal ceramics.

Characterization of optical mineralogy (petrography) and paste chemistry provide complementary information about the composition of ceramic pastes. Optical mineralogy or petrography yields information on the kind, size, and shape of inclusions present in the ceramic fabric. Often, mineral inclusions that occur consistently in wares can be correlated with specific geological formations in the study region (Douglass 1987; Lombard 1986; Rugge and Doyel 1980; Shepard 1936; Shepard in Judd 1954; Toll and others 1980; Warren 1969;

Zedeño and others 1993). Size and shape of mineral grains indicate the extent of mechanical and physical weathering of individual inclusions and also reflect natural factors such as source lithology, climate, and depositional processes, being, therefore, possible diagnostics of procurement location (Bishop, Rands, and Holley 1982; Darvill and Timby 1982; Middleton and others 1985; Peacock 1970; Streeten 1982; Wandibba 1982). Mineralogical analysis is useful for the broadest range of low-fired pottery and is usually considered a preliminary step in provenience studies, providing the necessary criteria to decide whether more sensitive methods of ceramic characterization are necessary for addressing a particular problem (Rice 1987: 415).

On the other hand, paste chemistry studies identify and quantify elements or element compounds that constitute the ceramic paste, including rare earths that occur in trace amounts in the clay fraction (Bishop 1980; Bishop and Neff 1989; Bishop, Harbottle, and Sayre 1982; Bishop, Rands, and Holley 1982; Harbottle 1976; Neff 1992; Perlman and Asaro 1969; Rands and Bishop 1980). This type of analysis provides a highly sensitive approach to the discrimination between local and nonlocal pottery by identifying the variability in clays used for its manufacture. It works particularly well when background knowledge of regional geology and mineralogy of the ceramics under study are at hand.

Most methods commonly used for chemical characterization are performed on bulk samples, where clay and temper particles are combined. In such cases, especially if coarse-textured ceramics are being characterized, information on the mineralogical composition of aplastic inclusions is critical, in particular when temper and clay matrix are chemically heterogeneous (Neff and others 1988, 1989; Tani 1989). Chemical heterogeneity in clay beds, which is a product of both depositional and weathering processes, may introduce confusion unrelated to ceramic provenience (Tani 1989). Nevertheless, chemical analysis is a powerful alternative to mineralogical analysis because it enables identification of subtle differences between clays that may not be discovered otherwise.

Chemical characterization relies on several premises and assumptions. First, the "provenience postulate" assumes that identifiable chemical differences exist between sources of raw material and that the analytical approach chosen can recognize these differences. A corollary assumption maintains that compositional variation within a source is usually less than the variation between sources (Weigand and others 1977: 24). For identifying local and nonlocal ceramics, it is assumed that vessels manufactured from the same clay source will be more similar chemically to one another than to vessels manufactured from a different clay source.

Second, the "criterion of abundance" is widely used for identifying local ceramics, and the assumption is that those wares or types of vessels that are present in significant numbers at a site are the most likely to have been locally manufactured (Colton and Hargrave 1937; Judd 1954; Kidder 1936). In provenience studies, the chemical "center of gravity" or statistical centroid of a site's ceramics is based on elemental abundances rather than frequency of archaeologically defined pottery categories. It represents the analytical counterpart, that is, the chemical fingerprint, of ceramics presumed to be local because of their abundance. The chemical "center of gravity" can be contrasted against other chemically defined and statistically derived compositional groups (Bishop, Rands, and Holley 1982: 301).

A third assumption used in provenience studies is based on the "principle of least effort" (Zipf 1949): vessels rather than raw materials were circulated among prehistoric settlements (Arnold 1985; Rice 1987; Shepard 1985). A compositional group is often interpreted as representing not just a raw material source but a ceramic group from a given locus of manufacture. Knowledge of available raw materials in the study area should provide general baselines for comparison with the ceramics presumed to be of local origin and should serve to evaluate the probability of movement of raw materials.

Several methods with varying degrees of precision, accuracy, and sensitivity available for performing both chemical and mineralogical analyses on ceramics have been reviewed in detail by many authors (for example, Bishop, Rands, and Holley 1982; Olin and Franklin 1982; Rice 1987; Tite 1972). Here I only refer to those used in this research: instrumental neutron activation analysis (INAA), inductively coupled plasma emission (ICP) spectroscopy, and petrographic analysis.

Instrumental Neutron Activation Analysis

Instrumental Neutron Activation Analysis (INAA) identifies the chemical composition of clays used in the manufacture of ceramics. It is a powerful analytical approach that combines low sample-preparation time, sensitivity below the parts per million range for some elements, and automated counting and recording (Bishop, Rands, and Holley 1982: 292). A small sample (40–100 mg) of powdered ceramic fabric is bombarded by neutrons that are captured by target nuclei, resulting in a radioisotope for each element, each decaying with its own half-life and characteristic radiation. Emitted gamma rays are specific to an isotope and can be measured to determine the number of radionuclei in a sample (Bishop, Rands, and Holley 1982; Glascock 1992; Harbottle 1976). Although 75 elements can be identified through this procedure, most laboratories commonly determine only 33 of them. Data provided by INAA generally require statistical manipulation before they can be interpreted archaeologically (Bishop and Neff 1989; Glascock 1992).

A sample that included 102 sherds from broken vessels and 16 clays was submitted to INAA. Cibola White Ware was assigned first priority in the analysis, because even though it is the most abundant decorated ware at Chodistaas Pueblo (51 vessels, or 15.4% of the total assemblage and 46.0% of the decorated assemblage), the ware is presumed to have been brought into Chodistaas from north of the Mogollon Rim. Furthermore, Cibola White Ware displays a wide range of variation in design styles, so it provides an excellent opportunity to evaluate the extent to which stylistic and compositional variability are positively correlated. Samples from 47 Cibola vessels from Chodistaas Pueblo, 5 vessels from Grasshopper Pueblo, 2 vessels from Grasshopper Spring Pueblo, and 1 vessel from site AZ P:14:197 were submitted to INAA. Additionally, 50 samples that included Roosevelt Red Ware, brown corrugated, gray corrugated, painted corrugated, and red plain sherds from broken vessels, and 16 clays, were selected to investigate compositional similarity between wares and their correspondence to local clays. To select these samples, a small sherd of each broken vessel was first refired, as explained in the previous section, and examined under a 40x binocular microscope. Sherds from each ware were then classified according to variations in color and texture. The classes so formed were, in turn, used as sampling strata for INAA. Vessels that were 75 percent complete, or more, had selective priority.

Sample preparation entailed a number of steps to avoid contamination. Edges of large sherds were cleaned and a powder from the sherd core was obtained by drilling small holes with a tungsten-carbide drill. If the sherd was too small, brittle, or thin for this procedure, a sherd chip of about one square centimeter was ground to fine powder in an agate mortar. Slip and dirt was removed from the surfaces and edges of the sherd chip with a tungsten carbide rotary file before grinding. Powdered paste was extracted from the bottom of whole vessels using a similar drill bit. Samples of about 100

mg to 150 mg were put in sterile glass vials, oven-dried for 24 hours, and then weighed.

A multielemental analysis of each sample was conducted as part of a program of collaborative research between the Smithsonian Institution's Conservation Analytical Laboratory and the National Bureau of Standards. As described by Crown and Bishop (1987), the samples and accompanying standard material (NBS Standard Reference Material SRM 1633 [Coal Fly Ash]) were irradiated for six hours at a neutron flux of 7.7 x 10^{13} n/cm^2/sec. Following a six-day decay, each sample was counted for one hour using a Ge-Li detector (FWHM at 1333 ^{60}Co of 1.71 kev). The resulting information was collected on an 8192–channel Nuclear Data ND6000 multichannel analyzer. The samples were allowed to decay for 30 days and then each sample was recounted for two hours using the same system. Subsequent data processing and reduction of the gamma peak data to elemental concentrations included corrections for pulse pileup and gamma peak interferences.

SPSS and Gauss software packages were used in the statistical analysis of the information obtained from INAA. Elemental concentrations of As, Ce, Co, Cr, Cs, Eu, Fe, Hf, K, La, Lu, Nd, Rb, Sb, Sc, Sm, Sr, Ta, Tb, Th, Yb, and Zn, for which determinations with few or no missing values were obtained, were transformed into logarithms to approximate a normal distribution and to compensate for the differences in the magnitudes between major elements and trace elements or rare earths (Glascock 1992; Harbottle 1976). The log data were then submitted to a complete linkage hierarchical cluster analysis using a matrix of Mean Euclidean Distances as the measure of similarity (Sneath and Sokal 1973). The resulting dendrogram gave a preliminary summary of grouping tendencies in the analytical data. Because such summaries are subject to varying degrees of "distortion" due to strongly correlated elemental pairs and to the inclination for cluster analysis to force data into hyperspherical groups, the largest lower level dendrogram groups showing the strongest tendencies for a single manufacturing locus were selected for more detailed examination (Bishop, Harbottle, and Sayre 1982; Bishop, Rands, and Holley 1982; Glascock 1992).

A principal component (PC) analysis based on a correlation matrix was used to evaluate initial clustering tendencies; the correlation matrix was chosen over the variance-covariance matrix to minimize the differences in the magnitudes between elements such as Fe and K and the rare earths. Bivariate plots were graphed to display the PCs as well as the original concentration data. Initial group membership was then refined using a technique based on a sample's Mahalanobis distance from the multivariate group centroid. Because most of the initial groups had fewer member samples than existing variables, Mahalanobis probabilities were calculated for each sample using the first seven PCs calculated over the total data set (Glascock 1992: 17). Samples outside the 95 percent confidence interval of each group were excluded and the group properties recalculated. When no further samples could be removed, probabilities of "outlier samples" were reevaluated as to the likelihood of belonging to the group (Bishop and Neff 1989: 67–69). A sample showing equal probability of belonging to more than one group was treated as an outlier. Discriminant function analysis applied to the analytical data provided additional information on group formation and an evaluation of the discriminatory power of each variable (Glascock 1992; Harbottle 1976). Clay samples were then projected to the groups' axes to obtain the best relative fit of these samples into the already defined compositional groups. The elemental concentrations of each sample are in Appendix B.

Inductively Coupled Plasma Emission Spectroscopy

Inductively Coupled Plasma Emission Spectroscopy (ICP) was conducted to acquire additional information on paste chemistry of vessel samples that were not submitted to INAA. The following samples were submitted to ICP: (a) 48 samples from Chodistaas Pueblo vessels; (b) 12 clays collected during survey, (c) 9 clays from Room 113 at Grasshopper Pueblo, (d) 14 samples of Cibola White Ware vessels from Grasshopper Pueblo, and (e) 4 samples of Cibola White Ware vessels from Grasshopper Spring Pueblo. Twenty-two samples of Cibola White Ware vessels that had been analyzed by INAA as well were included in this analysis to control for replicability of the chemical patterns obtained by both methods.

ICP analysis, carried out by the Laboratory of Archaeology at the University of Wisconsin, Madison, is a low-cost technique for the chemical characterization of ceramics that uses weak acid at ambient temperature to extract elements from the clay paste. According to Burton and Simon (1993: 45–48), the samples were prepared by removing dirt and any surface treatments from a small portion of the potsherd or fired clay lump and grinding this portion in an agate mortar. A 100–ml sample of ground sherd was placed with 20 ml of 1–molar hydrochloric acid in a polypropylene vial, which was shaken and allowed to remain at room temperature (26°C, 78.8°F) for two weeks. The solution was then analyzed by ICP. In this study, 21 elements were measured: Al, Ba, Ca, Ce, Cu, Cr, Fe, K, La, Lu, Mg, Mn, Na, P, S, Sc, Sr, Ti, V, Y, and Zn. Concentrations were calculated as micrograms of extractable ion per gram of sherd (ppm). Although the acid extraction provides precise quantitative results, it does not measure the same attributes that bulk methods such as INAA measure, and the quantitative data are not directly comparable to data obtained by bulk methods (Burton and Simon 1993: 48). The data are, however, comparable to data sets generated by using an identical extraction method. Acid extraction renders precisions of approximately 5 percent of the absolute value for most elements. The elemental concentrations of each sample are included in Appendix C.

Elemental concentrations obtained by ICP were submitted to a statistical analysis identical to that described for INAA. ICP produced broad groups comparable to those obtained by INAA, but the analysis tended to lump fine-grained compositional groups that had been isolated by INAA. For example, ICP clearly differentiated between local and nonlocal Cibola White Ware samples, but compositional groups within nonlocal samples could not be differentiated by this technique. ICP is an exploratory technique useful for acquiring an initial idea of the compositional variability of a ceramic assemblage, but the results obtained by this method need to be reinforced with INAA and temper analyses.

Temper Analysis

Identification of mineral inclusions from thin sections of ceramic samples has been a standard approach to provenience studies in the American Southwest ever since Shepard (1936, 1942, 1965) made a petrographic analysis of the pottery from the Rio Grande Valley. Two basic methods for identifying and quantifying mineral inclusions have been used in archaeology: one involves estimating the density of inclusions by visual comparison with known or prepared standards (Matson 1970: 595; Shepard in Judd 1954: 119; Stoltman 1989: 148), and the second entails point counting by superimposing a grid, ribbon, or line over a thin section and counting all mineral inclusions lying beneath intersection points. A variant of the second method superimposes a perimeter of varying dimensions and all the particles within the perimeter are then counted. Point counting can be done manually (Stoltman 1989: 148) or with an image analyzer interfaced with a petrological microscope, TV monitor, microcomputer, and digitizing

CHAPTER SEVEN

Manufacture and Circulation of Corrugated and Plain Pottery

Undecorated pottery constitutes a large portion of almost every prehistoric ceramic assemblage in the Southwest, and it is commonly assumed to have been made locally. Undecorated wares are often regarded as a "measure" of local ceramic manufacture, with which other wares of presumed nonlocal origin may be contrasted. Spatial variation in undecorated ceramics was traditionally thought to correlate with the cultural or ethnic affiliation of the potters. Undecorated or "index" wares (Colton 1953: 67) were used to assign archaeological sites to different prehistoric groups, and differential distribution of those wares helped delineate culture areas within the American Southwest.

More recent research has identified a number of regions where undecorated wares of different ceramic traditions are found together in a single site. Regions with mixed undecorated collections are commonly located along the boundaries of the distributions of particular ceramic traditions where distribution edges overlap, supporting the idea that such traditions tend to represent different groups. It is less common, however, to find two or more technological traditions represented in a whole-vessel assemblage from a small site occupied less than forty years, as one finds at Chodistaas Pueblo. This unusual situation provides the opportunity to investigate in detail the provenience and significance of technological variability observed in undecorated ceramics. The technological and compositional analyses of corrugated and plain wares from Chodistaas Pueblo are discussed below, along with the local manufacture and circulation of these wares in the Grasshopper region.

CORRUGATED WARES

There are two major corrugated wares in the Chodistaas assemblage, brown and gray (gray-orange); both are indented and obliterated. Red-slipped or Salado Red Corrugated pottery is a variant of brown corrugated, and the morphological and technological similarities between them are particularly evident in large jars and large bowls. In contrast, gray corrugated jars have technological and, to a certain extent, morphological

characteristics that are unique to that ware, even though in some instances the paste color of gray corrugated is similar to that of brown corrugated. Painted corrugated pottery is the decorated counterpart of gray and brown corrugated (including Salado Red Corrugated), and it is discussed together with unpainted corrugated wares.

The presence of gray and brown corrugated wares in room assemblages at Chodistaas Pueblo and Grasshopper Spring pueblo is but one example of the complex distribution of these wares along the Mogollon Rim, recognized archaeologically as the boundary between the Anasazi–gray ware and Mogollon–brown ware traditions. Mixed assemblages are found in a large portion of east-central Arizona and west-central New Mexico, particularly in the area between the Upper Little Colorado River and the Mogollon Rim (Danson 1957). Here, the relative percentages of gray and brown corrugated not only vary spatially but temporally. Gray corrugated percentages decrease as one moves toward the mountains and are higher in assemblages earlier than the late Pueblo II period; the opposite is characteristic of brown corrugated (Beeson 1966; Crown 1981b; Dittert and Ruppé 1951; Gratz 1980; Longacre 1961; Martin, Rinaldo, and Longacre 1961; Rugge and Doyel 1980; Wendorf 1953).

Variation in manufacturing loci of brown and gray corrugated pottery is evident within relatively short distances. Rugge and Doyel's (1980) petrographic analysis of Pueblo II period brown and gray corrugated wares from Springerville, east-central Arizona, indicated differences in temper technology: brown corrugated and smudged corrugated vessels were consistently tempered with stream or dune sand with a high quartz content, and gray corrugated pottery appeared to have been tempered with a mixture of sand and crushed sherds. The variability in temper used in brown and gray corrugated wares also indicated that at least some vessels of each ware were introduced into the Springerville settlements from the Plateau (Rugge and Doyel 1980: 203). In addition to temper, these wares differed from one another in surface manipulation and rim form, corroborating the traditional assumption that they represented different manufacturing technologies and perhaps even different ceramic traditions and peoples (Rugge and Doyel 1980: 185).

Technological, functional, and stylistic analyses of Pueblo II and early Pueblo III period gray and brown corrugated wares from the Platt Ranch sites in the St. Johns area, about 60 km (37 miles) north of Springerville, also indicated distinct manufacturing technologies. Petrographic analysis showed that gray corrugated ware was tempered with a mixture of crushed sherds and quartz, and that brown corrugated ware had primarily quartz and chert temper, with secondary amounts of sherd, plagioclase, basalt, and muscovite. Here, however, the homogeneity exhibited in gray ware in contrast to the variability observed in brown ware was interpreted as indicating that gray ware was locally produced and brown ware was traded into the area, perhaps from several specific locations south of the study area (Crown 1981b: 267, 269). The analysis of sherds from two sites located south of the Platt Ranch sites suggested that brown ware tempered with chert, quartz, and muscovite was probably manufactured in the Mogollon Rim area. Additionally, gray and brown corrugated vessels differed in number of coils and indentations, direction of indentations, wall thickness, surface manipulation, and bowl-to-jar ratios, reinforcing Crown's (1981b: 267, 269) conclusion that members of different cultural traditions who inhabited different regions produced the two wares.

Local manufacture of brown corrugated ware on the Colorado Plateau has been recorded in Pueblo II and Pueblo III period sites in the Snowflake-Mesa Redonda area, where petrographic analysis and comparison of refired sherds with local clays indicate that the majority of brown corrugated pottery was local to the area and that gray corrugated, found in small numbers, probably was not (Neily 1988: 162). Locally manufactured brown plain and corrugated wares were also identified in pueblo settlements of the Petrified Forest National Monument, where brown wares constituted a long-standing ceramic tradition (Fowler 1989; Mera 1934; Reed 1980; Vint and Burton 1990; Wendorf 1953).

South of the Mogollon Rim, the late Pueblo III and Pueblo IV "brown indented obliterated corrugated" pottery is commonly found north of the Salt River in Lower Cherry Creek, in the Sierra Ancha, and in the Grasshopper region, decreasing west of Tonto Creek and south of the Salt River (Wood and McAllister 1982: 92). In sites located around Pinal Creek, DeVore Wash, and Pinto Creek, Tonto Corrugated, a presumably local variant of this type, constitutes a large percentage of the

ceramic assemblages (Wood and McAllister 1982: 91–92). Brown indented obliterated corrugated decreases dramatically east of the Grasshopper region and is almost absent in Cibecue Creek sites and in the Forestdale Valley. However, late Pueblo III period sites located in the eastern portion of the White Mountain Apache Reservation have brown ware assemblages with finely corrugated pottery that is rare in the Grasshopper region and westward (Reid and others 1993).

Salado Red Corrugated has a distribution similar to brown corrugated; it is concentrated in the Sierra Ancha and Grasshopper regions, decreasing in abundance toward the south and west (Wood and McAllister 1982). A small amount of Salado Red Corrugated has been reported from the Forestdale Valley (Stafford and Rice 1980) and from Point of Pines (Wasley 1952).

Ceramic assemblages in the Arizona mountains with gray ware components occur in Pueblo III period sites along Cibecue Creek and in the Forestdale Valley (AZ P:16:9). Here, gray-orange indented corrugated pottery similar to pots at Chodistaas Pueblo constitutes over 60 percent of the undecorated sherds from surface collections. Mixed assemblages are common in the Grasshopper region, where gray-orange indented corrugated pottery varies from less than 10 percent to over 40 percent of undecorated surface sherds. To the west, however, gray corrugated vessels are virtually absent (Reid and others 1993).

Painted corrugated pottery is a long-lived decorated ceramic tradition in the Arizona mountains. The Chodistaas Pueblo whole-vessel assemblage includes McDonald Painted Corrugated, Salado White-on-red Corrugated, and Cibicue Painted Corrugated. In distribution, the most eastern and northern type is McDonald Painted Corrugated, which was described by Haury (1931) at the Forestdale Valley. He observed that McDonald was best known from the Upper Gila and that it was common at Showlow and Pottery Hill. It is also abundant in the White Mountain and Upper Silver Creek areas (Colton and Hargrave 1937: 62).

A smooth variety of what is now named Cibicue Painted Corrugated (recorded in abbreviated form as Cibicue Polychrome in the Grasshopper excavations) was identified by Haury (1934) at Canyon Creek Ruin, and Mauer (1970) studied several varieties of Cibicue Painted Corrugated (Cibicue Polychrome), including indented corrugated that was found in burial offerings at Grasshopper Pueblo. Little is known about its distribution prior to the A.D. 1300s. The westernmost painted corrugated type, Salado White-on-red Corrugated, is common from Grasshopper to the Tonto-Roosevelt area in central Arizona. Painted corrugated paste colors, brown and gray, mirror the distribution of their undecorated counterparts.

The cases mentioned above indicate that variation in the distribution of corrugated wares occurs not only between the plateau and the mountains, but within each geographic area as well. This variability, and the presence of mixed undecorated assemblages, could have been caused by a number of mechanisms. If differential distribution of each ware indeed represents a distinct ceramic tradition, and perhaps a distinct group of people, then mixed assemblages are indicating movement of pots, movement of people, or both. Ethnic coresidence within a particular region also could have produced side-by-side differential distributions of both wares and mixed assemblages.

Alternatively, these distribution patterns could be associated with the availability of certain kinds of clay and temper, which would have restricted local manufacture to either brown or gray ware, as in the case of the "Anasazi Brown Ware Tradition" mentioned above. Sherd-tempered corrugated wares are an exception, because sherd temper is characteristic of pottery manufactured in the Colorado Plateau area. For these reasons, it is important to consider not only paste color and temper, but also other technological and morphological attributes that could indicate production of brown and gray wares under different manufacturing criteria. In the Chodistaas Pueblo case, technological analysis of corrugated wares was useful for identifying two manufacturing technologies in the assemblage, and compositional analysis provided the necessary information to infer the manufacturing loci of both corrugated wares.

Technological Analysis

The original classification of the Chodistaas Pueblo floor assemblage by Crown (1981a: 71–73) grouped most of the corrugated pots into the descriptive category "brown indented obliterated corrugated." Examination of corrugated pots recovered after 1979, however, led to a reevaluation of the variability present in the undecorated assemblage. The partition of Chodistaas corrugated vessels into gray-orange corrugated and brown-red corrugated involved sorting by visual inspection, refiring of sherds from every broken vessel, and evaluating statistically the technological attributes thought to be diagnostic of each ware. Samples for compositional analysis were chosen only after both wares had been clearly defined and their differences tested experimentally and statistically.

Sorting

The preliminary identification of brown and gray corrugated vessels involved observations of paste color and texture. Even though in many cases paste color was deceiving because of variation in original firing atmosphere, texture differences were relatively simple to identify: brown corrugated ware (slipped and unslipped) had poorly sorted coarse to medium heterogeneous inclusions that often included muscovite, whereas gray corrugated ware had large amounts of quartz inclusions that gave the paste a sandy, sugarlike texture. A wide range of variation in texture was observed within each of the wares. Using these sorting criteria made it possible to initially classify 135 corrugated vessels (81.8 percent of the total unpainted corrugated assemblage of 165 vessels); 50 pots were gray corrugated and 85 pots were brown corrugated. The 30 remaining vessels were classified as indeterminate paste color and then submitted to more detailed testing. In addition, 17 of the 20 painted corrugated vessels were classified according to paste color and texture: 8 pots were identified as "brown" and 9 pots as "gray."

Refiring Experiments

A small sherd of every broken vessel was refired in an oxidizing atmosphere in order to standardize paste color. I expected to find clear differences in paste color among brown, red-slipped, and gray corrugated wares, both painted and unpainted, and to be able to determine the range of variation in paste color within each ware. Paste groups so defined, in turn, could be useful as sampling strata for chemical analysis. I refired 157 sherds at 950°C (1742°F) in an oxidizing atmosphere and then examined them under a 40x binocular microscope to classify them by texture.

Refiring revealed a continuous range of paste color, from dark red to light orange, with the darker hues generally associated with the brown paste. A limited degree of overlap in color was observed, but clear texture differences helped separate both brown and gray paste categories: 143 corrugated vessels were classified as brown corrugated (93 pots, including 12 Salado Red Corrugated and 4 painted corrugated) and gray corrugated (50 pots, including 5 painted corrugated). Left unclassified were 32 vessels, 16 of which are whole and could not be refired. Both gray and brown paste categories were subdivided into color and texture groups (Table 7.1) that were evaluated further by microscopic analysis.

Table 7.1. Texture and Color Groups of Sherds after Refiring Experiment
(n = 143)

| Texture | Brown | | Gray | |
	n	Paste color	n	Paste color
Coarse	25	2.5YR 3/6 Dark red	28	5YR 6/8 Reddish yellow
Medium	51	2.5YR 4/6, 4/8 Red	11	2.5YR 5/8 Red
Fine	17	2.5YR 5/6 Red	11	2.5YR 5/8 Red

Statistical Analysis

A statistical analysis was conducted to determine if attributes other than paste color and texture were unequivocally correlated to brown and gray corrugated categories. Following the methodology for sorting corrugated pottery used by Crown (1981a, 1981b) and by Gifford and Smith (1978) and my own observations, five attributes were recorded for each category: number of corrugations, number of indentations, shape of indentations, neck length, and wall thickness. Visual inspection of surface treatment on large jars revealed that brown corrugated vessels typically exhibit greater obliteration of coils and indentations than gray corrugated vessels. In addition, the shape of indentations is different in each ware. Four indentation shape categories were observed: triangular, narrow elongated, broad elongated, and square. Triangular indentations are characteristic of gray corrugated, whereas the remaining three categories are almost exclusively associated with brown corrugated (Table 7.2).

During preliminary sorting it was observed that large brown corrugated jars tended to have thicker walls and longer necks than gray corrugated jars of comparable size. Measurements of average wall thickness and neck length were taken for further testing.

The average number of coils and indentations per 4 square centimeters was counted for every corrugated

Table 7.2. Shape and Obliteration of Indentations on Brown Corrugated and Gray Corrugated Jars

Shape	Brown Corrugated	Gray Corrugated	Total
Triangular	6	32	38
Narrow elongated	13	2	15
Broad elongated	21	1	22
Square	6	1	7
Highly obliterated	7		7
Total	53	36	89

vessel. Brown corrugated jars have wider, fewer coils and indentations than gray corrugated jars. Large Salado Red Corrugated bowls (with a rim diameter larger than 35 cm) and jars are almost identical to brown corrugated vessels, but small corrugated bowls show more variation in both size and shape of corrugations and indentations.

In her analysis of variability in number of corrugations, number of indentations, and wall thickness, Crown (1981a: 133–146) suggested that some correlation existed between these attributes and vessel size, form, and type for the Chodistaas Pueblo assemblage. A larger sample of vessels was needed to reevaluate this observation, in particular because Crown (1981b) later demonstrated that these attributes were useful for isolating distinct manufacturing technologies in mixed undecorated assemblages.

To investigate if the number of corrugations, the number of indentations, neck length, and wall thickness were significantly different for each ware, I first had to test whether these attributes were correlated with vessel form and size. To do so, I chose all the corrugated jars (painted and unpainted) included in the brown and gray paste categories after the refiring experiments and used maximum diameter as an approximation of vessel size, because this measurement is available for most jars. Small (less than 20 cm maximum diameter), medium (20 to 29 cm maximum diameter), and large (more than 30 cm maximum diameter) jars were equally represented in both paste categories, and 75 brown paste jars and 43 gray paste jars were included in the tests. Corrugated bowls were not used for statistical testing because they constituted only 14.05 percent (32 of 182) of all the corrugated wares, and only 10 brown paste bowls had the necessary measurements.

Correlation Tests

The Pearson Correlation Coefficient between maximum diameter and each quantitative attribute was calculated using the SPSS-X Statistical Program to eliminate the possibility that observed differences between paste color categories were strongly correlated with vessel size. The coefficients and one-tailed significance levels, summarized in Table 7.3, indicate very low, even negative correlations between vessel size and number of corrugations and indentations for both wares. The correlation coefficient for number of corrugations on gray corrugated jars is particularly interesting, because it suggests that these jars were consistently built with thin coils regardless of size. Similarly, neck length,

Table 7.3. Pearson Correlation Coefficient Calculated for Brown Corrugated and Gray Corrugated Pottery

Variables	Pearson Coefficient Maximum Diameter	1-Tailed Significance
Brown Corrugated (n = 75)		
Maximum diameter	1.0000	
Wall thickness	0.4828	p < .001
Neck length	−0.4411	p < .001
Number of indentations	−0.3019	p < .01
Number of corrugations	0.2238	p < .01
Gray Corrugated (n = 43)		
Maximum diameter	1.0000	
Wall thickness	0.4206	p < .01
Neck length	−0.1098	p < .01
Number of indentations	−0.3225	p < .01
Number of corrugations	−0.0688	p < .01

which is consistently shorter for gray corrugated jars, appears to be independent of size. Brown ware, on the other hand, has a more ambiguous correlation coefficient for neck length than gray ware. The highest correlation coefficients are for average wall thickness in both wares. However, the test suggests that there is moderate to negative correlation between jar size and the four tested attributes and, therefore, these attributes may be used to assess differences between both manufacturing technologies independently from size.

Descriptive Statistics and Comparison of Means

The mean, standard deviation, kurtosis, and skewness of number of corrugations, number of indentations, neck length, and wall thickness were calculated for each paste color category using the SPSS-X Statistical Program. The Student T-test was used to compare the means of each attribute and determine whether attribute differences between the paste color categories were statistically significant. The results of this test, summarized in Table 7.4, indicate that the means of the num-

Table 7.4. Student T-Tests: Brown Corrugated (n = 75) versus Gray Corrugated (n = 43)

Variables	F Value	2-Tail P > F	t Value	Degrees of Freedom	2-Tail P > t
Neck length	1.05	.833	2.53	116	.014
Wall thickness	1.16	.601	1.78	116	.078
Number of corrugations	1.28	.347	3.16	116	.003
Number of indentations	1.78	.031	2.99	116	.003*

*Separate variance estimate

ber of corrugations, number of indentations, and neck length are significantly different for each category, suggesting that these attributes may indeed be diagnostic of different manufacturing technologies (Fig. 7.1).

Frequencies and histograms were also obtained to check for the presence and absence of normal distributions. Overall, descriptive statistics confirm preliminary observations on the distinctive characteristics of brown and gray corrugated pottery. By looking at the mean values and relative frequency of number of corrugations (Fig. 7.2), it became evident that brown corrugated jars were manufactured with thicker, fewer coils than gray corrugated jars. In addition, they exhibit narrow variation in the number of corrugations: 73 percent of the measured jars have 3 to 4 corrugations per 4 square centimeters, which contrasts with gray corrugated jars with 80 percent of the measurements from 4 to 6 corrugations per 4 square centimeters. Mean values and relative frequency of number of indentations per 4 square centimeters (Fig. 7.3) parallel those of number of corrugations, underscoring the direct proportionality that exists between the two attributes, but reinforcing the differences between brown and gray corrugated.

The mean value and relative frequency of neck length measurements (Fig. 7.4), on the other hand, show that gray corrugated jars have consistently smaller necks whose dimensions vary within a much narrower range than those of brown corrugated jars; 90 percent of the gray jars vary between 11 mm and 30 mm, whereas only 60 percent of the brown jars are within this range. Wall thickness is the only attribute that seems to be a weak measure of difference between the two wares. Both categories have similar mean and standard deviation values (Fig. 7.5). Relative frequency of wall thickness measurements indicate that almost one-half (45%) of the gray corrugated vessels are 6 mm thick and roughly one-half (58%) of the brown corrugated vessels are 6 mm to 7 mm thick; brown vessels also have a wider range of variation in thickness.

To summarize, technological analysis of corrugated pottery, which involved sorting, refiring, and statistical testing, indicates that the differences between brown corrugated ware and gray corrugated ware are not limited to paste color and texture. They extend to vessel construction and surface treatment, as measured in neck length, number of corrugations, and number and shape of indentations, and they should be considered as two separate wares rather than variations within a single ware. The analysis also suggests the possibility that there are two distinctive manufacturing technologies

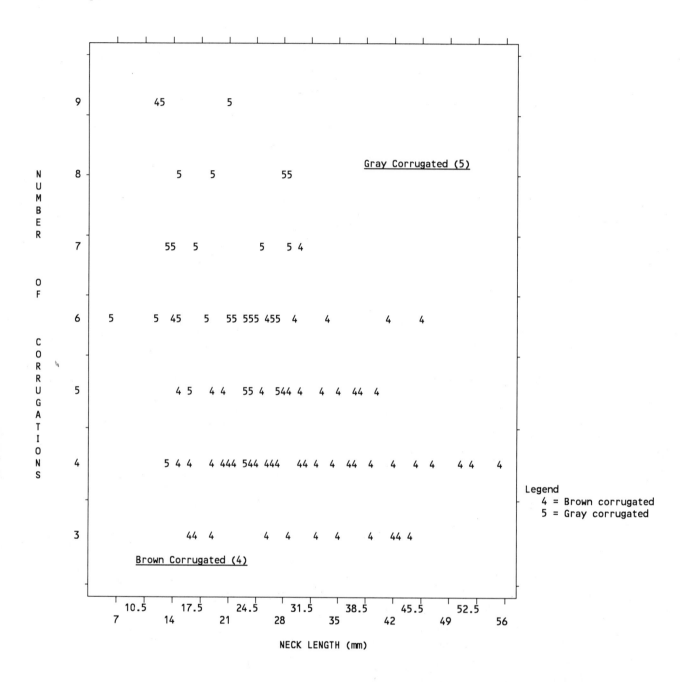

Figure 7.1. Bivariate representation of the relationship between number of corrugations and neck length for brown corrugated and gray corrugated jars.

represented in the corrugated whole-vessel assemblage at Chodistaas Pueblo: brown corrugated and gray corrugated. This pattern of variability is also present in room assemblages of the contemporaneous, neighboring pueblo of Grasshopper Spring, where six of eight excavated rooms have both wares represented in the floor assemblages. The observed technological differences between brown and gray corrugated wares, however, do not tell us whether they were locally made or imported into the Grasshopper region. Compositional analysis provided the information necessary for inferring the probable manufacturing loci of these wares.

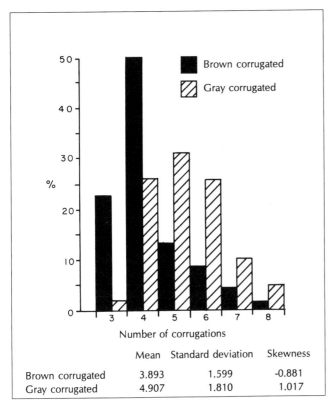

Figure 7.2. Number of corrugations per 4 square centimeters on brown corrugated and gray corrugated jars.

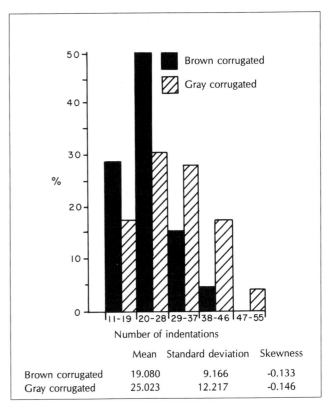

Figure 7.3. Number of indentations per 4 square centimeters on brown corrugated and gray corrugated jars.

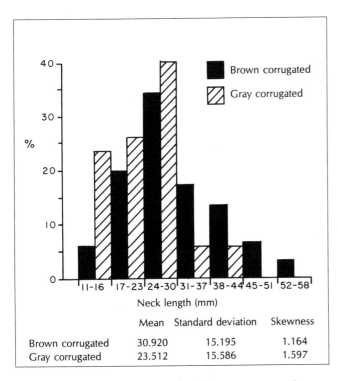

Figure 7.4. Neck length of brown corrugated and gray corrugated jars.

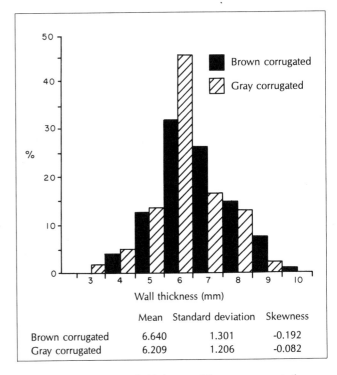

Figure 7.5. Wall thickness of brown corrugated and gray corrugated jars.

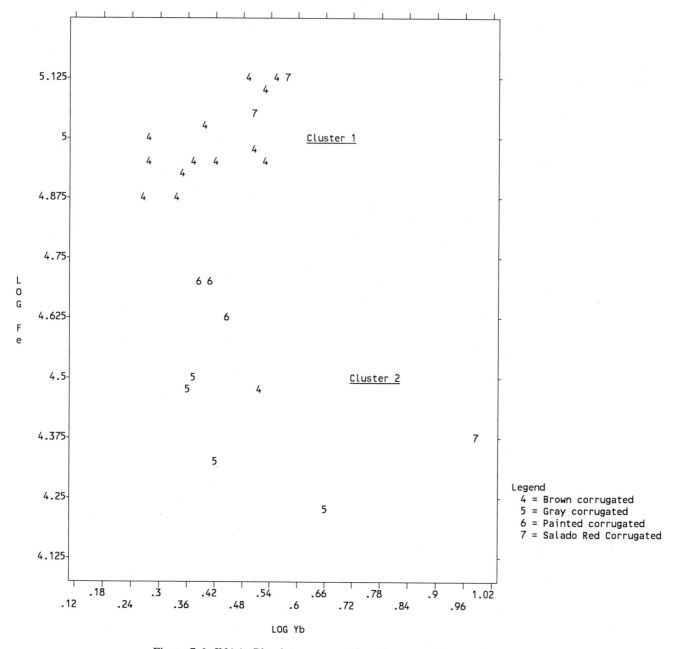

Figure 7.6. INAA: Bivariate representation of corrugated ware clusters.

Compositional Analysis

Detailed information on paste composition of corrugated wares was crucial for determining whether both brown and gray corrugated wares were manufactured on the Grasshopper Plateau or were acquired elsewhere. The analysis involved chemical characterization of paste by INAA and ICP and microscopic characterization of mineral inclusions. Although the sample of vessel sherds submitted to both chemical analyses was small, it provided insights about the compositional differences between gray and brown corrugated wares. Qualitative analysis of temper inclusions in refired sherds from every broken vessel not only reinforced the results of chemical characterization but was critical for interpreting chemical patterns and for pinpointing possible temper sources for each corrugated ware.

Instrumental Neutron Activation Analysis (INAA)

A sample of 24 corrugated sherds from room vessels (14 brown, 4 gray, 3 Salado Red Corrugated, and 3 painted) was selected from the color and texture subgroups of brown and gray pastes defined after refiring and submitted to INAA. Information on 16 clays was added to this sample for comparative purposes. Elemental concentrations of La, Yb, Eu, Sc, As, Lu, Ce, Fe,

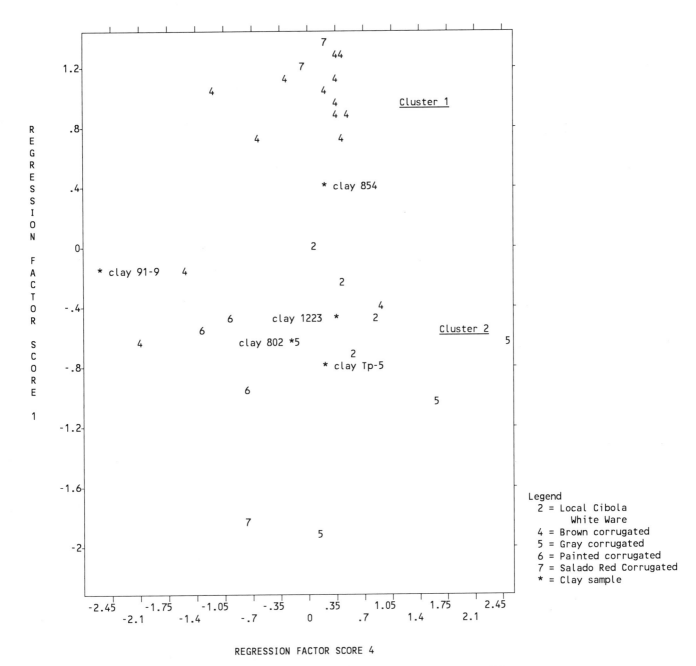

Figure 7.7. INAA: Corrugated wares and local Cibola White Ware clusters and clays, as defined by principal components.

Ta, Nd, Co, Hf, Sm, Cr, Th, K, Na, Zn, and Cs, for which no missing values were found, were converted to logarithmic values and then submitted to a complete linkage hierarchical cluster analysis to observe preliminary group tendencies. A bivariate plot of iron (log Fe) and ytterbium (log Yb) illustrates preliminary grouping tendencies (Fig. 7.6).

To refine group tendencies, the data were submitted to a Principal Component analysis. Samples from three archaeological clays (numbers 854, 802, 1223) and two survey clays (Tp–5 and 91–9) were included. Mahalanobis distances calculated for these clay samples

relative to either cluster indicate that: (a) the clay samples have at least a 79 percent probability of fitting into Cluster 2, and (b) clay 854 has a 31.5 percent probability of fitting in Cluster 1 and a 62.3 percent probability of belonging in Cluster 2 (Fig. 7.7). I refer to these as "clusters" rather than "compositional groups" because the small sample size precludes further statistical evaluation of group formation.

Cluster 1 includes ten brown corrugated and two Salado Red Corrugated. The samples in Cluster 2 are more dispersed than in Cluster 1, and Cluster 2 includes all other samples with lower elemental concentrations

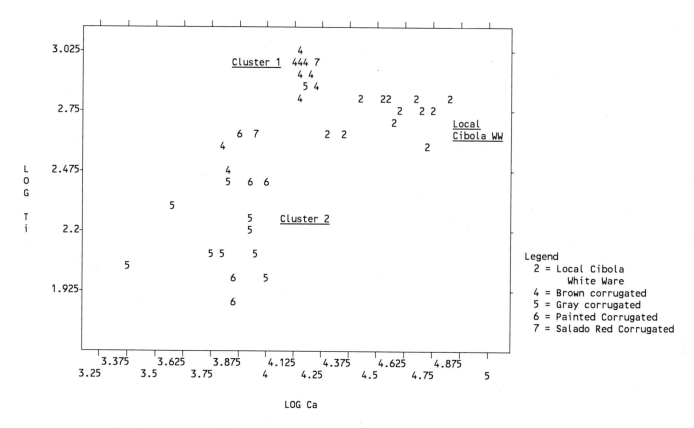

Figure 7.8. ICP: Bivariate representation of corrugated ware clusters and local white wares.

than the former one, including four Cibola White Ware samples with brown paste (Chapter 8). This cluster hints at the existence of broader compositional variability among corrugated types than is represented in such a small sample.

Inductively Coupled Plasma
Emission Spectroscopy (ICP)

Twenty-seven samples from corrugated vessels at Chodistaas Pueblo were submitted to ICP (10 gray, 10 brown, 2 Salado Red Corrugated, and 5 painted corrugated). In addition, twelve samples from survey clays and nine samples of clays from Room 113 in Grasshopper Pueblo (Triadan 1989) were also analyzed. A bivariate graph representing elemental concentrations (log) of titanium (Ti) and calcium (Ca) illustrates the differences in chemical paste composition between brown and gray paste categories (Fig. 7.8), and their compositional relationship with brown paste Cibola White Ware samples from Chodistaas and Grasshopper pueblos (see Chapter 8).

A Principal Component analysis that included log concentrations of Al, Ba, Ca, Cr, Cu, Fe, K, La, Mg,

Mn, Na, P, Sr, Ti, and Zn reinforced this pattern. In Figure 7.9, Cluster 1 includes brown paste sherds (brown corrugated and Salado Red Corrugated) and one gray paste sherd that group tightly around a sample of tempered clay (1906) from Room 113 in Grasshopper Pueblo. In contrast, sherds of gray corrugated and painted corrugated in Cluster 2 appear more widespread in the bivariate plots, indicating greater heterogeneity in raw material used in the manufacture of these vessels than of Cluster 1 vessels.

Mahalanobis distances calculated for two survey clay samples (GS1 and Tp–5) indicate that they have over a 75 percent probability of belonging in Cluster 2. A much larger number of samples is needed to determine more accurately how many raw material sources are represented in the gray corrugated vessels from Chodistaas Pueblo. One gray sherd clustered with the brown paste samples. This could have been caused by an erroneous sorting of the vessels or it could be due to more significant patterns in its manufacture.

As illustrated in the figures presented above, INAA and ICP yielded highly comparable grouping tendencies, regardless of different extraction methods. Only three samples overlapped across both analytical techniques

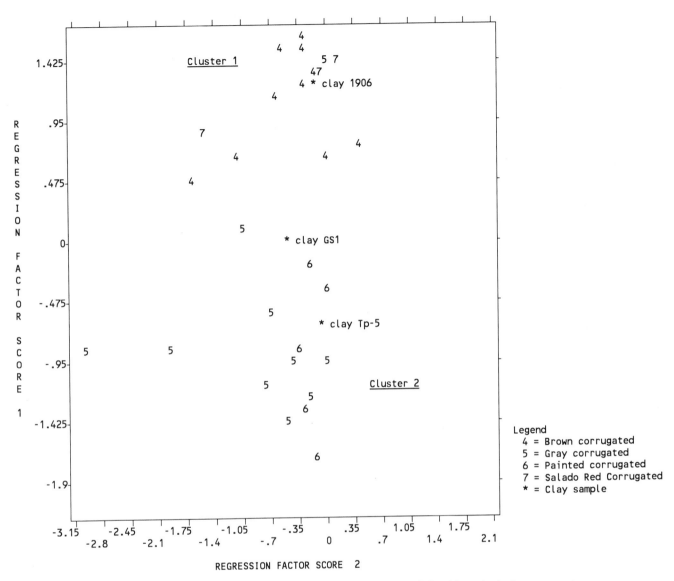

Figure 7.9. ICP: Corrugated ware clusters and local clays, as defined by principal components.

and they were classified in similar ways; two brown corrugated fit in Cluster 1 in both ICP and INAA, and one painted corrugated fit in Cluster 2. This comparability is particularly important for Cluster 1 vessels, because the clay sample (1906) that "matches" this cluster was only analyzed through ICP.

Petrographic Analysis

Qualitative characterization of mineral inclusions was recorded for 151 refired sherds from corrugated vessels. The analysis included microscopic examination of samples from two quartz sand sources collected in the Forestdale Valley and in Cibecue Creek, and from three sources of weathered diabase and diabase sands col-

lected in Canyon Creek and Q Ranch. Crushed sherds were also examined for comparison with sherd-tempered vessels.

Temper Types

Two major temper types were identified petrographically, each showing gradual variation in particle size and in presence or absence of quartz sand particles. Type 1 includes brown paste vessels tempered with diabase minerals and has three variants: 1a is coarse-grained diabase (more than 95% of the inclusions), 1b is medium to fine-grained diabase (more than 95% of the inclusions), and 1c is diabase plus quartz. The first two variants are almost identical to the diabase samples collected from weathering outcrops in Canyon Creek

Table 7.5. Temper Type 1 by Pottery Ware and Type

Pottery	Type 1a Coarse Diabase	Type 1b Medium Diabase	Type 1c Diabase + Quartz	Total
Brown corrugated	21	37	19	77
Gray corrugated			9	9
Unclassified corrugated			1	1
Salado Red Corrugated	12	1		13
Salado White-on-red Corrugated	4		3	7
Cibicue Painted Corrugated			1	1
McDonald Painted Corrugated			1	1
Total	37	38	34	109

Table 7.6. Temper Types 2 and 3 by Pottery Ware and Type

Pottery	Type 2a Quartz	Type 2b Quartz + Plagioclase	Type 2c Quartz + Pyroxene	Type 3 Ground Sherds	Total
Gray corrugated	19	11	3	1	34
Salado Red Corrugated				1	1
Cibicue Painted Corrugated			1		1
McDonald Painted Corrugated	3	2			5
Gray painted corrugated	1				1
Total	23	13	4	2	42

and Q Ranch, which are distinctive because of the presence of small amounts of muscovite; diabase deposits are extensive from the Canyon Creek escarpment westward. The third variant is similar to the fine diabase sand collected from the banks of Q Ranch Creek. The presence of water-worn quartz grains in this variant indicates that the parent materials were transported rather than weathered in situ as in types 1a and 1b. Diabase-quartz sand, therefore, must have come from farther south or west, where the drainages form soft sand banks. Table 7.5 summarizes the distribution of brown paste corrugated vessels by Temper Type 1 variants. One vessel formerly left unclassified and nine vessels classified as "gray corrugated" are actually tempered with diabase-quartz sand.

Temper Type 2 includes gray paste corrugated vessels tempered with quartz sand and also has three variants: 2a consists of well-sorted, rounded, water-worn quartz sand (more than 95% quartz), 2b has quartz and small amounts of plagioclase, and 2c has mainly quartz and small amounts of pyroxene. Variant 2b is similar to the sand sample collected from a bank in Cibecue Creek, which is the closest known source of sands. There are no sand deposits on the Grasshopper Plateau; Salt River Draw and Spring Creek cut through clayey loam soils and weathered limestone into bedrock. The sources of Type 2, therefore, may have been located to the east, around Cibecue Creek or farther south, because the amounts of quartz relative to other mineral inclusions increase as one approaches the lower reaches of a drainage. Table 7.6 summarizes the distribution of gray paste corrugated vessels among Temper Type 2 variants. One Salado Red Corrugated and one gray corrugated have sherd temper.

Chemical and Petrographic Variability

Comparison between clusters (INAA and ICP) and temper types indicates a strong correlation between clay and temper used for the manufacture of gray and brown corrugated wares. As indicated in Table 7.7, all the *brown paste* vessels in Cluster 1 have diabase-derived temper materials (Type 1). Clay 1906, which belongs in Cluster 1, is also tempered with fine weathered diabase (Temper Type 1b), and the single gray corrugated sample is tempered with diabase sand. Conversely, 12 *gray paste* samples in Cluster 2 are tempered with quartz sands (Type 2).

A comparison of INAA clusters and temper types supports these observations: all the samples from Cluster 1 are tempered with diabase-derived materials. In contrast, Cluster 2 includes more temper variation: two samples have quartz sand temper, seven samples have diabase-derived temper, and two (outliers), including one Salado Red Corrugated and one gray corrugated, have sherd temper (Table 7.8).

Table 7.7. Temper Types by ICP Clusters

Pottery	Temper Type 1	Temper Type 2	Total
Cluster 1			
Brown corrugated	10		10
Gray corrugated	1		1
Salado Red Corrugated	3		3
Cluster 2			
Gray corrugated		9	9
Painted Corrugated	2	3	5
Total	16	12	28

Table 7.8. Temper Types by INAA Clusters

Pottery	Temper Type 1	Temper Type 2	Temper Type 3	Total
Cluster 1				
Brown corrugated	11			11
Salado Red Corrugated	2			2
Cluster 2				
Brown corrugated	3			3
Gray corrugated	1	2		3
Painted corrugated	3			3
Outliers				
Gray corrugated			1	1
Salado Red Corrugated			1	1
Total	20	2	2	24

Brown versus Gray Corrugated Wares

The results of these analyses indicate differential selection of raw materials for the manufacture of brown and gray corrugated vessels. The probable sources of clays used for making brown and gray corrugated pottery and the presence of diabase-derived temper in brown corrugated and of quartz sand in gray corrugated suggest that both wares may have been manufactured within a radius of 10 km (about 6 miles) from Chodistaas Pueblo. The closest known diabase sources are located in the Canyon Creek drainage at Oak Creek Ranch, about 3 km (1.8 mile, straight line) west of Chodistaas, and the closest known quartz sand deposits are along Cibecue Creek, approximately 9 km (5.6 miles, straight line) from the site. Archaeological recovery of diabase-tempered clays that match the chemical composition of brown corrugated pottery (clay 1906) and gray corrugated pottery (clays 802, 854) further supports the manufacturing of these wares locally as well as regionally and suggests continuity in resource exploitation throughout the occupation of Chodistaas and Grasshopper pueblos. These findings are reinforced by the identification of at least three highly probable clay source locations (GS1, Tp–5, and 91–9) in the region.

Chodistaas is one of the westernmost late Pueblo III period sites on the Grasshopper Plateau; only a small cluster of approximately contemporaneous sites has been located immediately north of Oak Creek Ranch and west of Chodistaas. It is possible that diabase deposits were located within the "primary exploitation threshold" (Browman 1976) or territory where potters could obtain their resources at minimum energy cost and maximum benefit. Furthermore, iron pigments that produce a raspberry red slip are available locally. One can infer, therefore, that the manufacturing loci of brown corrugated, Salado Red Corrugated, and at least one-half of the painted corrugated vessels (seven of eleven Salado White-on-red Corrugated, one Cibicue Painted Corrugated, and one McDonald Painted Corrugated) were within the Grasshopper Plateau. Chemical differences between painted and unpainted brown corrugated samples may be signaling differential selection of clays, but the sample analyzed is too small to identify any significant pattern. On the other hand, the homogeneity of temper type in brown unpainted, slipped, and painted corrugated clearly indicates that these vessels were manufactured under similar technological criteria.

Gray corrugated ware presents a different situation. Quartz sand sediments similar to the temper used in the manufacture of gray corrugated vessels are present in Cibecue Creek. These deposits are located close to the "primary exploitation threshold" of Chodistaas and Grasshopper Spring pueblos and could have been easily exploited. However, two factors should be considered before any inference about the manufacturing loci of this ware is suggested: (1) the Cibecue Valley was populated during the late A.D. 1200s, and (2) gray corrugated ware is much more abundant in the Cibecue Valley than on the Grasshopper Plateau. Gray corrugated pottery constitutes 60 to 90 percent of undecorated surface collections of Pueblo III period sites in the Cibecue area (Montgomery and Reid 1994; Reid and others 1993). Local availability of temper sources for the gray corrugated vessels suggests that at least some of them were manufactured in the Cibecue Valley, but this suggestion cannot be adequately demonstrated without further testing. The wide range of variation in the chemical composition of gray paste, even when observed in a small sample, suggests that gray corrugated ware was probably made in more than one manufacturing locus.

The "anomalous" clustering of a few samples of brown and gray corrugated was thought at first to be the product of sorting error. Two alternative explanations for this anomaly may be offered: (1) considering the geological similarity between the Grasshopper Plateau and the Cibecue Valley, it is highly possible that chemical overlap of clays from these regions may occur, and (2) considering the geographical proximity between the two regions, it is likely that resource procurement zones for clay exploitation overlapped.

Information from the petrographic analysis indicates that the temper types of these samples are consistent with the sorting criteria. Cluster 1 has exclusively diabase-derived temper, whereas Cluster 2 includes all quartz-sand and some diabase temper types. Of the gray corrugated vessels, 21 percent (9 of 43) have diabase temper, indicating that, if my interpretation of a local use of diabase is correct, Grasshopper Plateau settlers not only manufactured brown corrugated but also gray corrugated pottery. Thus, petrographic data also support the interpretation of multiple sources of gray corrugated ware.

I suggest, on the basis of technological and compositional data, that the majority of corrugated vessels present in the assemblage from Chodistaas Pueblo were manufactured within a restricted area that included at least two geographically adjacent regions: the Grasshopper Plateau and the Cibecue Valley. The technological and compositional distinctiveness of brown corrugated and gray corrugated wares further indicates that they were made under different technological criteria. Coresidence of potters who were manipulating both manufacturing technologies is a plausible explanation that would account for the use of local raw materials in the manufacture of both brown and gray corrugated vessels.

It is difficult to infer whether each of these wares represents a socially or ethnically bounded ceramic "tradition" or whether this case of side-by-side variation in ceramic technology signals multiethnic occupation of a restricted area, because no Cibecue sites have been excavated. Grasshopper and Cibecue settlements were located within a short distance of each other, and it would not be surprising if strong relationships existed among them. The presence of gray corrugated ware at Chodistaas and other contemporaneous pueblos on the Grasshopper Plateau is but one indication of these relationships. In this regard, Reid (in Reid and others 1993) suggests that people from the Cibecue Valley moved onto the Grasshopper Plateau during the fourteenth century. What makes the above hypothesis critical for further research is the possibility that inhabitants of two adjacent regions, perhaps culturally or socially related, managed to maintain their own separate ceramic technologies.

The movement of corrugated vessels, however, was not exclusively unidirectional; both brown and gray corrugated vessels are present at Forestdale, Grasshopper, Cibecue, and Q Ranch. If most brown and gray corrugated wares were manufactured in different regions, as the marked differential distribution of surface ceramic materials and compositional data suggest, then one may further infer that relationships of reciprocal exchange between these regions existed. Compositional analysis of brown and gray wares from Cibecue Valley sites is necessary to reinforce this interpretation.

The differential distribution of gray and brown corrugated in the southern Colorado Plateau and the Arizona mountains, and the introduction of gray corrugated vessels and the technological criteria for their manufacture into the Grasshopper region and adjacent areas to the west, may be signaling, according to Montgomery and Reid (1994), the direction of the movement of people into the mountains during the late Pueblo III period. They observe that differences between gray corrugated sherd and vessel frequencies in surface collections and floor assemblages at Chodistaas Pueblo closely mirror a similar pattern observed for Roosevelt Red Ware (Chapter 8), and they postulate the movement of people as a probable mechanism of circulation of these wares.

Although the information and discussion presented here are far from sufficient for reconstructing the relationships that existed between Chodistaas Pueblo and other settlements, they nonetheless corroborate the importance of prehistoric ceramic technology for distinguishing between local and nonlocal ceramics.

RED PLAIN WARE

Red-slipped plain pottery occurs throughout the Arizona mountains and in the Salt-Gila Basin and surrounding areas. Red plain generally displays a high degree of technological variability, particularly in temper, wall thickness, and surface manipulation (Doyel 1978), indicating that this ware was manufactured in a number of locations. Perhaps the most widely distributed and best known thirteen-century red plain ceramics are Gila Red, a paddled, slipped, and polished pottery found in Hohokam assemblages but ultimately derived from an unknown Mogollon source (Haury 1940: 39–90, 1945: 81), and Salado Red, a coiled, smoothed, and slipped pottery distributed throughout the Arizona mountains (Doyel 1978: 34; Gladwin and Gladwin 1930; Haury 1934). The existence of other less well-known, more localized red plain types, such as Inspiration Red (Doyel 1978: 96), Tonto Red (Colton and Hargrave 1937: 166), and the later Kinishba Red (Haury and Hargrave 1931), suggests that red plain ware was ubiquitous in most prehistoric assemblages south of the Colorado Plateau.

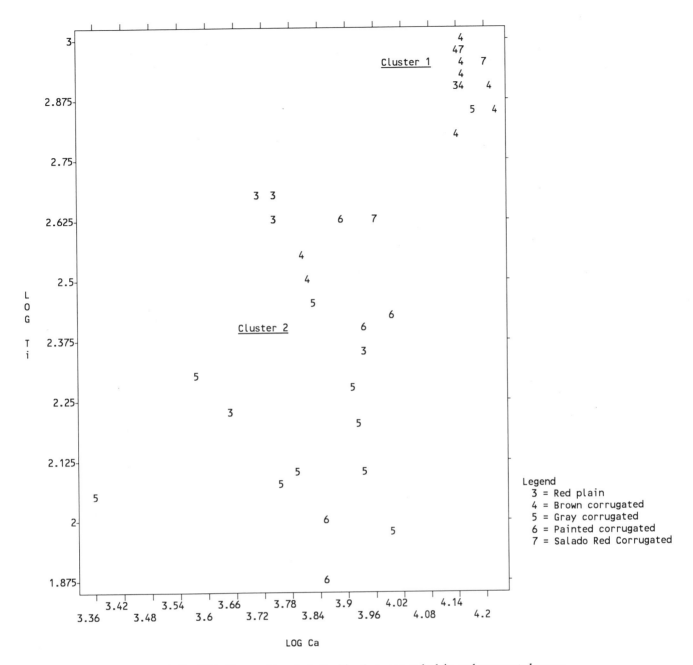

Figure 7.10. ICP: Compositional similarities between red plain and corrugated wares.

Technology and Provenience

At Chodistaas Pueblo, red plain ware constitutes 18.4 percent of undecorated vessels (40 of 217) and 12.1 percent of the total whole-vessel assemblage. Technologically, most red plain vessels are homogeneous in paste color and texture, wall thickness, and slip color; size and shape of jars (35 of 40 vessels) display more variability. Generally, red plain jars are distinct from the local brown indented obliterated corrugated jars because they were tempered with medium to coarse quartz-feldspar and muscovite sand rather than with diabase, and most were thinned by the paddle and anvil

technique. Several red plain jars have unique shapes with shoulders and long necks, and even elliptical bodies. Based on their distinctiveness, specifically the use of paddle and anvil for wall thinning, Crown (1981a) suggested that red plain vessels may have been introduced into the pueblo from elsewhere. Temper identification of 32 refired sherds from broken jars and chemical characterization of samples from 12 vessels (ICP: n = 6; INAA: n = 6) indicate that only a small number of pots can be positively identified as local.

One diabase-tempered sample and five sand-tempered samples of red plain jars were analyzed by ICP (Fig. 7.10). This sample is small but interesting. At least

[69]

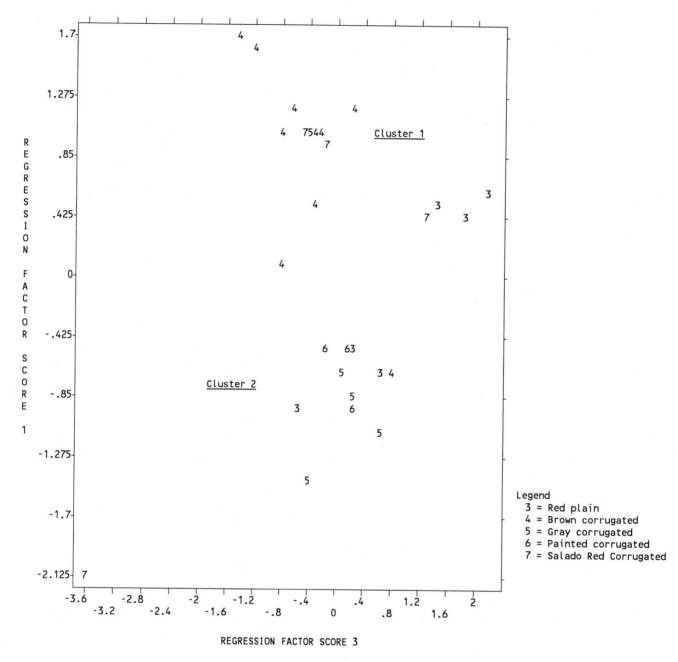

Figure 7.11. INAA: Compositional similarities between red plain and corrugated wares, as defined by principal components.

three sand-tempered red plain samples are chemically different from the local gray corrugated (Cluster 2), and the diabase-tempered red plain sample clusters with the brown corrugated (Cluster 1). Results from INAA of six red plain samples (Fig. 7.11) also revealed a considerable degree of compositional variation. Three sand-tempered red plain samples form a separate grouping with one Salado Red Corrugated out of Cluster 1, and two diabase-tempered red plain samples belong in

Cluster 2. Overall, these analyses were useful for identifying compositional differences between brown corrugated and red plain wares and for indicating local manufacture of a limited number of vessels.

Temper in 23 of the jars and 4 of the bowls is medium to coarse quartz sand with small amounts of feldspar and muscovite. As mentioned previously, sand deposits are not found on the Grasshopper Plateau. The sampled Cibecue Creek sands do not include visible muscovite particles, but these sands are similar in size and sorting to the temper in the red plain vessels. However, red plain pottery (Inspiration Red) tempered with quartz-feldspar sand and muscovite was reported as locally produced in the Miami-Globe area, south of the Grass-hopper Plateau (Doyel 1978: 96). Only five red plain jars are tempered with coarse weathered diabase (Temper Type 1a). These jars have a dark, almost brown paste (2.5YR 3/6 Dark Red), whereas all the sand-tempered jars and bowls have light red-to-orange paste (2.5YR 5/6 Red).

Morphological and technological attributes such as presence and absence of sharp "Gila" shoulders, neck length, paddle and anvil marks, and wall thickness were recorded for red plain jars to determine whether these attributes covary with paste color and temper type and to observe if sharp-shouldered jars had consistently larger necks than rounded jars within a temper type. Nine vessels had sharp shoulders, but their neck lengths varied from 35 mm to 104 mm. "Gila" shoulders and long necks appear in both sand- and diabase-tempered jars. In contrast, walls are generally thicker in diabase-tempered jars (9 mm to 10 mm) than in sand-tempered jars (5 mm to 6 mm) of comparable size, which are distinctive because of their consistently thin walls.

These observations agree with Whittlesey's (1982a: 18–21) analysis of vessel thinning techniques in mixed assemblages from the Tonto-Roosevelt region, where both the paddle-and-anvil and coil-and-scrape methods crosscut wares and types. Red plain, however, is the only ware in the Chodistaas assemblage that has been consistently thinned by the paddle-and-anvil technique, including those vessels positively identified as local. This information does not pinpoint the provenience of sand-tempered red plain vessels, but the particular characteristics of this ware and the reported occurrence of red plain pottery (Inspiration Red) with similar temper, surface manipulation, and range of shapes in other areas of east-central Arizona (such as in the Miami-Globe area; Doyel 1978) lead me to suggest that the red plain vessels in the whole-vessel assemblage at Chodistaas Pueblo were manufactured somewhere in the mountains, perhaps just west of the Grasshopper Plateau.

To recapitulate, there are three distinct technological traditions represented in the corrugated and plain vessels at Chodistaas Pueblo: brown corrugated, gray corrugated, and red plain. Salado Red Corrugated is a slipped variant of brown corrugated. Both gray and brown corrugated wares include painted vessels. Paste chemistry and temper mineralogy indicate that at least one of these traditions, brown corrugated, was local to the Grasshopper Plateau: brown indented obliterated corrugated, Salado Red Corrugated, and painted corrugated types such as Salado White-on-red Corrugated represent local ceramic manufacture. Technological and compositional differences between the local ceramics and the gray corrugated and red plain, coupled with relative abundance of these wares in areas east and west of the Grasshopper Plateau respectively, suggest that the local settlers obtained a number of gray corrugated and red plain vessels from their neighbors. Considering the hypothesis of relative mobility of mountain populations during the late 1200s, it is possible that inhabitants of small settlements on the Grasshopper Plateau maintained reciprocal relationships with other groups in and beyond the mountains. Furthermore, the local adoption of gray corrugated technology may be signaling a movement of people into the region at the end of the thirteenth century.

That the local potters were able to manufacture both gray corrugated ware and red plain ware is evident in the use of locally available clays and diabase temper in up to 21 percent of gray corrugated pottery and 16 percent of red plain pottery. However, they seemingly had a strong preference for brown corrugated vessels. Reproduction of presumably nonlocal wares using local raw materials could be evidence for coresidence of people from different backgrounds. Of more general interest for interpreting ceramic variability is the coexistence of several technological traditions within a relatively small area of interaction. The information presented here provides initial support to the traditional interpretation of technological variation in prehistoric Southwestern ceramics: that the manufacturing technology of undecorated wares may represent geographic and perhaps social and ethnic boundaries.

CHAPTER EIGHT

The Circulation of Cibola White Ware, White Mountain Red Ware, and Roosevelt Red Ware

Decorated pottery usually constitutes a small part of any prehistoric ceramic assemblage. In the American Southwest, however, archaeologists rely heavily on attributes of painted pottery to infer aspects of prehistoric behavior such as social organization, community interaction, or information transfer. Unfortunately, the ceramic record is mainly composed of fragmentary vessels and sherds that seldom depict enough of the painted designs to make those inferences. At Chodistaas Pueblo, 113 whole and restored vessels, representing four decorated wares (Cibola White Ware, Roosevelt Red Ware, White Mountain Red Ware, and painted corrugated ware) provide sufficient material for an examination of the range of variation in design style and technology that occurred in this small pueblo during a limited time interval. By integrating this information with data on ceramic composition and archaeological evidence from Chodistaas and other sites in the Grasshopper region, it is possible to propose a reconstruction of the manufacture and circulation of decorated wares throughout these mountain settlements during the late Pueblo III period. Compositional, technological, and stylistic information on three polished and painted wares from Chodistaas Pueblo is presented, and the probability of local manufacture for each ware and the possible mechanisms of circulation of nonlocal wares are discussed.

CIBOLA WHITE WARE

Cibola White Ware was the dominant decorated ware over most of eastern Arizona and western New Mexico for at least six centuries (about A.D. 700–1300). This mineral-painted white ware had a wide geographic distribution, which extended south from Dolores, Colorado to the Mogollon Rim of Arizona, and from the Rio Grande Valley of New Mexico west to the Lower Little Colorado River and the Chevelon drainage in Arizona (Fowler 1989: 2; S. Plog 1980: 65).

Available information on the provenience of Cibola White Ware from sites on the Colorado Plateau indicate that this ware was manufactured in numerous regions, such as the Upper Puerco river valley (Zedeño and others 1993), the San Juan Basin (Franklin 1982; Toll 1985; Toll and others 1980; Windes 1984; Zedeño and others 1992), Pinedale (Haury and Hargrave 1931; Lightfoot and Jewett 1984); Mineral Creek and Hooper Ranch (Martin and others 1961), the Springerville area (Doyel 1984; Rugge and Doyel 1980), the Snowflake-Mesa Redonda area (Neily 1988), and as far west as the Chevelon drainage (S. Plog 1980). Furthermore, the prehistoric communities in these and other plateau regions apparently not only manufactured Cibola White Ware vessels but also obtained them from other communities, and intraregional and interregional circulation of this ware occurred throughout the duration of its manufacture.

Evidence that long-distance circulation of Cibola White Ware began as early as A.D. 800 comes from Basketmaker to Pueblo I period sites in Dolores, Colorado, where Wilson and Blinman (1988: 366–368) identified nonlocal Cibola White Ware sherds. The movement of Cibola White Ware vessels extended southward into the mountains of east-central and central Arizona during the Pueblo II to III interval. Compositional analyses of ceramics from Q Ranch (Tuggle and others 1982) and from the Tonto Basin (Lightfoot and Jewett 1984; Lindauer, in press) suggest that the majority of these materials were manufactured elsewhere. These nonlocal vessels are stylistically and technologically similar to those found on the Grasshopper Plateau.

The emphasis I place on compositional, technological, and stylistic variability of Cibola White Ware from Chodistaas Pueblo and other sites on the Grasshopper Plateau stems from the belief that a ware that was manufactured in so many places and had such wide circulation must record key information about the movement of people, materials, and ideas across a vast landscape. Understanding such behaviors is crucial for reconstructing episodic changes in the Arizona mountains at the end of the thirteenth century.

Compositional Analysis

The most complete set of data on paste composition of vessels from Chodistaas Pueblo was obtained for Cibola White Ware. At Chodistaas, Cibola White Ware is the most abundant decorated ware: 45.1 percent of the decorated assemblage and 15.4 percent of the total whole-vessel assemblage. Traditionally, the relative abundance of Cibola vessels at the site would have been interpreted as indicating local manufacture, but as discussed previously, this criterion is misleading. The information from several regions presented above suggests that, when local, Cibola White Ware commonly shares technological and even compositional characteristics with other decorated and undecorated wares. At Chodistaas, however, Cibola vessels contrast sharply with the rest of the ceramic assemblage in paste color, temper type, pigment type, and firing technology. One may question, therefore, whether the local people were actually manufacturing pottery under two distinctive technological and stylistic criteria or were obtaining Cibola White Ware vessels elsewhere.

To find an answer for this question, samples from 56 Cibola White Ware vessels were submitted to INAA. Binocular examination of sherds from reconstructible vessels indicated that they did not have large amounts of temper that could affect seriously the results of the analysis (Neff and others 1988, 1989). The sample was selected to control for spatial as well as temporal variability and was divided as follows:

47 whole and partial Cibola White Ware vessels from Chodistaas Pueblo, including 8 bowls, 10 pitchers, 28 jars, and 1 canteen (two unclassified and two Snowflake vessels were excluded from the analysis);

3 Cibola White Ware vessels from rooms excavated at two sites contemporaneous with Chodistaas Pueblo: 2 jars from Grasshopper Spring Pueblo and 1 jar from site AZ P:14:197;

5 Cibola White Ware vessels from Grasshopper Pueblo, included for temporal comparison: 3 jars had design and paste characteristics similar to those of Chodistaas Pueblo black-on-white pots, and 2 jars were similar in design but different in paste color and texture (these last 2 jars are representative of the majority of whole and reconstructible Cibola jars from Grasshopper Pueblo).

In addition, samples of unfired clays collected from the vicinity of Chodistaas Pueblo and areas farther away were included in the analysis. Six clays were chosen on the basis of firing color (light gray to buff), plasticity,

and shrinkage properties (Chapter 6). Of these clays, two were collected in the vicinity of Grasshopper, two came from the Forestdale Valley and surroundings (approximately 60 km, 37 miles, to the northeast), one was recovered from Room 10 at Chodistaas Pueblo, and one was from Room 113, a storage-manufacturing room in Grasshopper Pueblo. Red-firing clays were also included in the analysis to compare them to brown paste samples.

In the following presentation of the results of this analysis, it is important to stress the conceptual and empirical difference between analytically defined sources, geological raw material sources, and actual manufacturing loci. *Analytically defined sources* are hypothetical raw material sources that are identified chemically and are represented by "compositional groups." They differ from *geological clay and temper sources* in that their chemical composition results from the artificial combination of all ceramic paste components, whereas geological raw material sources are discrete sedimentary units that occur naturally. Geological sources and analytical sources, in turn, may or may not directly correspond to specific *manufacturing loci*.

For example, a potter or community of potters may have exploited more than one raw material source to manufacture a specific ware. In such a case, multiple raw material sources used in the past may be represented archaeologically by multiple compositional groups that do not necessarily indicate the existence of multiple manufacturing loci. The opposite case, several communities using raw material sources that are geologically similar and chemically indistinguishable from one another, could also occur. Therefore, interpretations of chemical or mineralogical variability within a specific ware should take these complex relationships into consideration.

Determination of Compositional Groups

Fifty-three samples (94.6% of the total analyzed) were unequivocally assigned to one of four compositional groups. In a bivariate space, the graphic representation of group separation through reference to log concentrations (Fig. 8.1) of europium (Eu) and iron (Fe) and to principal components (Fig. 8.2) clearly illustrates the analytical distinctiveness of each group: Group 1 has 27 members, Group 2 has 9 members, Group 3 has 13 members, and Group 4 has 4 members. Groups 2 and 4 are too small to evaluate how well they represent their analytical source. Two samples were left as outliers because of their low probability of belonging to any of

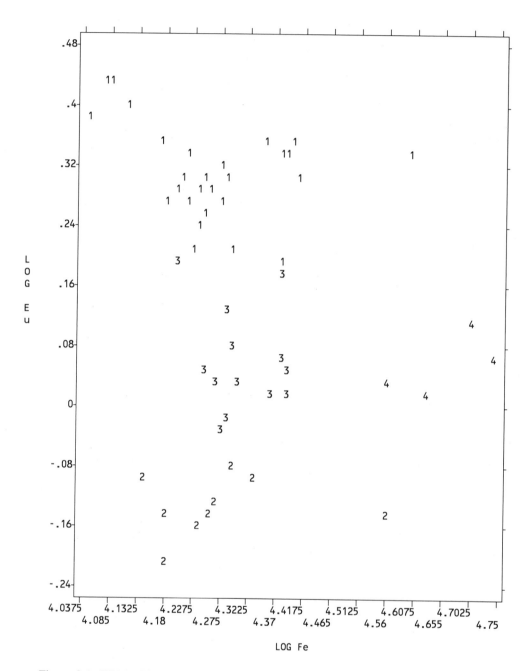

Figure 8.1. INAA: Bivariate representation of Cibola White Ware compositional groups.

the groups, and one was omitted because it had almost equal probability of belonging to Group 1 or Group 3.

Group 4 has only four members but presents an important compositional characteristic, high iron (Fe) content, that clearly indicates a different analytical source. Group 4 includes samples of two jars from Grasshopper Pueblo and two from Chodistaas Pueblo. The Grasshopper jars are technologically distinct from those in the remaining compositional groups and, although small, this group hinted at the existence of a

separate source for a majority of Cibola White Ware vessels at Grasshopper Pueblo. To investigate further this possibility, 32 Cibola vessels were submitted to ICP: 14 from Chodistaas, 4 from Grasshopper Spring Pueblo, and 14 from Grasshopper Pueblo. The last samples were chosen from those vessels that had paste color, shape, and design different from the former ones.

The results of ICP clearly separated white-paste samples from brown-paste ones. The analysis revealed that Cibola White Ware samples from Chodistaas and

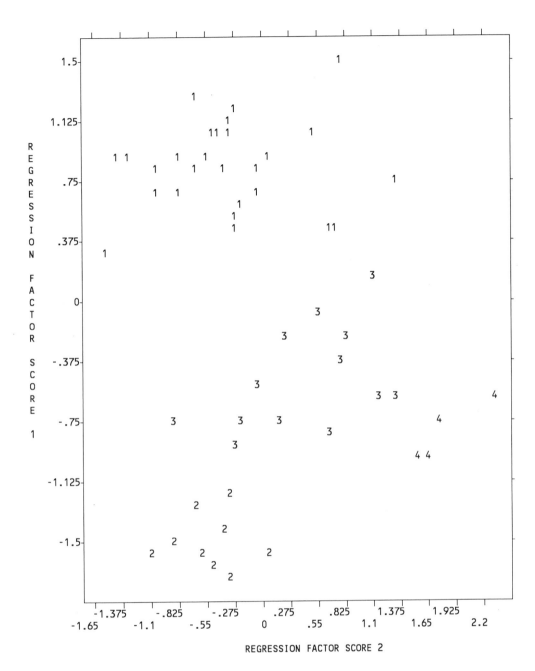

Figure 8.2. INAA: Cibola White Ware compositional groups, as defined by principal components.

Grasshopper Spring represent an analytical source or related sources whose chemical composition is completely different from the sources of all but three of the Grasshopper Pueblo samples. A bivariate representation of ICP log concentrations for two elements, zinc (Zn) and iron (Fe), illustrates these differences (Fig. 8.3). However, the fine-grained group formation seen in INAA was not replicated by ICP, probably because elemental concentrations were measured by different extraction techniques (Fig. 8.4).

Neither ICP nor INAA revealed matches between light-firing clays and white-paste samples. However, calculation of Mahalanobis distances in a discriminant function analysis, using INAA data, revealed matches between Group 4 and two clay samples from Room 113 (clays 854 and 1223), one of which is diabase-tempered (854). A sample from the sterile layer of Test pit 88–5 (Tp–5) at Chodistaas Pueblo also has strong chemical similarities with Group 4 (Fig 8.5). The compositional relationships among a local clay deposit, clays recov-

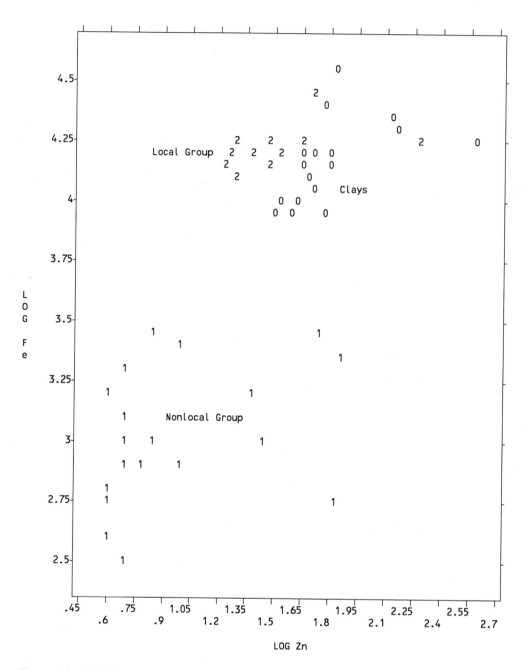

Figure 8.3. ICP: Bivariate representation of local and nonlocal Cibola White Ware samples.

ered in archaeological contexts, and Group 4 vessels indicate that at least some of the brown-paste Cibola White Ware vessels from Grasshopper Pueblo and the two vessels from Chodistaas Pueblo were manufactured with local clays. As shown in Chapter 7, brown paste white ware vessels are compositionally similar to gray corrugated, painted corrugated and Roosevelt Red Ware samples included in Cluster 2 (INAA), suggesting manufacture on the Grasshopper Plateau or in its immediate vicinity.

In summary, the compositional variation evident in these analyses indicates that: (1) Cibola White Ware vessels from Chodistaas Pueblo represent at least four analytical sources; (2) two other contemporaneous sites, Grasshopper Spring and AZ P:14:197, also contain white ware vessels that represent the same analytical sources as those from Chodistaas; (3) although a few vessels from Grasshopper Pueblo were chemically similar to at least one compositional group identified in the Chodistaas sample, the majority of Cibola White Ware

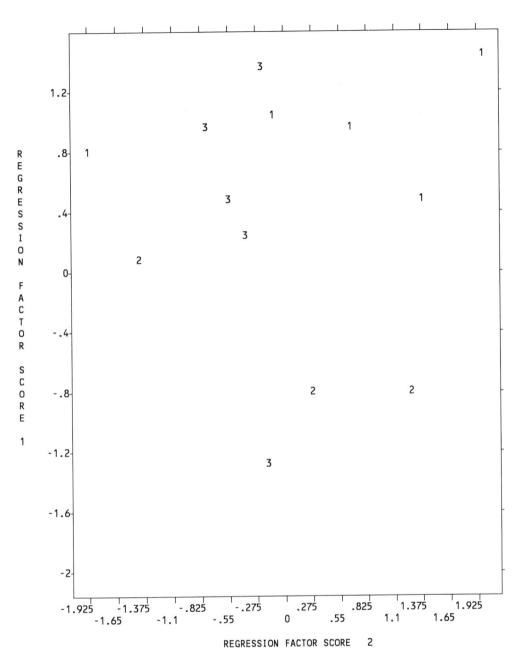

Figure 8.4. ICP: Principal Components scatter plot showing nonlocal Cibola White Ware samples. Sample numbers 1 to 3 indicate compositional groups defined by INAA.

vessels at Grasshopper (which have brown paste rather than white paste) represent a source that is completely different from those identified for the three earlier sites; only two brown paste Cibola jars were found in the Chodistaas assemblage. The chemical similarities among brown paste black-on-white pottery from Chodistaas and Grasshopper, local gray corrugated, and local clay sources suggest that these vessels were probably manufactured in the region.

Variation in paste composition of Cibola White Ware in the Grasshopper region occurs both spatially and temporally. Cibola White Ware vessel clays from late Pueblo III sites came from at least three chemically distinct, presumably nonlocal sources. Later, a shift to local manufacture of this ware is indicated by the use of local clays. This shift took place sometime during the Pueblo IV occupation of Grasshopper Pueblo. Data on manufacturing technology support these observations.

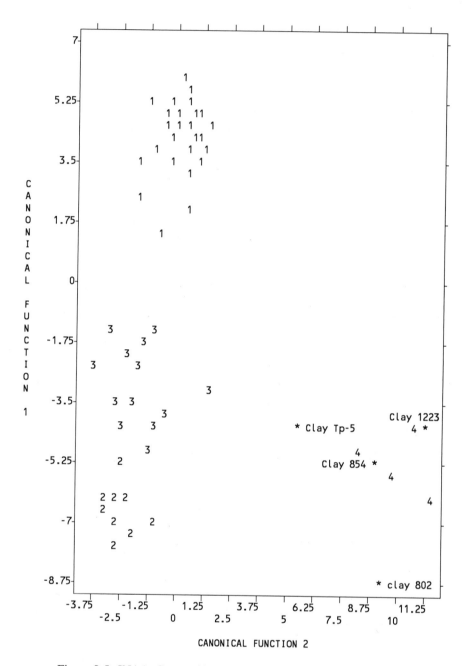

Figure 8.5. INAA: Compositional similarities between clays and local
Cibola White Ware samples, as defined by discriminant functions.

Technological Analysis

An analysis of manufacturing technology of Cibola White Ware was conducted to evaluate the probability that this ware was manufactured locally. Compositional analysis alone was insufficient, because no clay "matches" were found for white-paste samples, whereas there were matches between brown paste samples and local clays. Working under the premise that ceramic technology may signal variation in actual manufacturing loci more accurately than design style, I sought first to find out whether Cibola White Ware shared technological characteristics with other wares in the assemblage, and second, whether those characteristics varied spatially and temporally relative to the procurement sources for this ware. To do so, I used geological information relevant to clay sources in the Grasshopper region and adjacent areas, observations of temper technology, and data obtained from experimental refiring of sherd samples from all the broken vessels. Observations of forming techniques and vessel morphology provided additional information for reconstructing the manufacturing technology of this ware. Integration of compositional and technological data shows that Cibola White Ware *was not* manufactured in the Grasshopper region during the late Pueblo III period.

Raw Materials: Clays, Temper, and Pigments

All but two Cibola White Ware vessels from Chodistaas Pueblo were manufactured with white-firing clays. As James Burton advised me in 1990, these clays have low concentrations of elements and chemical compounds, in particular calcium, which is a characteristic of clays (specifically kaolinites) formed in acidic environments. No clay mineral analysis to identify kaolinites was performed, but low calcium concentrations or absence thereof were also detected by INAA. In contrast, the Grasshopper Plateau is situated on the western edge of the Upper Supai Formation, Cibeque Member, which is characterized by highly calcareous sandstone and shale, with limestone lenses (Finnell 1966). Outcrops of Naco Limestone are present in the southern and western portions of the region. According to Winters (1963: 17, 73), occasional thin beds of white clay and highly calcareous claystone occur in the Supai Formation, but in general kaolin clay and accessory minerals are almost absent.

The closest known white-firing clays and kaolinite beds are restricted to a narrow east-west zone of Cretaceous sediments parallel to the Mogollon Rim, all south of State Highway 260 (Moore 1968, map). Of these, the only outcrops that have been sampled and tested were in Cretaceous Shales along Corduroy Creek, immediately south of the Forestdale Valley, about 60 km (37 miles) northeast of Grasshopper (Moore 1968: 73). There are no geological formations likely to have white acidic clays in a radius of 15 km to 20 km (9 to 12 miles) from Chodistaas Pueblo. There is a Cretaceous Shale outcrop about 15 km northeast of Chodistaas; the terrain between Chodistaas and this location is extremely rugged, so in walking distance it is probably no closer than 25 km to 30 km (15 to 19 miles; USGS Chediski Quadrangle topographic sheet, T9N/R16E). To date, no such clays have been located there.

Three of the compositional groups determined for the Chodistaas Pueblo assemblage represent a type of clay (acidic, white-firing, perhaps kaolinite) of probable cretaceous origin, of restricted availability in the Arizona mountains and southern Colorado Plateau. It is probable, then, that the chemical characteristics of compositional groups 1, 2, and 3 represent different clay sources located not too far from one another. Although compositional differences between Group 1 and Groups 2 and 3 are large enough to suggest exploitation of two geologically and even geographically discrete clay sources, differences between Groups 2 and 3 represent a continuum of variation and may be indicating different outcrops of a single source. Without a clay match, however, these observations remain speculative. Identification of manufacturing loci from analytical sources would require careful sampling and analysis of white-firing clays across their zone of occurrence and relative to prehistoric settlements nearby. Only then could one get a relatively accurate idea of the true spatial significance of the observed compositional variation.

Temper technology is homogeneous across the three compositional groups, suggesting that they are technologically related. Twenty-seven sherds from white paste vessels representing Chodistaas Pueblo (n = 21), Grasshopper Spring Pueblo (n = 3), and Grasshopper Pueblo (n = 3) were refired and examined under a 40x binocular microscope to identify temper types. The paste of these sherds has a fine, compact texture, with small amounts of orange-red crushed sherds and quartz sand. Positive determination of sherd temper was made for all but one sherd; sherd temper became visible only after refiring the sherds. Sherd and quartz temper occurs across the three compositional groups, but in varying proportions. Group 1 has one sample with only sand temper, and Group 2 has one sample with only sherd temper. Results of the petrographic analysis reported by Crown (1981a) were compared with the compositional groups. The presence of ground sherds was noted in only two of Crown's samples. However, her temper groups overlap across the compositional groups, supporting my observation that black-on-white vessels from Chodistaas have similar temper technology, regardless of chemical paste composition. Homogeneity in temper technology may have been a generalized characteristic of Cibola White Ware manufactured on the Colorado Plateau. Recent chemical and petrographic analyses of over a hundred Cibola White Ware samples from sites on the upper Puerco River and in the San Juan Basin area produced similar results (Zedeño and others 1993: 212; Table 56).

Thirteen sherds from brown paste black-on-white vessels were also refired and examined microscopically.

Table 8.1. Paste Color, Temper, and Pigments of Refired Cibola White Ware Sherds by Compositional Group

Compositional Group	Paste color	Temper (n)	Pigment (n)
1 (n = 12)	10YR 8/1 White 10YR 8/2 White 5YR 8/2 Pinkish white	Sherd + sand (11) Sand (1)	Iron (7) Manganese (4)
2 (n = 5)	2.5Y 8/2 White 5Y 8/1 White	Sherd + sand (5)	Iron (1) Manganese (1)
3 (n = 8)	10YR 8/1 White 10YR 8/4 Very pale brown	Sherd + sand (7) Sherd (1)	Iron (6) Manganese (1)
4 (n = 13)*	10YR 5/3 Brown 10YR 6/4 Light yellowish brown 5Y 6/3 Pale olive	Sherd (1) Sherd + sand (3) Diabase + sherd + opaque minerals (9)	Iron (1) Manganese (4)
Outliers (n = 2)	10YR 8/1 White 5Y 8/1 White	Sherd + sand (2)	Iron (1) Manganese (1)

* Includes 11 sherds from Grasshopper Pueblo.

The sample included sherds from Chodistaas Pueblo (n = 2) and Grasshopper Pueblo (n = 11). Most brown paste vessels were made with dark gray, probably carbonaceous clay. All sherds were refired and they turned dull buff to orange in color; some of them retained a dark core. The three temper types identified were sherd, sherd and sand, and a heterogeneous admixture of sherd, diabase, opaque minerals (iron oxides), and occasional muscovite flakes. Diabase, muscovite, and iron oxides are common on the Grasshopper Plateau. When chemical groups defined by ICP are represented graphically, brown paste samples cluster tightly (see Fig 8.3). However, variation in temper type and color of brown paste samples suggests greater compositional heterogeneity than that determined in this study.

Identification of black mineral pigments on refired sherds of white paste samples revealed that iron (Fe) pigments were used far more commonly than manganese (Mn) pigments for vessel decoration. In the decorated brown paste group, however, there are more manganese occurrences than iron ones. This pattern may be a function of the small sample size used to determine pigment types. The results of temper and pigment identification are presented in Table 8.1.

To summarize, an evaluation of raw materials used in the manufacture of Cibola White Ware from the Grasshopper Plateau indicates that the sources of clay for manufacturing Cibola White Ware during the late Pueblo III period were not located on the Grasshopper Plateau and were well beyond the hypothetical "primary exploitation threshold" (Browman 1976) or territory where potters could obtain their resources at minimum energy cost and maximum benefit. Local potters could have exploited more distant sources, however. The zone where white-firing clays are located was occupied prehistorically, and it has important late Pueblo III period settlements in it (from east to west, AZ P:16:9 in Forestdale, upper Cibecue Creek sites, the Pinedale Ruin, and Chevelon sites), but there is no evidence to indicate that trade in clays occurred, certainly not in the quantities required to manufacture the large number of vessels already excavated.

In the absence of convincing evidence of manufacture of white paste pottery at Chodistaas Pueblo, the most parsimonious interpretation of these data is that Cibola White Ware vessels were introduced into the settlement from the north. The occurrence of clays with similar firing color and similar temper and of vessels with similar black mineral pigments in the black-on-white pottery from Chodistaas suggests that the three analytical sources of these pots may in turn represent localities within a geographically restricted area.

Sherd temper cannot be easily traced to procurement sources, but it is known to occur in ceramics made on the Colorado Plateau. Sherd temper is restricted to polished and painted pottery in the Chodistaas assemblage. Although local vessels were made with orange-firing and red-firing clays, ceramics of this color range were also manufactured in many areas of the Colorado Plateau, such as Pinedale, Fourmile (Lightfoot and Jewett 1984), Snowflake–Mesa Redonda (Neily 1988), Petrified Forest National Monument (Fowler 1989), and the Middle Little Colorado River (Zedeño and others 1993), among others. One starting point for tracing the provenience of Cibola White Ware pottery tempered with ground orange sherds would involve determining those areas where both white-firing and orange-firing clays were used for local ceramic production. Chemical characterization of sherd temper particles by Scanning Electron Microprobe (Olin and Franklin 1982) would be necessary to assess accurately the composition, and perhaps provenience, of the ground sherds.

In contrast, the raw material sources of most late black-on-white pots from Grasshopper Pueblo are obviously distinct from the earlier ones, and at least one of these sources is local. Further tests are necessary to assess how many sources are represented in the brown paste Cibola White Ware vessels from Grasshopper Pueblo. The analysis here illustrates the difficulties of identifying intraregional manufacturing loci from chemical analysis, refiring experiments, and petrographic observations.

Forming Techniques and Vessel Morphology

The relative homogeneity of Cibola White Ware from Chodistaas Pueblo is also present in vessel shape. Even though it is difficult and often impossible to find observable traces of primary forming techniques on smoothed-polished pottery, slight ripples from original coils can be felt along vessel walls. Crown (1981a: 124) suggested that a large broken potsherd or plate-shaped vessel or basket may have been used to turn the jars during construction. She observed that large black-on-white jars:

> almost uniformly show evidence of a slight slump at a point above the vessel base. The "slump" is often so slight that it can be felt better than seen, but is clearly present. This slump is unquestionably caused by the slight collapse of the drying vessel wall at the point where it was no longer supported by a base (Crown 1981a: 124).

Most large jars are "egg-shaped," with wide shoulders and pointy bases that make the pots unstable and that suggests some sort of support must have been used to free the potter's hands. At Chodistaas Pueblo there is slight variation in jar and pitcher shapes, from semiglobular to egg-shaped, and few are squat; various jar and pitcher sizes are represented in every compositional group, but bowls are restricted to Group 1. Conversely, all the later brown paste Cibola jars from Grasshopper Pueblo are relatively homogeneous in size and shape;

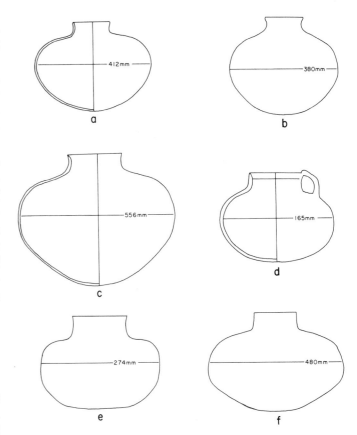

Figure 8.6. Shapes of Cibola White Ware jars and a pitcher from Chodistaas Pueblo (*a-d*) and jars from Grasshopper Pueblo (*e, f*); *b, e, f* are whole vessels.

they typically have a wide, rounded base and squat body. Except for six especially large, wide-shouldered jars, all brown paste and white paste jars from this site are of medium size. Figure 8.6 illustrates the range of variation in vessel shapes from Chodistaas and Grasshopper pueblos.

Surface Treatment and Finish

It is difficult to identify unequivocally the presence of white slip on the exterior surface of black-on-white pottery at Chodistaas Pueblo because the paste is white. Sometimes, however, slip was applied to the rim interior, and a slight difference in color and texture of the interior surface revealed the presence of a white slip. Surface polishing varies from smoothing that gives exterior surfaces a dull appearance, to moderately high polish. Black-on-white pottery at Grasshopper Pueblo, on the other hand, has a dark gray paste and was treated with a thick, chalky white slip; vessels are all evenly polished.

Firing Techniques

Refiring of 25 sherds from broken vessels was helpful for making observations on the original firing atmosphere and temperature of Cibola White Ware. The sherds were refired at 950°C (1742°F) and left to cool in the oven. The white paste sherds from Chodistaas Pueblo vessels did not change visibly, with the exception of two that turned light pink. Unfortunately, it was not possible to estimate, on the basis of changes in paste color alone, what type of atmosphere was present during the last stage of the original firing process.

Changes in the color of iron paint, however, indicate that vessels painted with this pigment were fired in a nonoxidizing atmosphere. Eleven sherds from Grasshopper Pueblo vessels changed from dark gray to dull buff or orange, indicating that these, too, were fired in a nonoxidizing atmosphere. Changes in paint color also suggested that the original firing temperature must have been no lower than 750°C (1382°F), because moderately high temperatures are needed to reduce iron pigments and turn them black (Shepard 1985). Only two Cibola pots from Chodistaas were fired in an oxidizing atmosphere; they have reddish brown paint instead of black. High temperatures must have been achieved in the original firing of the vessels, because four jars have glassy surfaces and two of them became warped from over-firing.

Hardness of 5 to 7 on the Mohs scale and conchoidal fracture of many of the pots also suggest moderately high firing temperatures for the black-on-white pottery. Fire clouds are not common but occur in the black-on-white assemblage. These stains could have appeared on the pots during firing or during the burning of the pueblo rooms. Observations on the firing process of Cibola White Ware support the traditional view that this ware represents a distinctive firing technology (Colton 1939; Shepard 1985), in particular when contrasted with other wares in the assemblage.

Spatial and Temporal Variability in Procurement Sources of Cibola White Ware

The reconstruction of critical stages in the manufacture of black-on-white vessels at Chodistaas Pueblo indicate that, although they may have been made at three different locations outside the Grasshopper region, most, if not all, of the pots were produced with a similar technology. Because white-firing clay sources have a restricted geographic distribution, it is likely that these pots were manufactured in a few, perhaps geographically and socially related, loci. Sources of Cibola White Ware may have been located not farther than 100 km (62 miles) to the north.

Vessels of room floor assemblages at Chodistaas Pueblo can be considered contemporaneous in the sense that they were all in use until shortly before abandonment. However, the partition of Cibola White Ware vessels by shape and compositional characteristics may be used to argue that these vessels did not all enter the room assemblages at the same time and that a shift in procurement sources began to occur toward the end of the occupation of Chodistaas.

A comparison of the percentages of Roosevelt Red Ware and Cibola White Ware bowls from the surface and room floors at Chodistaas Pueblo has led to the hypothesis that black-on-white bowls were replaced by Pinto Black-on-red and Pinto Polychrome bowls sometime after A.D. 1285 (Montgomery and Reid 1990). The replacement of black-on-white bowls by polychrome bowls was also observed by Haury and Hargrave (1931) at the Pinedale Ruin. All the black-on-white bowls in room assemblages at Chodistaas included in this analysis (n = 8) fit into Compositional Group 1; Groups 2 and 3 include jars and pitchers from Chodistaas, Grasshopper Spring, and Grasshopper pueblos and site AZ P:14:197 (Table 8.2).

The unequal distribution of black-on-white bowls across compositional groups may be related to the replacement event: the source of vessels from Group 1 perhaps contributed to the ceramic assemblage throughout the occupation of Chodistaas, whereas vessels from Groups 2 and 3 may have entered the assemblage at a different time in the occupation of the pueblo, when

Table 8.2. Vessel Shape Distribution by Site Across Compositional Groups

Site	Group 1	Group 2	Group 3	Group 4
Chodistaas Pueblo	14 jars 8 bowls 3 pitchers	4 jars 1 pitcher	7 jars 3 pitchers	1 jar 1 canteen
Grasshopper Spring Pueblo		1 jar	1 jar	
AZ P:14:197			1 jar	
Grasshopper Pueblo		2 jars	1 jar	2 jars 9 jars* 2 bowls*

*ICP

Table 8.3. Frequencies of Design Styles on Cibola White Ware at Chodistaas Pueblo by INAA Compositional Groups

Design style	Group 1			Group 2		Group 3		Group 4		Outliers		Total
	Bowls	Jars	Pitchers	Jars	Pitchers	Jars	Pitchers	Jars	Canteen	Jars	Pitchers	
Red Mesa									1			1
Puerco	1				1		1					3
Snowflake*	1	3				1	1					6
Tularosa		6	2	1		4	1	1		1		16
Kayenta-Tusayan	1			1		1						3
Roosevelt	1	5	1	1		1						9
Pinedale	2		1	1						1		5
Unclassified	2										2	4
Total	8	14	4	4	1	7	3	1	1	2	2	47

* Two Snowflake vessels and two unclassified vessels were not included in the INAA sample.

black-on-white bowls were no longer manufactured. Compositional analysis of surface bowl sherds from Chodistaas and Grasshopper is necessary to test whether the absence of bowls in Groups 2 and 3 is related to the replacement event. The scarcity of surface bowl sherds at Grasshopper Pueblo (Montgomery and Reid 1990: 93, Table 2) suggests that few black-on-white bowls were being manufactured by about A.D. 1300.

In addition, there is an unequal distribution of the vessels represented in Groups 2 and 3 across rooms in Chodistaas Pueblo. Vessels in Group 1 were present in almost every room, whereas all but three Chodistaas vessels in Groups 2 and 3 were in the southern room block, in Rooms 3, 5, 8, 9, and 6, all of which were built after A.D. 1280. Two explanations for this pattern may be suggested. First, Groups 1, 2, and 3 may be signaling differences in exchange partnerships, where the occupants of the north room block had little or no access to the kinds of vessels represented in Groups 2 and 3. Because the south room block was built at a later date than the north one, it is possible that an exchange partnership that involved only one sector of the pueblo's inhabitants (represented archaeologically by vessels from Groups 2 and 3) developed sometime during the occupation of Chodistaas, Grasshopper Spring, and site AZ P:14:197 and continued through the first years of occupation of Grasshopper Pueblo. If this explanation is correct, then the temporal difference suggested by the absence of bowls and the presence of Grasshopper Pueblo vessels in these groups would be reinforced. A second explanation, which accords with the general trend of population movement into the Arizona mountains at the end of the thirteenth century, is that vessels represented in Groups 2 and 3 were brought into the area by immigrants from the north. Differences in con-

struction dates as well as in architectural layout of the north and south room blocks brings into consideration the likely possibility that late in its brief history Chodistaas Pueblo sheltered an immigrant group.

What is relevant for understanding the dynamics of manufacture and circulation of Cibola White Ware on the Grasshopper Plateau is that the locally produced black-on-white pottery, although different in raw material, morphology, and style of decoration (all of which can be explained in terms of geographical and temporal context of manufacture) still had important technological similarities with the nonlocal Cibola White Ware. These similarities include use of ground sherds along with local tempering materials and firing technology.

Having established tentative spatial and temporal boundaries for the manufacture of Cibola White Ware recovered from sites on the Grasshopper Plateau, I turn to design styles to consider how stylistic variation on black-on-white pottery from Chodistaas and Grasshopper pueblos highlights these arguments.

Design Style Analysis

The compositional groups described above were used as analytical units within which variation in Cibola White Ware design styles was observed (Table 8.3). I treated Group 1, Groups 2 and 3, and Group 4 as representing discrete ceramic manufacturing loci. The criteria followed here for classifying Cibola black-on-white vessels into formal styles were first provided by Crown (1981a: 296–302); additional references to formal style definitions were incorporated from Neily (1988: 143–161). I made slight changes to Crown's (1981a) classification in order to incorporate the decorated vessels

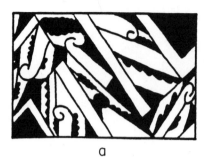 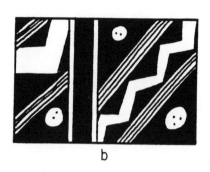 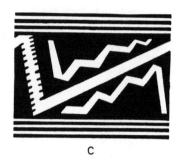

Figure 8.7. Cibola White Ware design styles at Chodistaas Pueblo. *a*, Red Mesa style, Group 4; *b*, Puerco style, Group 3; *c*, Puerco style, Group 2. (Not to scale; see Appendix A: *a*, Case 229; *b*, 187; *c*, 126.)

recovered in recent years, but most of her classification was left intact. I adhered strictly to diagnostic attributes recognized for each formal style, leaving unclassified those designs that did not display attributes clearly diagnostic of any style. The original classification was designed for Chodistaas Pueblo black-on-white vessels, but I included also those vessels from Grasshopper Pueblo, Grasshopper Spring Pueblo, and AZ P:14:197 for which compositional data were available. The stylistic classification that follows focuses specifically on jars and pitchers, which constitute the overwhelming majority (42 of 51) of the Cibola White Ware whole-vessel assemblage from Chodistaas. Styles of bowl designs were classified independently and are discussed separately. The following styles were identified; they are listed chronologically, from early to late.

Red Mesa Style
(Crown 1981a: 301)

Red Mesa style is characterized by lines of medium width in a banded layout. All solid elements are elaborated with pendant dots. Typical design elements include small interlocking curvilinear scrolls (Jernigan 1982; Sullivan 1984; Wilson 1976). At Chodistaas Pueblo, only one vessel is of this style (Fig. 8.7*a*); it is a small canteen with high shoulders and handles at each side of the neck. Crown considered this vessel to be aberrant in form, style, and technology: "Technologically, the vessel exhibits a grayish wash instead of a slip, is poorly polished, and too highly fired. The vessel is the only canteen in the collection, and is probably an heirloom" (Crown 1981a: 305). This canteen is also one of the two Cibola vessels from Chodistaas made with brown paste. One Red Mesa jar was also recovered from Grasshopper Spring Pueblo.

Puerco Style
(Crown 1981a: 301)

Puerco style was described by Carlson (1970), Sullivan (1984), and Wasley (1959), and has three varieties: Puerco, Gallup, and Escavada. Puerco style is generally characterized by banded, vertically sectioned designs, separated by panels of parallel vertical lines. Elements are negative, although unopposed hatched elements may occur. Squares, checkerboards, parallelograms, triangles, negative lightning, and negative bullseyes are common, and ticked bands are sometimes present. This style seems to have developed from the Red Mesa style, and it is closely related to the Reserve style (Neily 1988: 149). At Chodistaas Pueblo there are two Puerco style pitchers, one is Puerco variety (Fig. 8.7*b*; Wasley 1959: 269) and the other is Escavada variety (Fig. 8.7*c*; Neily 1988: 149). Both pitchers are characterized by heavy use of black that gives the designs a bold effect.

Snowflake Style
(Crown 1981a: 300)

The controversial Snowflake style was first defined by Longacre (1964), but his definition of Snowflake was too inclusive to be useful for distinguishing this style from the Puerco style. Colton (1941b) and Wasley (1959), among others, equated Snowflake Black-on-white designs with the carbon-painted Sosi. A single attribute was used here to identify Snowflake style: solid ribbonlike designs with or without interlocking rectilinear scrolls and stepped edges. Sosi, on the other hand, combines ribbonlike designs with barbed edges. At Chodistaas Pueblo, four jars and one pitcher of Snowflake style typically exhibit ribbonlike rectangular scrolls with or without stepped edges, in which black

Figure 8.8. Snowflake style designs on Cibola White Ware at Chodistaas Pueblo. *a*, *b*, *d*, Group 1; *c*, *e*, Group 3. (Not to scale; see Appendix A: *a*, Case 63; *b*, 263; *c*, 144; *d*, 151; *e*, 243.)

solids are equal or slightly larger than the white background. Secondary elaborations include triangular scrolls (Fig. 8.8*a*, *b*), stepped elements (Fig. 8.8*c*); checkerboard-filled triangles (Fig. 8.8*d*), or solid triangles (Fig. 8.8*e*). One Snowflake jar was recovered at Grasshopper Spring Pueblo.

Tularosa Style
(Crown 1981a: 296)

Tularosa style is characterized by interlocking solid and hatched designs, in which diagonally hatched units are larger than or equal to the solid unit. The basic motif is repeated six to eight times. Elements often exhibit stepped edges and motifs include scrolls, double terraces, frets, birds, and vertical zigzags. Tularosa style vessels have medium to fine hatching work, and framing lines are as thin as hatching lines (Carlson 1970: 90-91; Colton 1953; Colton and Hargrave 1937; Wasley 1959). Thirteen jars and three pitchers from Chodistaas Pueblo are of Tularosa style. Although variability in layout, complexity, and execution of the designs is evident, most vessels have balanced solid and hatched interlocked stepped designs (Figs. 8.9, 8.10). Two Tularosa style jars were recovered at Grasshopper Spring Pueblo (Fig. 8.10*d*, *f*).

Kayenta-Tusayan Style

The Kayenta style was defined first by Colton and Hargrave (1937) and was further elaborated by Beals, Brainerd, and Smith (1945: 103–121). According to these authors, Kayenta style is characterized by negative designs that have interlocking "S" scrolls and usually occur as interlocking rectilinear scrolls attached to terraces or triangles with sawteeth. White areas within the design are normally smaller than black areas and occur in the form of straight, curved, or zigzag lines and sometimes in the form of small parallelograms. Kayenta style is also characterized by true pleated or "diaper" designs that form diamonds of complex internal elaboration. Secondary elaborations on framing bands are also common. Two jars from Chodistaas display intricate pleated designs with negative effect (Fig. 8.10*g*, *h*).

Roosevelt Style
(Crown 1981a: 300)

Roosevelt is perhaps one of the most inclusive styles and thus there has been considerable disagreement over its definition and usage. According to Pomeroy (1962: 30–38), Roosevelt style displays banded designs with

Figure 8.9. Tularosa style designs on Cibola White Ware at Chodistaas Pueblo. *a-e*, *g*, *h*, Group 1; *f*, *i*, *j*, *l*, Group 3; *k*, Group 2. (Not to scale; see Appendix A: *a*, Case 106; *b*, 186; *c*, 1; *d*, 181; *e*, 231; *f*, 301; *g*, 78; *h*, 127; *i*, 109; *j*, 36; *k*, 190 *l*, 218.)

Figure 8.10. Tularosa style designs (*a–f*) and Kayenta-Tusayan style designs (*g, h*) on Cibola White Ware at Chodistaas Pueblo (*a–c, e, g, h*) and Grasshopper Spring Pueblo (*d, f*). *a*, Outlier; *b, d, h*, Group 3; *c*, Group 1; *e*, Group 4; *f, g*, Group 2. (Not to scale; see Appendix A: *a*, Case 68; *b*, 272; *c*, 267; *d*, GS–332; *e*, 6; *f*, GS–331; *g*, 198; *h*, 101.)

Figure 8.11. Roosevelt style designs on Cibola White Ware at Chodistaas Pueblo. *a–d*, *g*, *h*, Group 1; *e*, Group 3; *f*, Group 2. (Not to scale; see Appendix A: *a*, Case 222; *b*, 254; *c*, 295; *d*, 300; *e*, 32 *f*, 217; *g*, 223; *h*, 285.)

diagonally or vertically sectioned layout, interlocking solid motifs, use of frets, stepped terraces, scrolls, and opposed sawteeth. Hatching is infrequent, and solids exhibit negative designs. Pomeroy's definition of Roosevelt style includes a heterogeneous array of layouts and motifs that dilutes the concept of Roosevelt style. He included designs of ribbonlike interlocking solid rectangular scrolls combined with stepped elements that actually represent the diagnostic attribute of the Snowflake style (Crown 1981a: 300–301). Pomeroy's Roosevelt style functions as a useful category by comprising a number of Kayenta-Tusayan stylistic attributes such as negative "S" scrolls, parallel hatching, and opposed sawteeth, thereby separating out those solid dark designs that have a Tusayan "flavor" but that do not truly belong with any of the northern styles.

At Chodistaas, Roosevelt style pots have two subcategories. One includes three examples: simple solid banded designs with opposed sawteeth (Figs. 8.11*a*, *b*), and interlocked barbed units combined with secondary stepped units (Fig. 8.11*c*) reminiscent of Sosi style; it is characterized by the boldness and simplicity of the designs, which have no internal or secondary elaborations. In contrast, the second subcategory (five jars) is characterized by negative designs of diagonal and diamond layout with intricate elaborations, including many Kayenta-Tusayan stylistic attributes. Here, interlocking rectangular scrolls have internal elaborations, including spurred triangles; interlocked barbed units; negative units such as parallelograms, lightning, and bullseyes; parallel hatching; opposed sawteeth; and stepped terraces (Figs. 8.11*d*, *f–h*). One jar exhibits a diaperlike pleated layout (Fig. 8.11*e*). Snowflake designs at Chodistaas, then, differ from Roosevelt designs in that their interlocked solid rectangular scrolls have little or no internal elaborations, nor complex secondary elaborations.

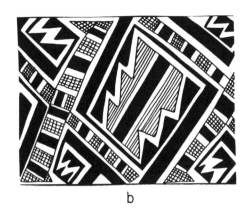

a   b   c

Figure 8.12. Pinedale style designs on Cibola White Ware at Chodistaas Pueblo. *a*, Group 2; *b*, Outlier; *c*, Group 1. (Not to scale; see Appendix A: *a*, Case 53; *b*, 269; *c*, 150.)

Pinedale Style
(Crown 1981a:299)

According to Carlson (1970: 91–93), Pinedale style is characterized by interlocking solid and hatched units, but, unlike Tularosa, the solid unit is as large or larger than the hatched unit, giving the design a bolder, darker effect. Units are large and are repeated only two to four times. Elements still exhibit stepped edges, but internal elaborations of the elements are more common. Carlson pointed out that the double terrace motif no longer appears, and the running diamond motif first occurs on this style. Two Pinedale style jars, two bowls, and one pitcher are in the Chodistaas assemblage. One jar has the diagnostic interlocked solid and hatched curvilinear "S" scrolls (Fig. 8.12*a*) and two pots have running diamonds (Fig 8.12*b*, *c*). Most of the Grasshopper Pueblo jars are painted in the Pinedale style. The hallmark of these designs is the combination of Kayenta-Tusayan complex diamond elaborations and secondary line elaborations with interlocked solid and hatched curvilinear scrolls (Carlson 1970:108).

One jar and two pitchers were left unclassified (Fig. 8.13*a–c*). The jar (8.13*a*) exhibits typical Tusayan parallel hatching (Beals, Brainerd, and Smith 1945: 102), but has diagonal paneling not common to any style.

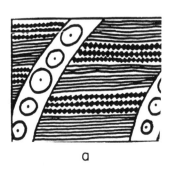

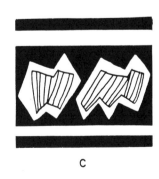

a   b   c

Figure 8.13. Unclassified design styles on Cibola White Ware at Chodistaas Pueblo. *a*, Group 2; *b*, *c*, Outliers. (Not to scale; see Appendix A: *a*, Case 29; *b*, 266; *c*, 143.)

Figure 8.14. Pinedale style designs on Cibola White Ware at Grasshopper Pueblo. *a*, Group 4; *b*, Group 2. (Not to scale; see Appendix A, Grasshopper Pueblo: *a*, Case 340; *b*, 339.)

Design Styles and Compositional Variation

Cibola White Ware design styles from Chodistaas Pueblo have several characteristics that unite them as a stylistically consistent corpus of vessels. All jars and pitchers have two fields of decoration: neck and body. The body designs are most commonly framed above and below the band of decoration by a thick solid band, and occasionally with several thin solid bands, which leave the base of the jar unpainted. At Chodistaas, the most common neck designs are panels of vertical bars. At Grasshopper Pueblo neck decoration is usually more elaborate and varied.

Another important characteristic of this Cibola White Ware assemblage is the strong preference for diagonal layouts that form diamonds. Diagonally laid out designs, for example, form Puerco style vertical panels or Roosevelt style horizontal sections. There is also a tendency, observable in numerous Chodistaas pots but most evident in Grasshopper Pueblo vessels, to pack or fill in all remaining spaces once the primary layout has been painted. These secondary elaborations may range from single solids to hatched, opposed, or interlocked designs. Finally, the variability in creativity, complexity, and execution of designs, even within one compositional group or within one particular style, is a remarkable feature of the black-on-white assemblage.

Examination of the design variation in each of the three compositional groups defined by INAA indicates that Groups 1, 2, and 3 share several stylistic features. They all include Tularosa, Puerco, and Roosevelt designs. Furthermore, there is use of specific stylistic

configurations or *schemata* (Jernigan 1986) and the relative balance of solid and hatched designs with its characteristic light (as opposed to bold) effect. Groups 1 and 3 have Snowflake ribbonlike solid interlocking rectangular scrolls with or without stepped edges. In contrast, the large Pinedale solid and hatched interlocking curvilinear scrolls are absent in Group 1, but appear in one jar (Group 2) from Chodistaas and in four jars from Grasshopper Pueblo that belong to Groups 2 and 3. This schema, in turn, occurs alone or in combination with intricate Kayenta-Tusayan style diamonds in both local and nonlocal vessels (Fig. 8.14*a*, *b*).

Group 1 includes all of the single-motif banded Roosevelt designs, but the most complex and elaborated Roosevelt designs occur in every nonlocal group. When observing the Tularosa style designs from all four groups, it is readily apparent that the designs from Group 1 have larger hatched and white areas than black solid areas. Conversely, Tularosa designs from Groups 2 and 3 tend to incorporate black solid areas that are as large or larger than hatched ones. Also, large Pinedale solid-and-hatched vessels of Groups 2 and 3 (including Grasshopper Pueblo pots) have a bolder, darker effect than vessels of Group 1. The addition of Kayenta-Tusayan style diamonds with massive black areas or negative designs to Pinedale style vessels from Grasshopper Pueblo also results in darker designs. Designs in Groups 2 and 3, therefore, show a trend in the use of color contrast that became a hallmark of Cibola White Ware during the Pueblo IV period.

The variation observed in design styles of black-on-white vessels from Chodistaas and Grasshopper pueblos supports a hypothesis of a temporal shift in the manufacture of Cibola White Ware sometime at the end of the thirteenth century. The single most important marker of this temporal shift is the appearance of Pinedale style designs on black-on-white vessels, particularly jars, at Chodistaas and Grasshopper pueblos.

An aspect restricted to jars from Grasshopper Pueblo is the blending of Kayenta-Tusayan and Wingate-Tularosa stylistic configurations to create an intricate, bold Pinedale style. The use of northern stylistic criteria is even more evident in the Pinedale style jars from Group 4, where rectangular panels and triangular spaces filled with Tusayan parallel hatching (Beals, Brainerd, and Smith 1945: 104) are often used as focus or filler of the designs (Fig. 8.14b). At Chodistaas, "classic" stylistic expressions such as Puerco, Snowflake, and Tularosa dominate the white ware assemblage, and the Kayenta-Tusayan influence is entirely restricted to the Roosevelt style. At Grasshopper Pueblo, however, the blending of northern and southern stylistic criteria is pervasive and constitutes in itself a different style. As Colton and Hargrave (1937: 17–18) noted, prehistoric Southwestern potters were conservative: they expressed their creativity by borrowing and recombining motifs in a whole design, as seen in the Pinedale style, while keeping the style of elements, motifs, and patterns remarkably constant, generation after generation.

There are two Pinedale style bowls at Chodistaas Pueblo and only ten Pinedale Black-on-white bowls in the large bowl assemblage from Grasshopper Pueblo. A sharp contrast in the degree of stylistic variation can be observed between the black-on-white bowl designs from the two sites. Designs on bowls at Chodistaas are of Puerco (Fig. 8.15*a*), Tusayan (Fig. 8.15*b*), Snowflake (Fig. 8.15*c, d*), Roosevelt (Fig. 8.15*e*), and Pinedale (Fig. 8.15*f*) styles, and two bowls do not have diagnostic attributes of any particular style (Fig. 8.15*g, h*). Design execution as well as shape and size of these bowls also show variability: rim diameter ranges between 7.5 cm and 30.0 cm, suggesting that they were not being manufactured in a standardized fashion. One need only examine Pueblo II or early Pueblo III period black-on-white bowls to find how consistent the form and how elaborate the decoration were during the height of their manufacture. This consistency had ceased by late Pueblo III times.

Black-on-white bowls from Grasshopper Pueblo are generally smaller than polychrome bowls and are not "nestable," as are White Mountain Red Ware bowls (Whittlesey 1974). They have one important characteristic that places them apart from Pueblo II and III period bowls: their interior and exterior decoration is similar

Figure 8.15. Design styles on Cibola White Ware bowls at Chodistaas Pueblo; all Group 1 except *c* (not analyzed by INNA). *a*, Puerco; *b*, Tusayan; *c, d*, Snowflake; *e*, Roosevelt; *f*, Pinedale; *g, h*, unclassified. (Not to scale; see Appendix A: *a*, Case 283; *b*, 37; *c*, 50; *d*, 176; *e*, 230; *f*, 148; *g*, 26; *h*, 142.)

to Pinedale Black-on-red bowls rather than to Pinedale style Roosevelt Red Ware. Conversely, contemporaneous Pinedale Black-on-white bowls from other regions, such as the Tonto Basin, are almost identical to Roosevelt Red Ware (Zedeño 1992).

Were black-on-white bowls being made in certain regions while being discontinued in others? Probably so, as indicated by the large number of nonlocal Pinedale Black-on-white bowls recovered from Roosevelt–Gila phase sites in the Tonto Basin. However, most bowls from Grasshopper Pueblo as well as from Roosevelt Lake sites were recovered from burials, which generally tend to include heirloom items.

In summary, design variation on Cibola White Ware from Chodistaas Pueblo shows that there is a significant overlap between styles and procurement sources during a restricted period of time: Puerco, Tularosa, Snowflake, Roosevelt, and Kayenta-Tusayan styles are present in more than one compositional group. On the other hand, there is a definite association between sources and Pinedale style. Styles on Pueblo IV period Cibola White Ware on the Grasshopper Plateau differ from styles on late Pueblo III period vessels; Pueblo IV pots, local or not, incorporate stylistic criteria not only from other black-on-white ceramic traditions but also from contemporaneous polychrome traditions *on a single pot*. The sharp contrast between designs on black-on-white vessels from Chodistaas and Grasshopper Spring pueblos and on those from Grasshopper Pueblo suggests that the coming together of people, materials, and ideas during the Pueblo IV period, as exemplified in the aggregation at Grasshopper Pueblo, indeed contributed to the blending of stylistic traditions in fourteenth-century Cibola White Ware designs. As Crown (1981a: 359) pointed out, the sharp decrease in stylistic variability during Pueblo IV times may be reflecting changes in the social, and perhaps ritual (Adams 1991b), context of manufacture of decorated vessels.

This analysis also reveals that prehistoric potters were able to manipulate a broad spectrum of designs and to readily copy, modify, and blend "foreign" representations, such as Kayenta-Tusayan, with their own traditional styles. All of this was expressed in a short period of time, and perhaps even in a restricted geographic region. It is reasonable to ask, then, if these particular ceramic styles could possibly represent prehistoric boundaries of any sort, messages encoded in designs, or symbols of political, social, or religious status.

We may never be able to achieve the quality of evidence that Haury (1958) produced for a Kayenta migration at Point of Pines, but, it is clear that the southward movement of northern people was felt in many regions of the Arizona mountains and that it certainly influenced people's ideas on how to decorate black-on-white pottery (Carlson 1970: 109). That the designs on Cibola White Ware from Grasshopper Pueblo show a Kayenta-Tusayan influence even more markedly than those from Chodistaas Pueblo only demonstrates that a particular stylistic "trend" could be reproduced regardless of technological traditions and cultural or ethnic boundaries. Style, therefore, may be a useful marker of temporal change and of the spread of ideas and influences, but it is definitely not a good indicator of pottery manufacturing loci at this time period in the Arizona mountains. Demonstration of local origin of decorated ceramics constitutes a crucial methodological step for constructing any inference based on stylistic attributes.

Implications for Ceramic Circulation

Evidence from the Grasshopper Plateau and the Q Ranch region (Tuggle and others 1982) indicates that Cibola White Ware circulated into the mountain settlements of east-central Arizona from the north during the late Pueblo III period. Two mechanisms of ceramic circulation can be postulated: movement of pots and movement of people. There is no evidence to suggest that Cibola White Ware was distributed in the mountains through a formal trade network, because small mountain pueblos of this period did not have the population density nor the organizational requirements to sustain a constant flow of trade goods. However, the relative proximity of these settlements to the probable manufacturing localities of some of the Cibola White Ware pottery (less than 100 km, or 62 miles, to the north) may have facilitated the movement of black-on-white vessels on a fairly regular basis. Considering the mobility or short-term sedentism of this time, this pottery could have been transported from its sources by the mountain settlers, brought into the mountains by people from the north, or both.

The relative abundance of *nonlocal* Cibola White Ware at Chodistaas Pueblo indicates that its inhabitants maintained long-distance relationships with communities from the Colorado Plateau. It is likely, therefore, that these Cibola vessels were acquired through reciprocal exchange. This mechanism of circulation of decorated ceramics may have served to obtain access to products of different ecological zones and to reinforce intercommunity relationships among close and distant settlements.

That such relationships lasted until at least the first decade of the fourteenth century is suggested by the presence of black-on-white vessels from a common source in Chodistaas Pueblo and contemporaneous settlements, and in Grasshopper Pueblo slightly later.

Considering the restricted distribution of white-firing clays, the interruption in the supply of nonlocal vessels could have been related to the abandonment of the communities that used this type of clay to make black-on-white pottery during the late 1200s. Cibola White Ware continued to be used in Grasshopper Pueblo, but by then it was manufactured locally and perhaps obtained from sources different from the earlier ones.

I contend that the shift toward local manufacture of Cibola White Ware marks two crucial population trends that characterized the late Pueblo III to Pueblo IV transition period: (1) abandonment of a number of regions on the Colorado Plateau followed by southward migration, and (2) aggregation of ethnically diverse populations in large pueblos. These trends are evident in the ceramic record, where a halt in the manufacture of Cibola White Ware may have occurred when the regions where this ware was manufactured were abandoned; access to white-firing clays probably ended once people moved away from their former residences.

Abandonment and migration likely caused well-established exchange partnerships and long-distance relationships to weaken; continuity in the supply of Cibola White Ware from nonlocal sources was definitely broken sometime during the 1300s. Furthermore, the shift toward production of local black-on-white vessels, distinct from the earlier ones but nonetheless produced with similar tempering and firing techniques, seems to indicate that this pottery was made or introduced into the local ceramic repertoire by people bearing a foreign technological tradition.

WHITE MOUNTAIN RED WARE

The Circulation of St. Johns Polychrome

St. Johns Polychrome has long been recognized as the most widespread of Southwestern pottery types: according to Carlson (1970: 37), St. Johns Polychrome extends south from Mesa Verde (Colorado) on the north to about Casas Grandes (Mexico), and from the Pecos River (New Mexico) west to the Chino Valley in western Arizona. Little is known of its manufacturing loci; however, the largest concentrations of St. Johns pottery occur in the Cibola area, west-central New Mexico and within an 80-km (50-mile) radius of the town of St. Johns in east-central Arizona. Outside the core area, St. Johns Polychrome is most commonly distributed to the south and west, along the Tularosa and San Francisco rivers as far south as the Gila River and between the

Little Colorado River and the Mogollon Rim. It is rare south of the Mogollon Rim (Breternitz 1966; Carlson 1970; Colton and Hargrave 1937; Gladwin and Gladwin 1931; Mera 1934).

Information is meager on ceramic manufacture in the Cibola area, thought to have been the most significant manufacturing locus of St. Johns Polychrome (Carlson 1970: 39; Graves 1982: 327). The strongest evidence for its manufacture comes from east-central Arizona; at Hooper Ranch Pueblo an unfired St. Johns Polychrome bowl, clay, and St. Johns sherds had strong mineralogical similarities (Martin and others 1961: 132). In addition, petrographic analysis of the earlier Wingate Polychrome from Springerville (Doyel 1984; Rugge and Doyel 1980) suggested local production of White Mountain Red Ware in the Upper Little Colorado–Mogollon Rim area. St. Johns Polychrome, a type that shows some degree of technological homogeneity throughout its area of distribution (Bronitski 1986), is technologically identical to Heshota Polychrome in the Cibola area. St. Johns also shows striking affinities to the late Pueblo III period Springerville Polychrome (a variety of St. Johns), which is distributed along the Upper Little Colorado River (Carlson 1970: 39, 44). These affinities indicate continuity in manufacturing technology in both the northern and southern core areas of this pottery.

The known manufacturing loci of Cibola White Ware and White Mountain Red Ware overlap along the Arizona–New Mexico border, both wares being similar in paste composition and design style (Carlson 1970; Doyel 1984; Lightfoot and Jewett 1984; Martin and others 1961). However, large quantities of locally made Cibola White Ware pottery extend beyond the distribution limits of St. Johns Polychrome. Apparently, the manufacture of St. Johns was restricted mainly to the Upper Little Colorado–Puerco area and the Upper Gila drainages, whereas the contemporary Cibola ware was produced locally as far west as the Chevelon drainage in central Arizona. St. Johns Polychrome is relatively abundant within 40,000 square kilometers (15,440 square miles) of its presumed production centers, located along the Arizona–New Mexico border, but is scarce elsewhere (Graves 1982: 319, 327, Appendix 1). On the Grasshopper Plateau and in the Cibecue Valley only a few St. Johns Polychrome sherds (1 to 5%) are reported from surface collections; there are only two St. Johns Polychrome bowls in the whole-vessel assemblage at Chodistaas Pueblo, and another two in the whole-vessel assemblage at Grasshopper Spring Pueblo.

The scarcity of Pueblo III period White Mountain Red Ware in the Arizona mountains, particularly from the Grasshopper Plateau, may be related to the absence of local manufacture of this ware in the regions with which mountain settlers maintained reciprocal relationships. At Chodistaas Pueblo, two St. Johns Polychrome bowls have gray-buff paste that is different from the paste of nonlocal Cibola White Ware vessels. This hypothesis is consistent with the inference that Cibola White Ware from the Grasshopper Plateau and in the Q Ranch region was manufactured in areas farther west than the manufacturing loci of St. Johns Polychrome. There is reference to local manufacture of Cibola White Ware at Pinedale (Haury and Hargrave 1931; Lightfoot and Jewett 1984) and at Chevelon (S. Plog 1980; Tuggle and others 1982), but not of St. Johns Polychrome. On the other hand, the manufacturing loci of the later Pinedale Polychrome appear to have been centered in the Pinedale area (Lightfoot and Jewett 1984), directly north of the Grasshopper Plateau. Daniela Triadan's ongoing research on the production and distribution of Pueblo IV period White Mountain Red Ware from the Grasshopper Plateau, which entails extensive chemical and petrographic analysis, also shows that nonlocal White Mountain Red Ware in the region is different compositionally from the nonlocal Cibola White Ware included in this study. One implication of her findings is that Pueblo IV communities participated in networks that were established only after A.D. 1300.

The overall distribution of St. Johns Polychrome indicates that exchange of this type of bowl occurred mainly within the core production zones and occasionally with peripheral zones; Graves (1982: 329) suggests that noncomplex, down-the-line sporadic trading ventures were responsible for the wide distribution of St. Johns Polychrome.

ROOSEVELT RED WARE

Local Adoption of a Foreign Ceramic Tradition

Roosevelt Red Ware, of which Pinto Polychrome and Pinto Black-on-red are the earliest manifestations, was first identified and named by Harold Gladwin and Winifred MacCurdy (Gladwin and Gladwin 1930: 5) as a ware characteristic of the Salado culture. The presence of Salado traits (cobble masonry, compound walls, inhumation, Roosevelt Red Ware, Roosevelt Black-on-white, paddled plain wares) from the Verde Valley in Arizona to southwestern New Mexico, and from the Little Colorado River to Casas Grandes (Mexico), has stimulated a number of alternative explanations of the identity of Salado pottery-making people. The Gladwins

(1930, 1931, 1934, 1935), and later Haury (1945), considered Salado pottery to be a product of groups who moved from the Little Colorado into the Salt–Gila Basin around A.D. 1100 to 1250. Haury proposed that the Salado culture emerged from a combined Mogollon-Anasazi base in the area south of the Mogollon Rim (Haury 1945: 205). Mc.Gregor (1941, 1965) also viewed the Salado as a polythetic development with influences from two or more cultures, most probably Mogollon and Anasazi.

Alternative positions have subsumed Salado under the broad term of Western Pueblo (Gumerman and Weed 1976; Reed 1948) or have explained Salado occupations in both the Tonto Basin (Doyel 1977; Wasley 1966; Weaver 1976) and the Salt–Gila Basin (Wood 1980; Wood and McAllister 1982) as an in situ, evolutionary development of the Hohokam. Finally, many archaeologists have viewed Salado as a variant of the Sinagua (Schroeder 1952), as a product of influences from Casas Grandes (Di Peso 1958; Ferdon 1955; LeBlanc and Nelson 1976), or as a mountain Mogollon-derived manifestation (Young in Lindsay and Jennings 1968; Whittlesey and Reid 1982b). The confusing character of the Salado phenomenon, its prominence in contemporary archaeological research, and the central role of ceramic analysis in Southwestern prehistory require a critical evaluation of the introduction and spread of Roosevelt Red Ware (Crown 1990, 1994; Crown and Bishop 1987; Reid and others 1992).

Efforts to elucidate the manufacturing loci of Roosevelt Red Ware have been concentrated primarily on Gila Polychrome, which was made in a number of localities during the fourteenth century (Crown and Bishop 1987; Danson and Wallace 1956; Di Peso 1976; LeBlanc and Nelson 1976; Lightfoot and Jewett 1984). The origin of the earliest Roosevelt Red Ware, however, was practically unknown until recently.

According to Doyel and Haury (1976: 128) a "Pinto Polychrome horizon," that is, the occurrence of this type without Gila Polychrome, has been recorded at Point of Pines, Grasshopper, Vosberg, and the Tonto-Globe areas. Results of chemical and petrographic analyses of Pinto Polychrome sherds from Point of Pines, Besh-Ba-Gowah (Globe), and the Vosberg Valley, in central Arizona, are currently interpreted by White and Burton (1992) as representing local production of Pinto bowls within each of these regions and also perhaps importation from a manufacturing center located above the Mogollon Rim. Their data accord with the hypothesis of a northern origin of Pinto Black-on-red and Pinto Polychrome.

The Gladwins thought that Pinto Polychrome "appeared full-fledged as an outgrowth of the Little Colorado Culture" (Gladwin and Gladwin 1931: 48) as a result of people moving southward from the Middle Little Colorado into the Tonto–Roosevelt region. Mera (1934), on the other hand, based his argument of an Anasazi origin of this pottery on the stylistic similarities between Pinto Polychrome and St. Johns Polychrome and on the technological similarities of Pinto Polychrome with Woodruff Brown Ware in northeastern Arizona. Mera observed that Pinto Polychrome was almost identical to Showlow Black-on-red, a Pueblo II carbon paint type of brown ware technology. This ceramic sequence, Woodruff Brown–Showlow Red Ware–Pinto, has been recently examined and reinforced with additional technological and stylistic data from the Zuni region (Fowler 1989; Fowler and Sant 1990).

Although the proposed sequence may approximate the probable evolutionary development of Roosevelt Red Ware, no one to date has identified locally made Pinto Polychrome or Pinto Black-on-red in sites located on the Colorado Plateau. All the available information on the provenience of these types comes from sites on the Mogollon Rim. The technological and stylistic characteristics of the Roosevelt Red Ware assemblage at Chodistaas Pueblo are undoubtedly "Anasazi," but a large number of them were manufactured on the Grasshopper Plateau. The information presented below suggests that Roosevelt Red Ware technology and style were adopted by local potters as a result of direct contact with immigrants from the north.

Roosevelt Red Ware at Chodistaas Pueblo

Chodistaas Pueblo currently provides the most complete and accurately dated early Roosevelt Red Ware assemblage in the Southwest; 8 Pinto Polychrome and 32 Pinto Black-on-red complete and partial bowls make up 35.4 percent of the decorated assemblage and 12.1 percent of the total whole-vessel assemblage. Detailed investigation of Roosevelt Red Ware centered on its provenience and time of appearance at Chodistaas. Vessels of Pinto types seemingly appeared suddenly sometime after A.D. 1285. Comparison of floor vessels with surface sherds revealed that within less than five years Cibola White Ware bowls were almost completely replaced with Pinto bowls. This replacement was pervasive, as indicated by the distribution of Pinto bowls throughout Chodistaas Pueblo and by the low numbers of Cibola White Ware bowl sherds in the surface collection and excavated assemblages from Grasshopper Pueblo (Montgomery and Reid 1990: 93, 95, Table 2).

Information on the chemical composition of Pinto bowls from Chodistaas Pueblo indicates that the vessels represent both local and nonlocal sources. The characteristics of these bowls (in particular, design style, temper technology, and carbon paint) and the circumstances of their appearance on the Grasshopper Plateau suggest that Roosevelt Red Ware was adopted in the Arizona mountains as a result of a movement of people from north of the Mogollon Rim. Roosevelt Red Ware technology may have been readily assimilated by local potters once Cibola White Ware bowls were no longer available (Reid and others 1992). Stylistic, compositional, and technological data support this hypothesis.

Design Style

Pinto Black-on-red and Pinto Polychrome bowls are strikingly homogeneous in design style: all but four Pinto Black-on-red bowls are decorated in the Pinedale style, in the tradition of Wingate and Tularosa designs on White Mountain Red Ware (Carlson 1970: 93, Fig. 49). As Crown (1981a: 305–306) observed, Pinedale designs on these bowls are characterized by large solid and hatched curvilinear scrolls repeated two, three, or four times. This is probably one of the earliest and best dated occurrences of the Pinedale style in the Southwest. Four bowls are painted in the Tularosa style, with solid and finely hatched rectilinear units. Two black-on-red bowls also have white and black ribbonlike designs on the exterior, respectively, a variant that is also found on Pinto bowls from Grasshopper Spring Pueblo and that is characteristic of St. Johns Polychrome. The homogeneity in Roosevelt Red Ware design styles (Figs. 8.16, 8.17) has been interpreted by Crown (1981a: 366; 1994) as being functionally related, perhaps indicating manufacture under ritual constraints or production for exchange.

Temper Technology

The most obvious characteristic of Roosevelt Red Ware from Chodistaas Pueblo is its homogeneity: in paste color, red slip color, shape, and paint. In essence, the only variable aspect of the manufacture of Pinto Black-on-red and Pinto Polychrome bowls is temper technology (Table 8.4). Microscopic analysis of refired sherds indicated that sherd-tempered bowls (19, 47.5% of all Pinto in the assemblage) have minute amounts of

Figure 8.16. Roosevelt Red Ware design styles on Pinto Black-on-red bowls at Chodistaas Pueblo. (Not to scale; see Appendix A: *a*, Case 49; *b*, 9; *c*, 242; *d*, 206; *e*, 214; *f*, 189; *g*, 58; *h*, 201; *i*, 204; *j*, 107; *k*, 207; *l*, 100.)

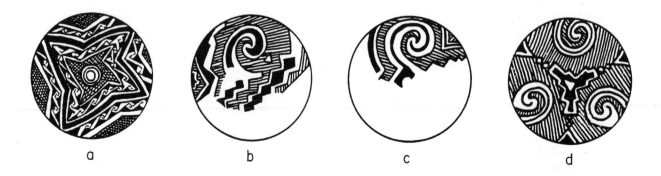

Figure 8.17. Roosevelt Red Ware design styles on Pinto Polychrome bowls at Chodistaas Pueblo. (Not to scale; see Appendix A: *a*, Case 86; *b*, 22; *c*, 59; *d*, 12.)

Table 8.4. Temper Types in Pinto Black-on-red and Pinto Polychrome Bowls

Bowls (n = 34)	Sherd	Sherd + quartz sand	Quartz sand	Diabase + quartz sand
Pinto Black-on-red (n = 27)	17	3	6	1
Pinto Polychrome (n = 7)	2	3	2	
Total	19	6	8	1

quartz. By observing carefully the white sherd temper particles it was noticed, in turn, that these were originally tempered with ground, pink-orange sherds, as are a number of Cibola White Ware vessels in the assemblage. Six sherd-tempered bowls (15% of all Pinto) have equal amounts of quartz and ground sherd temper. Sand-tempered bowls, on the other hand, present the same range of variation observed in the temper of gray corrugated pots: all variants of Temper Type 2 are represented in the eight bowls (20% of all Pinto). Only one Pinto Black-on-red bowl has diabase-sand temper (Type 1c).

The presence of two distinctive temper technologies, ground sherds and sand admixtures, in a ware that entered the room assemblages at Chodistaas a few years before abandonment, suggests that mountain potters were able to readily incorporate Roosevelt Red Ware, a ceramic tradition of northern affiliation, into their own repertoire once black-on-white bowls were no longer available.

Analytical Sources: INAA

Sixteen samples of Pinto Black-on-red and Pinto Polychrome bowls were submitted to INAA analysis (Fig. 8.18). A Principal Component analysis of these and other samples from corrugated vessels and clays indicates that 13 Pinto bowls show strong chemical similarities with Cluster 2, which includes local black-on-white pottery, brown and gray corrugated, red plain vessels, and three clays. Of the 13 bowls, 2 are tempered with sand, 10 with crushed sherds, and 1 with sand and sherds. One additional sample is in Cluster 1 and two are outliers.

The chemical composition of these bowls mirrors the variability observed in local undecorated wares. What is most interesting from this pattern is that the overwhelming majority of samples are compositionally similar to gray corrugated and local Cibola White Ware,

suggesting that Roosevelt Red Ware was made under technological criteria (with sherd temper and organic paint) similar to wares that were not originally part of the mountain technological tradition. The decorated and undecorated pots, the technical knowledge to make these pots, or both, may have been introduced on the Grasshopper Plateau through reciprocal exchange with immediate neighbors as well as through a movement of people.

Firing Technology

Refiring of 17 sherds from Pinto Black-on-red and Pinto Polychrome bowls at different temperature intervals indicated that this ware was fired in a partially oxidizing atmosphere. Original dark cores began to oxidize at temperatures that ranged between 550°C (1022°F) and 700°C (1292°F), which was similar to the atmosphere and temperature range obtained for corrugated and plain wares (Chapter 6, Table 6.4). Organic paint in the bowl interiors began to fade around 500°C and to disappear above 700°C, which is the approximate temperature needed to completely volatilize carbon (Rice 1987: 88). The desire to maintain carbon-painted designs on interior surfaces, therefore, required that Roosevelt Red Ware bowls be fired at low temperatures that nonetheless allowed the oxidation of red iron-based slips on black-on-red bowls. Blackened surfaces and faded paint are common in the Roosevelt Red Ware assemblage, suggesting that perhaps potters were experimenting with firing technology (Crown 1981a: 366). This observation should be taken with caution, however, because fire-related changes in the appearance of these bowls also could have resulted from the burning of the pueblo.

Low-temperature firing produced heavy, relatively soft, and highly breakable Pinto bowls. Mohs hardness scale was 3 to 4 for Pinto bowls and 5 to 7 for black-on-white bowls. Similarly, a Pinto bowl with a maximum diameter of 26.0 cm weighs approximately 300 grams more than a black-on-white bowl of the same dimension. Preliminary strength tests by Mark Neupert (Reid and others 1992), measuring the modulus of rupture of sample sherds, indicated that early Roosevelt Red Ware bowls were 40 percent less resistant to catastrophic impact than were Cibola White Ware bowls. The combination of raw materials and moderately high firing temperature is a technological factor that may have contributed to the production of a lightweight, hard, and breakage-resistant Cibola White Ware, better suited for transport than Roosevelt Red Ware.

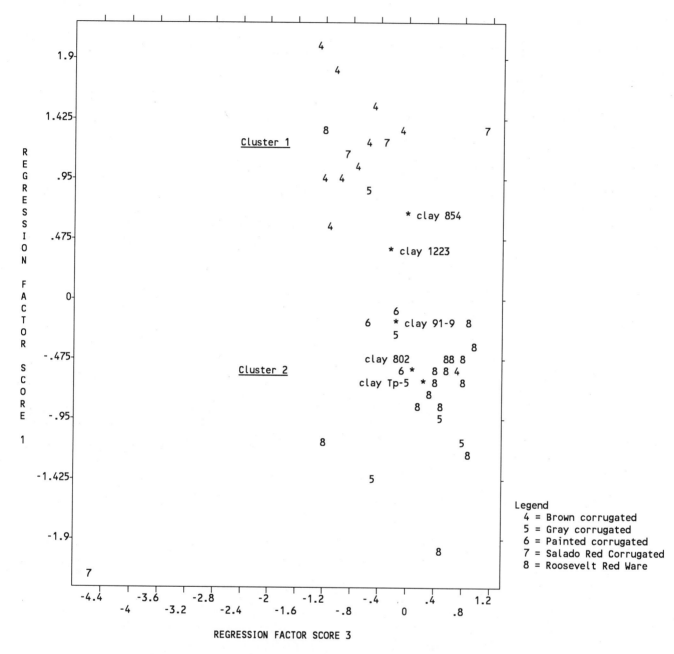

Figure 8.18. INAA: Compositional similarities among Roosevelt Red Ware, corrugated wares, and local clays, as defined by principal components.

Cibola White Ware required a control of firing technology to reduce black iron paint without blackening the white surface background, and Roosevelt Red Ware required that temperatures be kept low and atmospheres neutral in order to avoid the volatilization of organic pigments. Both technologies, although distinct, are derived from the Colorado Plateau ceramic traditions such as the Little Colorado and Tusayan white wares and Showlow Red Ware.

Although the manufacture of Roosevelt Red Ware, a low-fired, incompletely oxidized ware, required no truly specialized technology, it did introduce innovations into the mountain ceramic tradition. By the A.D. 1300s, this ware was made locally in almost every inhabited region of the mountains and desert basins in Arizona.

Did early Roosevelt Red Ware circulate in a manner similar to Cibola White Ware? The fragility of Pinto bowls argues against regular long-distance movement, but these red ware vessels could have circulated among immediate neighbors, as suggested for gray corrugated ware. Because groups from the Colorado Plateau abandoned their villages and came to the mountains at the end of the thirteenth century, it is reasonable to propose that immigrants brought bowls with them or manufactured Pinto bowls with local raw materials. Ethnic coresidence, in turn, stimulated local potters to adopt "foreign" design styles and technical practices such as sherd-temper and organic paint.

To conclude this chapter, it should be underscored that the painted and polished wares present in the whole-vessel assemblage at Chodistaas Pueblo illustrate the operation of different mechanisms of circulation. Cibola White Ware probably was obtained regularly through reciprocal exchange with communities located north of the Mogollon Rim.

White Mountain Red Ware, the classic "trade" ware, is poorly represented at Chodistaas Pueblo and many other sites in the Arizona mountains, indicating that during the thirteenth century small mountain communities obtained St. Johns Polychrome bowls through sporadic, "down-the-line trading ventures" (Graves 1982: 329). Roosevelt Red Ware, on the other hand, is a key indicator of the movement of people from the north into the Arizona mountains. At Chodistaas Pueblo both local and foreign technologies were detected in Pinto bowls, suggesting a local adoption of this ware that perhaps was a result of direct contact between potters of different cultural and ethnic backgrounds. That all these wares can be traced to the Colorado Plateau indicates either that mountain and plateau populations were similar or that they maintained strong relationships throughout the late Pueblo III period.

CHAPTER NINE

Archaeological Ceramics and Prehistoric Behavior

Prehistoric pottery contains information on the flow of people, materials, and ideas through time and space and is the most useful artifact category that archaeologists have at hand for reconstructing behavior in village-farming societies. Valuable insights on issues of prehistoric economics, demography, social inequality, and ritual may be ascertained once the specific behaviors that generated ceramic variation are understood. Identifying local and nonlocal ceramics is the first step for decoding ceramic variation.

This report has a strong focus on the methodological aspects of ceramic analysis. The research was originally designed to explore and expand the study of design style, technology, and physical-chemical composition for distinguishing local from nonlocal pottery. Chodistaas Pueblo, a small, exceptionally well-dated, and well-preserved site, provided an ideal ceramic assemblage for refining methods of pottery analysis and for gaining insights into the nature of ceramic variability (Chapter 4). The wealth of information on the prehistory of the region and on ceramic-related behavior that this basic exercise produced was unanticipated. The assemblage from Chodistaas Pueblo provided answers to many questions about the specific mechanisms of ceramic circulation. Even though this study did not explore the full range of cultural and behavioral information that archaeologists discern from prehistoric pottery, it opened new avenues of inquiry that are worthy of a detailed review.

In this concluding chapter, it is useful to reemphasize the importance of understanding the transfer of stylistic and technological information when interpreting complex patterns of ceramic variation and their behavioral correlates. In the sections below I underscore the main contributions of the study of the Chodistaas ceramic assemblage for reconstructing regional prehistory and the value of ceramics for addressing current issues in Southwestern prehistory.

CHODISTAAS PUEBLO IN PERSPECTIVE

More than a decade ago, Crown emphasized the unique potential of Chodistaas Pueblo and its whole vessel assemblage for investigating aspects of prehistoric behavior. The assemblage provided information on contexts of pottery manufacture, use, and ownership that could not be inferred from sherd collections and discard contexts (Crown 1981a: 379). The unusual circumstances surrounding the abandonment of Chodistaas are but one example of the processes that resulted in the formation of its remarkable ceramic record.

Chodistaas Pueblo illustrates a broad spectrum of behaviors that likely characterized many prehistoric Southwestern communities of similar size, date, and level of economic and sociopolitical development. For those archaeologists who are interested in the prehistory of small, short-lived communities, whose inhabitants practiced hunting, gathering, and cultivation in marginal environments, Chodistaas provides a model for deriving inferences about a way of life that was pervasive in most regions of the northern Southwest and throughout most of the prehistory of the area. For those concerned with the adequacy of gradualistic notions of change, Chodistaas represents a strong case in prehistory where episodic, rapid change can be closely monitored from the ceramic record. For archaeologists who study prehistoric pottery in other areas of the world, the study of ceramics from Chodistaas offers a comparative model of the mechanisms of transfer of information on style and technology.

The Chodistaas Pueblo ceramic assemblage provides useful comparative information on pottery manufacture and circulation during the late Pueblo III period. In this research, I have attempted to reconstruct the behaviors that brought ceramics into Chodistaas and contemporan-

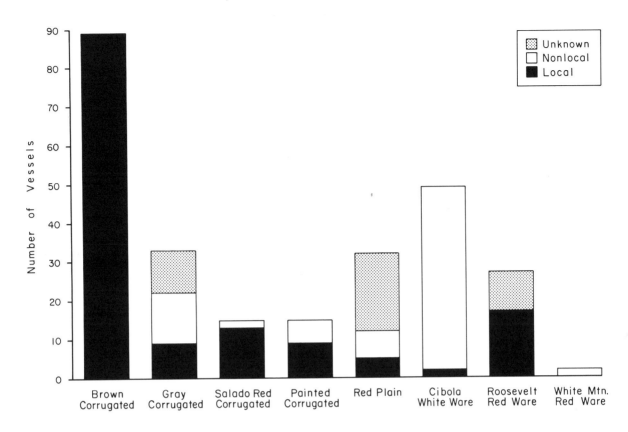

Figure 9.1. Local and nonlocal ceramics at Chodistaas Pueblo.

eous settlements on the Grasshopper Plateau. If my interpretation of the information presented here is correct (Fig. 9.1), then Chodistaas Pueblo illustrates a case in which a small, short-lived mountain community obtained at least one-third of its pots from close as well as from distant neighbors. Practically all Cibola White Ware, White Mountain Red Ware, and many gray corrugated and red plain vessels are nonlocal. Although Chodistaas potters were able to produce vessels similar to those obtained from other sources, they had a strong preference for manufacturing a relatively limited but consistent repertoire of unpainted, painted, and red-slipped brown corrugated pottery. Evidence concerning the manufacture of Roosevelt Red Ware at Chodistaas is especially intriguing, because its interpretation requires a consideration of broad interregional processes such as migration and ethnic coresidence as the principal agents for the transfer of information necessary for producing this ware locally.

Pots circulated onto the Grasshopper Plateau, specifically into Chodistaas Pueblo, through at least three mechanisms: sporadic trading episodes, reciprocal exchange among relatively mobile communities, and movement of people into the region. This reconstruc-

tion, in turn, accords with current notions of prehistoric adaptations of mountain communities during the late A.D. 1200s.

Based on information gathered from recent excavations at Grasshopper Spring Pueblo, site AZ P:14:197 (ASM), and from a survey and study of surface ceramics from late Pueblo III sites at Q Ranch, Grasshopper, Cibecue, Forestdale, and Corn Creek (Reid and others 1993), I suggest that many of these sites approximate Chodistaas Pueblo in the diversity of their pottery and that processes similar to those outlined for Chodistaas may have brought nonlocal pots to many contemporaneous mountain settlements.

The evidence from Chodistaas Pueblo contributes to the growing consensus among Southwestern archaeologists that ceramic containers circulated within and between regions on a fairly regular basis, regardless of settlement size, degree of residential stability, or relative proximity of a community to large population centers (Chapter 1). That the nature and scale of exchange relationships changed significantly after aggregation occurred cannot be denied. However, the fact that large numbers of nonlocal pots were recovered from a 20-room pueblo occupied for only 40 years indicates that distributions of nonlocal ceramics alone are not evidence of sociopolitical complexity. Rather, the relative abundance of nonlocal ceramics in small settlements may be signaling reciprocal relationships among prehistoric communities whose survival largely depended on their ability to establish and maintain a system of social interactions. This network facilitated exploitation of diverse resources in a marginal environment. Residential mobility was a common adaptive strategy of small mountain communities, and it is likely that people carried pots from one residence to another and that they manufactured their traditional pottery with raw materials available in their new residential location. A corollary process is ethnic coresidence and the transfer of pottery-making knowledge.

Chodistaas Pueblo, then, represents a most unusual archaeological case in which formation processes resulted in perhaps the best preserved and most complete ceramic record in the American Southwest. Such exceptional conditions for data recovery and analysis proved invaluable for obtaining strict chronological control that, in turn, was essential for reconstructing aspects of prehistoric behavior that may not be at all visible under less favorable circumstances. Long-term research at Chodistaas made it possible to obtain a sample of whole vessels that closely approximates a population, thereby providing a solid data base for constructing inferences about ceramic-related behavior. Chodistaas Pueblo is, in this sense, a rare finding. However, I believe that many of the behaviors that brought ceramics to Chodistaas are not unique; on the contrary, the site illustrates processes of ceramic manufacture and circulation that were common to other contemporaneous communities in the mountains of east-central Arizona, and the analysis of Chodistaas pots provides comparative data for future research in the area.

A REVIEW OF METHODS AND TECHNIQUES

Establishing a direct connection between prehistoric pottery and the populations who made and discarded it requires the use of an analytic unit that conveys technological variation relevant for identifying local and nonlocal ceramics (Chapter 2). Wares may be viewed as analogous to "natural" groups, in the sense that they allow the partition of an assemblage into few, obviously distinct, groups of vessels. The all-inclusive quality of wares facilitates the isolation and comparison of aspects of ceramic manufacture common to more than one ware as well as those restricted to a single ware. This inclu-

siveness proved to be extremely useful for ready identification of nonlocal wares, such as Cibola White Ware, that had unique technological characteristics when compared with the remainder of the assemblage. Similarly, identification of technological and compositional variation within a single ware helped to isolate local and nonlocal aspects of Roosevelt Red Ware technology, on which the hypothesis of local manufacture of a foreign tradition was built (Chapter 8). Ware provided sufficient analytical flexibility to isolate only those aspects of variation that were relevant for identifying local and nonlocal ceramics. However, ware did not always correlate with provenience and could not be used for making a priori inferences about manufacturing loci. The unit does serve, then, as a preliminary classificatory criterion, which subsequently must be tested by compositional analysis. This observation is critical for further research, because it cautions against "visual" identifications of local and nonlocal ceramics.

Analysis of the manufacturing technology of vessels from Chodistaas Pueblo covered a wide range of attribute variability in all wares and was complemented by experimental and statistical testing. Analysis of the design styles of decorated pots was limited to qualitative assessment of design style variation in Cibola White ware, and many of the observations derived from it may not be directly applicable to other wares nor to other assemblages that lack whole vessels. Nonetheless, the analysis illustrates the wealth of information that complete designs may provide and the inherent danger of deriving inferences about style-related past behavior solely from fragmentary materials.

The research was designed originally to include a detailed study of compositional variability encountered in a single site occupied for a short time interval. Therefore, a number of analyses (qualitative petrography, INAA, and ICP) were carried out simultaneously on a large number of samples. The results showed that complementary information on qualitative petrography and paste chemistry are needed when identification of raw material sources and the establishment of a direct correlation between those sources and the prehistoric pottery are essential for meeting research goals. In the Chodistaas Pueblo case, where each ware presents a particular set of questions regarding its manufacturing loci, the need for conducting a complete compositional analysis varied from ware to ware. For example, the results revealed that petrographic analysis would have sufficed for identifying the local brown corrugated ware, but it would have been insufficient for establishing local manufacture of Roosevelt Red Ware. This analysis underscores the importance of a preliminary assessment of the variability present in ceramic paste (Bishop, Rands, and Holley 1982) and of careful selection of a particular analytical method.

Similarly, the methods followed for locating and sampling potential raw material sources must be tailored according to the particular geographic and geological characteristics of the region under study and to the nature of prehistoric settlement patterns. Arnold's (1985) cross-cultural analysis of the procurement of raw materials for ceramic manufacture provided valuable criteria for conducting the survey. I was fortunate to have been able to locate and sample clay and temper sources that matched the clays and vessels used prehistorically. However, the information obtained from the clay survey and compositional analysis indicates that a resource procurement area larger than the one suggested by Arnold's research may have been exploited in the past and that future research in neighboring regions is necessary for rounding out the present study.

TRANSFER OF CERAMIC INFORMATION AND RECONSTRUCTION OF BEHAVIOR

Some of the most useful information obtained from this research bears on the mechanisms of technological and stylistic transfer. Technology and style are the two fundamental dimensions that archaeologists use to partition variation in a ceramic assemblage, and the behaviors involved in the generation of variability across these dimensions must be well understood. As discussed in Chapter 5, the transfer of technology, a complex system of knowledge and experimentation, requires a direct "teaching framework" (Schiffer and Skibo 1987) in which the sequence of behaviors that result from specific technical and cultural choices cannot be learned by visual inspection but only from direct interaction among potters. In the American Southwest, long-lived technological traditions resulted from the intergenerational transmission of this knowledge.

Through the observation of differences in manufacturing technologies of several ceramic wares, I was able to detect definite indicators of technological traditions that were foreign to mountain potters. Tempering ceramic paste with crushed sherds has long been recognized as common practice among prehistoric potters on the Colorado Plateau. The presence of sherd temper in Roosevelt Red Ware and Cibola White Ware, therefore, was interpreted as evidence of northern technology. At least in the case of Cibola White Ware, manufacturing technology, paste composition, and information on the

regional geology were used to infer that the ware was manufactured north of the Mogollon Rim. In the case of Roosevelt Red Ware, in which a match was found between local clays and a group of Pinto bowls, a more complex inference that involved movement of people into the region around the estimated time of appearance of this ware is postulated. Although compositional analysis accurately measures variability in procurement sources of prehistoric pottery, technological information is indispensable for recognizing culturally determined behaviors involved in ceramic manufacture.

Cibola White Ware design styles crosscut three analytical sources and are similar to styles displayed on black-on-white and polychrome vessels made in several regions, suggesting that there is no apparent correlation between design variation and manufacturing loci. An important implication of this observation is that stylistic information in the prehistoric Southwest crossed ethnic and territorial boundaries, and that styles could be readily incorporated into any ceramic tradition with or without direct contact between potters. Prehistoric potters were able to create new design styles, such as Pinedale, in short periods of time, by copying foreign motifs and recombining the newly acquired stylistic criteria with their own traditional designs. The widespread distribution of design styles displayed on pottery as well as on other decorated items argues against the existence of restrictive mechanisms for the transfer of such information in at least some contexts in the prehistoric Southwest.

Consider, for example, how much effort has been placed on identifying socially significant patterns of design variation in the archaeological record. For at least a decade, Southwestern archaeologists recorded countless design elements and motifs, looking for patterns of social organization, community interaction, boundaries, and social distance, but, as Stephen Plog (1980: 124) has pointed out, to date no one has adequately demonstrated that such patterns existed. It is revealing that patterned distributions of ceramic designs do not appear among settlements that are located less than 50 km to 80 km (30 to 50 miles) apart, whereas consistent differences in ceramic technology may be established between communities located less than 10 km (6 miles) apart.

Failure in explaining ceramic design variation in the American Southwest is not only a result of incorrect assumptions about the provenience of the ceramics under study, lack of examination of formation processes, or spurious use of statistical testing; it is the result of indiscriminate application of ethnographic analogy and theoretical constructs to the ceramic record without an adequate understanding of the behaviors that produced such variation. What was observed in Cibola White Ware designs fits well with what Colton and Hargrave observed back in 1937: that style is a sensitive marker of temporal change and of the transfer and acceptance of ideas among culturally and ethnically diverse groups of people. On the other hand, many answers to archaeological issues that require the establishment of a direct connection between prehistoric pottery and its makers (ethnicity, boundary maintenance, population movement) can be found in the ceramic technology, by tracing the development of technological traditions, their distribution in space, and the patterns of transfer of technological knowledge. It was perhaps through technology rather than style that prehistoric Southwestern societies expressed their social and cultural distinctions.

CHODISTAAS PUEBLO CERAMICS AND REGIONAL PREHISTORY

Chodistaas Pueblo was occupied during a critical period in Southwestern prehistory. The last decades of the thirteenth century witnessed changes in subsistence strategies, demographic shifts, and social reorganization in broad areas of the northern Southwest that culminated in the aggregation of culturally and ethnically diverse peoples in large mountain pueblos. The character of the late Pueblo III period in the Arizona mountains is highlighted by episodes of sudden change that immediately preceded the aggregation period. These episodic changes left subtle material evidence that can be recovered only when temporal and contextual associations are well controlled, and when formation processes are incorporated into archaeological analysis and interpretation.

At Chodistaas Pueblo, where these analytical conditions are met, it was possible to monitor episodic changes from the ceramic assemblage. Research by Montgomery and Reid (1990) identified an instance of rapid replacement of Cibola White Ware bowls by Roosevelt Red Ware bowls sometime after A.D. 1285. Exploring the provenience of these wares allowed me to postulate a probable correlation between the replacement event and temporal shifts in the manufacture of Cibola White Ware and incorporation of Roosevelt Red Ware into the local ceramic tradition. Changes were thus evident not only in the replacement of one ware by another, but in specific discontinuities in paste composition, technology, and design style.

This instance of episodic change appears to have been symptomatic of demographic reorganization that resulted from the abandonment of many areas on the Colorado Plateau and the movement of people into the mountains. Ceramic replacement did not go unnoticed by Haury and Hargrave (1931) at the Pinedale Ruin. The Gladwins (Gladwin and Gladwin 1934) and Haury (1945) thought that the appearance of Roosevelt Red Ware in the Arizona mountains was directly related to population movement from the north. More recently, Carlson (1970: 224) and Graves (1982: 333) observed that design styles on Southwestern pottery were extremely sensitive to demographic shifts and concomitant discontinuities in regional ceramic traditions between A.D. 1275 and 1300. The episodic events recorded in the ceramic assemblage from Chodistaas Pueblo, therefore, are by no means unique, but stand as an excellent example of one of the major trends that characterized the last decades of the thirteenth century.

Identification of nonlocal ceramics at Chodistaas Pueblo revealed that this small community, located in an isolated backwoods area, maintained contact with communities to the north, east, and west of the Grasshopper Plateau. Cibola White Ware was acquired regularly throughout the occupation of Chodistaas, until the pueblo burned. As Reed (1958: 7), and more recently Johnson (1989: 384) observed, long-term, long distance relationships established among relatively mobile populations probably influenced migration routes and choices of destinations and formed the basis for the development of trade networks during the fourteenth century.

Temporal discontinuities in the manufacture of Cibola White Ware on the Grasshopper Plateau are strongly correlated with the abandonment of northern settlements and subsequent migration of northern people into the Arizona mountains. Similarly, the introduction and spread of Roosevelt Red Ware appears to have been brought about by direct interaction or ethnic coresidence of plateau and mountain potters. On the other hand, it was not until the establishment of Grasshopper Pueblo that mountain communities began to participate regularly in the trade network that distributed White Mountain Red Ware. Thus, the vessels from Chodistaas illustrate different mechanisms of ceramic circulation in operation during the late A.D. 1200s, and the assemblage is a good indicator of the intensity and diversity of intercommunity relationships.

One particular case of intercommunity relationships that should be explored in further research is suggested by the compositional and technological differences between brown corrugated and gray-orange corrugated pottery. I interpreted these ware differences as indicating reciprocal relationships between Chodistaas inhabitants, their Cibecue neighbors, and perhaps other nearby community residents. That these relationships existed is not unlikely, considering the geographical proximity between Grasshopper and Cibecue settlements. What is significant from the "ceramic" perspective is the possibility that interacting communities that otherwise shared a number of material culture traits (masonry, settlement orientation, room layout, and presence or absence of decorated and undecorated wares) appear to have had different ceramic technologies.

Consistent technological differences that go beyond the exploitation of immediately available raw material sources suggest a number of behavioral possibilities. One possibility is the existence of cultural or ethnic differences manifest in ceramic manufacture. As discussed previously, archaeologists generally acknowledge that ceramic technology is a diagnostic aspect of cultural or ethnic affiliation. However, the preservation of side-by-side technological differences in ceramic manufacture among settlements with otherwise similar cultural traits may be signaling the persistence of separate teaching frameworks. Restricting the flow of technological information to specific residential groups may have allowed interacting communities to maintain boundaries and acknowledge social distance. If this interpretation is correct, then technology transfer was restricted not just between broad archaeological areas such as the Colorado Plateau and the Mogollon Rim, but between localities less than 10 km (6 miles) apart.

It is less clear where the manufacturing loci of other nonlocal wares were situated. Nevertheless, the correlation between ceramic paste composition of these wares and regional geology suggests that Chodistaas settlers obtained some of their ceramics from near as well as relatively distant regions (within 100 km, 62 miles). In this case, the distinction of local versus nonlocal ceramics was not just a "binary" issue, but became an issue of scale, in which undecorated wares may represent interaction among immediate and close neighbors, and decorated wares may signal long-distance community relationships.

To summarize, identifying local and nonlocal pottery from Chodistaas Pueblo constituted a crucial starting point for building inferences about the mechanisms of ceramic circulation, such as reciprocal exchange and population movement (mobility as well as migration) and their relevance for delineating intercommunity relationships and episodic change during a critical transitional period in the prehistory of the Grasshopper Plateau. The range of variation encountered in the Chodistaas ceramic assemblage is not an exception, but one important characteristic of many late Pueblo III mountain settlements that have assemblages with great potential for reconstructing aspects of this transition.

SOUTHWESTERN POTTERY AND PREHISTORIC BEHAVIOR

Redefining large-scale, interregional developments in the prehistory of the American Southwest is the central goal of contemporary Southwestern archaeology. This goal does not imply the abandonment of intrasettlement or small-scale research, but it requires an evaluation of even the most restricted data sets in light of major trends that characterized prehistoric developments at different times. For example, current emphasis on the reevaluation of the "Salado Culture" requires that information from three major areas of the Southwest, plateau, mountains, and desert basins, be pieced together in order to uncover the origins and spread of this prehistoric phenomenon. The technological analysis of Roosevelt Red Ware from Chodistaas Pueblo provides valuable information on this subject.

As has been demonstrated, ceramics play a pivotal role in investigating developments such as the Salado, with its multiregional evolvement. Because ceramic manufacture is both restricted and enhanced by natural environment, cultural choice, technical knowledge, and stylistic behavior, ceramic materials constitute the "fingerprint" of a particular group of pottery-making people. In the American Southwest, where demographic dynamics (mobility, abandonment, migration, aggregation) are at the core of archaeological interpretation, ceramics have proved especially useful for tracing the movement and identifying coresidence of culturally and ethnically diverse groups. Similarly, determining the direction and timing of ceramic exchange is currently considered crucial for understanding the interregional economic and sociopolitical organization of prehistoric Southwestern communities. Here, too, the establishment of a direct connection between pottery and people is necessary for delineating the dynamics of production and distribution of ceramic materials and for tracing the spread of ideas and influences encoded in them.

Pottery also provides information on transitions and episodic changes in prehistory that are seldom preserved in other components of the archaeological record. Lack of strict temporal control often gives archaeologists the illusion that most cultural and social changes are gradual. However, a detailed reconstruction of the formation of the ceramic record may reveal episodes of rapid change that, in turn, are good indicators of shifts in subsistence, demography, and community organization.

In the American Southwest, archaeologists have traditionally recognized that technology and style provide two distinct lines of evidence for tracing the movement of people, materials, and ideas over time and space. Similarly, many issues of current interest, such as population movement, were explored decades ago. By using ideas proposed by traditional archaeologists in combination with modern analytical techniques, the ceramic as-

semblage from Chodistaas Pueblo could be exploited more thoroughly, and the ceramic information from this small settlement could be incorporated into a broader Southwestern perspective, than would have been possible by pursuing the methods of "old" or "new" or "post-processual" archaeology separately. This critical reevaluation of concepts and inferences, developed within the context of the history of archaeological thought in the Southwest, provided surprisingly well-integrated results and unexpected insights to long-standing problems of relevance to archaeological interpretation.

Identification of Chodistaas Pueblo Vessels by Provenience, Ware, Form, and Temper

The whole and partial vessels from Chodistaas Pueblo, Grasshopper Spring Pueblo, site AZ P:14:197, and Grasshopper Pueblo that are described in Appendix A constitute the data base used for the analyses in this book. Information on clay samples that were submitted to compositional analysis is also included.

The variables selected for vessel description provide detailed provenience information, typological assignment, vessel shape, size measurements, compositional group membership, and temper type.

1. The Case number identifies each vessel illustrated in the text and each vessel and clay sample analyzed by Instrumental Neutron Activation Analysis (Appendix B) and Inductively Coupled Plasma Emission Spectroscopy (Appendix C).

2. Vessel provenience includes room number designation (Room #), individual pot number assigned in the field or laboratory (Pot Id.), and individual field number (Field #). Vessel proveniences from Grasshopper Pueblo correspond to catalog numbers of the Arizona State Museum (Catalog no.).

3. Typological designations include Ware, Type, and Style as identified for this study.

4. Vessel indicates shape (jar, bowl, pitcher), followed by measurements in centimeters of maximum diameter (Max. diam.) and interior aperture (Int.) for whole or reconstructed vessels.

5. The Cluster (Cls.) or Group (Grp.) membership of each vessel selected for ICP and INAA analyses is provided. The last column includes a brief description of temper.

Case	Room #	Pot Id.	Field #	Ware - Type - Style	Vessel	Max. (cm)	Int. (cm)	ICP	INAA	Temper
1	1	1	97	Cibola White Ware - Tularosa	Ellip. Jar	40.0	12.0	Nonocal	Grp. 1	Quartz Sand and Sherd
2	1	2	193	Cibicue Painted Corrugated	Bowl	28.8	8.0	Cls. 2		Diabase and Quartz Sand
3	1	3	286	Gray-orange indented corrugated	Jar	17.1	10.0			95% Quartz Sand
4	1	4	330	Brown indented obliterated corrugated	Jar	28.0	26.0	Cls. 2		Diabase and Quartz Sand
5	1	5	336	McDonald Painted Corrugated	Bowl	41.7	12.0		Grp. 4	99% Quartz Sand
6	1	6	338	Cibola White Ware - Tularosa	Jar	41.0	15.4	Cls. 2	Cls. 2	Quartz Sand and Sherd
7	2	1	55	Red plain	Jar	40.0	28.0	Cls. 1	Cls. 1	Diabase and Quartz Sand
8	2	2	84	Brown indented obliterated corrugated	Jar	27.0	26.0		Cls. 2	Coarse Diabase
9	2	3	120	Roosevelt Red Ware - Pinto Black-on-red	Bowl					Sand
10	2	4	137	Brown indented obliterated corrugated	Jar	36.0	20.0		Cls. 1	Medium Diabase
11	2	5	232	Unclassified corrugated (gray?)	Bowl	7.3	6.5			
12	2	6	233	Roosevelt Red Ware - Pinto Polychrome	Bowl	33.8	31.6			Quartz Sand
13	2	7	234	Unclassified corrugated	Plate	24.0	22.4			
14	2	8	235	Red plain	Jar	36.0	11.0		Cls. 2	Quartz, Feldspar, Muscovite
15	2	9	238	Brown indented obliterated corrugated	Jar	40.0	20.0			Medium Diabase
16	2	10	241	Cibicue Painted Corrugated	Bowl	35.7	33.9	Cls. 1		Quartz and Pyroxene Sand
17	2	11	829	Gray-orange indented corrugated	Jar	48.0	17.6	Cls. 2		99% Quartz Sand
18	2	12	433	Red plain	Jar	41.3	28.0			Quartz, Feldspar, Muscovite
19	2	13	532	Gray-orange indented corrugated	Jar	22.0	34.0	Outlier		99% Quartz Sand
20	2	14	692	Brown plain	Jar	58.0	27.0			Medium Diabase
21	2	15	693	Brown indented obliterated corrugated	Jar	50.0	22.0			Medium Diabase
22	2	16	695	Roosevelt Red Ware - Pinto Polychrome	Bowl	27.7	22.0		Cls. 2	Sherd
23	2	17	699	Brown indented obliterated corrugated	Jar	40.0	30.0			Coarse Diabase
24	2	18	743	Brown indented obliterated corrugated	Jar					Medium Diabase
25	2	19	747	Gray-orange indented corrugated	Jar				Grp. 1	Quartz and Plagioclase Sand
26	2	20	535	Cibola White Ware - unclassified	Bowl	13.9	12.5			
27	2	21	432	Brown indented obliterated corrugated	Jar	30.0	16.0			Medium Diabase
28	3	1	24	Brown plain	Jar					
29	3	2	26	Cibola White Ware - unclassified	Jar	48.4	28.0	Nonlocal	Grp. 2	Quartz Sand and Sherd
30	3	3	59	Red plain	Jar	42.0	13.4			Quartz, Feldspar, Muscovite
31	3	4	61	Gray-orange indented corrugated	Jar	46.0	20.0			Diabase and Quartz Sand
32	3	5	63	Cibola White Ware - Roosevelt	Jar	42.0	32.0	Nonlocal	Grp. 3	Quartz Sand and Sherd
33	3	6	74	Salado Red Corrugated	Jar	41.7	11.9			Coarse Diabase
34	3	7	95	McDonald Painted Corrugated	Bowl	12.7	10.2		Cls. 2	Diabase and Quartz Sand
35	3	8	126	Brown indented obliterated corrugated	Bowl	8.2	7.3			
36	3	9	135	Cibola White Ware - Tularosa	Jar	33.3	10.7	Nonlocal	Grp. 3	Quartz Sand and Sherd
37	3	10	139	Cibola White Ware - Kayenta-Tusayan	Bowl	21.3	20.6		Grp. 1	Quartz Sand
38	3	11	144	McDonald Painted Corrugated	Bowl	21.4	19.7			99% Quartz Sand
39	3	12	162	Gray-orange indented corrugated	Jar	54.0	34.0			99% Quartz Sand
40	3	13	163	Salado Red Corrugated	Jar	50.2	18.0		Outlier	Sherd
41	3	14	164	Red plain	Jar	52.0	21.0		Outlier	Coarse Diabase
42	3	15	167	Brown indented obliterated corrugated	Jar	56.0	27.0			Medium Diabase
43	3	16	168	Brown indented obliterated corrugated	Jar	50.0	24.0			Medium Diabase
44	3	17	170	Brown indented obliterated corrugated	Jar	31.3	15.3	Cls. 1	Cls. 1	Diabase and Quartz Sand
45	3	18	214	Brown plain	Bowl	9.0	7.0			
46	3	19	215	Brown indented obliterated corrugated	Jar	8.7	5.4			
47	3	20	216	Salado White-on-red Corrugated	Jar	8.8	4.9			Coarse Diabase

Case	Room #	Pot Id.	Field #	Ware - Type - Style	Vessel	Max. (cm)	Int. (cm)	ICP	INAA	Temper
48	3	48	232	Gray-orange indented corrugated	Jar	40.0				99% Quartz Sand
49	3	49	236	Roosevelt Red Ware - Pinto Black-on-red	Bowl	28.3	27.2			Quartz Sand
50	3	50	241	Cibola White Ware - Snowflake	Laddle Bowl	7.5	6.8			
51	3	51	258	Brown indented obliterated corrugated	Jar	48.0	21.0		Cls. 1	Medium Diabase
52	3	52	259	Brown indented obliterated corrugated	Jar	42.0	25.0			Diabase and Quartz Sand
53	3	53	260	Cibola White Ware - Pinedale	Jar	46.1	15.7	Nonlocal	Grp. 2	Sand and Sherd
54	3	54	262	Brown indented obliterated corrugated	Jar	48.0	27.0			Diabase and Quartz Sand
55	3	55	265	Brown indented obliterated corrugated	Jar	48.0	26.0			Diabase and Quartz Sand
56	3	56	266	Brown indented obliterated corrugated	Jar	42.0	22.0			Medium Diabase
57	3	57	282	Brown indented obliterated corrugated	Jar	22.0	19.0			Diabase and Quartz Sand
58	3	58	387	Roosevelt Red Ware - Pinto Black-on-red	Bowl	17.0	16.0		Cls. 2	Sherd
59	3	59	388	Roosevelt Red Ware - Pinto Polychrome	Bowl	33.0				Sand
60	3	60	134	Red plain	Jar	36.0	24.0			Diabase and Quartz Sand
61	3	61	174	Brown indented obliterated corrugated	Jar	48.0	27.0	Cls. 1		Sand?
62	4	1	65	Roosevelt Red Ware - Pinto Black-on-red	Bowl				Grp. 1	
63	4	2	183	Cibola White Ware - Snowflake	Jar	55.6	16.4			Sand and Sherd
64	4	3	394	Roosevelt Red Ware - Pinto Black-on-red	Bowl	30.0	29.0			Sherd
65	4	4	72	Salado White-on-red Corrugated	Jar	42.6	17.4			Coarse Diabase
66	4	5	259	Roosevelt Red Ware - Pinto Black-on-red	Bowl	30.0			Outlier	Sherd
67	4	6	73	Salado White-on-red Corrugated	Jar	34.2	13.0			Coarse Diabase
68	4	7	74	Cibola White Ware - Tularosa	Jar	41.2	11.4		Outlier	Sand and Sherd
69	4	8	75	Salado Red Corrugated	Jar					Coarse Diabase
70	4	9	75	Gray-orange indented corrugated	Jar	14.6	9.6			
71	4	10	319	Unclassified corrugated (gray?)	Jar	8.5	5.0			
72	4	11	338	Brown indented obliterated corrugated	Jar	9.9	4.8			
73	4	12	337	Brown indented obliterated corrugated	Jar	22.6	16.3	Cls. 1		Coarse Diabase
74	4	13	389	Brown indented obliterated corrugated	Jar	20.0	13.0			Medium Diabase
75	4	14	335	Gray-orange indented corrugated	Jar		11.6			
76	4	15	336	Gray-orange indented corrugated	Jar	56.0	28.0		Grp. 1	99% Quartz Sand
77	5	62	100	Unclassified corrugated	Pitcher	11.1	5.3			Quartz, Feldspar, Muscovite
78	5	63	101	Cibola White Ware - Tularosa	Jar	38.0	17.0		Cls. 2	99% Quartz Sand
79	5	64	102	Red plain	Jar	38.0	33.0			
80	5	65	103	Gray-orange indented corrugated	Jar	46.0	34.0	Cls. 2	Cls. 2	99% Quartz Sand
81	5	66	127	Cibola White Ware - unclassified	Stirrup Jar					Quartz, Feldspar, Muscovite
82	5	67	136	Gray-orange indented corrugated	Jar	50.0	20.0	Cls. 2	Cls. 2	99% Quartz Sand
83	5	68	137	Gray-orange indented corrugated	Jar	46.0	28.0			99% Quartz Sand
84	5	69	138	Brown plain	Jar	48.0				Coarse Diabase
85	5	70	140	Brown indented obliterated corrugated	Jar	30.4	18.0	Cls. 1	Cls. 1	Sherd
86	5	71	142	Roosevelt Red Ware - Pinto Polychrome	Bowl	34.0	28.7		Cls. 2	
87	5	72	149	Brown indented obliterated corrugated	Jar	22.0	17.0			Diabase and Quartz Sand
88	5	73	205	Brown indented obliterated corrugated	Jar					Diabase and Quartz Sand
89	5	74	210	Brown indented obliterated corrugated	Jar	24.0	22.0			Medium Diabase
90	5	75	215	Brown indented obliterated corrugated	Jar	52.0	24.0		Cls. 1	Medium Diabase
91	5	76	216	Brown indented obliterated corrugated	Jar	40.0	24.0	Cls. 1		Coarse Diabase
92	5	77	224	Brown painted corrugated	Jar	36.0	15.0			
93	5	78	225	Brown indented obliterated corrugated	Jar	50.0	30.0			
94	5	79	226	Brown indented obliterated corrugated	Jar	49.0	26.0	Cls. 1		Coarse Diabase

Case	Room #	Pot Id.	Field #	Ware - Type - Style	Vessel	Max. (cm)	Int. (cm)	ICP	INAA	Temper
95	5	80	227	Gray-orange indented corrugated	Jar	52.0	26.0			Quartz and Pyroxene Sand
96	5	81	228	Brown indented obliterated corrugated	Jar	42.0	24.0			Coarse Diabase
97	5	82	230	Gray-orange indented corrugated	Jar	42.0				Quartz and Plagioclase Sand
98	5	83	231	Red plain	Jar	36.0	16.0			Quartz, Feldspar, Muscovite
99	5	84	232	Brown indented obliterated corrugated	Jar	16.1	8.6			
100	5	85	260	Roosevelt Red Ware - Pinto Black-on-red	Bowl	36.0	34.0	Nonlocal	Cls. 2	Diabase and Quartz Sand
101	5	86	263	Cibola White Ware - Kayenta-Tusayan	Jar	41.1	9.9		Grp. 3 3	Sherd
102	5	87	264	Gray-orange indented corrugated	Jar	38.0				
103	5	88	269	Brown painted corrugated	Bowl	10.2	8.9			
104	5	89	282	Gray-orange indented corrugated	Bowl	9.0	8.2	Cls. 2	Outlier	99% Quartz Sand
105	5	90	297	Red plain	Bowl	35.0	33.0		Grp. 1	Quartz, Feldspar, Muscovite
106	5	91	301	Cibola White Ware - Tularosa	Pitcher	13.7	8.0			
107	5	92	302	Roosevelt Red Ware - Pinto Black-on-red	Bowl	32.4	31.0			
108	5	93	303	Brown indented obliterated corrugated	Jar	13.0	5.0			Diabase and Quartz Sand
109	5	94	304	Cibola White Ware - Tularosa	Pitcher	16.0	8.0			Sand and Sherd
110	5	95	370	Gray-orange indented corrugated	Jar		30.0		Grp. 3	Quartz and Plagioclase Sand
111	5	96	371	Brown indented obliterated corrugated	Jar	34.0	18.0			Diabase and Quartz Sand
112	5	97	372	Salado White-on-red Corrugated	Jar	32.0	16.0			Coarse Diabase
113	6	1	370	Red plain	Jar	38.0	18.0			Quartz, Feldspar, Muscovite
114	6	2	317	Red plain	Jar	39.0	17.4			Quartz, Feldspar, Muscovite
115	6	3	268	Brown plain	Ladle	7.5	6.8			
116	6	4	391	Brown indented obliterated corrugated	Bowl	10.5	9.6			
117	6	5	369	Brown indented obliterated corrugated	Jar	41.0	25.2	Cls. 1	Cls. 2	Medium Diabase
118	6	6	378	Roosevelt Red Ware - Pinto Black-on-red	Bowl	33.4	30.4			Sand
119	6	7e	396	Brown indented obliterated corrugated	Jar	45.0	20.4			Diabase and Quartz Sand
120	6	7w	397	Gray-orange indented corrugated	Jar	64.0	28.8			Diabase and Quartz Sand
121	6	8	395	Roosevelt Red Ware - Pinto Black-on-red	Bowl	32.0	30.0			Sherd
122	6	9	394	Salado Red Corrugated	Bowl	37.6	33.4	Cls. 1		Coarse Diabase
123	6	10	318	Brown indented obliterated corrugated	Jar	44.0	20.2			
124	6	11	351	Gray-orange indented corrugated	Jar	21.0	12.4	Cls. 2		Quartz and Pyroxene Sand
125	6	12	328	Salado White-on-red Corrugated	Bowl	25.0	24.0			Diabase and Quartz Sand
126	6	13	313	Cibola White Ware - Puerco	Pitcher	16.5	6.6	Nonlocal	Grp. 2	Sand and Sherd
127	6	14	346	Cibola White Ware - Tularosa	Jar	16.0	5.5		Grp. 1	
128	6	15	314	Unclassified corrugated (gray?)	Bowl	20.0	19.0			
129	6	16a	345	Gray-orange indented corrugated	Jar	54.6	26.6			Quartz and Plagioclase Sand
130	6	16b	345	Unclassified corrugated	Jar	46.0	26.0			Diabase and Quartz Sand
131	6	17	316	Red plain	Jar	38.6	16.3			Quartz, Feldspar, Muscovite
132	6	18	326	Brown indented obliterated corrugated	Jar	30.0	19.0			Diabase and Quartz Sand
133	6	19	315	Red plain	Bowl	31.0	29.0			Quartz, Feldspar, Muscovite
134	6	20	323	Red plain	Jar	41.0	19.6			Quartz, Feldspar, Muscovite
135	6	21	323	Brown indented obliterated corrugated	Jar	44.4	28.0			Diabase and Quartz Sand
136	6	22	341	Brown indented obliterated corrugated	Jar	21.0	14.0			Medium Diabase
137	6	23	330	Unclassified corrugated	Jar	21.9	15.0			
138	6	24	336	Brown indented obliterated corrugated	Jar	41.4	26.6			Medium Diabase
139	6	25	343	McDonald Painted Corrugated	Bowl	32.0	31.0			Quartz and Plagioclase Sand
140	6	26	322	Salado Red Corrugated	Bowl	46.0	45.0			Coarse Diabase
141	6	29	365	Roosevelt Red Ware - Pinto Black-on-red	Bowl	34.4	32.0			Sherd

Case	Room #	Pot Id.	Field #	Ware - Type - Style	Vessel	Max. (cm)	Int. (cm)	ICP	INAA	Temper
142	6	30	392	Cibola White Ware - unclassified	Bowl	15.0	14.0		Grp. 1	
143	6	31	256	Cibola White Ware - unclassified	Pitcher	13.0			Outlier	
144	6	32	339	Cibola White Ware - Snowflake	Pitcher	12.4			Grp. 3	
145	6	33	441	Brown plain	Bowl	9.0	8.6			
146	6	pv2	346	Roosevelt Red Ware - Pinto Black-on-red	Bowl	34.0	32.0			
147	6	pv3	382	Roosevelt Red Ware - Pinto Black-on-red	Bowl	33.6	32.0			
148	6	pv4	393	Cibola White Ware - Pinedale	Bowl	30.0	28.8		Grp. 1	Sand and Sherd
149	7	1	156	White Mt. Red Ware - St. Johns Polychrome	Bowl	32.0	30.2			
150	7	2	157	Cibola White Ware - Pinedale	Pitcher	12.6	5.0		Grp. 1	
151	7	3	158	Cibola White Ware - Snowflake	Jar	28.0	10.8		Grp. 1	
152	7	4	159	Roosevelt Red Ware - Pinto Polychrome	Bowl	26.4	26.0	Cls. 1		Sand and Sherd
153	7	5	591	Brown indented obliterated corrugated	Jar	58.0	28.0			Medium Diabase
154	7	6	592	Brown indented obliterated corrugated	Jar	23.8	13.4			Medium Diabase
155	7	7	593	Gray-orange indented corrugated	Jar					Quartz and Pyroxene Sand
156	7	8	597	Gray-orange indented corrugated	Jar	18.2	14.0			
157	7	9	599	Salado Red corrugated	Bowl	42.0	40.8			
158	7	10	594	Red plain	Ellip. Jar	37.0	12.4			
159	7	11	607	Red plain	Jar	54.6	30.4	Cls. 1		Coarse Diabase
160	7	12	615	Salado Red Corrugated	Jar	35.8	13.0	Cls. 1		Coarse Diabase
161	7	13	619	Red plain	Jar	32.6	12.0			Quartz, Feldspar, Muscovite
162	7	14	614	Salado White-on-red Corrugated	Bowl	24.0	22.6	Cls. 2	Cls. 2	Diabase and Quartz Sand
163	7	15	613	Red plain	Jar	29.0	10.8			
164	7	16	612	Brown indented obliterated corrugated	Jar	56.6	24.3			Medium Diabase
165	7	17	610	Roosevelt Red Ware - Pinto Black-on-red	Bowl	17.4	16.0			Sherd
166	7	18	611	Unclassified corrugated	Jar	9.8	4.0			
167	7	19	602	Gray-orange indented corrugated	Jar	32.0	20.2			Quartz and Plagioclase Sand
168	7	20	601	Unclassified corrugated	Jar	45.4	18.6			
169	7	21	606	Brown indented obliterated corrugated	Jar					Coarse Diabase
170	7	22	605	Gray-orange indented corrugated	Jar	38.6	22.4			Diabase and Quartz Sand
171	7	23	616	Roosevelt Red Ware - Pinto Black-on-red	Bowl					Sherd
172	7	24	603	Gray-orange indented corrugated	Jar	24.2	17.8			Quartz and Plagioclase Sand
173	7	25	604	Gray-orange indented corrugated	Jar	29.6	15.1		Outlier	Sherd and Sand
174	7	26	598	Roosevelt Red Ware - Pinto Black-on-red	Bowl	32.4	28.6			Sand
175	7	27	591	Roosevelt Red Ware - Pinto Black-on-red	Bowl	26.0	30.0			Sand
176	7	28	595	Cibola White Ware - Snowflake	Bowl	33.0	25.0		Grp. 1	
177	7	29a	608	Roosevelt Red Ware - Pinto Black-on-red	Bowl	8.2	5.2		Cls. 2	Sand and Sherd
178	7	30	600	Cibola White Ware - unclassified	Pitcher	58.0	32.0		Cls. 1	
179	8	98	31	Brown indented obliterated corrugated	Jar	48.0	36.0	Cls. 2		Diabase and Quartz Sand
180	8	99	50	Gray-orange indented corrugated	Jar	48.0	12.0		Grp. 1	Quartz and Plagioclase Sand
181	8	100	350	Cibola White Ware - Tularosa	Jar	38.0	13.0			Sand and Sherd
182	8	101	76	Salado Red Corrugated	Jar	34.0	25.0			Coarse Diabase
183	8	102	96	Brown plain	Bowl					Quartz and Plagioclase Sand
184	8	103	100	Brown indented obliterated corrugated	Jar	10.5	4.0	Cls. 1		Coarse Diabase
185	8	104	102	Salado Red Corrugated	Jar	36.7	11.5	Nonlocal		Medium Diabase
186	8	105	107	Cibola White Ware - Tularosa	Jar	15.9	6.6		Grp. 1	Sand and Sherd
187	8	106	108	Cibola White Ware - Puerco	Pitcher				Grp. 3	Sand and Sherd
188	8	107	129	Red plain	Jar	18.0	10.0			Quartz, Feldspar, Muscovite

Case	Room #	Pot Id.	Field #	Ware - Type - Style	Vessel	Max. (cm)	Int. (cm)	ICP	INAA	Temper
189	8	108	130	Roosevelt Red Ware - Pinto Black-on-red	Bowl	27.1	24.8		Cls. 2	Sherd
190	8	109	131	Cibola White Ware - Tularosa	Jar	46.9	13.4		Grp. 2	Quartz, Feldspar, Muscovite
191	8	110	132	Red plain	Jar	38.0				Medium Diabase
192	8	111	178	Brown indented obliterated corrugated	Jar		29.0			Diabase and Quartz Sand
193	8	112	185	Gray-orange indented corrugated	Jar	24.0	20.0			Diabase and Quartz Sand
194	8	113	186	Gray-orange indented corrugated	Jar	26.0	17.0			Coarse Diabase
195	8	114	197	Brown indented obliterated corrugated	Jar	58.0	34.0		Cls. 1	Coarse Diabase
196	8	115	266	Brown indented obliterated corrugated	Jar	58.0				Sherd and Sand
197	8	116	307	Roosevelt Red Ware - Pinto Polychrome	Bowl	34.5	33.6		Cls. 1	Sand and Sherd
198	8	117	310	Cibola White Ware - Kayenta-Tusayan	Jar	51.9	12.4		Grp. 2	Quartz, Feldspar, Muscovite
199	8	118	314	Red plain	Ellip. Jar	30.0	12.0			99% Sand
200	8	119	326	Red plain	Jar	46.0	22.0		Cls. 2	Sherd
201	8	120	327	Roosevelt Red Ware - Pinto Black-on-red	Bowl	24.0	26.0		Cls. 2	99% Quartz Sand
202	8	121	329	Gray-orange indented corrugated	Jar	40.0	24.7			99% Quartz Sand
203	8	122	340	McDonald Painted Corrugated	Bowl	26.0	28.0	Cls. 2		Sherd
204	8	123	345	Roosevelt Red Ware - Pinto Black-on-red	Bowl	31.0			Cls. 2	Coarse Diabase
205	8	124	356	Brown indented obliterated corrugated	Jar					Sherd
206	8	125	361	Roosevelt Red Ware - Pinto Black-on-red	Bowl	37.0	35.0		Cls. 2	Sherd
207	8	126	365	Roosevelt Red Ware - Pinto Black-on-red	Bowl	19.0	18.0			Sand
208	8	127	373	Red plain	Bowl	25.0	24.0			Quartz, Feldspar, Muscovite
209	8	128		Salado Red Corrugated	Bowl	16.6	16.0			Coarse Diabase
210	8	129	370	Gray-orange indented corrugated	Jar	22.0	17.0	Cls. 2		99% Quartz Sand
211	8	130	375	Brown indented obliterated corrugated	Jar	52.0				Medium Diabase
212	8	131	377	Red plain	Jar	46.0				Quartz, Feldspar, Muscovite
213	8	132	384	Red plain	Jar	48.0	18.0			Quartz, Feldspar, Muscovite
214	8	133	325	Roosevelt Red Ware - Pinto Black-on-red	Bowl	34.0	32.0			Sherd and Sand
215	8	134	298	Gray-orange indented corrugated	Jar					Diabase and Quartz Sand
216	9	135	35	Gray-orange indented corrugated	Jar	10.6	6.2		Grp. 2	Sand and Sherd
217	9	136	80	Cibola White Ware - Roosevelt	Jar	41.3	10.8		Grp. 3	Quartz, Feldspar, Muscovite
218	9	137	136	Cibola White Ware - Tularosa	Jar	38.9	11.5		Outlier	Diabase and Quartz Sand
219	9	138	137	Red plain	Jar	36.0	18.0	Outlier		Quartz, Feldspar, Muscovite
220	9	139	141	Gray-orange indented corrugated	Jar	19.8	10.8			Sand and Sherd
221	9	140	172	Red plain	Jar	40.0	18.0		Grp. 1	Sand and Sherd
222	9	141	173	Cibola White Ware - Roosevelt	Jar	36.0	12.5		Grp. 1	
223	9	142	175	Cibola White Ware - Roosevelt	Jar	44.0	12.6	Nonlocal		99% Quartz
224	9	143	176	Unclassified corrugated	Plate	25.8	24.2			Coarse Diabase
225	9	144	187	Gray-orange indented corrugated	Jar	28.0	14.0			Quartz, Feldspar, Muscovite
226	9	145	192	Brown indented obliterated corrugated	Jar	60.0	34.0			Medium Diabase
227	9	146	206	Red plain	Jar	15.0	8.0			Diabase Sand and Opaques
228	9	147	300	Brown indented obliterated corrugated	Jar	40.0	23.0	Local	Grp. 4	Sand and Sherd
229	9	148	308	Cibola White Ware - Red Mesa	Canteen	20.0	6.5		Grp. 1	
230	9	149	237	Cibola White Ware - Roosevelt	Bowl	34.0	32.0		Grp. 1	Coarse Diabase
231	9	150	310	Cibola White Ware - Tularosa	Jar	40.6	10.8			Quartz, Feldspar, Muscovite
232	9	151	311	Red plain	Jar	36.0	14.0			Diabase and Quartz Sand
233	9	152	312	Red plain	Jar	40.0	22.0	Outlier	Outlier	Quartz, Feldspar, Muscovite
234	9	153	365	Gray-orange indented corrugated	Jar	22.0	19.0	Cls. 1		
235	9	154	367	Red plain	Bowl	9.4	8.3			

Case	Room #	Pot Id.	Field #	Ware - Type - Style	Vessel	Max. (cm)	Int. (cm)	ICP	INAA	Temper
236	9	155	375	Red plain	Bowl	49.1	47.8			99% Quartz Sand
237	9	156	388	Gray-orange indented corrugated	Jar	40.0	20.0			Coarse Diabase
238	10	1	378	Brown indented obliterated corrugated	Jar	46.8	20.8			99% Quartz Sand
239	10	2	254	Gray-orange indented corrugated	Jar	10.8	5.4			Diabase and Quartz Sand
240	10	pv1	302	Brown indented obliterated corrugated	Jar	36.0	25.4			99% Quartz Sand
241	10	pv2	288	Gray-orange indented corrugated	Jar	31.0	19.3			Sherd
242	11	157	409	Roosevelt Red Ware - Pinto Black-on-red	Bowl		20.0			Sand and Sherd
243	11	158	253	Cibola White Ware - Snowflake	Jar	52.0	10.0	Nonlocal	Grp. 3	
244	11	159	284	Brown painted corrugated	Effigy pot	50.0	15.0			
245	11	160	307	Brown indented obliterated corrugated	Jar	54.0	27.0		Cls. 2	Coarse Diabase
246	11	161	308	Brown indented obliterated corrugated	Jar		22.0			Medium Diabase
247	11	162	334	Roosevelt Red Ware - Pinto Polychrome	Bowl	32.0	30.0			Sherd
248	11	163	361	Brown indented obliterated corrugated	Jar	60.0	26.0			Medium Diabase
249	11	164	368	Salado Red Corrugated	Jar	40.0	13.0		Cls. 1	Coarse Diabase
250	11	165	367	Brown indented obliterated corrugated	Jar	36.0	24.0			Medium Diabase
251	11	166	368	Brown indented obliterated corrugated	Jar	34.0	19.0			Medium Diabase
252	11	167	376	Brown indented obliterated corrugated	Jar	34.0	18.0			Medium Diabase
253	11	168	382	Roosevelt Red Ware - Pinto Black-on-red	Bowl	24.0	20.0			Sherd
254	11	169	385	Cibola White Ware - Roosevelt	Jar	34.0			Grp. 1	Diabase and Quartz Sand
255	11	170	396	Gray-orange indented corrugated	Jar	39.0	26.0		Cls. 1	99% Quartz Sand
256	11	171	393	McDonald Painted Corrugated	Bowl	31.0	30.0			
257	13	1	160	Roosevelt Red Ware - Pinto Black-on-red	Bowl	27.4	26.0		Cls. 2	Sherd and Sand
258	13	2	229	Roosevelt Red Ware - Pinto Black-on-red	Bowl	27.4	25.0			
259	13	3	235	Red plain	Ellip. Jar	45.4	13.3	Cls. 2		Quartz, Feldspar, Muscovite
260	13	4		Roosevelt Red Ware - Pinto Black-on-red	Bowl	28.0	25.0	Outlier		Sherd
261	13	5	190	Gray-orange indented corrugated	Jar	33.4	11.6	Cls. 2		99% Quartz
262	13	6	239	Gray-orange indented corrugated	Jar	34.4	18.4		Grp. 1	
263	13	8	236	Cibola White Ware - Snowflake	Jar	32.8	11.4			
264	13	9	315	McDonald Painted Corrugated	Bowl	18.6	17.8			
265	13	10	316	Gray-orange indented corrugated	Jar	47.0	31.0			99% Quartz Sand
266	13	11	334	Cibola White Ware - unclassified	Pitcher	12.3	3.2	Nonlocal	Outlier	Sand and Sherd
267	14	1	392	Cibola White Ware - Tularosa	Jar	42.8	12.0		Grp. 1	Sand and Sherd
268	14	2	391	Unclassified corrugated	Jar		23.2			
269	14	3	390	Cibola White Ware - Pinedale	Jar	36.0	11.4		Grp. 1	
270	14	4	423	Gray painted corrugated	Jar	34.0	11.2	Cls. 2		Sand and Sherd
271	14	5	424	Brown indented obliterated corrugated	Jar	37.5	31.4			99% Quartz Sand
272	14	6	425	Cibola White Ware - Tularosa	Jar	40.1	9.8			
273	14	7	426	Brown indented obliterated corrugated	Jar	34.0	15.8		Grp. 3	Sand and Sherd
274	14	8	427	Salado White-on-red Corrugated	Bowl	47.0	46.0			Diabase Coarse
275	14	9	428	Brown indented obliterated corrugated	Jar	40.0	23.4			Medium Diabase
276	14	10	429	Brown indented obliterated corrugated	Jar	34.6	25.4			Medium Diabase
277	14	11	534	Red plain	Jar	41.6	13.0			Diabase and Quartz Sand
278	14	12	535	Gray-orange indented corrugated	Jar	41.4	27.0			Quartz and Plagioclase Sand
279	14	13	666	Brown indented obliterated corrugated	Jar		24.4			Diabase and Quartz Sand
280	14	14	667	Cibola White Ware - Pinedale	Bowl	16.0	15.4			Sherd and Sand
281	14	15	700	Roosevelt Red Ware - Pinto Polychrome	Bowl	26.5	25.5		Grp. 1	
282	14	16	744	Gray-orange indented corrugated	Jar	14.5	11.0			Quartz and Plagioclase Sand

Case	Room #	Pot Id.	Field #	Ware - Type - Style	Vessel	Max. (cm)	Int. (cm)	ICP	INAA	Temper
283	15	172	130	Cibola White Ware - Puerco	Bowl	18.0	17.0		Grp. 1	Sand and Sherd
284	15	173	133	Red plain	Jar	32.0	18.0			
285	15	174	134	Cibola White Ware - Roosevelt	Jar	37.0	14.0	Nonlocal	Grp. 1	Sand
286	15	175	135	Gray-orange indented corrugated	Jar	34.0	24.0	Cls. 2		Quartz and Plagioclase Sand
287	15	176	136	Roosevelt Red Ware - Pinto Black-on-red	Bowl	28.0	26.0		Cls. 2	Sherd
288	15	177	149	Brown indented obliterated corrugated	Jar	28.0	20.0			Coarse Diabase
289	15	178	159	White Mt. Red Ware - St. Johns Polychrome	Bowl	23.2	21.1			
290	15	179	221	Roosevelt Red Ware - Pinto Black-on-red	Bowl	26.0	24.0			
291	15	180	239	Gray-orange indented corrugated	Jar	46.0	26.0			Quartz and Plagioclase Sand
292	15	181	240	Salado Red Corrugated	Bowl	19.0	18.0			Coarse Diabase
293	15	182	241	Brown plain	Plate	12.4	10.5			
294	15	183	243	Salado Red Corrugated	Bowl	50.0	48.0		Cls. 1	Coarse Diabase
295	15	184	265	Cibola White Ware - Roosevelt	Pitcher	11.4	6.0		Grp. 1	Quartz, Feldspar, Muscovite
296	15	185	266	Red plain	Jar	35.0	18.0			Coarse Diabase
297	15	186	267	Brown indented obliterated corrugated	Jar	58.0	28.0		Cls. 1	
298	16	187	104	Brown plain	Jar	3.3	1.5			Diabase Coarse
299	16	188	152	Brown indented obliterated corrugated	Jar	28.0	20.0			
300	16	189	172	Cibola White Ware - Roosevelt	Jar	46.0	12.0		Grp. 1	Sand and Sherd
301	16	190	177	Cibola White Ware - Tularosa	Jar	44.0			Grp. 3	Diabase and Quartz Sand
302	16	191	263	Brown indented obliterated corrugated	Jar	40.0	24.0		Cls. 2	Medium Diabase
303	16	192	264	Brown indented obliterated corrugated	Jar	34.0	18.0		Cls. 1	
304	16	193	265	Brown indented obliterated corrugated	Jar	50.0	30.0			Quartz, Feldspar, Muscovite
305	16	194	266	Red plain	Jar	32.0	17.0			Medium Diabase
306	16	195	267	Brown indented obliterated corrugated	Jar	44.0	28.0			Quartz, Feldspar, Muscovite
307	16	196	268	Red plain	Jar	54.0	20.0	Nonlocal		99% Quartz Sand
308	16	197	270	Gray-orange indented corrugated	Jar	32.0	18.0	Cls. 2		99% Quartz
309	17	1	164	Gray-orange indented corrugated	Jar	34.0		Cls. 1		Coarse Diabase
310	17	2	255	Red plain	Jar	60.0	31.0			Coarse Diabase
311	17	3	256	Salado Red Corrugated	Jar	48.0	17.9			Medium Diabase
312	17	4	170	Brown indented obliterated corrugated	Jar	47.0	23.2			Medium Diabase
313	17	5	158	Brown indented obliterated corrugated	Jar	47.0	20.2			
314	17	6	157	Brown indented obliterated corrugated	Jar	49.4	23.0			Diabase and Quartz Sand
315	17	7	171	Brown indented obliterated corrugated	Jar	54.0	17.2			Medium Diabase
316	17	8	163	Brown indented obliterated corrugated	Jar					
317	17	9	159	Unclassified corrugated (gray?)	Jar					Quartz, Feldspar, Muscovite
318	17	10	255	Red plain	Jar					Medium Diabase
319	17	11	129	Brown indented obliterated corrugated	Jar					Medium Diabase
320	17	12	28	Brown indented obliterated corrugated	Jar					Coarse Diabase
321	17	13	152	Brown indented obliterated corrugated	Jar		16.2			Coarse Diabase
322	17	14	193	Brown indented obliterated corrugated	Jar					Coarse Diabase
323	17	15	26	Brown indented obliterated corrugated	Jar		16.4			
324	17	16	413	Brown indented obliterated corrugated	Jar		30.2			
325	Tp-1	1	25	Gray-orange indented corrugated	Jar	39.0	21.4			99% Quartz Sand
326	Tp-1	2	150	Brown plain	Bowl	6.5	5.8			
327	Tp-1	3	144	Brown plain	Jar	54.6	20.8			Coarse Diabase
238	Tp-1	4	123	Roosevelt Red Ware - Pinto Black-on-red	Bowl	18.0	17.0			
329	Tp-1	pv1	145	Brown indented obliterated corrugated	Jar					Medium Diabase

Case	Room #	Pot Id.	Field #	Ware - Type - Style	Vessel	Max. (cm)	Int. (cm)	ICP	INAA	Temper
330	Tp-1	pv2	143	Brown indented obliterated corrugated	Jar					Medium Diabase
Grasshopper Spring Pueblo										
331	2	6		Cibola White Ware - Tularosa	Jar				Grp. 2	
332	2	10		Cibola White Ware - Tularosa	Jar				Grp. 3	
333	3		133	Cibola White Ware - Pinedale	Jar			Nonlocal		Sherd
334	5		57	Cibola White Ware - Red Mesa	Jar			Nonlocal		
335	5	pv1		Cibola White Ware - Unclassified	Jar			Nonlocal		Sand and Sherd
Site AZ P:14:197 (ASM)										
336	1	6		Cibola White Ware	Jar					
Grasshopper Pueblo										
	Cat. No.									
337	11.841			Cibola White Ware	Jar				Grp. 2	
338	39.034			Cibola White Ware	Jar				Grp. 3	
339	32.891			Cibola White Ware	Jar				Grp. 2	
340	28.506			Cibola White Ware	Jar			Local	Grp. 4	Diabase, Sherd, Opaques
341	23.718			Cibola White Ware	Jar			Local	Grp. 4	Diabase, Sherd, Opaques
342	41.403			Cibola White Ware	Bowl			Local		Diabase, Sherd, Opaques
343	28.512			Cibola White Ware	Jar			Local		Diabase, Sherd, Opaques
344	42.267			Cibola White Ware	Jar			Local?		Sherd, Quartz, Biotite
345	13.661			Cibola White Ware	Jar			Local		Sherd
346	34.964			Cibola White Ware	Jar			Local?		Sherd, Biotite, Opaques
347	34.982			Cibola White Ware	Jar			Local		Diabase?, Sherd, Opaques
348	35.361			Cibola White Ware	Jar			Local		Quartz, Opaques, Sherd?
349	29.545			Cibola White Ware	Jar			Local		Diabase, Sherd, Opaques
350	39.096			Cibola White Ware	Bowl			Nonlocal		Sherd
351	28.515			Cibola White Ware	Jar			Local		Sand and Sherd
352	29.943			Cibola White Ware	Jar			Nonlocal		Sherd
353	28.505			Cibola White Ware	Jar			Nonlocal		Sherd
Clay samples										
354			1	Grasshopper Spring Creek				x	x	
355			4	Grasshopper Spring Creek				x	x	
356			5	Grasshopper Spring Creek				x		
357			6	Hop Canyon					x	
358			8	Grasshopper Spring Creek				x	x	
359			9	Cibecue					x	
360			13	Grasshopper Butte				x		
361			17	Spring Creek				x	x	
362			21	Chediski Farms					x	
363			22	Forestdale Valley (at Tundastusa)				x	x	
364			23	Spring Creek						
365			30	Chodistaas Room 10				x	x	
366			31	Chodistaas Test pit 88-5 (Tp-5)				x	x	
367			199	Chodistaas burnt clay from adobe wall				x	x	
368			200	Chodistaas (vicinity)				x	x	
Clays excavated in Room 113 at Grasshopper Pueblo										
369	113		469	Raw clay				x		
370	113		730	Raw clay				x		

Case	Room #	Pot Id.	Field #	Ware - Type - Style	Vessel	Max. (cm)	Int. (cm)	ICP	INAA	Temper
371	113		802	Tempered clay				x	x	
372	113		854	Tempered clay				x	x	
373	113		907	White pigment clay				x	x	
374	113		1223	Raw clay				x	x	
375	113		1448	Raw clay				x		
376	113		1509	Raw clay				x		
377	113		1609	Tempered clay				x		

Instrumental Neutron Activation Analysis

Elemental Concentrations of Samples from Decorated and Undecorated Vessels

Instrumental Neutron Activation analysis provides precise, accurate, and highly sensitive measurements of the concentrations of different chemical elements in ceramic pastes. The raw elemental concentrations for each vessel and clay sample analyzed for this study are presented in parts per million (ppm). The data provided here must be converted into logarithms of base 10 before performing statistical analyses comparable to those discussed in the text.

For vessel identification, each sample listed in Appendix B has been assigned a case number (Case) that corresponds to the Case number in Appendix A. "ID #" refers to the laboratory sample identification number.

Case	ID #	As	La	Lu	Nd	Sm	U	Yb	Ce	Co	Cr	Cs	Eu	Fe
1	PCN097	1.880	72.300	.596	69.800	10.300	4.860	3.940	126.000	7.350	64.100	15.800	1.860	16700
6	PCN338	5.450	35.200	.473	28.800	5.120	12.000	2.630	62.400	24.400	90.400	9.270	1.060	36500
7	PCN055	16.800	31.800	.332	19.700	4.780	1.390	2.630	50.100	20.700	65.800	7.960	.951	40500
8	PCN084	2.290	19.800	.285	12.300	5.420	.000	2.240	39.000	35.400	31.600	1.560	1.760	85300
9	PCN120	6.410	47.800	.451	32.400	7.330	2.260	3.270	87.100	16.700	60.100	14.300	1.380	28700
10	PCW137	2.400	23.300	.260	10.700	4.420	.000	1.870	38.900	56.000	29.600	1.940	1.410	101000
14	PCW235	17.400	34.400	.398	22.100	5.010	1.820	3.160	58.900	15.500	70.600	7.830	1.010	38400
22	PCN695	19.200	39.700	.382	22.900	5.740	3.050	3.010	65.300	12.500	79.300	9.380	1.090	37800
26	PCN535	12.000	77.300	.564	46.300	10.600	5.610	3.910	129.000	13.100	70.100	17.200	1.830	17700
29	PCN026	4.480	33.600	.347	18.600	3.890	5.130	2.440	54.200	11.500	61.500	14.000	.735	18400
32	PCN063	5.470	54.000	.453	37.300	5.660	3.710	3.030	82.800	6.080	43.900	10.900	1.120	24300
34	PCN095	26.700	30.000	.373	19.000	4.350	2.480	2.780	49.800	10.100	75.900	8.150	.853	43200
36	PCN135	4.320	49.700	.352	20.200	5.480	3.150	2.900	76.600	23.500	39.500	10.400	1.040	24700
37	PCN139	7.910	60.500	.476	63.400	8.870	4.050	3.460	109.000	7.360	64.900	20.900	1.570	23900
40	PCN163	31.200	18.600	1.490	20.800	5.820	.836	9.590	45.500	6.900	39.600	5.560	1.110	23900
41	PCN164	19.000	97.700	.474	55.500	11.500	.000	3.940	167.000	19.700	34.000	4.790	2.010	48900
44	PCN170	25.100	16.500	.278	14.300	3.560	.000	1.820	30.300	37.900	61.400	11.100	1.090	74300
51	PCN258	3.840	13.500	.242	7.310	3.760	.000	1.890	25.200	53.300	22.800	1.210	1.320	89900
53	PCW260	4.470	33.700	.346	18.800	3.910	5.140	2.430	53.900	11.400	60.800	13.900	.738	18700
58	PCN387	9.440	46.000	.470	30.500	7.480	1.230	3.370	81.800	16.000	58.900	11.000	1.460	34500
63	PCN183	7.240	68.200	.612	42.800	11.600	2.730	4.470	121.000	21.500	80.700	12.100	2.180	39800
66	PCN259	16.300	27.400	.305	14.200	3.440	2.890	2.310	44.600	5.300	35.500	12.900	.824	34800
68	PCN074	6.550	84.300	.682	62.700	12.800	5.050	4.910	150.000	6.380	65.600	28.300	2.140	21200
78	PCN101	22.600	75.900	.557	75.200	11.100	4.840	4.040	125.000	6.370	69.300	15.800	1.920	17300
80	PCN103	11.700	82.000	.736	66.200	12.400	5.710	4.510	137.000	9.680	81.800	13.000	2.160	16700
82	PCN136	3.890	40.000	.301	28.200	5.420	4.030	2.660	64.000	22.400	54.800	11.700	1.000	21600
85	PCN140	2.420	18.600	.336	14.900	5.000	.000	2.660	35.100	46.700	155.000	2.010	1.520	87100
86	PCN142	5.600	47.800	.481	27.800	7.330	1.950	3.310	89.300	16.600	59.200	16.900	1.420	30000
91	PCN216	2.690	21.900	.490	22.100	6.430	.000	3.550	47.200	78.900	153.000	2.660	1.910	133000
94	PCN226	2.650	20.000	.485	19.800	6.180	.000	3.100	42.600	71.100	146.000	2.440	1.770	134000
100	PCN260	3.370	34.400	.288	14.800	4.020	4.940	2.370	54.500	19.600	55.000	12.800	.783	21700
101	PCN263	4.400	49.900	.498	41.900	7.710	5.010	3.270	89.300	6.900	67.500	19.400	1.580	15700
105	PCN297	18.400	99.100	.485	38.500	12.000	.000	3.900	179.000	30.700	40.000	4.670	1.910	47800
106	PCN301	6.310	94.200	.614	106.000	15.800	6.110	5.120	170.000	18.300	78.000	19.900	2.720	12100
109	PCN304	2.890	45.600	.468	34.000	5.770	5.530	3.740	72.800	16.700	65.800	15.700	1.090	20300
118	PCN378	7.870	44.100	.463	29.000	6.680	2.670	3.360	78.500	11.100	60.100	10.800	1.330	34000
125	PCN328	20.800	27.900	.369	16.600	4.430	1.480	2.430	47.500	17.500	98.600	9.950	1.000	50400
126	PCN313	1.240	30.800	.454	15.400	3.210	6.040	2.230	48.200	3.300	48.800	12.700	.627	15100
127	PCN346	13.100	64.100	.530	48.400	9.710	3.710	3.910	112.000	5.890	60.300	12.900	1.710	17200
142	PCN392	7.480	85.300	.627	65.500	13.600	4.790	4.580	156.000	8.240	70.800	18.500	2.390	11100
143	PCN256	2.820	24.300	.286	17.100	3.560	2.970	2.130	58.700	21.600	64.300	12.900	.879	22900
144	PCN339	5.700	50.000	.486	31.100	7.830	2.690	3.880	88.100	21.000	47.000	20.700	1.490	23800
148	PCN393	1.820	86.100	.665	51.200	10.800	7.180	3.760	111.000	8.730	53.600	16.900	2.020	17800
150	PCN157	5.810	81.800	.664	62.700	12.900	4.840	5.040	140.000	17.300	71.100	15.100	2.140	16500
151	PCN158	5.980	81.500	.670	64.900	12.900	5.090	4.710	149.000	16.600	70.300	19.100	2.210	14700
162	PCN614	19.700	22.200	.377	13.300	3.890	1.570	2.580	37.600	15.900	98.900	9.420	.986	51200
173	PCN604	8.490	30.200	.339	19.300	3.410	2.010	2.280	55.300	6.370	52.600	10.400	.625	30300
176	PCN595	3.760	94.400	.687	106.000	15.700	5.770	5.020	171.000	10.400	78.200	18.900	2.700	11900
177	PCN608	12.500	47.900	.424	34.700	6.780	3.100	2.980	86.100	14.100	55.600	21.600	1.300	40100
179	PCN031	3.470	16.900	.351	13.100	4.980	.000	2.480	35.100	54.700	232.000	2.330	1.520	108000
181	PCN350	24.200	88.100	.594	85.700	11.900	5.270	4.160	136.000	6.490	69.300	25.500	2.000	19300
183	PCN096	4.350	33.400	.348	17.500	3.520	4.920	2.200	49.200	3.930	64.900	15.000	.671	16100
186	PCN107	7.060	79.300	.955	94.200	11.100	5.160	5.920	124.000	4.950	56.400	10.000	1.860	19000
187	PCN108	4.290	41.200	.447	25.500	5.060	4.570	2.870	67.300	4.470	54.800	11.000	1.020	23100
189	PCN130	21.700	40.200	.404	29.100	5.700	2.930	3.320	65.800	10.400	66.400	9.310	1.080	31300
190	PCN131	3.330	37.700	.335	24.600	4.380	4.650	2.390	60.400	4.810	65.600	14.100	.845	19500
195	PCN197	4.160	21.500	.414	17.900	6.280	.000	3.330	46.300	74.000	107.000	2.420	1.940	124000
197	PCW307	3.450	14.200	.202	10.100	3.460	.000	1.670	23.600	38.300	75.000	1.970	1.230	87100
198	PCN310	1.850	32.600	.382	20.100	4.230	5.360	2.490	57.400	3.940	65.200	14.600	.794	14000
200	PCN326	13.900	35.300	.346	23.300	5.190	2.770	2.660	58.100	17.000	34.500	11.000	.984	32500
201	PCN327	22.300	40.400	.393	30.800	5.920	2.130	3.090	65.500	12.300	69.200	9.080	1.000	30900
204	PCN345	8.130	45.400	.426	30.400	6.820	1.960	3.370	83.000	13.800	54.700	14.900	1.320	29700

Case	ID #	Hf	Rb	Sb	Sc	Ta	Tb	Th	Zn	Zr	Ba	Ca	K	Na
1	PCN097	6.730	53.100	.838	15.500	1.610	1.450	19.800	55.70	244.0	533.0	0	7980.0	1510.0
6	PCN338	5.550	119.000	.729	15.700	1.660	.689	13.200	71.10	239.0	524.0	84100	19100.0	4160.0
7	PCN055	8.220	51.300	1.120	11.300	.897	.678	9.730	63.20	261.0	659.0	0	14300.0	4980.0
8	PCN084	3.240	.000	.000	19.900	.767	.927	2.030	54.50	.0	279.0	22700	7870.0	20300.0
9	PCN120	6.170	124.000	1.040	14.100	1.440	.966	15.100	90.80	246.0	807.0	0	20500.0	3460.0
10	PCW137	3.670	.000	.000	17.300	.748	.490	2.900	101.00	.0	350.0	443004	610.0	11600.0
14	PCW235	9.120	59.200	1.320	11.300	1.520	.773	10.400	63.20	273.0	509.0	0	12700.0	2840.0
22	PCN695	8.320	78.700	1.360	12.900	1.420	.752	11.600	60.70	220.0	610.0	34700	14800.0	2470.0
26	PCN535	6.790	57.400	1.320	15.600	2.070	1.170	19.300	73.30	229.0	502.0	0	9910.0	1630.0
29	PCN026	7.940	56.400	1.210	13.500	1.640	.556	20.400	52.80	219.0	337.0	0	11100.0	1460.0
32	PCN063	5.920	58.600	.975	13.100	1.320	.723	14.100	55.30	181.0	711.0	0	10500.0	875.0
34	PCN095	7.870	77.300	1.430	12.700	1.080	.555	11.600	78.30	242.0	1000.0	0	13900.0	3050.0
36	PCN135	5.960	49.200	.895	12.400	2.440	.659	13.300	48.30	184.0	607.0	0	9840.0	863.0
37	PCN139	6.750	82.000	.962	15.600	1.850	1.040	21.200	71.40	239.0	522.0	0	11700.0	839.0
40	PCN163	2.210	61.800	1.940	12.600	.409	1.340	9.060	85.30	.0	456.0	0	6350.0	838.0
41	PCN164	8.950	.000	1.090	13.600	.931	1.310	9.770	108.00	268.0	826.0	0	19100.0	20200.0
44	PCN170	5.270	.000	.767	17.500	.698	.662	5.830	76.40	126.0	392.0	37200	7460.0	10300.0
51	PCN258	3.010	.000	.000	18.300	.492	.000	2.290	98.40	.0	409.0	43500	4000.0	12200.0
53	PCW260	7.040	55.800	1.230	13.600	1.610	.542	20.300	53.60	217.0	341.0	0	11600.0	1420.0
58	PCN387	7.080	124.000	1.390	12.600	1.380	.785	14.100	88.90	236.0	836.0	0	21400.0	3700.0
63	PCN183	6.590	57.800	.925	18.600	1.450	1.400	16.400	89.30	245.0	895.0	0	8280.0	5850.0
66	PCN259	4.370	91.200	1.160	10.100	.809	.382	10.400	59.20	121.0	519.0	0	15700.0	899.0
68	PCN074	7.310	144.000	1.560	16.300	1.880	1.730	28.100	82.60	239.0	935.0	0	19900.0	1070.0
78	PCN101	5.930	51.900	1.580	14.000	1.400	1.330	17.300	62.40	183.0	431.0	0	7820.0	1880.0
80	PCN103	7.310	36.100	1.160	14.700	1.670	1.450	20.600	71.10	278.0	644.0	0	6350.0	1770.0
82	PCN136	6.650	75.700	.951	13.200	1.350	.703	16.100	66.10	193.0	409.0	0	10400.0	1050.0
85	PCN140	4.070	.000	.000	27.500	.887	.773	3.140	109.00	.0	284.0	43200	7910.0	18500.0
86	PCN142	6.500	130.000	1.050	13.800	1.640	.962	15.600	93.10	185.0	684.0	0	19000.0	3800.0
91	PCN216	4.610	.000	.000	26.900	.607	1.170	2.930	151.00	.0	471.0	34800	22000.0	7030.0
94	PCN226	4.220	.000	.000	26.800	.515	1.120	2.900	157.00	.0	587.0	28600	14600.0	6190.0
100	PCN260	6.400	65.800	1.140	13.500	1.470	.583	17.900	55.60	184.0	418.0	0	11400.0	1660.0
101	PCN263	6.110	72.800	1.370	19.500	1.670	1.000	17.600	81.10	184.0	457.0	0	13000.0	1110.0
105	PCN297	9.590	.000	.818	13.000	2.120	1.240	11.600	112.00	254.0	693.0	0	21700.0	20300.0
106	PCN301	7.050	38.900	.863	16.400	1.730	1.830	21.800	75.20	264.0	405.0	0	7080.0	1350.0
109	PCN304	8.240	61.800	1.070	14.500	1.820	.962	21.300	58.20	259.0	389.0	0	10200.0	920.0
118	PCN378	5.740	118.000	1.000	12.700	1.270	1.060	14.600	94.40	185.0	713.0	30800	21200.0	2280.0
125	PCN328	7.180	.000	1.170	14.800	.853	.615	9.310	70.30	230.0	598.0	19000	11800.0	6400.0
126	PCN313	7.240	61.700	.700	13.400	1.660	.423	16.100	43.70	202.0	277.0	0	9460.0	889.0
127	PCN346	6.560	52.800	1.140	13.500	1.420	1.170	19.000	65.60	226.0	612.0	0	10700.0	1410.0
142	PCN392	6.950	58.100	1.250	15.100	1.680	1.710	20.600	104.00	253.0	469.0	0	7100.0	1480.0
143	PCN256	10.400	38.400	.859	14.800	1.940	.716	29.600	122.00	280.0	608.0	0	5550.0	968.0
144	PCN339	8.390	76.900	.966	13.300	1.440	1.100	19.800	72.30	279.0	377.0	0	14600.0	1070.0
148	PCN393	7.110	69.800	.982	16.300	1.730	1.530	19.600	71.60	222.0	607.0	11700	9120.0	731.0
150	PCN157	7.890	42.600	1.280	15.300	1.650	1.600	22.900	84.70	269.0	497.0	0	7820.0	1090.0
151	PCN158	7.290	42.800	1.160	16.300	1.610	1.490	21.000	78.90	264.0	531.0	0	7050.0	1190.0
162	PCN614	6.980	55.300	.993	15.500	.811	.542	6.610	71.00	224.0	501.0	0	13200.0	5280.0
173	PCN604	7.310	63.800	1.020	9.160	.899	.485	10.900	57.90	191.0	468.0	0	9930.0	570.0
176	PCN595	7.050	60.500	.975	16.900	1.760	1.790	21.600	101.00	262.0	505.0	0	8110.0	1320.0
177	PCN608	4.700	147.000	1.570	14.900	1.160	.871	15.700	136.00	.0	735.0	33700	22800.0	1610.0
179	PCN031	4.460	.000	.000	27.200	1.030	.817	3.030	118.00	.0	618.0	28800	7130.0	9020.0
181	PCN350	6.150	69.300	1.810	13.900	1.400	1.360	17.300	62.40	214.0	398.0	0	10800.0	1410.0
183	PCN096	8.200	48.100	.918	14.800	1.820	.471	20.800	54.80	209.0	213.0	0	7670.0	540.0
186	PCN107	10.900	47.800	1.530	13.800	2.010	1.640	29.600	56.10	269.0	346.0	0	5850.0	643.0
187	PCN108	6.240	54.500	.887	13.300	1.380	.641	16.200	58.20	206.0	525.0	0	10900.0	1490.0
189	PCN130	10.000	76.900	1.340	12.100	1.560	.745	13.800	64.00	214.0	575.0	0	11400.0	2200.0
190	PCN131	7.830	52.100	.982	14.100	1.620	.519	18.500	56.00	210.0	483.0	0	9790.0	908.0
195	PCN197	4.910	.000	.000	28.200	1.250	.998	3.090	138.00	.0	690.0	29100	20700.0	7060.0
197	PCW307	4.140	.000	.000	17.500	.759	.652	3.020	81.80	.0	518.0	28100	5650.0	13700.0
198	PCN310	9.040	49.700	.849	13.700	1.730	.596	19.200	65.20	274.0	290.0	0	7780.0	710.0
200	PCN326	4.210	122.000	1.930	11.400	.920	.719	12.000	56.90	.0	662.0	0	16900.0	1270.0
201	PCN327	9.400	53.200	1.230	11.600	1.630	.804	13.500	62.20	286.0	622.0	0	11700.0	2090.0
204	PCN345	6.750	127.000	1.090	13.400	1.360	1.010	14.900	88.50	190.0	811.0	0	19800.0	3370.0

Case	ID #	As	La	Lu	Nd	Sm	U	Yb	Ce	Co	Cr	Cs	Eu	Fe
206	PCN361	9.910	45.900	.430	31.700	7.010	1.880	2.960	83.800	14.200	57.900	16.400	1.250	38200
217	PCN080	3.530	33.900	.382	14.500	3.850	4.970	2.330	52.000	4.420	62.500	14.700	.721	17900
218	PCW136	13.000	35.700	.361	22.000	4.020	2.550	2.640	62.700	18.000	58.300	14.100	.728	36600
219	PCX137	9.640	43.100	.162		4.550	.000	1.450	60.100	19.700	32.800	4.490	.815	31800
222	PCN173	14.000	75.500	.641	56.000	11.700	4.390	4.350	121.000	10.500	80.200	15.000	2.030	25600
223	PCN175	7.360	76.000	.736	80.200	12.500	3.840	5.150	141.000	15.300	74.600	12.800	2.210	22400
229	PCN308	5.790	36.500	.439	29.600	5.650	1.850	2.740	63.800	9.400	117.000	11.900	1.040	42300
230	PCN237	13.800	74.000	.605	66.200	11.200	4.760	4.370	127.000	7.760	71.400	12.700	1.970	15700
231	PCX310	13.400	73.300	.646	47.900	11.200	4.560	4.060	119.000	8.850	74.600	12.700	1.970	18200
233	PCN312	25.900	109.000	.545	71.800	13.200	.000	4.350	195.000	21.900	42.300	5.270	2.380	61000
243	PCN253	1.980	42.100	.457	25.200	5.730	4.360	3.100	69.300	5.550	62.800	18.100	1.130	17600
245	PCN307	5.830	46.200	.507	31.900	7.060	1.930	3.310	83.400	14.600	60.100	18.000	1.320	30000
249	PCN368	5.710	24.500	.421	20.600	7.570	.000	3.200	48.000	52.200	60.800	6.030	2.050	111000
254	PCN385	9.760	77.800	.646	91.300	11.800	.000	4.660	132.100	8.040	65.300	15.210	2.028	16300
255	PCN396	19.400	39.100	.320	24.300	5.020	1.480	2.330	66.100	9.840	36.600	11.500	1.200	32100
257	PCN160	10.600	46.000	.521	34.500	6.870	3.420	3.840	87.900	11.200	57.400	11.400	1.390	33800
260	PCX173	9.820	76.400	.638	60.800	10.800	6.250	3.980	122.000	8.670	75.500	14.100	1.860	17000
263	PCN236	12.000	67.000	.692	53.700	9.100	5.500	3.950	109.000	7.310	71.000	14.600	1.610	16900
266	PCN334	3.860	58.700	.766	38.400	8.110	6.270	4.580	100.000	7.330	49.100	28.500	1.390	22800
267	PCX392	10.100	87.500	.706	95.100	14.000	5.660	4.550	150.000	8.040	77.300	14.000	2.470	12900
269	PCN390	2.810	69.500	.791	57.800	9.270	4.920	5.160	116.000	7.660	54.300	16.100	1.640	19700
272	PCN425	5.050	46.700	.474	40.300	6.080	5.140	3.080	78.900	5.360	66.200	20.700	1.190	19600
280	PCN667	10.200	82.000	.875	76.600	12.200	4.170	5.640	134.000	10.500	67.300	9.570	2.150	24700
283	PCW130	1.910	71.800	.595	69.600	10.500	4.830	3.930	126.000	7.440	63.900	15.800	1.910	14900
285	PCN134	11.000	71.400	.590	72.600	12.600	4.040	4.070	126.000	11.300	74.000	14.500	2.260	24900
287	PCX136	8.810	48.600	.470	41.900	7.430	2.330	3.220	81.300	11.400	53.300	12.800	1.410	32000
294	PCN243	3.060	23.300	.530	14.400	7.230	.000	3.750	48.900	69.800	121.000	2.520	2.050	132000
295	PCN265	11.400	73.600	.655	50.700	11.600	5.150	4.160	128.000	9.680	75.500	13.200	2.070	18700
297	PCN267	4.110	23.700	.290	14.300	5.310	.000	2.370	45.700	53.800	152.000	2.740	1.690	88700
300	PCN172	7.830	72.100	.687	55.600	10.600	4.820	4.060	125.000	7.780	88.500	13.200	1.900	15000
301	PCN177	5.940	45.500	.440	30.500	5.920	4.410	2.980	74.800	21.800	60.100	13.800	1.150	23800
302	PCW263	59.200	17.300	.293	9.400	3.180	1.130	2.190	30.100	28.200	125.000	23.600	.773	75200
303	PCN264	7.480	26.600	.441	13.900	6.920	.000	3.410	54.100	38.000	43.900	3.370	1.910	89100
306	PCW267	11.800	21.600	.508	11.200	6.000	.000	3.160	42.600	51.300	118.000	10.800	1.810	95100
331	PCG206	4.560	39.500	.350	24.400	4.520	3.980	2.210	59.700	4.780	58.900	12.900	.813	21400
332	PC2010	4.160	41.000	.349	28.200	4.950	4.300	2.560	65.200	4.830	59.800	13.300	.946	19000
336	PCN006	3.880	43.800	.436	28.700	5.690	4.610	3.240	73.800	4.540	57.300	16.900	1.090	18600
337	PCN841	4.000	33.300	.352	23.400	3.440	4.730	2.050	48.300	4.890	62.700	13.300	.689	17300
338	PCN034	2.590	49.300	.410	42.400	6.710	5.000	2.690	80.400	6.380	61.100	13.000	1.340	19200
339	PCN891	4.240	31.700	.360	15.300	3.800	4.470	2.380	51.100	4.060	61.200	12.400	.706	15000
340	PCN506	7.500	30.300	.446	29.700	5.460	.881	2.900	53.800	20.100	122.000	7.210	1.150	55100
341	PCN718	8.390	31.000	.430	28.000	5.940	1.370	2.880	55.600	22.200	94.800	7.640	1.300	50000
354	PCCGS1	1.560	32.600	.499	18.700	5.110	2.260	3.270	54.500	10.800	91.600	7.280	.957	20600
355	PCCGS4	14.900	26.800	.288	18.600	4.190	2.490	1.920	47.300	9.710	58.100	3.780	.769	17700
357	PCC006	1.990	23.300	.263	20.300	2.810	5.650	1.380	29.400	3.300	105.000	7.500	.540	16100
359	PCC009	1.470	20.700	.173	13.900	2.480	5.780	1.070	24.400	2.480	64.600	4.260	.489	61900
361	PCC017	6.440	29.000	.471	19.400	4.250	12.800	2.670	53.200	9.400	67.600	4.710	.845	27200
362	PCC021	5.623	26.182	.315	22.491	3.837	7.015	1.941	44.875	9.036	59.566	9.036	.767	14388
363	PCC022	6.124	46.026	.582	38.905	7.228	8.650	3.741	81.658	12.589	47.315	12.794	1.489	18707
364	PCCSC8	1.030	32.700	.353	21.900	5.110	2.800	2.770	57.500	8.340	97.300	7.050	.968	28800
365	PCC010	2.110	24.700	.327	18.700	3.780	8.200	2.100	44.100	8.670	67.100	5.640	.767	14700
366	PCCTP5	9.440	33.000	.451	36.000	5.080	3.040	2.770	62.200	11.000	88.700	8.170	.975	39400
367	PCC199	2.830	25.900	.371	18.700	3.850	11.500	2.490	47.800	11.200	74.600	4.900	.782	16500
368	PCC200	2.810	35.600	.524	18.600	5.130	2.340	3.130	64.100	10.000	56.200	3.680	.923	19200
371	PCC802	8.380	32.900	.357	17.900	5.140	1.710	2.790	58.600	10.100	66.100	6.220	1.020	24200
372	PCC854	13.800	40.600	.463	29.900	7.330	1.160	3.410	65.800	22.300	86.500	7.530	1.640	59800
373	PCC907	80.168	95.940	.908	73.790	12.190	5.675	6.166	153.109	3.243	51.286	25.003	1.991	30409
374	PC1223	14.400	40.700	.519	30.100	6.310	6.080	3.000	72.400	13.200	90.400	7.400	1.150	28700

Case	ID #	Hf	Rb	Sb	Sc	Ta	Tb	Th	Zn	Zr	Ba	Ca	K	Na
206	PCN361	5.270	97.500	1.290	15.100	1.310	.910	16.000	97.70	152.0	625.0	0	18800.0	1690.0
217	PCN080	8.130	59.000	.902	14.900	1.640	.541	20.500	65.00	200.0	370.0	0	9350.0	776.0
218	PCW136	8.180	112.000	1.320	10.700	1.080	.570	12.400	31.50	202.0	281.0	0	12200.0	871.0
219	PCX137	7.830	.000	1.120	8.690	1.910	.556	11.700	57.30	205.0	650.0	0	17200.0	16300.0
222	PCN173	6.930	72.800	1.360	16.700	1.590	1.460	20.400	74.60	234.0	391.0	0	8130.0	1790.0
223	PCN175	7.600	44.700	1.070	17.100	1.790	1.540	19.600	70.50	239.0	481.0	0	5850.0	3050.0
229	PCN308	5.240	158.000	.927	14.100	1.040	.710	11.400	56.90	142.0	251.0	61700	22400.0	2870.0
230	PCN237	7.030	50.900	1.170	14.100	1.590	1.280	19.800	58.50	252.0	605.0	0	1800.0	1580.0
231	PCX310	6.640	51.900	1.510	14.300	1.500	1.310	18.200	65.00	193.0	589.0	0	9330.0	1150.0
233	PCN312	11.000	.000	.989	16.600	1.320	1.530	10.800	119.00	387.0	719.0	0	19500.0	8300.0
243	PCN253	7.210	90.600	1.080	16.800	1.550	.740	16.400	90.80	198.0	250.0	0	12800.0	935.0
245	PCN307	6.150	95.100	1.160	13.800	1.420	1.000	15.100	95.30	163.0	796.0	0	20300.0	3760.0
249	PCN368	4.720	67.100	.000	27.700	.826	1.180	4.970	89.50	112.0	562.0	20320	.0	3800.0
254	PCN385	7.080	48.200	.000	15.700	1.700	1.600	20.200	67.30	256.0	491.0	0	8600.0	1410.0
255	PCN396	4.100	149.000	1.890	10.400	1.150	.824	10.600	52.50	.0	802.0	0	27300.0	3050.0
257	PCN160	6.400	109.000	1.140	13.300	1.370	.914	15.600	122.00	220.0	695.0	0	17700.0	3070.0
260	PCX173	7.280	50.400	1.400	15.700	1.730	1.200	20.900	74.80	226.0	736.0	0	7800.0	1300.0
263	PCN236	8.280	39.200	1.420	17.000	2.040	1.060	25.200	69.70	233.0	733.0	0	6040.0	1870.0
266	PCN334	7.640	147.000	1.410	15.600	1.690	1.200	23.100	80.20	236.0	291.0	0	18100.0	811.0
267	PCX392	6.810	53.200	1.230	15.000	1.671	1.600	20.890	67.30	256.0		0	7230.0	1300.0
269	PCN390	8.130	113.000	1.190	15.800	1.560	1.490	21.600	83.80	300.0	466.0	0	17500.0	1500.0
272	PCN425	7.100	94.800	1.480	16.900	1.720	.995	18.400	68.40	195.0	354.0	0	13600.0	1400.0
280	PCN667	10.100	43.600	1.750	14.800	1.910	1.530	27.200	72.10	317.0	583.0	0	7360.0	4360.0
283	PCW130	6.720	53.200	.796	15.800	1.590	1.460	19.900	58.10	247.0	528.0	0	7940.0	1530.0
285	PCN134	6.590	64.900	1.210	16.100	1.470	1.550	16.900	78.00	210.0	348.0	0	9080.0	3010.0
287	PCX136	6.010	108.000	1.280	13.200	1.390	.931	15.400	78.30	187.0	767.0	22600	18800.0	2770.0
294	PCN243	4.810	.000	.321	29.400	.621	1.200	3.280	162.00	.0	735.0	23000	15100.0	8280.0
295	PCN265	6.980	47.200	1.400	15.300	1.690	1.330	19.500	86.30	240.0	711.0	0	6370.0	2610.0
297	PCN267	4.060	.000	2.450	18.300	.802	.687	2.410	95.10	.0	269.0	39300	6150.0	17300.0
300	PCN172	7.960	49.000	1.190	13.900	1.600	1.220	20.600	62.80	242.0	991.0	0	9400.0	1140.0
301	PCN177	6.310	94.400	1.160	15.200	2.920	.802	16.600	59.80	177.0	463.0	19600	13600.0	995.0
302	PCW263	6.370	.000	1.110	20.500	1.280	.000	6.470	88.30	.0	258.0	25200	9980.0	6620.0
303	PCN264	5.050	.000	.492	26.900	.995	1.230	4.900	84.10	.0	366.0	19500	13200.0	20200.0
306	PCW267	4.540	.000	.000	29.400	.711	.966	2.990	136.00	.0	535.0	51200	13600.0	17800.0
331	PCG206	8.130	67.000	.925	13.800	1.620	.537	20.100	60.00	210.0	509.0	0	11000.0	841.0
332	PC2010	7.500	66.700	.973	13.300	1.450	.650	18.100	54.00	218.0	568.0	0	10200.0	942.0
336	PCN006	6.980	104.000	1.090	13.800	1.410	.769	17.000	60.50	184.0	488.0	0	12600.0	998.0
337	PCN841	7.210	73.500	1.040	14.400	1.710	.497	19.300	65.90	211.0	328.0	0	9080.0	1170.0
338	PCN034	8.050	47.900	1.100	16.800	1.840	.902	20.300	68.10	212.0	350.0	0	7310.0	640.0
339	PCN891	7.890	57.400	1.040	13.100	1.720	.526	17.900	47.50	242.0	407.0	0	8690.0	995.0
340	PCN506	5.300	139.000	.760	18.300	1.060	.815	9.120	79.60	133.0	348.0	67300	18700.0	4120.0
341	PCN718	5.410	136.000	.760	16.100	.865	.807	8.930	81.80	129.0	461.0	42700	19400.0	6210.0
354	PCCGS1	10.400	140.000	.676	12.400	1.140	.830	12.500	49.80	292.0	.0	24000	1760.0	3780.0
355	PCCGS4	5.500	49.300	.895	7.130	.604	.611	7.000	471.00	200.0	68.9	173000	8070.0	3670.0
357	PCC006	2.770	75.700	.774	5.930	.481	.465	4.620	46.70	123.0	.0	232000	10700.0	650.0
359	PCC009	1.980	45.500	.587	3.790	.256	.333	2.960	32.80	74.3	.0	275000	6350.0	543.0
361	PCC017	7.210	91.600	.893	8.870	.861	.652	8.910	48.40	240.0	.0	99800	14600.0	6440.0
362	PCC021	4.150	85.507	.480	7.943	.631	.638	6.918	44.98	143.9	117.0	172982	12106.0	3040.9
363	PCC022	6.622	144.877	1.259	10.990	1.219	1.030	13.305	65.62	222.8	507.0	0	19588.4	2009.1
364	PCCSC8	5.090	122.000	.619	11.700	.998	.655	9.710	54.30	171.0	.0	90600	19900.0	2410.0
365	PCC010	3.820	105.000	.390	10.300	.769	.506	8.040	48.30	152.0	155.0	139000	17300.0	2840.0
366	PCCTP5	8.570	120.000	.979	13.800	.867	.634	12.200	69.70	234.0	394.0	0	15800.0	2880.0
367	PCC199	6.080	116.000	.345	9.400	.971	.573	8.890	61.20	261.0	283.0	156000	15800.0	5780.0
368	PCC200	13.500	77.600	.778	6.840	1.050	.740	10.500	49.30	406.0	384.0	0	14900.0	6340.0
371	PCC802	7.000	80.400	.723	9.080	.851	.867	8.950	69.70	195.0	331.0	78700	17100.0	540086.0
372	PCC854	5.830	80.000	.879	15.700	.893	1.040	9.080	89.50	249.0	353.0	23600	11900.0	6220.0
373	PCC907	5.508	143.880	1.901	13.213	1.879	1.778	28.576	53.21	187.9	.0	0	14996.9	341.2
374	PC1223	6.670	108.000	.914	11.700	1.000	.839	11.600	164.00	242.0	340.0	26100	14300.0	2910.0

Inductively Coupled Plasma Emission Spectroscopy

Elemental Concentrations of Samples from Decorated and Undecorated Vessels

Inductively Coupled Plasma Emission Spectroscopy is a precise and expedient method of measuring chemical elemental concentrations in ceramic pastes. ICP and INAA (Appendix B) use different extraction methods to derive these measurements. The ICP raw elemental concentrations for each vessel and clay sample are given in parts per million (ppm). The data provided here must be converted into logarithms of base 10 before performing statistical analyses comparable to those discussed in the text.

Each sample listed in Appendix C has been identified with a case number (Case) that corresponds to the Case number for vessel identification in Appendix A. Sample refers to the laboratory sample identification number.

Case	Sample	Al	Ba	Ca	Cr	Cu	Fe	K	La	Mg	Mn	Na	P	Sr	V	Zn	Y	Sc	Ti	Ce	Lu	S
1	14	3677	160	2894	0	0	667	209	7	150	9	282	63	15	1	4	2	0	59	.86	.00	114
2	60	37652	455	9846	51	30	25370	4293	113	5455	198	838	479	57	55	51	10	7	273	108.74	2.98	138
5	61	44504	412	8620	42	25	22144	3252	117	2525	75	598	593	45	41	52	17	5	255	133.05	2.74	130
7	34	33742	256	8624	30	23	24430	2927	105	5092	216	673	448	58	37	43	8	5	221	55.01	2.10	129
8	46	55313	193	14118	42	33	35377	2621	1379	658	374	1241	1779	73	82	31	12	9	781	99.30	3.86	146
15	40	55364	339	14192	46	49	54620	3318	190	13754	880	1136	1275	95	77	76	11	7	842	98.27	4.97	145
17	49	58132	349	15128	43	50	45219	3369	164	13794	849	2003	1504	120	45	79	11	7	693	98.86	4.36	151
18	38	36185	183	5556	33	26	24645	3043	105	3908	196	778	298	45	42	66	5	6	468	59.65	2.20	125
29	7	4165	57	1659	0	0	1508	522	21	197	10	183	59	21	4	24	1	0	44	22.56	.00	106
32	8	3182	99	2442	0	3	784	345	17	216	16	221	141	14	2	6	2	0	59	24.39	.00	107
36	6	5088	236	4439	0	8	2016	407	14	418	27	295	191	20	6	5	2	0	92	19.12	.00	120
43	42	59711	333	13718	46	58	53828	2623	194	14405	831	1225	1462	103	60	76	12	7	942	95.56	5.04	138
53	9	1706	35	1133	0	0	586	175	7	60	5	206	41	7	0	4	1	0	54	.59	.00	105
61	47	21935	82	6607	30	23	17284	1583	80	3735	183	844	537	44	39	22	7	4	318	90.30	2.36	118
73	48	29189	136	6375	35	29	26197	2210	110	5857	264	899	893	48	49	37	9	5	365	99.37	2.98	132
83	52	36346	223	8224	36	22	17438	2631	103	4029	110	587	437	47	41	33	14	5	188	117.35	2.48	126
85	43	31608	211	16162	61	53	25522	2561	107	8021	419	1802	1319	90	63	44	11	8	775	92.35	3.13	166
91	45	51468	311	16567	54	55	50639	6338	187	11349	750	871	1821	61	70	82	24	3	728	212.24	4.93	149
101	12	4062	104	3506	0	14	993	359	17	251	15	241	110	19	3	5	3	0	79	24.48	.00	124
104	58	37486	427	9927	44	21	22343	2824	105	1912	44	608	665	76	47	37	5	6	94	103.04	2.74	128
117	39	52736	322	13776	40	43	51450	2063	198	12346	766	1489	1499	106	54	68	10	6	633	54.10	4.24	139
122	64	35558	301	1432	46	17	46585	3384	168	12094	655	1196	1400	68	71	85	14	8	948	103.08	4.54	139
124	56	26218	319	8392	44	24	18000	3437	87	2804	101	515	494	42	46	37	7	5	154	74.09	2.33	132
126	5	2442	69	3141	0	0	412	370	8	125	12	211	77	12	1	4	1	0	44	18.34	.00	110
153	41	37956	382	14316	51	45	48071	5468	181	11200	614	428	2500	55	97	61	28	19	1023	121.98	4.70	139
159	33	34660	297	13649	38	47	48820	3329	187	9263	466	561	2441	54	66	83	25	9	794	72.32	4.19	132
160	66	33626	198	9031	26	23	25105	1198	96	5449	319	719	818	56	34	60	6	4	414	51.30	2.40	120
162	59	35837	199	7713	65	31	31069	3138	122	5285	124	688	607	53	107	56	10	9	425	100.79	3.34	121
180	55	34496	176	5756	36	22	16995	2858	86	3245	86	464	223	31	46	37	7	5	116	102.54	2.35	124
184	44	50478	293	14200	51	53	50565	2601	180	14024	951	1440	1361	104	59	73	13	8	879	92.56	4.73	146
186	1	15500	201	19111	3	1	2944	897	47	339	22	255	189	18	6	7	5	1	41	71.30	.00	190
203	62	42607	435	7071	44	21	19340	3779	99	1715	51	480	398	43	44	42	5	5	101	106.75	2.52	132
210	53	44742	257	6234	42	22	20340	2937	114	2814	62	360	323	41	42	35	10	6	123	128.96	2.63	120
219	35	32450	271	5128	29	21	22717	2734	99	3502	155	664	485	46	39	49	5	5	484	50.38	2.02	121
223	3	3977	163	2634	0	0	1254	316	34	311	20	405	244	18	5	5	4	0	117	54.31	.00	106
229	13	38140	92	32201	33	10	13059	2856	58	2703	55	1708	388	98	25	11	5	2	464	24.36	1.27	190
233	36	34978	238	5496	38	35	33517	3597	206	5698	528	669	795	45	53	80	25	8	419	223.28	3.05	117
234	50	53765	65	3733	24	16	12262	1359	74	2234	71	438	195	22	43	18	8	3	201	93.25	2.10	113
243	11	1828	40	1027	0	0	557	482	16	103	7	191	63	7	2	4	2	0	43	38.98	.00	102
259	37	21720	105	4432	20	12	13818	2655	99	2107	136	629	254	27	25	39	14	4	165	134.32	1.55	121
262	57	26417	126	6811	39	26	22142	2257	96	4025	196	722	505	42	52	30	6	6	278	86.27	2.62	124
267	2	1551	265	10955	7	13	2760	1127	72	896	35	395	354	42	14	54	8	2	107	89.80	.00	147
270	63	53862	284	7069	40	24	21601	3052	116	1952	63	606	445	46	39	45	10	7	77	134.21	2.61	132

Case	Sample	Al	Ba	Ca	Cr	Cu	Fe	K	La	Mg	Mn	Na	P	Sr	V	Zn	Y	Sc	Ti	Ce	Lu	S
285	4	3214	74	4103	0	6	2414	319	31	518	34	337	257	20	7	10	4	0	115	46.89	.00	111
286	51	10616	44	2317	15	15	14576	1315	67	1159	38	227	177	15	35	14	4	3	110	81.18	2.12	109
301	10	6039	76	6444	0	4	1581	429	18	218	12	233	224	30	3	4	2	0	83	20.65	.00	132
309	54	42312	365	8678	43	31	24472	3649	118	2320	198	500	550	50	51	91	15	8	127	116.45	2.91	126
311	65	41177	312	15857	60	75	46475	3024	170	11495	795	1619	1314	72	67	204	14	9	882	96.78	4.52	155
331	18	1934	88	1188	0	0	767	335	17	149	15	166	65	10	4	5	1	0	42	27.99	.00	102
333	16	2008	49	2448	0	0	819	381	11	196	18	193	80	12	2	10	2	0	49	14.76	.00	111
334	15	1832	102	1828	0	0	1000	232	13	218	20	150	47	9	2	27	1	0	70	17.30	.00	105
335	17	2006	71	1403	0	0	1034	331	35	191	12	183	93	9	3	7	5	0	47	58.51	.00	102
340	24	32581	189	44390	42	18	17158	3242	77	3853	107	1031	1097	89	42	24	7	4	496	53.83	1.98	252
341	22	32732	234	37226	41	20	17502	3061	78	4391	137	1572	1408	100	43	45	9	5	667	48.26	1.94	238
342	20	41067	345	47021	38	24	16941	3572	84	6779	196	1810	3540	130	45	189	10	6	562	43.67	2.01	243
343	21	34705	167	41330	42	27	14580	3386	66	3673	113	1371	1038	107	41	29	8	4	604	37.40	1.77	242
344	30	54024	203	59255	45	18	12826	4916	68	3396	79	1060	1079	117	31	20	9	4	558	57.60	1.95	271
345	27	53629	431	68537	52	46	17968	11480	95	6919	155	1525	2634	178	48	29	12	7	540	57.07	2.15	359
346	32	42164	241	60710	39	19	15782	3251	79	5243	131	1995	1654	133	41	18	10	5	658	54.05	2.11	298
347	26	38646	167	41153	43	16	14252	3048	68	3025	118	1778	925	98	46	17	8	4	615	45.44	1.79	234
348	19	40885	213	40958	38	14	18039	3446	78	4148	150	1865	1967	124	33	20	9	4	5	45.29	2.10	5
349	23	27337	209	30130	33	14	17700	2576	80	3675	138	1422	924	82	40	20	8	4	443	39.76	1.88	185
350	28	1481	54	756	0	0	328	571	19	284	3	174	75	6	4	5	0	0	41	24.26	.00	155
351	31	46925	255	64004	71	19	27655	10807	126	8847	314	810	1815	123	60	51	10	8	395	67.13	3.00	336
352	25	47830	371	83378	49	19	16651	6226	90	6042	252	2483	1866	215	54	33	13	6	667	66.49	2.49	37
353	29	50452	107	45969	42	13	15261	2588	73	2410	87	1528	1135	106	28	24	9	2	655	46.43	2.02	219
354	75	24131	42	16774	41	7	8498	5807	56	9370	88	871	853	99	29	31	5	6	57	69.97	1.48	179
355	76	13457	72	23187	28	10	9582	3102	60	13108	187	588	355	71	32	35	6	4	210	64.55	1.55	209
356	77	20663	97	56243	41	12	9567	4279	68	17552	207	819	533	111	51	43	10	6	193	83.25	2.08	330
358	78	23641	55	214182	53	20	21707	3694	111	20483	438	880	734	554	44	376	13	7	122	124.08	3.80	5521
360	67	49884	184	9133	81	17	14200	13048	125	53822	413	1452	825	59	84	137	8	9	294	101.37	2.64	153
361	73	28287	86	117580	49	25	8510	6094	87	24492	287	1284	594	297	42	46	11	6	228	89.45	2.74	508
363	68	28688	331	6567	31	14	16190	4552	80	4486	170	493	334	43	50	57	18	6	82	121.66	1.43	624
364	74	28348	48	89434	69	34	12712	8656	100	10922	270	1021	757	163	47	44	12	8	77	98.31	2.63	350
365	69	38806	101	191805	74	195	15371	8598	90	12660	293	1112	875	298	66	47	13	8	219	95.02	3.09	598
366	72	38826	142	6079	47	14	14850	5334	89	6365	248	739	416	28	58	52	17	9	265	66.85	1.92	162
367	71	33093	109	161826	65	18	18047	7578	92	14552	430	1468	709	255	56	58	11	7	283	99.73	3.11	517
368	70	4949	35	4376	2	3	1562	636	27	472	114	615	583	21	11	5	5	2	65	55.65	.00	117
369	84	29218	132	141674	55	20	16383	4899	109	14231	279	792	1212	136	75	61	14	7	243	126.42	3.52	442
370	81	31688	142	42440	63	28	19225	5582	113	12318	332	729	1133	57	61	149	16	8	196	95.69	2.83	264
371	87	22961	129	35623	49	20	14665	5083	87	16531	469	825	1281	77	51	65	11	6	212	116.73	2.57	236
372	80	33142	240	24842	51	26	23963	3772	125	9354	260	660	1560	68	91	60	22	8	336	90.32	2.87	203
373	83	54362	104	7005	39	12	3957	6455	126	2546	60	365	650	90	57	36	17	6	27	222.12	1.37	351
374	86	32763	166	42104	74	32	20210	5616	110	12756	719	750	1355	76	63	149	17	9	207	97.62	2.94	266
375	82	22033	167	263875	43	37	11365	3993	83	10456	303	619	1221	161	47	51	11	5	213	122.32	3.45	666
376	79	26960	76	165686	113	155	8588	4223	75	12278	343	803	673	213	50	39	12	7	157	122.55	2.62	521
377	85	52901	167	14308	43	47	36399	3478	140	12322	764	1253	1768	81	71	69	12	7	729	101.52	3.87	174

References

ABBOTT, DAVID R.
1988   Form, Function, Technology, and Style in Hohokam Ceramics. In "The 1982–1984 Excavation at Las Colinas," by David R. Abbott, Kim E. Beckwith, Patricia L. Crown, R. Thomas Euler, David A. Gregory, J. Ronald London, Marilyn B. Saul, Larry A. Schwalbe, Mary Bernard-Shaw, Christine R. Szuter, and Arthur W. Vokes. *Arizona State Museum Archaeological Series* 162(4): 73–197. Tucson: Arizona State Museum, University of Arizona.

1993   Clarifying Hohokam Socioeconomic Organization: Ceramic Results from Pueblo Grande and Elsewhere. Paper presented at the annual meeting of the Arizona Archaeological Council, Flagstaff.

ADAMS, E. CHARLES
1991a   Homol'ovi II in the 14th Century. In "Homol'ovi II: Archaeology of an Ancestral Hopi Village, Arizona," edited by E. Charles Adams and Kelley A. Hays. *Anthropological Papers of the University of Arizona* 55: 116–121. Tucson: University of Arizona Press.

1991b   *The Origin and Development of the Pueblo Katsina Cult.* Tucson: University of Arizona Press.

ADAMS, E. CHARLES, AND KELLEY A. HAYS, Editors
1991   Homol'ovi II: Archaeology of an Ancestral Hopi Village, Arizona. *Anthropological Papers of the University of Arizona* 55. Tucson: University of Arizona Press.

ADAMS, E. CHARLES, DEBORAH S. DOSH,
AND MIRIAM T. STARK
1987   Spatial Organization in the Hopi Mesas–Hopi Buttes–Middle Little Colorado River Valley, A.D. 1300–1600. MS on file, Arizona State Museum, University of Arizona, Tucson.

ADAN-BAYEWITZ, D., AND ISADORE PERLMAN
1985   Local Pottery Provenience Studies: A Role for Clay Analysis. *Archaeometry* 27(2): 203–217.

ALLEN, WILLIAM L., AND JAMES B. RICHARDSON III
1971   The Reconstruction of Kinship from Archaeological Data: The Concepts, the Methods, and the Feasibility. *American Antiquity* 36(1): 41–53.

AMBLER, J. RICHARD
1961   Archaeological Survey and Excavations at Casa Grande National Monument, Arizona. *The Kiva* 27(4): 10–23.

AMSDEN, CHARLES A.
1936   An Analysis of Hohokam Pottery Design. *Medallion Papers* 23. Globe: Gila Pueblo.

ARNOLD, DEAN E.
1975   Ceramic Ecology of the Ayacucho Basin: Implications for Prehistory. *Current Anthropology* 16(2): 183–206.

1980   Localized Exchange: An Ethnoarchaeological Perspective. In "Models and Methods in Regional Exchange," edited by Robert E. Fry. *Society for American Archaeology Papers* 1: 147–150.

1981   A Model for the Identification of Nonlocal Ceramic Distribution: View from the Present. In "Production and Distribution: A Ceramic Viewpoint," edited by Hilary Howard and Elaine L. Morris. *BAR International Series* 120: 31–44. Oxford.

1985   *Ceramic Theory and Cultural Process.* Cambridge: Cambridge University Press.

BEAGLEHOLE, ERNEST
1937   Notes on Hopi Economic Life. *Yale University Publications in Anthropology* 15. New Haven: Yale University.

BEALS, RALPH L., GEORGE W. BRAINERD, AND WATSON SMITH
1945   Archaeological Studies in Northeast Arizona. *University of California Publications in American Archaeology and Ethnology* 44(1). Berkeley: University of California Press.

BEESON, WILLIAM J.
1966   Archaeological Survey near St. Johns, Arizona: A Methodological Study. MS, Doctoral Dissertation, University of Arizona, Tucson.

BENNETT, JOHN W.
1968   Reciprocal Economic Exchanges among North American Agricultural Operations. *Southwestern Journal of Anthropology* 24(3): 276–309.

BERNARD, H. RUSSELL, AND PERTTI J. PELTO, Editors
1987   *Technology and Social Change.* 2nd edition. New York: MacMillan.

BINFORD, LEWIS R.
1962   Archaeology as Anthropology. *American Antiquity* 28(2): 217–225.

1963   "Red Ochre" Caches from the Michigan Area: A Possible Case of Cultural Drift. *Southwestern Journal of Anthropology* 19(1): 89–108.

1965   Archaeological Systematics and the Study of Cultural Process. *American Antiquity* 31(2): 203–210.

1980   Willow Smoke and Dogs' Tails: Hunter-gatherer Settlement Systems and Archaeological Site Formation. *American Antiquity* 45(1): 4–20.

BISHOP, RONALD L.
1980   Aspects of Ceramic Compositional Modeling. In "Models and Methods in Regional Exchange," edited

BISHOP, RONALD L. (Continued)
　　by Robert E. Fry. *Society for American Archaeology Papers* 1: 47–66.

BISHOP, RONALD L., AND HECTOR NEFF
1989　Compositional Data Analysis in Archaeology. In "Archaeological Chemistry IV," edited by Ralph O. Allen, pp. 57–86. *Advances in Chemistry Series* 220. Washington: American Chemical Society.

BISHOP, RONALD L., GARMAN HARBOTTLE, AND EDWARD V. SAYRE
1982　Chemical and Mathematical Procedures Employed in the Maya Fine Paste Ceramics Project. In "Excavations at Seibal, Analysis of Fine Paste Ceramics," edited by Jeremy A. Sabloff. *Memoirs of the Peabody Museum of Archaeology and Ethnology, Harvard University,* 15(2): 272–282. Cambridge: Peabody Museum.

BISHOP, RONALD L., ROBERT L. RANDS, AND GEORGE R. HOLLEY
1982　Ceramic Compositional Analysis in Archaeological Perspective. In *Advances in Archaeological Method and Theory,* Vol. 5, edited by Michael B. Schiffer, pp. 276–329. New York: Academic Press.

BISHOP, RONALD L., VELETTA CANOUTS, SUZANNE DE ATLEY, ALFRED QOYAWAYMA, AND C. W. AIKINS
1988　The Formation of Ceramic Analytical Groups: Hopi Pottery Production and Exchange, A.D. 1300–1600. *Journal of Field Archaeology* 15: 317–337.

BLINMAN, ERIC, AND C. DEAN WILSON
1988　Overview of A.D. 600–800 Ceramic Production and Exchange in the Dolores Project Area. *Dolores Archaeological Program 1: Supporting Studies: Additive and Reductive Technologies,* compiled by Eric Blinman, Carl J. Phagan, and Richard H. Wilshusen, pp. 395–424. Denver: Engineering and Research Center, Bureau of Reclamation, Department of the Interior.

1992　Ceramic Production and Exchange during the Basketmaker III and Pueblo I Periods in the Northern San Juan Region. In *Ceramic Production and Distribution: An Integrated Approach,* edited by George J. Bey III and Christopher A. Pool, pp. 155–173. Boulder: Westview Press.

BOHRER, VORSILA
1982　Plant Remains from Rooms at Grasshopper Pueblo. In "Multidisciplinary Research at Grasshopper Pueblo, Arizona," edited by William A. Longacre, Sally J. Holbrook, and Michael W. Graves. *Anthropological Papers of the University of Arizona* 40: 97–105. Tucson: University of Arizona Press.

BRADFIELD, WESLEY
1931　Cameron Creek Village: A Site in the Mimbres Area in Grant County, New Mexico. *Monographs of the School of American Research* 1. Santa Fe: School of American Research.

BRAUN, DAVID P.
1983　Pots as Tools. In *Archaeological Hammers and Theories,* edited by Arthur S. Keene, pp. 107–134. New York: Academic Press.

BRAUN, DAVID P., AND STEPHEN PLOG
1982　Evolution of "Tribal" Social Networks: Theory and Prehistoric North American Evidence. *American Antiquity* 47(3): 504–525.

BRETERNITZ, DAVID A.
1960　Excavations at Three Sites in the Verde Valley, Arizona. *Museum of Northern Arizona Bulletin* 34. Flagstaff: Northern Arizona Society of Science and Art.

1966　An Appraisal of Tree-ring Dated Pottery in the Southwest. *Anthropological Papers of the University of Arizona* 10. Tucson: University of Arizona Press.

BREW, JOHN O.
1946　Archaeology of Alkali Ridge, Southeastern Utah, with a Review of the Prehistory of the Mesa Verde Division of the San Juan and Some Observations on Archaeological Systematics. *Papers of the Peabody Museum of American Archaeology and Ethnology, Harvard University,* 21. Cambridge: Peabody Museum.

BRONITSKI, GORDON
1986　Compressive Texting of Ceramics: A Southwestern Example. *The Kiva* 51(2): 85–99.

BROWMAN, DAVID L.
1976　Demographic Correlations of the Wari Conquest of Junin. *American Antiquity* 41(4): 465–477.

BROWN, JEFFREY L.
1973　The Origin and Nature of Salado: Evidence from the Safford Valley, Arizona. MS, Doctoral Dissertation, University of Arizona, Tucson.

BRUNSON, JUDITH
1985　Corrugated Ceramics as Indicators of Interaction Spheres. In *Decoding Prehistoric Ceramics,* edited by Ben A. Nelson, pp. 102–177. Carbondale: Southern Illinois University Press.

BUNZEL, RUTH L.
1929　The Pueblo Potter: A Study of Creative Imagination in Primitive Art. *Columbia University Contributions to Anthropology* 8. New York: Columbia University Press.

BURTON, JAMES, AND ARLYN W. SIMON
1993　Acid Extraction as a Simple and Inexpensive Method for Compositional Characterization of Archaeological Ceramics. *American Antiquity* 58(1): 45–69.

CARLSON, ROY L.
1970　White Mountain Redware: A Pottery Tradition of East-Central Arizona and Western New Mexico. *Anthropological Papers of the University of Arizona* 19. Tucson: University of Arizona Press.

1982　The Polychrome Complexes. In "Southwestern Ceramics: A Comparative Review," edited by Albert H. Schroeder. *The Arizona Archaeologist* 15: 210–234. Phoenix: Arizona Archaeological Society.

CARTLEDGE, THOMAS R.
1976 Prehistory in Vosberg Valley, Central Arizona. *The Kiva* 42(1): 95–104.

CHAGNON, NAPOLEON
1968 *Yanomamo: The Fierce People*. New York: Holt, Rinehart, and Winston.

CHAPMAN, KENNETH M.
1936 The Pottery of Santo Domingo Pueblo: A Detailed Study of Its Decoration. *Memoirs of the Laboratory of Anthropology* 1. Santa Fe: Laboratory of Anthropology.

CHEAL, DAVID J.
1988 *The Gift Economy*. London: Routledge.

CIBOLA WHITEWARE CONFERENCE
1958 Concordances and Proceedings. MS on file, Museum of Northern Arizona, Flagstaff.

CIOLEK-TORRELLO, RICHARD
1978 A Statistical Analysis of Activity Organization: Grasshopper Pueblo, Arizona. MS, Doctoral Dissertation, University of Arizona, Tucson.
1985 A Typology of Room Function at Grasshopper Pueblo, Arizona. *Journal of Field Archaeology* 12: 41–63.

COLTON, HAROLD S.
1939 The Reducing Atmosphere and Oxidizing Atmosphere in Prehistoric Southwestern Ceramics. *American Antiquity* 4(3): 224–231.
1941a Prehistoric Trade in the Southwest. *The Scientific Monthly* 32: 308–319.
1941b Winona and Ridge Ruin, Part 2. Notes on the Technology and Taxonomy of the Pottery. *Museum of Northern Arizona Bulletin* 19. Flagstaff: Northern Arizona Society of Science and Art.
1953 Potsherds: An Introduction to the Study of Prehistoric Southwestern Ceramics and Their Use in Historic Reconstruction. *Museum of Northern Arizona Bulletin* 25. Flagstaff: Northern Arizona Society of Science and Art.
1955 Checklist of Southwestern Pottery Types. *Museum of Northern Arizona Ceramic Series* 2. Flagstaff: Northern Arizona Society of Science and Art.
1956 Pottery Types of the Southwest. *Museum of Northern Arizona Ceramic Series* 3C. Flagstaff: Northern Arizona Society of Science and Art.

COLTON, HAROLD S., AND LYNDON L. HARGRAVE
1937 Handbook of Northern Arizona Pottery Wares. *Museum of Northern Arizona Bulletin* 11. Flagstaff: Northern Arizona Society of Science and Art.

COLTON, MARY-RUSSELL F.
1931 Technique of the Major Hopi Crafts. *Museum of Northern Arizona, Museum Notes* 3(12). Flagstaff: Northern Arizona Society of Science and Art.

CORDELL, LINDA S.
1991 Anna O. Shepard and Southwestern Archaeology: Ignoring a Cautious Heretic. In *Ceramic Analysis and Social Inference in American Archaeology: The Ceramic Legacy of Anna O. Shepard*, edited by Ronald L. Bishop and Frederick Lange, pp. 132–153. Boulder: University of Colorado Press.

CORDELL, LINDA S., AND FRED T. PLOG
1979 Escaping the Confines of Normative Thought: A Reevaluation of Puebloan Prehistory. *American Antiquity* 44(3): 405–429.

COSTIN, KATHY
1991 Craft Specialization: Issues in Defining, Documenting, and Explaining the Organization of Production. *Archaeological Method and Theory*, Vol. 3, edited by Michael B. Schiffer, pp. 1-56. Tucson: University of Arizona Press.

CRONIN, CONSTANCE
1962 An Analysis of Pottery Design Elements Indicating Possible Relationships between Three Decorated Types. In "Chapters in the Prehistory of Eastern Arizona," edited by Paul S. Martin. *Fieldiana: Anthropology* 53: 105–114. Chicago: Chicago Natural History Museum

CROWN, PATRICIA L.
1981a *Variability in Ceramic Manufacture at the Chodistaas Site, East-Central Arizona*. MS, Doctoral Dissertation, University of Arizona, Tucson. Ann Arbor: University Microfilms.
1981b The Ceramic Assemblage. In "Prehistory of the St. Johns Area, East Central Arizona," edited by Deborah A. Westfall. *Arizona State Museum Archaeological Series* 153: 233–290. Tucson: Arizona State Museum, University of Arizona.
1990 Converging Traditions: Salado Polychrome Ceramics in Southwestern Prehistory. Paper presented at the 55th annual meeting of the Society for American Archaeology, Las Vegas.
1994 *Ceramics and Ideology: Salado Polychrome Pottery*. Albuquerque: University of New Mexico Press.

CROWN, PATRICIA L., AND RONALD L. BISHOP
1987 Convergence in Ceramic Manufacturing Traditions in the Late Prehistoric Southwest. Paper presented at the 52nd annual meeting of the Society for American Archaeology, Toronto.

CROWN, PATRICIA L., LARRY A. SCHWALBE, AND J. RONALD LONDON
1986 An X-ray Fluorescence Analysis of the West Branch Site Ceramics. In "Archaeological Investigations at the West Branch Site: Early and Middle Rincon Occupation in the Southern Tucson Basin," edited by Frederick W. Huntington. *Institute for American Research Anthropological Papers* 5: 411–428. Tucson: Institute for American Research.
1988 X-ray Fluorescence Analysis of Materials Variability in Las Colinas Ceramics. In "The 1982–1984 Excavation at Las Colinas," by David R. Abbott, Kim E. Beckwith, Patricia L. Crown, R. Thomas Euler, David A. Gregory, J. Ronald London, Marilyn B. Saul, Larry A. Schwalbe, Mary Bernard-Shaw, Christine R. Szuter, and Arthur W. Vokes. *Arizona State Museum Archaeological Series* 162(4):

CROWN, PATRICIA L., LARRY A. SCHWALBE, AND J. RONALD LONDON (Continued)
30–72. Tucson: Arizona State Museum, University of Arizona.

CROWN-ROBERTSON, PATRICIA L.
1978   Migration Theory in Archaeology. MS on file, Arizona State Museum, University of Arizona, Tucson.

CUSHING, FRANK
1886   A Study of Pueblo Pottery as Illustrative of Zuni Culture Growth. *Bureau of Ethnology, 4th Annual Report, 1882–1883*, pp. 473–522. Washington: Smithsonian Institution.

DANSON, EDWARD B.
1957   An Archaeological Survey of West Central New Mexico and East Central Arizona. *Papers of the Peabody Museum of Archaeology and Ethnology, Harvard University,* 44. Cambridge: Peabody Museum.

DANSON, EDWARD B., AND ROBERTS M. WALLACE
1956   A Petrographic Study of Gila Polychrome. *American Antiquity* 22(2): 180–183.

DARVILL, TIM, AND JANE TIMBY
1982   Textural Analysis: A Review of Potentials and Limitations. In "Current Research in Ceramics: Thin-section Studies," edited by Ian C. Freestone, Catherine Johns, and Tim Potter, pp. 73–86. *The British Museum Seminar 1980.* London: The British Museum.

DEAN, JEFFREY S., AND WILLIAM J. ROBINSON
1982   Dendrochronology at Grasshopper Pueblo. In "Multidisciplinary Research at Grasshopper Pueblo," edited by William A. Longacre, Sally J. Holbrook, and Michael W. Graves. *Anthropological Papers of the University of Arizona* 40: 46–60. Tucson: University of Arizona Press.

DE ATLEY, SUZANNE P.
1973   A Preliminary Analysis of Patterns of Raw Material Use in Plainware Ceramics from Chevelon, Arizona. MS, Master's Thesis, Department of Anthropology, University of California, Los Angeles.
1990   Potter's Craft or Analyst's Tool? A Century of Ceramic Technology Studies in the American Southwest. In *Ceramic Analysis and Social Inference in American Archaeology: The Ceramic Legacy of Anna O. Shepard,* edited by Ronald L. Bishop and Frederick Lange, pp. 205–223. Boulder: University of Colorado Press.

DE ATLEY, SUZANNE P., AND RONALD L. BISHOP
1990   Toward an Integrated Interface for Archaeology and Archaeometry. In *Ceramic Analysis and Social Inference in American Archaeology: The Ceramic Legacy of Anna O. Shepard,* edited by Ronald L. Bishop and Frederick Lange, pp. 358–382. Boulder: University of Colorado Press.

DEBOER, WARREN
1984   The Last Pottery Show: System and Sense in Ceramic Studies. In *The Many Dimensions of Pottery: Ceramics in Archaeology and Anthropology,* edited by Sander E. van der Leeuw and Alison C. Pritchard, pp. 527–571. CINGULA 7. Amsterdam: Institute for Pre- and Proto-history, University of Amsterdam.

DEBOER, WARREN, AND DONALD LATHRAP
1979   The Making and Breaking of Shipibo-Conibo Ceramics. *Ethnoarchaeology: Implications of Ethnography for Archaeology,* edited by Carol Kramer, pp. 102–138. Carbondale: Southern Illinois University Press.

DEETZ, JAMES
1965   The Dynamics of Stylistic Change in Arikara Ceramics. *Illinois Studies in Anthropology* 4. Urbana: University of Illinois Press.

DEGARMO, GLENN
1975   *Coyote Creek Site 01: A Methodological Study of a Prehistoric Pueblo Population.* Doctoral Dissertation, University of California, Los Angeles. Ann Arbor: University Microfilms.

DEUTCHMAN, HAREE L.
1980   Chemical Evidence of Ceramic Exchange on Black Mesa. In "Models and Methods in Regional Exchange," edited by Robert E. Fry. *Society for American Archaeology Papers* 1: 119–134.

DI PESO, CHARLES C.
1958   The Reeve Ruin of Southeastern Arizona. *The Amerind Foundation* 8. Dragoon, Arizona: The Amerind Foundation.
1976   Gila Polychrome in the Casas Grandes Region. *The Kiva* 42(1): 57–64.

DITTERT, ALFRED E., JR.
1959   Culture Change in the Cebolleta Mesa Region, Central Western New Mexico. MS, Doctoral Dissertation, University of Arizona, Tucson.

DITTERT, ALFRED E., JR., AND REYNOLD J. RUPPÉ, JR.
1951   The Archaeology of Cebollita Mesa: A Preliminary Report. *El Palacio* 58(4): 116–129.

DOUGLASS, AMY
1987   Prehistoric Exchange and Sociopolitical Development: The Little Colorado Whiteware Production-Distribution System. MS, Doctoral Dissertation, Arizona State University, Tempe.

DOUGLASS, AMY, AND OWEN LINDAUER
1988   Hierarchical and Non-hierarchical Approaches to Ceramic Design Analysis: A Response to Jernigan. *American Antiquity* 53(3): 620–626.

DOWNUM, CHRISTIAN E., AND ALAN P. SULLIVAN III
1990   Settlement Patterns. In "The Wupatki Archaeological Inventory Survey Project: Final Report," compiled by Bruce A. Anderson. MS on file, Southwest Cultural Resources Center, Professional Paper 35.

DOYEL, DAVID E.
1976   Salado Cultural Development in the Tonto Basin and Globe-Miami Area, Central Arizona. *The Kiva* 42(1): 5–16.
1977   Classic Period Hohokam in the Escalante Ruin

Group. MS, Doctoral Dissertation, University of Arizona, Tucson.

1978 The Miami Wash Project: Hohokam and Salado in the Globe-Miami Area, Central Arizona. *Arizona State Museum Contributions to Highway Salvage Archaeology* 52. Tucson: Arizona State Museum, University of Arizona.

1980 Prehistory in Dead Valley, East Central Arizona: The TG&E Springerville Report. *Arizona State Museum Archaeological Series* 144. Tucson: Arizona State Museum, University of Arizona.

1984 Stylistic and Petrographic Variability in Pueblo II Period Cibola Whiteware from Upper Little Colorado. In "Regional Analysis of Prehistoric Ceramic Variation: Contemporary Studies of the Cibola Whitewares," edited by Alan P. Sullivan III and Jeffrey L. Hantman. *Arizona State University Anthropological Papers* 31: 4–16. Tempe: Arizona State University.

DOYEL, DAVID E., AND EMIL W. HAURY, Editors
1976 The Salado Conference. *The Kiva* 42(1).

DOZIER, EDWARD P.
1970 *The Pueblo Indians of North America.* New York: Holt, Rinehart, and Winston.

DUNNELL, ROBERT C.
1978 Style and Function: A Fundamental Dichotomy. *American Antiquity* 43(2): 192–202.

1986 Methodological Issues in Americanist Artifact Classification. In *Advances in Archaeological Method and Theory*, Vol. 9, edited by Michael B. Schiffer, pp. 149–208. Orlando: Academic Press.

EARLE, TIMOTHY K., AND JONATHON E. ERICSON, Editors
1977 *Exchange Systems in Prehistory.* New York: Academic Press.

ELSON, MARK D., AND WILLIAM H. DOELLE
1986 The Valencia Site Testing Project. *Institute for American Research Technical Report* 86-6. Tucson: Institute for American Research.

ERICSON, JONATHON E.
1977 Egalitarian Exchange Systems in California: A Preliminary View. In *Exchange Systems in Prehistory*, edited by Timothy K. Earle and Jonathon E. Ericson, pp. 109–126. New York: Academic Press.

ERICSON, JONATHON E., AND SUZANNE P. DE ATLEY
1976 Reconstructing Ceramic Assemblages: An Experiment to Derive the Morphology and Capacity of Parent Vessels from Sherds. *American Antiquity* 41(4): 484–489.

ERICSON, JONATHON E., DWIGHT W. READ, AND CHERYL BURKE
1971 Research Design: The Relationships between the Primary Functions and Physical Properties of Ceramic Vessels and Their Implications for Distributions on an Archaeological Site. *Anthropology UCLA* 3(2): 84–95.

FEINMAN, GARY M., STEADMAN UPHAM, AND KENT G. LIGHTFOOT
1981 The Production Step Measure: An Ordinal Index of Labor Input in Ceramic Manufacture. *American Antiquity* 46(4): 871–884.

FERDON, EDWIN N.
1955 A Trial Survey of Mexican-Southwestern Architectural Parallels. *Monographs of the School of American Research* 21. Santa Fe: School of American Research.

FEWKES, JESSE WALTER
1898 Archaeological Expedition into Arizona in 1895. *Bureau of American Ethnology, 17th Annual Report, 1895–1896.* Washington: Smithsonian Institution.

1904 Two Summers' Work in Pueblo Ruins. *Bureau of American Ethnology, 22nd Annual Report, 1900–1901.* Washington: Smithsonian Institution.

FINNELL, TONY
1966 *Geological Map of the Chediski Peak Quadrangle, Navajo County, Arizona.* Denver: U.S. Geological Survey.

FISH, PAUL R., SUZANNE K. FISH, STEPHANIE WHITTLESEY, HECTOR NEFF, MICHAEL D. GLASCOCK, AND J. MICHAEL ELAM
1992 An Evaluation of the Production and Exchange of Tanque Verde Red-on-Brown Ceramics in Southern Arizona. In "Chemical Characterization of Ceramic Pastes in Archaeology," edited by Hector Neff. *Monographs in World Archaeology* 7: 233–254. Madison: Prehistory Press.

FLANNERY, KENT, Editor
1976 *The Early Mesoamerican Village.* New York: Academic Press.

FONTANA, BERNARD L., WILLIAM J. ROBINSON, CHARLES W. CORMACK, AND ERNEST E. LEAVITT, JR.
1962 *Papago Indian Pottery.* Seattle: University of Washington Press.

FOWLER, ANDREW
1989 Ceramic Types of the Zuni Area. MS prepared for the New Mexico Archaeological Council Ceramic Workshop, Silver City, New Mexico, October 27-29.

FOWLER, ANDREW, AND MARK SANT
1990 The Development of an Anasazi Redware Tradition: The Regional Implications of Showlow Redware. Paper presented at the 55th annual meeting of the Society for American Archaeology, Las Vegas.

FRANKLIN, HAYWARD H.
1982 Ceramic Analysis of Nineteen Sites in the Bis Sa'ani Community. In "Bis Sa'ani: A Late Bonito Phase Community on Escavada Wash, Northwest New Mexico," edited by Cory D. Breternitz, David E. Doyel, and Michael P. Marshall. Prepared for the Alamito Coal Company, Tucson. *Navajo Nation Papers in Anthropology* 14(3): 873–934.

FRANKLIN, HAYWARD H., AND W. BRUCE MASSE
1976 The San Pedro Salado: A Case of Prehistoric Migration. *The Kiva* 42(1): 47–55.

FRIEDRICH, MARGARET H.
1970 Design Structure and Social Interaction: Archaeological Implications of an Ethnographic Analysis.

FRIEDRICH, MARGARET H. (Continued)
American Antiquity 35(3): 332–343.

FRISBIE, THEODORE R.
1982   The Anasazi–Mogollon Frontier? Perspectives from the Albuquerque Area or Brown Vs. Gray: A Paste Case from the Albuquerque Region. In *Mogollon Archaeology: Proceedings of the 1980 Mogollon Conference*, edited by Patrick H. Beckett, pp. 17–23. Ramona: Acoma Books.

GARRETT, ELIZABETH
1982   A Petrographic Analysis of Ceramics from the Apache-Sitgreaves National Forest, Arizona: On-site or Specialized Manufacture. MS, Doctoral Dissertation, Western Michigan University, Kalamazoo.

GIFFORD, EDWARD W.
1928   Pottery Making in the Southwest. *University of California Publications in American Archaeology and Ethnology* 23(8). Berkeley: University of California.

GIFFORD, JAMES C.
1957   Archaeological Explorations in Caves of the Point of Pines Region. MS, Master's Thesis, Department of Anthropology, University of Arizona, Tucson.

GIFFORD, JAMES C., AND WATSON SMITH
1978   Gray Corrugated Pottery from Awatovi and Other Jeddito Sites in Northeastern Arizona. *Papers of the Peabody Museum of Archaeology and Ethnology, Harvard University,* 69. Cambridge: Peabody Museum.

GLADWIN, HAROLD S.
1943   A Review and Analysis of the Flagstaff Culture. *Medallion Papers* 31. Globe, Arizona: Gila Pueblo.

GLADWIN, HAROLD S., EMIL W. HAURY, EDWIN B. SAYLES, AND NORA GLADWIN
1937   Excavations at Snaketown, Material Culture. *Medallion Papers* 25. Globe, Arizona: Gila Pueblo.

GLADWIN, WINIFRED J., AND HAROLD S. GLADWIN
1930   Some Southwestern Pottery Types, Series I. *Medallion Papers* 8. Globe, Arizona: Gila Pueblo.
1931   Some Southwestern Pottery Types, Series II. *Medallion Papers* 10. Globe, Arizona: Gila Pueblo.
1934   A Method for the Designation of Cultures and Their Variations. *Medallion Papers* 15. Globe, Arizona: Gila Pueblo.
1935   The Eastern Range of the Red-on-buff Culture. *Medallion Papers* 16. Globe, Arizona: Gila Pueblo.

GLASCOCK, MICHAEL D.
1992   Characterization of Archaeological Ceramics at MURR by Neutron Activation Analysis and Multivariate Statistics. In "Chemical Characterization of Ceramic Pastes in Archaeology," edited by Hector Neff, pp. 11–26. *Monographs in World Archaeology* 7. Madison: Prehistory Press.

GOLDSTEIN, JOSEPH I., AND HARVEY YAKOWITZ
1975   *Analytical Scanning Electron Microscopy.* New York: Plenum Press.

GOULD, RICHARD
1980   *Living Archaeology.* Cambridge: Cambridge University Press.

GRATZ, KATHLEEN E.
1980   Ceramics. In "Archaeological Investigations, Salt River Project Coronado Generating Station Project Plant Site and Access Road. Private and State Lands, Apache County, Arizona," prepared by J. E. Bradford, pp. 179–190. MS on file, Museum of Northern Arizona, Flagstaff.

GRAVES, MICHAEL W.
1981   Ethnoarchaeology of Kalinga Ceramic Designs. MS, Doctoral Dissertation, University of Arizona, Tucson.
1982   Breaking Down Ceramic Variation: Testing Models of White Mountain Redware Design Development. *Journal of Anthropological Archaeology* 1(4): 305–354.

GRAVES, MICHAEL W., WILLIAM A. LONGACRE, AND SALLY J. HOLBROOK
1982   Aggregation and Abandonment at Grasshopper Pueblo, Arizona. *Journal of Field Archaeology* 9(2): 193–206.

GREBINGER, PAUL
1976   Salado - Perspectives from the Middle Santa Cruz Valley. *The Kiva* 42(1): 39–46.

GUMERMAN, GEORGE J., AND CAROL S. WEED
1976   The Question of Salado in the Agua Fria and New River Drainages of Central Arizona. *The Kiva* 42(1): 105–112.

GUTHE, CARL E.
1925   *Pueblo Pottery Making: A Study at the Village of San Ildefonso.* Published for the Department of Archaeology, Phillips Academy. New Haven: Yale University Press.
1934   Introductory Essay. In "Standards of Pottery Description," by Benjamin March. *Occasional Contributions, University of Michigan Museum of Anthropology* 3: 7–10. Ann Arbor: University of Michigan Press.

HANGSTRUM, MELISSA
1985   Measuring Prehistoric Ceramic Craft Specialization: A Test Case in the American Southwest. *Journal of Field Archaeology* 12(1): 65–75.

HANTMAN, JEFFREY L., AND STEPHEN PLOG
1982   The Relationship of Stylistic Similarity to Patterns of Material Exchange. In *The Context for Prehistoric Exchange Systems*, edited by Jonathon E. Ericson and Timothy K. Earle, pp. 237–263. New York: Academic Press.

HANTMAN, JEFFREY L., KENT G. LIGHTFOOT, AND STEADMAN UPHAM
1979   The Implications of Changing Modes of Ceramic Production in the Prehistoric Plateau Southwest. Paper presented at the 44th annual meeting of the Society for American Archaeology, Vancouver, British Columbia.

HANTMAN, JEFFREY L., KENT G. LIGHTFOOT, STEADMAN UPHAM, FRED PLOG, STEPHEN PLOG, AND BRUCE DONALDSON
1984   Cibola Whitewares, A Regional Perspective. In "Regional Analysis of Prehistoric Ceramic Varia-

tion: Contemporary Studies of the Cibola White-wares," edited by Alan P. Sullivan III and Jeffrey L. Hantman. *Arizona State University Anthropological Papers* 31: 17–35. Tempe: Arizona State University.

HARBOTTLE, GARMAN
1976   Activation Analysis in Archaeology. In *Radiochemistry, A Specialist Periodical Report*, Vol. 3, edited by G. W. A. Newton, pp. 33–72. London: The Chemical Society, Burlington House.

HAURY, EMIL W.
1931   Showlow Black-on-red, Pinedale Polychrome, and Four-Mile Polychrome. In "Some Southwestern Pottery Types, Series 2," by Winifred J. and Harold S. Gladwin. *Medallion Papers* 9. Globe, Arizona: Gila Pueblo.
1932   The Age of Lead Glaze Decorated Pottery in the Southwest. *American Anthropologist* 34(3): 418–425.
1934   The Canyon Creek Ruin and the Cliff Dwellings of the Sierra Ancha. *Medallion Papers* 14. Globe, Arizona: Gila Pueblo.
1936   The Mogollon Culture of Southwestern New Mexico. *Medallion Papers* 20. Globe, Arizona: Gila Pueblo.
1940   Excavations in the Forestdale Valley, East-Central Arizona. *University of Arizona Bulletin* 11(4), *Social Science Bulletin* 12. Tucson: University of Arizona.
1945   The Excavation of Los Muertos and Neighboring Ruins in the Salt River Valley, Southern Arizona. *Papers of the Peabody Museum of American Archaeology and Ethnology, Harvard University,* 24(1). Cambridge: Peabody Museum.
1958   Evidence at Point of Pines for a Prehistoric Migration from Northern Arizona. In "Migrations in New World Culture History," edited by Raymond H. Thompson. *University of Arizona Bulletin* 29(2), *Social Science Bulletin* 27: 1-6. Tucson: University of Arizona.
1976   Salado: The View from Point of Pines. In "The 1976 Salado Conference," edited by David E. Doyel and Emil W. Haury. *The Kiva* 42(1): 81–84.

HAURY, EMIL W., AND LYNDON L. HARGRAVE
1931   Recently Dated Pueblo Ruins in Arizona. *Smithsonian Miscellaneous Collections* 82(11): 1–73. Washington: Smithsonian Institution.

HAWLEY, FLORENCE M.
1929   Prehistoric Pottery Pigments in the Southwest. *American Anthropologist* 31(4): 731–754.
1930   Chemical Examination of Prehistoric Smudged Wares. *American Anthropologist* 32(3): 500–502.
1938   Classification of Black Pottery Pigments and Paint Areas. *University of New Mexico Bulletin* 321. Albuquerque: University of New Mexico.

HAYS, KELLEY A.
1990   Symbol-minded Approaches to Prehistory: An Outline of Goals and Methods. Paper presented at the 55th annual meeting of the Society for American Archaeology, Las Vegas.

HEGMON, MICHELLE, WINSTON HURST, AND JAMES ALLISTON
1992   Production for Local Consumption and Exchange: Comparisons of Early Red and White Ware Ceramics in the San Juan Region. MS on file, New Mexico State University, Las Cruces.

HEIDKE, JAMES
1986a   Plainware Ceramics. In "Archaeological Investigations at the West Branch Site: Early and Middle Rincon Occupation in the Southern Tucson Basin," edited by Frederick W. Huntington. *Institute for American Research Anthropological Papers* 5: 165–196. Tucson: Institute for American Research.
1986b   Plainware Ceramics. In "Archaeological Investigations at the Tanque Verde Wash Site: A Middle Rincon Settlement in the Eastern Tucson Basin," by Mark Elson. *Institute for American Research Anthropological Papers* 7: 181–232. Tucson: Institute for American Research.

HEIDKE, JAMES, AND MIRIAM STARK
1994   Standardized Theories and Specialized Production: A View from the Tonto Basin. Paper presented at the 59th annual meeting of the Society for American Archaeology, Anaheim.

HERBICH, INGRID
1987   Learning Patterns, Potter Interaction, and Ceramic Style among the Luo of Kenya. *The African Archaeological Review* 5: 193–204.

HILL, JAMES N.
1965   Broken K: A Prehistoric Society in Eastern Arizona. MS, Doctoral Dissertation, University of Arizona, Tucson.
1968   Broken K Pueblo: Patterns of Form and Function. In *New Perspectives in Archaeology*, edited by Sally R. Binford and Lewis R. Binford, pp. 103–142. Chicago: Aldine.
1970   Broken K Pueblo: Prehistoric Social Organization in the American Southwest. *Anthropological Papers of the University of Arizona* 18. Tucson: University of Arizona Press.

HODDER, IAN
1982a   *Symbols in Action: Ethnoarchaeological Studies of Material Culture*. Cambridge: Cambridge University Press.
1982b   Sequences of Structural Change in the Dutch Neolithic. In *Symbolic and Structural Archaeology*, edited by Ian Hodder, pp. 177–192. Cambridge: Cambridge University Press.
1985   Post-processual Archaeology. In *Advances in Archaeological Method and Theory*, Vol. 8, edited by Michael B. Schiffer, pp. 1–26. Orlando: Academic Press.
1986   *Reading the Past*. Cambridge: Cambridge University Press.

HOLBROOK, SALLY J., AND MICHAEL W. GRAVES
1982   Modern Environment of the Grasshopper Region. In

HOLBROOK, SALLY J., AND MICHAEL W. GRAVES (Continued)
"Multidisciplinary Research at Grasshopper Pueblo, Arizona," edited by William A. Longacre, Sally J. Holbrook, and Michael W. Graves. *Anthropological Papers of the University of Arizona* 40: 5–12. Tucson: University of Arizona Press.

HOLMES, WILLIAM J.
1886   Pottery of the Ancient Pueblos. *Bureau of American Ethnology, 4th Annual Report, 1882–1883.* Washington: Smithsonian Institution.

HOUGH, WALTER
1930   Exploration of Ruins in the White Mountain Apache Indian Reservation, Arizona. *Proceedings of the U.S. National Museum* 78(2856): 1–21. Washington.

HOWARD, HILARY
1981   In the Wake of Distribution: Towards an Integrated Approach to Ceramic Studies in Prehistoric Britain. In "Production and Distribution: A Ceramic Viewpoint," edited by Hilary Howard and Elaine Morris. *BAR International Series* 120. Oxford.
1982   Clay and the Archaeologist. In "Current Research in Ceramics: Thin-section Studies," edited by Ian C. Freestone, Catherine Johns, and Tim Potter, pp. 145–158. *The British Museum Seminar 1980.* London: The British Museum.

JARMAN, M. R.
1972   A Territorial Model in Archaeology: A Behavioral and Geographical Approach. In *Models in Archaeology*, edited by David L. Clarke, pp. 705–733. London: Methuen.

JERNIGAN, WESLEY
1982   The White Mound–Kiatuthlanna–Red Mesa Stylistic Tradition. In "Cholla Project Archaeology: Ceramic Studies," edited by J. Jefferson Reid. *Arizona State Museum Archaeological Series* 161(5): 39–427. Tucson: Arizona State Museum, University of Arizona.
1986   A Non-hierarchical Approach to Ceramic Decoration Analysis: A Southwestern Example. *American Antiquity* 51(1): 3–20.

JOHNSON, ALFRED E.
1965   The Development of the Western Pueblo Culture. MS, Doctoral Dissertation, University of Arizona, Tucson.

JOHNSON, GREGORY
1989   Dynamics of Southwest Prehistory: Far Outside-Looking In. In *Dynamics of Southwest Prehistory*, edited by Linda S. Cordell and George J. Gumerman, pp. 371–390. Washington: Smithsonian Institution Press.

JUDD, NEIL M.
1954   The Material Culture of Pueblo Bonito. *Smithsonian Miscellaneous Collections* 124. Washington: Smithsonian Institution.

JUDGE, W. JAMES
1979   The Development of a Complex Cultural Ecosystem in the Chaco Basin, New Mexico. In *Proceedings of the First Conference on Scientific Research in the National Parks*, edited by Robert M. Linn, pp. 901–905. Washington.

KELSO, GERALD K.
1982   Two Pollen Profiles from Grasshopper Pueblo. In "Multidisciplinary Research at Grasshopper Pueblo, Arizona," edited by William A. Longacre, Sally J. Holbrook, and Michael W. Graves. *Anthropological Papers of the University of Arizona* 40: 106–109. Tucson: University of Arizona Press.

KIDDER, ALFRED V.
1924   *An Introduction to the Study of Southwestern Archaeology, with a Preliminary Account of the Excavations at Pecos.* Published for the Department of Archaeology, Phillips Academy. New Haven: Yale University Press.
1936   Introduction. In *The Pottery of Pecos*, Vol. 2, by Alfred V. Kidder and Anna O. Shepard, pp. xvii–xxxi. Published for the Department of Archaeology, Phillips Academy. New Haven: Yale University Press.

KINTIGH, KEITH W.
1979   Social Structure, the Structure of Style, and Stylistic Patterns in Cibola Pottery. MS on file, Department of Anthropology, University of Michigan, Ann Arbor.
1985   Social Structure, the Structure of Style, and Stylistic Patterns in Cibola Pottery. In *Decoding Prehistoric Ceramics*, edited by Ben A. Nelson, pp. 36–74. Carbondale: Southern Illinois University Press.

KROEBER, ALFRED L.
1916   Zuni Potsherds. *Anthropological Papers of the American Museum of Natural History* 18(1): 1–37. New York: American Museum of Natural History.
1963   *Styles and Civilizations.* Ithaca: Cornell University Press.

LANGE, RICHARD C., AND STEPHEN GERMICK
1992   *Proceedings of the Second Salado Conference, Globe, AZ 1992.* Phoenix: Arizona Archaeological Society.

LATHRAP, DONALD
1983   Recent Shipibo-Conibo Ceramics and Their Implications for Archaeological Interpretation. In *Structure and Cognition in Art*, edited by Dorothy K. Washburn, pp. 25–39. Cambridge: Cambridge University Press.

LEBLANC, STEPHEN A.
1982   Temporal Change in Mogollon Ceramics. In "Southwestern Ceramics: A Comparative Review," edited by Albert H. Schroeder. *The Arizona Archaeologist* 15: 107–128. Phoenix: Arizona Archaeological Society.

LEBLANC, STEPHEN A., AND BEN A. NELSON
1976   The Salado in Southwestern New Mexico. *The Kiva* 42(1): 71–80.

LEBLANC, STEPHEN A., AND MICHAEL WHALEN
1980   An Archaeological Synthesis of South Central and

Southwestern New Mexico. MS on file, Office of Contract Archaeology, University of New Mexico, Albuquerque.

LECHTMAN, HEATHER
1977   Style in Technology - Some Early Thoughts. In *Material Culture: Styles, Organization, and Dynamics of Technology*, edited by Heather Lechtman and Robert S. Merrill, pp. 3–20. New York: West Press.

LEKSON, STEPHEN H.
1988   Regional Systematics in the Later Prehistory of Southern New Mexico. In *Fourth Jornada Mogollon Conference, Collected Papers*, edited by Meliha S. Duran and Karl W. Laumbach, pp. 1–36. Tularosa, New Mexico: Human Systems Research.

LEONE, MARK P.
1968   Neolithic Economic Autonomy and Sense of Distance. *Science* 129: 1150–1151.

LIGHTFOOT, KENT G., AND ROBERTA JEWETT
1984   Late Prehistoric Ceramic Distributions in East-Central Arizona: An Examination of Cibola Whiteware, White Mountain Redware, and Salado Redware. In "Regional Analysis of Prehistoric Ceramic Variation: Contemporary Studies of the Cibola Whitewares," edited by Alan P. Sullivan III and Jeffrey L. Hantman. *Arizona State University Anthropological Research Papers* 31: 36–73. Tempe: Arizona State University.

LINDAUER, OWEN
In   Explaining White Wares in the Tonto Basin: Broad
Press   Scale Exchange, Emulation, or Both? *Kiva* (1995).

LINDSAY, ALEXANDER J.
1969   The Tsegi Phase of the Kayenta Cultural Tradition in Northeastern Arizona. MS, Doctoral Dissertation, University of Arizona, Tucson.
1987   Anasazi Population Movements to Southeastern Arizona. *American Archeology* 6(3): 190–198.

LINDSAY, ALEXANDER J., AND CALVIN JENNINGS
1968   Salado Redware Conference: Ninth Southwestern Ceramic Seminar. *Museum of Northern Arizona Ceramic Series* 4. Flagstaff: Northern Arizona Society of Science and Art.

LINNÉ, SIGVALD
1925   The Technique of South American Ceramics. Handlingar (Kungl. Vetenskaps-och Vitterhets-samhalles) 4 földjen, Ser A. Bd. 29(5). Gotenberg.

LOMBARD, JAMES
1985   Temper Composition of the Valencia Site Plainwares. In "Excavations at the Valencia Site: A Preclassic Hohokam Village in the Southern Tucson Basin," edited by William H. Doelle. *Institute for American Research Anthropological Papers* 3: 297–304. Tucson: Institute for American Research.
1986   A Petrographic Analysis of Ceramics from the West Branch Site. In "Archaeological Investigations at the West Branch Site: Early and Middle Rincon Occupation in the Southern Tucson Basin," edited by

Frederick W. Huntington. *Institute for American Research Anthropological Papers* 5: 429–444. Tucson: Institute for American Research.

LONGACRE, WILLIAM A.
1961   An Archaeological Survey in the Upper Little Colorado Drainage of East-Central Arizona. In "Mineral Creek Site and Hooper Ranch Pueblo, Eastern Arizona," edited by Paul S. Martin, John B. Rinaldo, and William A. Longacre. *Fieldiana: Anthropology* 52: 147–163. Chicago: Chicago Museum of Natural History.
1964   Sociological Implications of the Ceramic Analysis. In "Chapters in the Prehistory of Eastern Arizona, II," edited by Paul S. Martin and others. *Fieldiana: Anthropology* 55: 155–170. Chicago: Chicago Museum of Natural History.
1970   Archaeology as Anthropology: A Case Study. *Anthropological Papers of the University of Arizona* 17. Tucson: University of Arizona Press.

LONGACRE, WILLIAM A., AND J. JEFFERSON REID
1974   The University of Arizona Archaeological Field School at Grasshopper: Eleven Years of Multidisciplinary Research and Teaching. *The Kiva* 40(1–2): 3–38.

LORENTZEN, LEON
1988   The Burning and Filling of a Room by Prehistoric Peoples. MS on file, Department of Anthropology, University of Arizona, Tucson.

LOWE, CHARLES H., Editor
1964   *The Vertebrates of Arizona*. Tucson: University of Arizona Press.

MARTIN, PAUL S.
1943   The SU Site: Excavations at a Mogollon Village, Western New Mexico, Second Season, 1941. *Field Museum of Natural History Anthropological Series* 32(2). Chicago: Field Museum of Natural History.

MARTIN, PAUL S., AND JOHN B. RINALDO
1940   The SU Site, Excavations at a Mogollon Village, Western New Mexico, 1939. *Field Museum of Natural History Anthropological Series* 32(1). Chicago: Field Museum of Natural History.
1950   Sites of the Reserve Phase: Pine Lawn Valley, Western New Mexico. *Fieldiana: Anthropology* 38(3). Chicago: Chicago Natural History Museum.

MARTIN, PAUL S., JOHN B. RINALDO, AND ERNST ANTEVS
1949   Cochise and Mogollon Sites, Pine Lawn Valley, Western New Mexico. *Fieldiana: Anthropology* 38(1). Chicago: Chicago Natural History Museum.

MARTIN, PAUL S., JOHN B. RINALDO,
AND WILLIAM A. LONGACRE
1961   Mineral Creek Site and Hooper Ranch Pueblo, Eastern Arizona. *Fieldiana: Anthropology* 52. Chicago: Chicago Natural History Museum.

MATHUR, K. K.
1967   *Nicobar Islands*. New Delhi: National Book Trust.

MATSON, FREDERICK R.
1965   [Editor] *Ceramics and Man*. Chicago: Aldine.

MATSON, FREDERICK R. (Continued)
1970   Some Aspects of Ceramic Technology. In *Science in Archaeology: A Survey of Progress and Research*, edited by Don Brothwell and Eric Higgs, pp. 592–602. New York: Praeger.

MAUER, MICHAEL D.
1970   Cibicue Polychrome, A Fourteenth Century Ceramic Type from East-Central Arizona. MS, Master's Thesis, Department of Anthropology, University of Arizona, Tucson.

MAYRO, LINDA L., STEPHANIE M. WHITTLESEY, AND J. JEFFERSON REID
1976   Observations on the Salado Presence at Grasshopper Pueblo. *The Kiva* 42(1): 85–94.

MC.GREGOR, JOHN C.
1941   *Southwestern Archaeology*. New York: John Wiley and Sons.
1965   *Southwestern Archaeology*. 2nd Edition. Urbana: University of Illinois Press.

MCGUIRE, RANDALL H.
1975   Central Heights: A Small Salado Site near Globe, Arizona. MS on file, Arizona State Museum, University of Arizona, Tucson.

MERA, HARRY P.
1934   Observations on the Archaeology of the Petrified Forest National Monument. *Laboratory of Anthropology Technical Series, Bulletin* 7. Santa Fe: Laboratory of Anthropology.

MIDDLETON, ANDREW P., IAN C. FREESTONE, AND MORWEN N. LEESE
1985   Textural Analysis of Ceramic Thin Sections: Evaluations of Grain Sampling Procedures. *Archaeometry* 27(1): 64–74.

MILLS, BARBARA J., AND JAMES VINT
1991   Settlement Stability and the Organization of Late Prehistoric–Early Historic Ceramic Production in the Zuni Area. Paper presented at the 56th annual meeting of the Society for American Archaeology, New Orleans.

MONTGOMERY, BARBARA K.
1992   Understanding the Formation of the Archaeological Record: Ceramic Variability at Chodistaas Pueblo, Arizona. MS, Doctoral Dissertation, University of Arizona, Tucson.
1993   Ceramic Analysis as a Tool for Discovering Processes of Pueblo Abandonment. In *Abandonment of Settlements and Regions: Ethnoarchaeological and Archaeological Approaches*, edited by Catherine M. Cameron and Steve A. Tomka, pp. 157–164. Cambridge: Cambridge University Press.

MONTGOMERY, BARBARA K., AND J. JEFFERSON REID
1990   An Instance of Rapid Ceramic Change in the American Southwest. *American Antiquity* 55(1): 88–97.
1994   The Brown and the Gray: People, Pots, and Population Movement in East-Central Arizona. Paper presented at the 59th annual meeting of the Society for American Archaeology, Anaheim.

MOORE, RICHARD T.
1968   Mineral Deposits of the Fort Apache Indian Reservation, Arizona. *Arizona State Bureau of Mines Bulletin* 177. Tucson: Arizona State Bureau of Mines.

MORRIS, EARL H.
1939   Archaeological Studies in the La Plata District, Southwestern Colorado and Northwestern New Mexico. *Carnegie Institution of Washington, Publication* 519. Washington: Carnegie Institution.

MUNSELL COLOR COMPANY
1975   *Munsell Soil Color Charts*. Baltimore: Munsell Color Company.

NEALE, WALTER
1977   Reciprocity and Redistribution in an Indian Village. In *Peasant Livelihood: Studies in Economic Anthropology and Cultural Ecology*, edited by Rhonda Halperin and James Daw, pp. 147–163. New York: St. Martin's Press.

NEFF, HECTOR, Editor
1992   Chemical Characterization of Ceramic Pastes in Archaeology. *Monographs in World Archaeology* 7. Madison: Prehistory Press.

NEFF, HECTOR, RONALD L. BISHOP, AND EDWARD V. SAYRE
1988   Simulation Approach to the Problem of Tempering in Compositional Studies of Archaeological Ceramics. *Journal of Archaeological Science* 15: 159–172.
1989   More Observations on the Problem of Tempering in Compositional Studies of Archaeological Ceramics. *Journal of Archaeological Science* 16: 57–69.

NEILY, ROBERT B.
1988   Archaeological Investigations in the Snowflake-Mesa Redonda Area, East-Central Arizona: The Apache–Navajo South Project. *Arizona State Museum Archaeological Series* 173. Tucson: Arizona State Museum, University of Arizona.

NEITZEL, JILL E., AND RONALD L. BISHOP
1990   Neutron Activation of Dogoszhi Style Ceramics: Production and Exchange in the Chacoan Regional System. *Kiva* 56(1): 67–86.

NELSON, BEN A., Editor
1985   *Decoding Prehistoric Ceramics*. Carbondale: Southern Illinois University Press.

NELSON, GLENN C.
1984   *Ceramics: A Potter's Handbook*. 5th Edition. New York: CBS College Publishing.

NELSON, NELS C.
1916   Chronology of the Tano Ruins, New Mexico. *American Anthropologist* 18(2): 159–180.

NEUPERT, MARK A.
1994   Strength Testing Archaeological Ceramics: A New Perspective. *American Antiquity* 59(4). (In Press.)

NICKLIN, KEITH
1979   The Location of Pottery Manufacture. *Man* 14: 436–458.

NORDENSKIÖLD, GUSTAV E. A.
1893   *The Cliff Dwellers of the Mesa Verde, Southwestern Colorado*. Stockholm: P. A. Norstedt and Söner.

OLIN, JACQUELINE S., AND ALAN D. FRANKLIN, Editors
1982   *Archaeological Ceramics*. Washington: Smithsonian Institution Press.

ORLOVE, BENJAMIN
1977   Inequality among Peasants: The Forms and Uses of Reciprocal Exchange in Andean Peru. In *Peasant Livelihood: Studies in Economic Anthropology and Cultural Ecology*, edited by Rhonda Halperin and James Daw, pp. 201–214. New York: St. Martin's Press.

PEACOCK, DAVID P. S.
1970   The Scientific Analysis of Ancient Ceramics: A Review. *World Archaeology* 1(3): 375–389.

PEIRCE, H. WESLEY
1985   Arizona's Backbone: The Transition Zone. *Fieldnotes of the Arizona Bureau of Geology and Mineral Technology* 15(3): 1–6.

PERLMAN, ISADORE, AND F. ASARO
1969   Pottery Analysis by Neutron Activation. *Archaeometry* 11: 21–53.

PLOG, FRED T.
1977   Modeling Economic Exchange. In *Exchange Systems in Prehistory*, edited by Timothy K. Earle and Jonathon E. Ericson, pp. 127–140. New York: Academic Press.
1983   Political and Economic Alliances on the Colorado Plateau, A.D. 400–1450. In *Advances in World Archaeology* 2: 289–330.
1989   The Sinagua and Their Relations. In *Dynamics of Southwest Prehistory*, edited by Linda S. Cordell and George J. Gumerman, pp. 263–292. Washington: Smithsonian Institution Press.

PLOG, FRED T., JAMES N. HILL,
AND DWIGHT W. READ, Editors
1976   Chevelon Archaeological Research Project, 1971-72: *Monograph 2, Archaeological Survey*. Los Angeles: University of California.

PLOG, STEPHEN
1976   Measurement of Prehistoric Interaction between Communities. In *The Early Mesoamerican Village*, edited by Kent Flannery, pp. 255–272. New York: Academic Press.
1977   A Multivariate Approach to the Explanation of Ceramic Design Variation. MS, Doctoral Dissertation, Department of Anthropology, University of Michigan, Ann Arbor.
1978   Social Interaction and Stylistic Similarity: A Reanalysis. In *Advances in Archaeological Method and Theory*, Vol. 1, edited by Michael B. Schiffer, pp. 143–182. New York: Academic Press.
1980   *Stylistic Variation in Prehistoric Ceramics*. Cambridge: Cambridge University Press.
1983   Analysis of Style in Artifacts. *Annual Review of Anthropology* 12: 125–142.

POLANYI, KARL
1957   The Economy as Instituted Process. In *Trade and Market in the Early Empires*, edited by Karl Polanyi, Conrad Arensberg, and Harry Pearson, pp. 243–269. Glencoe, Illinois: Free Press.

POMEROY, JOHN A.
1962   A Study of Black-on-white Painted Pottery in the Tonto Basin, Arizona. MS, Master's Thesis, Department of Anthropology, University of Arizona, Tucson.

RANDS, ROBERT L., AND RONALD L. BISHOP
1980   Resource Procurement Zones and Patterns of Ceramic Exchange in the Palenque Region, Mexico. In "Models and Methods of Regional Exchange," edited by Robert E. Fry. *Society for American Archaeology Papers* 1: 19–46.

RAVESLOOT, JOHN C.
1987   The Archaeology of the San Javier Bridge Site (AZ BB:13:14), Tucson Basin, Southwestern Arizona. *Arizona State Museum Archaeological Series* 171. Tucson: Arizona State Museum, University of Arizona.

REDMAN, CHARLES L.
1977   The "Analytical Individual" and Prehistoric Style Variability. In *The Individual in Prehistory: Studies of Variability in Style and Prehistoric Technologies*, edited by James N. Hill and Joel Gunn, pp. 41–53. New York: Academic Press.
1978   Multivariate Artifact Analysis: A Basis for Multidimensional Interpretations. In *Social Archaeology: Beyond Subsistence and Dating*, edited by Charles L. Redman, pp. 159–192. New York: Academic Press.
1992   Pursuing Southwestern Social Complexity in the 1990s. In "Developing Perspectives on Tonto Basin Prehistory," edited by Charles L. Redman, Glen E. Rice, and Kathryn E. Pedrick. Roosevelt Monograph Series 2. *Anthropological Field Studies* 26: 5–10. Tempe: Arizona State University.

REED, ERIK K.
1942   Implications of the Mogollon Concept. *American Antiquity* 8(1): 27–32.
1948   The Western Pueblo Archaeological Complex. *El Palacio* 55(1): 9–15.
1950   Eastern-Central Arizona Archaeology in Relation to the Western Pueblos. *Southwestern Journal of Anthropology* 6(2): 120–138.
1958   Comment on Emil W. Haury's "Evidence at Point of Pines for a Prehistoric Migration from Northern Arizona." In "Migrations in New World Culture History," edited by Raymond H. Thompson. *University of Arizona Bulletin* 29(2), *Social Science Bulletin* 27: 7–8. Tucson: University of Arizona.
1980   Special Report on Review of Archaeological Survey Potsherd Collections, Petrified Forest National Monument, Arizona. In "An Archaeological Overview of Petrified Forest National Park," by Ivonne G. Steward. *Publications in Anthropology* 10: 191–221. Tucson: Western Archeological and Conservation Center, National Park Service.

REID, J. JEFFERSON
1973   *Growth and Response to Stress at Grasshopper Pueblo, Arizona.* Doctoral Dissertation, University of Arizona, Tucson. Ann Arbor: University Microfilms.
1982   [Editor] Cholla Project Archaeology. *Arizona State Museum Archaeological Series* 161. Tucson: Arizona State Museum, University of Arizona.
1984   What is Black-on-white and Vague All Over? In "Regional Analysis of Prehistoric Ceramic Variation: Contemporary Studies of the Cibola Whitewares," edited by Alan P. Sullivan III and Jeffrey L. Hantman. *Arizona State University Anthropological Research Papers* 31: 135–152. Tempe: Arizona State University.
1985   Formation Processes for the Practical Prehistorian: An Example from the Southeast. In *Structure and Process in Southeastern Archaeology*, edited by Roy S. Dickens, Jr., and H. Trawick Ward, pp. 11–33. Birmingham: University of Alabama Press.
1989   A Grasshopper Perspective on the Mogollon of the Arizona Mountains. In *Dynamics of Southwest Prehistory*, edited by Linda S. Cordell and George J. Gumerman, pp. 65–97. Washington: Smithsonian Institution Press.

REID, J. JEFFERSON, AND DAVID H. TUGGLE
1982   Cross-dating Cibola Whitewares. In "Cholla Project Archaeology: Ceramic Studies," edited by J. Jefferson Reid. *Arizona State Museum Archaeological Series* 161(5): 8–17. Tucson: Arizona State Museum, University of Arizona.
1988   Settlement Pattern and System in the Late Prehistory of the Grasshopper Region. Paper prepared for the Seminar "From Pueblo to Apache: The People of the Arizona Mountains." MS on file, Department of Anthropology, University of Arizona, Tucson.

REID, J. JEFFERSON, AND STEPHANIE WHITTLESEY
1982   Determining Functional Equivalence in Settlement Analysis. Paper presented at the 47th annual meeting of the Society for American Archaeology, Minneapolis.
1992   New Evidence for Dating Gila Polychrome. In *Proceedings of the Second Salado Conference, Globe, AZ 1992*, edited by Richard C. Lange and Stephen Germick, pp. 223–229. Phoenix: Arizona Archaeological Society.

REID, J. JEFFERSON, BARBARA K. MONTGOMERY, AND M. NIEVES ZEDEÑO
1989   The Birth of Roosevelt Redware. Paper prepared for the Fall Conference of the Arizona Archaeological Council, Phoenix. MS on file, Department of Anthropology, University of Arizona, Tucson.

REID, J. JEFFERSON, BARBARA K. MONTGOMERY, M. NIEVES ZEDEÑO, AND MARK A. NEUPERT
1992   The Origin of Roosevelt Redware. In *Proceedings of the Second Salado Conference, Globe, AZ 1992*, edited by Richard C. Lange and Stephen Germick,

pp. 212–215. Phoenix: Arizona Archaeological Society.

REID, J. JEFFERSON, DAVID H. TUGGLE, JOHN R. WELCH, BARBARA K. MONTGOMERY, AND M. NIEVES ZEDEÑO
1993   Demographic Overview in the Late Pueblo III Period in the Mountains of East-Central Arizona. MS on file, Department of Anthropology, University of Arizona, Tucson.

RENFREW, COLIN
1975   Trade as Action at a Distance: Questions of Integration and Communication. In *Ancient Civilization and Trade*, edited by Jeremy Sabloff and C. Carl Lamberg-Karlovsky, pp. 3–59. Albuquerque: University of New Mexico Press.

RICE, PRUDENCE M.
1976   Rethinking the Ware Concept. *American Antiquity* 41(4): 538–543.
1980   Peten Postclassic Pottery Production and Exchange: A View From Macanche. In "Models and Methods in Regional Exchange," edited by Robert E. Fry. *Society for American Archaeology Papers* 1: 67–82.
1982   Pottery Production, Classification, and the Role of Physicochemical Analysis. In *Archaeological Ceramics*, edited by Jacqueline S. Olin and Alan D. Franklin, pp. 47–56. Washington: Smithsonian Institution Press.
1984   Change and Conservatism in Pottery Producing Systems. In *The Many Dimensions of Pottery: Ceramics in Archaeology and Anthropology*, edited by Sander E. van der Leeuw and Alison C. Pritchard, pp. 231–293. CINGULA 7. Amsterdam: Institute for Pre- and Proto-history, University of Amsterdam.
1987   *Pottery Analysis: A Source Book.* Chicago: University of Chicago Press.

RIES, HEINRICH
1927   *Clays, Their Occurrence, Properties, and Uses, with Special Reference to Those of the United States of Canada.* 3rd Edition. New York: John Wiley.

RINALDO, JOHN B., AND ELAINE A. BLUHM
1956   Late Mogollon Pottery Types. *Fieldiana: Anthropology* 36(7). Chicago: Chicago Natural History Museum.

ROBERTS, FRANK H. H., JR.
1937   Archaeology in the Southwest. *American Antiquity* 3(1): 3–33.

ROGERS, MALCOLM J.
1936   Yuman Pottery Making. *San Diego Museum Papers* 2. San Diego: San Diego Museum.

ROHN, ARTHUR H.
1971   Mug House, Mesa Verde National Park, Colorado. *U.S. National Park Service Archaeological Research Series* 7-D. Washington: Department of the Interior.

RUGGE, DALE, AND DAVID E. DOYEL
1980   Petrographic Analysis of Ceramics from Dead Valley. In "Prehistory in Dead Valley, East-Central Arizona: The TG&E Springerville Project," edited by David E. Doyel and Sharon Debowski. *Arizona*

State Museum Archaeological Series 144: 189–203. Tucson: Arizona State Museum, University of Arizona.

RYE, OWEN
1981 Pottery Technology: Principles and Reconstruction. *Manuals on Archaeology* 4. Washington: Taraxacum.

SAHLINS, MARSHALL D.
1965 On the Sociology of Primitive Exchange. In "The Relevance of Models for Social Anthropology," edited by M. Banton. *Association of Social Anthropology Monograph* 1: 15–56. London: Tavistock.

SCARBOROUGH, ROBERT, AND IZUMI SHIMADA
1974 Geological Analysis of Wall Composition at Grasshopper with Behavioral Implications. *The Kiva* 40(1–2): 49–66.

SCHIFFER, MICHAEL B.
1987 *Formation Processes of the Archaeological Record.* Albuquerque: University of New Mexico Press.

SCHIFFER, MICHAEL B., AND JAMES M. SKIBO
1987 Theory and Experiment in the Study of Technological Change. *Current Anthropology* 28(5): 595–619.

SCHROEDER, ALBERT H.
1952 *The Excavations at Willow Beach, Arizona, 1950.* Santa Fe: National Park Service.
1982 [Editor] Southwestern Ceramics: A Comparative Review. *The Arizona Archaeologist* 15. Phoenix: Arizona Archaeological Society.

SHANKS, MICHAEL, AND CHRISTOPHER TILLEY
1987a *Social Theory and Archaeology.* Cambridge: Polity Press.
1987b Re-constructing Archaeology. Cambridge: Cambridge University Press.

SHEPARD, ANNA O.
1936 The Technology of Pecos Pottery. In *The Pottery of Pecos*, Vol. 2, by Alfred V. Kidder and Anna O. Shepard, pp. 389–587. Published for the Department of Archaeology, Phillips Academy. New Haven: Yale University Press.
1942 Rio Grande Glaze Paint Ware, A Study Illustrating the Place of Ceramic Technological Analyses. *Carnegie Institution of Washington, Publication* 573. Washington: Carnegie Institution.
1954 Rebuttal. In "The Material Culture of Pueblo Bonito," by Neil Judd. *Smithsonian Miscellaneous Collections* 124: 236–238. Washington: Smithsonian Institution.
1956 Ceramics for the Archaeologist. *Carnegie Institution of Washington, Publication* 609. Washington: Carnegie Institution.
1965 Rio Grande Glaze-paint Pottery: A Test of Petrographic Analysis. In *Ceramics and Man*, edited by Frederick R. Matson, pp. 62–87. Chicago: Aldine.
1985 *Ceramics for the Archaeologist.* 6th Edition. Washington: Carnegie Institution.

SIMON, ARLYN W., JEAN-CHRISTOPE KOMOROWSKI, AND JAMES H. BURTON
1992 Patterns of Production and Distribution of Salado Wares as a Measure of Complexity. In "Developing Perspectives on Tonto Basin Prehistory," edited by Charles L. Redman, Glen E. Rice, and Kathryn E. Pedrick. Roosevelt Monograph Series 2. *Anthropological Field Studies* 26: 61–76. Tempe: Arizona State University.

SKIBO, JAMES M., AND MICHAEL B. SCHIFFER
1987 The Effects of Water on Processes of Ceramic Abrasion. *Journal of Archaeological Science* 14: 83–96.

SKIBO, JAMES M., MICHAEL B. SCHIFFER, AND NANCY KOWALSKI
1989 Ceramic Style Analysis in Archaeology and Ethnoarchaeology: Bridging the Analytical Gap. *Journal of Anthropological Archaeology* 8: 338–409.

SKIBO, JAMES M., MICHAEL B. SCHIFFER, AND KENNETH C. REID
1989 Organic-tempered Pottery: An Experimental Study. *American Antiquity* 54(1): 122–146.

SMITH, WATSON
1971 Painted Ceramics of the Western Mound at Awatovi. *Papers of the Peabody Museum of Archaeology and Ethnology, Harvard University,* 38. Cambridge: Peabody Museum.

SNEATH PETER H., AND ROBERT R. SOKAL
1973 *Numerical Taxonomy.* San Francisco: W. H. Freeman.

SPIER, LESLIE
1917 An Outline for a Chronology of Zuni Ruins. *Anthropological Papers of the American Museum of Natural History* 18(3): 207–331. New York: American Museum of Natural History.

STAFFORD, C. RUSSELL, AND GLEN E. RICE
1980 Studies in the Prehistory of the Forestdale Region, Arizona. *Anthropological Field Studies* 1. Tempe: Arizona State University.

STANISLAWSKI, MICHAEL B.
1973 Book Review of "Archaeology as Anthropology: A Case Study," by William A. Longacre. *American Antiquity* 38(1): 117–122.

STEVENSON, JAMES
1883 Illustrated Catalogue of the Collections Obtained from the Indians of New Mexico and Arizona in 1879. *Bureau of American Ethnology, 2nd Annual Report, 1880.* Washington: Smithsonian Institution.

STEVENSON, MATILDA C.
1904 The Zuni Indians: Their Mythology, Esoteric Fraternities, and Ceremonies. *Bureau of American Ethnology, 23rd Annual Report, 1901-1902.* Washington: Smithsonian Institution.

STOFFLE, RICHARD, MICHAEL EVANS, M. NIEVES ZEDEÑO, BRENT STOFFLE, AND CINDY KESEL
1994 American Indians and Fajada Butte: An Ethnographic Overview and Assessment for Fajada Butte and

STOFFLE, RICHARD, MICHAEL EVANS, M. NIEVES ZEDEÑO,
BRENT STOFFLE, AND CINDY KESEL (Continued)
   Traditional Use (Ethnobotanical) Study for Chaco Canyon National Historical Park. Report prepared for the New Mexico State Historic Preservation Division and the National Park Service Southwest Region. MS on file, Bureau of Applied Research in Anthropology, University of Arizona, Tucson.

STOLTMAN, JAMES B.
1989   A Quantitative Approach to the Petrographic Analysis of Ceramic Thin-sections. *American Antiquity* 54(1): 147–160.

STREETEN, ANTHONY D.
1982   Textural Analysis: An Approach to the Characterization of Sand-tempered Ceramics. In "Current Research in Ceramics: Thin-section Studies," edited by Ian C. Freestone, Catherine Johns, and Tim Potter, pp. 123–134. *The British Museum Seminar 1980*. London: The British Museum.

SULLIVAN III, ALAN P.
1980   Prehistoric Settlement Variability in the Grasshopper Region, East-Central Arizona. MS, Doctoral Dissertation, University of Arizona, Tucson.
1984   Design Styles and Cibola Whiteware: Examples from the Grasshopper Area, East-Central Arizona. In "Regional Analysis of Prehistoric Ceramic Variation: Contemporary Studies of the Cibola Whitewares," edited by Alan P. Sullivan III and Jeffrey L. Hantman. *Arizona State University Anthropological Research Papers* 31: 74–93. Tempe: Arizona State University.
1988   Prehistoric Southwestern Ceramic Manufacture: Limitations of Current Evidence. *American Antiquity* 53(1): 23–35.

SULLIVAN III, ALAN P., AND JEFFREY L. HANTMAN, Editors
1984   Regional Analysis of Prehistoric Ceramic Variation: Contemporary Studies of the Cibola Whitewares. *Arizona State University Anthropological Research Papers* 31. Tempe: Arizona State University.

TALBOT, P. T.
1984   Prospecting for Clay. *Bulletin of the American Ceramic Society* 63: 1047–1050.

TANI, MASAKASU
1989   Chemical Variability in Ceramics. An Experimental Assessment of Three Potential Sources. MS on file, Department of Anthropology, University of Arizona, Tucson.

TEAGUE, LYNN S., AND PATRICIA L. CROWN
1983   Hohokam Archaeology Along the Salt-Gila Aqueduct–Central Arizona. *Arizona State Museum Archaeological Series* 150. Tucson: Arizona State Museum, University of Arizona.

THOMPSON, RAYMOND H.
1958   Modern Yucatecan Maya Pottery Making. *Memoirs of the Society for American Archaeology* 15.
1991   Shepard, Kidder, and Carnegie. In *Ceramic Analysis and Social Inference in American Archaeology: The Ceramic Legacy of Anna O. Shepard*, edited by Ronald L. Bishop and Frederick Lange, pp. 11–41. Boulder: University of Colorado Press.

THOMPSON, RAYMOND H., AND WILLIAM A. LONGACRE
1966   The University of Arizona Archaeological Field School at Grasshopper, East-Central Arizona. *The Kiva* 31(4): 255–275.

TITE, M. S.
1972   *Methods of Physical Examination in Archaeology*. London: Seminar Press.

TOLL III, H. WOLCOTT
1981   Ceramic Comparisons Concerning Redistribution in Chaco Canyon, New Mexico. In "Production and Distribution: A Ceramic Viewpoint," edited by Hilary Howard and Elaine Morris, pp. 83–122. *BAR International Series* 120: 83–122. Oxford.
1985   *Pottery, Production, Public Architecture, and the Chaco Anasazi System*. Doctoral Dissertation, University of Colorado, Boulder. Ann Arbor: University Microfilms International.

TOLL III, H. WOLCOTT, THOMAS C. WINDES, AND PETER J. MCKENNA
1980   Late Ceramic Patterns in Chaco Canyon: The Pragmatics of Modeling Ceramic Exchange. In "Models and Methods in Regional Exchange," edited by Robert E. Fry. *Society for American Archaeology Papers* 1: 95–118.

TRIADAN, DANIELA
1989   Defining Local Ceramic Production at Grasshopper Pueblo, Arizona. Master's Thesis, Freie Universität Berlin. MS on file, Arizona State Museum, University of Arizona, Tucson.
1994   White Mountain Red Ware: An Exotic Trade Item or a Local Commodity? Perspectives from the Grasshopper Region, Arizona. Paper presented at the 59th annual meeting of the Society for American Archaeology, Anaheim.

TUGGLE, H. DAVID
1970   Prehistoric Community Relationships in East-Central Arizona. MS, Doctoral Dissertation, University of Arizona, Tucson.

TUGGLE, H. DAVID, KEITH W. KINTIGH, AND J. JEFFERSON REID
1982   Trace-element Analysis of White Wares. In "Cholla Project Archaeology: Ceramic Studies," edited by J. Jefferson Reid. *Arizona State Museum Archaeological Series* 161(5): 22–38. Tucson: Arizona State Museum, University of Arizona.

TUGGLE, H. DAVID, J. JEFFERSON REID, AND ROBERT C. COLE, JR.
1984   Fourteenth Century Mogollon Agriculture in the Grasshopper Region of Arizona. In "Prehistoric Agricultural Strategies in the Southwest," edited by Suzanne K. Fish and Paul R. Fish. *Arizona State University Anthropological Research Papers* 33: 101–110. Tempe: Arizona State University.

TURNER II, CHRISTY G., AND LAUREL LOFGREN
1966   Household Size of Prehistoric Western Pueblo In-

dians. *Southwestern Journal of Anthropology* 22(2): 117–132.

UPHAM, STEADMAN
1982 *Polities and Power: An Economic and Political History of the Western Pueblo.* New York: Academic Press.

UPHAM, STEADMAN, AND FRED T. PLOG
1986 The Interpretation of Political Complexity in the Central and Northern Southwest: Toward a Mending of the Models. *Journal of Field Archaeology* 13: 223–238.

UPHAM, STEADMAN, KENT G. LIGHTFOOT, AND GARY M. FEINMAN
1981 Explaining Socially Determined Ceramic Distributions in the Prehistoric Plateau Southwest. *American Antiquity* 46(4): 822–833.

VINT, JAMES M., AND JEFFERY J. BURTON
1990 Ceramics. In *Archaeological Investigations at Puerco Ruin, Petrified Forest National Park, Arizona*, by Jeffery J. Burton, pp. 97–126. Tucson: Western Archeological and Conservation Center, National Park Service.

WALKER, LINDA
1989 Workability and Firing Tests of Grasshopper Clays. Ms. on file, Department of Anthropology, University of Arizona. Tucson.

WALLACE, HENRY D.
1986 Rincon Phase Decorated Ceramics in the Tucson Basin - A Focus on the West Branch Site. *Institute for American Research Anthropological Papers* 1. Tucson: Institute for American Research.

WANDIBBA, SIMIYU
1982 Experiments on Textural Analysis. *Archaeometry* 24(1): 71–75.

WARREN, A. HELENE
1969 Tonque, One Pueblo's Glaze Pottery Industry Dominated Middle Rio Grande Commerce. *El Palacio* 76(2): 36–42.
1967 Petrographic Analyses of Pottery and Lithics. "An Archaeological Survey of the Chuska Valley and the Chaco Plateau, New Mexico, Part 1: Natural Science Studies," by Arthur H. Harris, James Schoenwetter, and A. Helene Warren. *Museum of New Mexico Research Records* 4. Santa Fe: Museum of New Mexico.

WASHBURN, DOROTHY K.
1977 A Symmetry Analysis of Upper Gila Area Ceramic Design. *Papers of the Peabody Museum of Archaeology and Ethnology, Harvard University*, 68. Cambridge: Peabody Museum.
1978 A Symmetry Classification of Pueblo Ceramic Design. In *Discovering Past Behavior: Experiments in the Archaeology of the American Southwest*, edited by Paul Grebinger, pp. 101–122. New York: Gordon and Breach.

WASHBURN, DOROTHY K., AND RICHARD V. N. AHLSTROM
1982 Review of "Stylistic Variation in Prehistoric Ceram-

ics: Design Analysis in the American Southwest," by Stephen Plog. *The Kiva* 48(1–2): 117–123.

WASLEY, WILLIAM W.
1952 The Late Pueblo Occupation at Point of Pines, East-Central Arizona. MS, Master's Thesis, Department of Anthropology, University of Arizona, Tucson.
1959 Cultural Implications of Style Trends in Southwestern Prehistoric Pottery: Basketmaker III to Pueblo II in West Central New Mexico. MS, Doctoral Dissertation, University of Arizona, Tucson.
1966 Classic Period Hohokam. Paper presented at the 31st annual meeting of the Society for American Archaeology, Reno.

WATSON, PATTY JO
1977 Design Analysis of Painted Pottery. *American Antiquity* 42(3): 381–393.

WEAVER, DONALD E., JR.
1976 Salado Influences in the Lower Salt River Valley. *The Kiva* 42(1): 17–26.

WEIGAND, PHIL C., GARMAN HARBOTTLE, AND EDWARD V. SAYRE
1977 Turquoise Sources and Source Analysis: Mesoamerica and the Southwestern U.S.A. In *Exchange Systems in Prehistory*, edited by Timothy K. Earle and Jonathon E. Ericson, pp.15–34. New York: Academic Press.

WELCH, JOHN R.
1991 Rapid Agricultural Commitment: Late Prehistoric Agrarian Ecology and Evolution in the Grasshopper Region, Arizona. Paper presented at the 1991 meeting of the Southwestern Anthropological Association, Tucson.

WENDORF, FRED
1953 Archaeological Studies in the Petrified Forest National Monument. *Museum of Northern Arizona Bulletin* 27. Flagstaff: Northern Arizona Society of Science and Art.

WEST, STEVEN
1990 Workability and Firing Tests of Grasshopper Clays and Temper. MS on file, Department of Anthropology, University of Arizona, Tucson.

WHALLON, ROBERT
1968 Investigations of Late Prehistoric Social Organization in New York State. In *New Perspectives in Archaeology*, edited by Sally R. Binford and Lewis R. Binford, pp. 223–244. Chicago: Aldine.

WHEAT, JOE BEN
1955 Mogollon Culture Prior to A.D. 1000. *Memoirs of the Society for American Archaeology* 10.

WHEAT, JOE BEN, JAMES C. GIFFORD, AND WILLIAM W. WASLEY
1958 Ceramic Variety, Type Cluster, and Ceramic System in Southwestern Pottery Analysis. *American Antiquity* 24(1): 34–47.

WHITE, DIANE, AND JAMES BURTON
1992 Pinto Polychrome: A Clue to the Origin of the Salado Polychromes. In *Proceedings of the Second Salado Conference, Globe, AZ 1992*, edited by

WHITE, DIANE, AND JAMES BURTON (Continued)
Richard C. Lange and Stephen Germick, pp. 216–222. Phoenix: Arizona Archaeological Society.

WHITTLESEY, STEPHANIE M.
1974   Identification of Imported Ceramics through Functional Analysis of Attributes. *The Kiva* 40(1–2): 101–112.
1978   Status and Death at Grasshopper Pueblo: Experiments toward an Archaeological Theory of Correlates. MS, Doctoral Dissertation, University of Arizona, Tucson.
1982a   Examination of Previous Work in the Q Ranch Region: Comparison and Analysis. In "Cholla Project Archaeology: The Q Ranch Region," edited by J. Jefferson Reid. *Arizona State Museum Archaeological Series* 161(3): 123–150. Tucson: Arizona State Museum, University of Arizona.
1982b   Vessel Thinning Techniques and Ethnic Identification. In "Cholla Project Archaeology: Ceramic Studies," edited by J. Jefferson Reid. *Arizona State Museum Archaeological Series* 161(5): 18–21. Tucson: Arizona State Museum, University of Arizona.

WHITTLESEY, STEPHANIE M., AND J. JEFFERSON REID
1982a   Cholla Project Settlement Summary. In "Cholla Project Archaeology: Introduction and Special Studies," edited by J. Jefferson Reid. *Arizona State Museum Archaeological Series* 161(1): 205–216. Tucson: Arizona State Museum, University of Arizona.
1982b   Cholla Project Perspectives on Salado. In "Cholla Project Archaeology: Introduction and Special Studies," edited by J. Jefferson Reid. *Arizona State Museum Archaeological Series* 161(1): 63–80. Tucson: Arizona State Museum, University of Arizona.

WILSON, C. DEAN
1988   An Evaluation of Individual Migration as an Explanation for the Presence of Smudged Ceramics in the Dolores Project Area. In *Dolores Archaeological Program: Supporting Studies: Additive and Reductive Technologies*, compiled by Eric Blinman, Carl J. Phagan, and Richard H. Wilshusen, pp. 425–433. Denver: Engineering and Research Center, Bureau of Reclamation, Department of the Interior.

WILSON, C. DEAN, AND ERIC BLINMAN
1988   Identification of Non-Mesa Verde Ceramics in Dolores Archaeological Program Collections. In *Dolores Archaeological Program: Supporting Studies: Additive and Reductive Technologies*, compiled by Eric Blinman, Carl J. Phagan, and Richard H. Wilshusen, pp. 363–371. Denver: Engineering and Research Center, Bureau of Reclamation, Department of the Interior.

WILSON, C. DEAN, VICKIE L. CLAY, AND ERIC BLINMAN
1988   Clay Resources and Resource Use In the Dolores Project Area. In *Dolores Archaeological Program: Supporting Studies: Additive and Reductive Technologies*, compiled by Eric Blinman, Carl J.

Phagan, and Richard H. Wilshusen, pp. 375–392. Denver: Engineering and Research Center, Bureau of Reclamation, Department of the Interior.

WILSON, JOHN P.
1976   An Early Pueblo II Design Style. *Awanyu* 4(2): 8–22.

WINDES, THOMAS C.
1977   Typology and Technology of Anasazi Ceramics. In *Settlement and Subsistence along the Lower Chaco River*, edited by Charles A. Reher, pp. 279–370. Albuquerque: University of New Mexico Press.
1984   A View of the Cibola Whiteware from Chaco Canyon. In "Regional Analysis of Prehistoric Ceramic Variation: Contemporary Studies of the Cibola Whitewares," edited by Alan P. Sullivan III and Jeffrey L. Hantman. *Arizona State University Anthropological Research Papers* 31: 94–119. Tempe: Arizona State University.

WINTERS, STEPHEN S.
1963   Geology of the Upper Supai Formation, Arizona. *Geological Society of America Memoir* 89.

WOBST, H. MARTIN
1977   Stylistic Behavior and Information Exchange. In "Papers for the Director: Research Essays in Honor of James B. Griffin," edited by Charles E. Cleland. *Anthropological Papers, Museum of Anthropology, University of Michigan* 61: 317–342. Ann Arbor: University of Michigan.

WOOD, J. SCOTT
1980   The Gentry Timber Sale: Behavioral Patterning and Predictability in the Upper Cherry Creek Area, Central Arizona. *The Kiva* 46(1–2): 99–119.

WOOD, J. SCOTT, AND MARTIN E. MCALLISTER
1982   The Salado: An Alternative View. In "Cholla Project Archaeology: Introduction and Special Studies," edited by J. Jefferson Reid. *Arizona State Museum Archaeological Series* 161(1): 81–95. Tucson: Arizona State Museum, University of Arizona.

WRIGHT, RITA P.
1984   Technology and Style in Ancient Ceramics. In *Ancient Technology to Modern Science*, Vol. 1, edited by W. David Kingery, pp. 5–27. Columbus, Ohio: The American Ceramic Society.

YOUNG, JON
1967   The Salado Culture in Southwestern Prehistory. MS, Doctoral Dissertation, University of Arizona, Tucson.

YOUNG, LISA, AND TAMY STONE
1990   The Thermal Properties of Textured Ceramics: An Experimental Study. *Journal of Field Archaeology* 17(2): 195–204.

ZASLOW, BERT
1977   Pattern Mathematics and Archaeology: A Guide to Analyzing Prehistoric Ceramic Decorations by Symmetry and Pattern Mathematics. In "Pattern Mathematics and Archaeology," by Bert Zaslow and Alfred E. Dittert, Jr. *Arizona State University*

Anthropological Research Papers 2. Tempe: Arizona State University.

ZASLOW, BERT, AND ALFRED E. DITTERT, JR.
  1977   Pattern Mathematics and Archaeology. *Arizona State University Anthropological Research Papers* 2. Tempe: Arizona State University.

ZEDEÑO, M. NIEVES
  1992   Roosevelt Black-on-white Revisited. In *Proceedings of the Second Salado Conference, Globe, AZ 1992*, edited by Richard C. Lange and Stephen Germick, pp. 206–211. Phoenix: Arizona Archaeological Society.

ZEDEÑO, M. NIEVES, JAMES BUSMAN, JAMES BURTON, AND BARBARA J. MILLS
  1993   Ceramic Compositional Analyses. In *Across the Colorado Plateau: Anthropological Studies for the Transwestern Pipeline Expansion Project*, Vol. 16, *Interpretation of Ceramic Artifacts*, by B. J. Mills, Christine Goetze, and M. N. Zedeño. Albuquerque: Office of Contract Archaeology and Maxwell Museum of Anthropology, University of New Mexico.

ZIPF, G.
  1949   *Human Behavior and the Principle of the Least Effort*. Cambridge: Addison Wesley.

Index

Abstract

Archaeologists traditionally use pottery to reconstruct a wide range of activities of prehistoric people. Economic, social, and political aspects of ancient lifeways are inferred from the patterning of ceramic variation. To make these inferences, the locus of pottery manufacture must first be identified.

This monograph focuses on the development of a broadly applicable methodology for identifying local and nonlocal ceramics and for reconstructing mechanisms of ceramic circulation. A ceramic assemblage of 330 whole and partial vessels from Chodistaas Pueblo, a late Pueblo III period masonry ruin located in the Grasshopper region, Arizona, constitutes the main body of data used in this research. This data base is expanded with comparative information from three excavated sites on the Grasshopper Plateau and with observations on surface ceramic distributions from several regions of the Arizona mountains.

A three-dimensional approach to the identification of ceramic manufacturing loci involved the integrated analysis of technology, paste composition, and design style of all wares present in the Chodistaas Pueblo assemblage. The analyses entailed (1): ceramic paste characterization by instrumental neutron activation analysis (INAA), inductively-coupled plasma emission spectroscopy (ICP), and temper identifications, combined with a systematic survey of clay and temper sources in the region; (2) reconstruction of the manufacturing technology of each decorated and undecorated ware; and (3) analysis of design style variability in polished-painted wares.

The combined results of these analyses suggest that Chodistaas settlers manufactured mainly brown corrugated pottery that included unslipped, slipped, and painted vessels. The community also obtained Cibola White Ware, White Mountain Red Ware, and many Roosevelt Red Ware, gray corrugated, and red plain pots from nonlocal sources. Pottery circulated between Chodistaas Pueblo and other proximate as well as distant contemporaneous settlements through at least three mechanisms: sporadic trading episodes, reciprocal exchange among relatively mobile communities, and the immigration of people into the mountains. This reconstruction accords with current notions of prehistoric adaptations of mountain communities during the late thirteenth century and with general organizational trends that characterized the transition toward Pueblo aggregation in the mountains of east-central Arizona.

Resumen

Tradicionalmente, los arqueólogos han utilizado cerámica para reconstruir el modo de vida de poblaciones prehistóricas; actividades económicas, sociales, y políticas han sido inferidas a través de la variación cerámica. Este tipo de inferencias requieren de la identificación del lugar de manufactura cerámica.

Esta monografía se ocupa de desarrollar una metodología de amplia aplicación para identificar cerámica local e importada y para reconstruir los mecanismos de circulación de cerámica prehistórica. Trescientas treinta vasijas completas y parciales recuperadas en Chodistaas, un pueblo de mampostería de piedra que data del período Pueblo III tardío en la región de Grasshopper, Arizona, constituyen el cuerpo principal de datos en esta investigación. Esta base de información está complementada con datos comparativos sobre la cerámica recuperada en excavaciones de tres sitios en la región de Grasshopper y con información sobre la distribuición de cerámica de superficie en varias regiones de las montañas de Arizona.

La identificación de lugares de manufactura cerámica se realizó a través de la aplicación de una perspectiva tridimensional, la cual comprende un análisis integrado de tecnología, composición de la pasta, y estilo de diseño de todas las vajillas presentes en el conjunto cerámico de Chodistaas. Este análisis incluyó: (1) caracterización química de la pasta a través del análisis de activación neutrónica (INAA), espectroscopía de emisión de plasma con conección inductiva (ICP), análisis de antiplástico, y prospección sistemática de fuentes de arcilla y antiplástico en la región; (2) reconstrucción de la tecnología de manufactura de cada vajilla decorada y ordinaria; y (3) análisis de variabilidad en el estilo de diseño de vajillas pintadas y pulidas.

Los resultados combinados de esta investigación sugieren que los habitantes de Chodistaas fabricaron principalmente cerámica marrón corrugada (ordinaria, engobada, y pintada). La comunidad a su vez obtuvo las vajillas blanca Cíbola, roja White Mountain, y un buen número de vasijas de la vajillas roja Roosevelt, gris corrugada, y roja pulida, de fuentes externas. Este estudio también sugiere que la cerámica circuló entre Chodistaas y otras comunidades contemporáneas, tanto vecinas como distantes, a través de por lo menos tres mecanismos: episodios esporádicos de intercambio, reciprocidad social entre comunidades relativamente móbiles, e inmigración de gente a las montañas.

Esta reconstrucción corresponde a nociones contemporáneas sobre la adaptación prehistórica de comunidades montañesas del final del siglo décimo tercero y sobre las tendencias generales organizativas que caracterizaron la transición hacia la aglomeración de grupos Pueblo en las montañas del centro-este de Arizona.

ANTHROPOLOGICAL PAPERS OF THE UNIVERSITY OF ARIZONA